Law for Professionals

More information about this series at https://link.springer.com/bookseries/16313

Héctor Hugo Juárez Allende

The World Customs Organization

Past, Present and Future

Foreword by Ricardo Treviño Chapa

Springer

Héctor Hugo Juárez Allende
Córdoba, Argentina

Translated by
Andrea María Paz
Victoria Martínez Adalid
Ciudad de Buenos Aires, Argentina

ISSN 2662-141X ISSN 2662-1428 (electronic)
Law for Professionals
ISBN 978-3-030-85295-5 ISBN 978-3-030-85296-2 (eBook)
https://doi.org/10.1007/978-3-030-85296-2

This Springer imprint is published by the registered company Springer Nature Switzerland AG.
The registered company address is: Gewerbestrasse 11, 6330 Cham, Switzerland

I dedicate this book to my wife Daniela and my children Paula and Mauro, for their enormous patience and understanding in the long hours spent writing.

Foreword by Ricardo Treviño Chapa (MBA), Deputy Secretary General of the World Customs Organization

Dear reader, I am pleased to welcome you to the reading of a wonderful work that will take you through the past, let you know the present, and guide you into the future of the flagship institution of the international customs community, the customs house in the world: the World Customs Organization (WCO).

This institution was created in 1952, under the name of Customs Cooperation Council, to optimize the efficiency and effectiveness of customs, especially concerning the harmonious treatment of the international flow of goods, as well as providing a uniform global solution in terms of tariff classification and customs valuation of goods. Initially made up of only 17 Customs Administrations, the WCO currently comprises 183 Members that treat 98% of global trade.

Throughout all these years, the only intergovernmental organization dedicated one hundred percent to customs issues has successfully led the many transformations and trends in processes and business models. The WCO has highlighted internationally the wide and complex customs functions that encompass tariffs, revenue collection, trade issues, as well as national security. Thanks to the technical discussions that take place in the WCO Working Groups, it is now possible to develop guides and tools that always seek to strengthen control and promote the facilitation of international trade. The implementation of these tools is the result of the commitment made by its members and, if necessary, through its extensive network of experts, as the WCO provides the necessary capacity building to achieve this.

On this occasion, in my capacity as Deputy Secretary General of the WCO, it is with great pride that I present to you this work written by Dr. Héctor H. Juárez Allende, a lawyer and prominent customs specialist, who is currently serving as Judge of the Argentine Tax Court, the jurisdictional body entrusted with reviewing (upon appeal) the resolutive acts of the customs administration of his country.

Before becoming a magistrate, the author had worked as a customs official for many years, and as such, reached the highest technical level at Customs. His

---

Ricardo Treviño Chapa (MBA) is Deputy Secretary General of the World Customs Organization.

extensive knowledge of international customs law allowed him to represent the Argentine Republic in the negotiation and drafting of the MERCOSUR Customs Code.

As a customs officer and university professor, he has repeatedly visited our headquarters in Brussels, which has enabled him to collect information "on-site" and consolidate a network of contacts and friends who, from different points of views, have provided him with the accurate and valuable data that the reader will find in these pages.

Small tints and hues reveal a researcher who has not only compiled rigorous information, but who has analyzed it methodically, and through the lens of an observer who has been in the operational field or, as it is usually said, in the trench. No one better than a godson of the House, to study it, apprehend it, and display it.

It is enriching the reading of the historical facts linked to the genesis of the Institution, its first moments, its first conformation, the embryonic development of its structure, its first press release, and the small details that have traced the outlines of the today mature and robust organization.

The author's teaching capacities are shown in how he introduces the structure and operation of the Organization, a very arduous topic, that he presents with diagrams and the right dose of theoretical content which aids understanding, in particular, of the aspects related to human resources and the administration of its budget.

The relations between the Organization and other international agencies must be mentioned separately. The author provides details that help understand the enormous task carried out before the international community by the WCO on behalf Customs worldwide.

In this line of interrelations, the author has dedicated a chapter to analyzing the relationship between the WCO and one of its strategic allies, the private sector, and, in particular, customs brokers.

The numerous normative instruments that the Organization uses on a daily basis in the performance of its functions have been grouped and analyzed in a comprehensive way, and their relevant, specific, and differentiating aspects have been highlighted.

Technical customs matters are also present when dealing with issues related to the tariff classification, customs valuation, and the origin of goods, highly specialized topics that identify the customs community.

The fight against customs fraud as well as issues related to the facilitation of international trade are harmoniously treated from the perspective that both are part of a delicate balance of forces that must enable the flow of goods and the development of legitimate trade.

Capacity building is emphasized as it is key for customs officers to perfect their respective profiles according to their competences, guaranteeing continuous, updated, and integrity-based training that favors an inclusive approach, greater cooperation with other customs, with the private sector and other intergovernmental organizations, as well as the achievement of sustainable development goals.

In this regard, I must point out that motivating leadership, collective decision-making, transparency of information for its members and strategic partners, consensus on common interests, inclusion in the development and execution of programs, the effectiveness and efficiency in the use of its resources, instruments and tools and clear accountability not only to members but also to their donors, constitute the highest world-class standards implemented by the WCO and are duly outlined in the work.

In addition, the evolution in the adaptation capacity of the WCO to constantly changing environments is verified through the development of the Strategic Plans of the Organization and its regions, as well as the constant updating of the Packages that provide Customs a wide range of instruments and tools for their application in their respective territories.

At the same time, it is highlighted in the text that the areas of research and performance measurement along with digital development and data governance have become essential to strengthen risk management and the advance information strategies that customs administrations around the world implement in their efforts to achieve excellence.

The current cross-border trade environment requires thinking about a comprehensive, visionary customs management, aware of the different realities and needs at the local, regional, and global level, with special emphasis on strategic management, communication, and collaboration, both nationally and internationally, and the use of innovation to mitigate risks, facilitate trade, ensure fair collection and protection of society, fight against transnational counterfeiting, terrorism, and crime, while increasing the security levels of supply chains as well as promoting sustainable initiatives for the care of our planet. The author's explorations in this work may offer insights in this regard.

Likewise, we must be aware that we are entering a new industrial era in which a series of innovations based on information technology and the Internet could have significant repercussions on production processes and on the way international trade develops. The "Internet of Things," artificial intelligence, 3D printing, blockchains, and other technologies, create new challenges for the Institution.

These dizzying and disruptive changes are analyzed in the final section of this volume, in the chapter dedicated to the WCO Future Agenda, where we are able to see the impact that these modern technologies will have on the evolution of customs activity. Advantages and disadvantages, risks, and opportunities are duly examined and presented.

The text presented in this brief foreword constitutes the culmination of an enormous effort to publicize the trajectory of an international organization based on cooperation and multilateralism, which permanently strives for the common good and development of its member administrations, providing them with the tools and technical assistance they may need.

World Customs Organization, Brussels, Belgium

Ricardo Treviño Chapa

Acknowledgment

During the development of the research and in the process of collecting information, I have received the support of numerous specialists in the field. I am especially thankful to all of them for generously sharing their experience and knowledge.

In particular, I am mainly grateful to María Luisa Carbonell, a high-ranking official of the Directorate General of Customs of the Argentine Republic, a specialist in international issues of the institution, with whom we share our fanaticism for the World Customs Organization, and in light of which, participated in lengthy inspiring discussions. Without her support, this text would not have been possible. Her guidance had a clarifying, lasting, and invaluable impact.

I am also indebted to Ana Hinojosa, hierarchical official of the Customs Service of the United States of America (Customs and Border Protection), who was in charge of the WCO's Compliance and Facilitation Directorate (2016/2019), and to whom I owe permanent support and motivation.

I must dedicate a separate paragraph to Edmond Galle, who was responsible for the WCO Library for more than 30 years—the living history of the Organization. Without his collaboration, it would have been impossible for me to navigate and dive into the historical aspects and details that only he remembers as he lived them first-hand. His contribution has been fundamental in understanding the early years of the organism. Slight nuances and stories come alive in his memories and tales.

My thanks also to the current Deputy Secretary General of the WCO, Ricardo Treviño Chapa, for reading the draft and for his accurate observations and comments that, in addition to providing tranquility to the author, have provided the text with richness and kept it up to date.

A special mention to María Teresa Rivas, a specialist in translation of international customs documents, who freeheartedly and kindly carried out the meticulous and arduous task of the final control of this work.

At this point, I must clarify that the responsibility for any errors in the book, both in its content and in its writing, rests solely and exclusively with the author.

Contents

Chapter 1
Introduction

The Customs Cooperation Council (CCA) was created in 1952 and constitutes an independent intergovernmental body with exclusive competence in customs matters and which today, under the name of World Customs Organization (WCO), brings together almost all of the world's customs, representing more than 98% of world trade.

In order to visualize this global representativeness, it is enough to mention that the number of States Parties[1] that comprise it (183)[2] exceeds the number of States Parties that make up the World Trade Organization (WTO) (164).[3]

From its inception to the present, international merchandise trade has multiplied 235 times, from 83,820 million dollars in 1953 to 19,670,000 million dollars in 2018.[4]

This rapid growth has not been without risks for society, so customs controls have always been necessary in order to protect citizens from the different scourges that plague their communities from abroad: illegal drugs, defective products, hazardous substances and materials, prohibited biological and bacteriological agents, and nuclear and radioactive elements, to name just a few.

These controls are also required to protect national products from unfair competition, which affects people's work and economic well-being. Revenue is threatened

[1]Clarification of concepts: In this text expressions such as "State Parties", "Contracting States", "Signatory States", "Signatory Countries", and similar wording that are used to refer to members of the World Customs Organization should be considered with the same scope and identical meaning as the expression "Contracting Parties"; i.e. without taking into account whether said parties are effectively "States" or constitute "Customs Unions" or "Separate Customs Territories" as it is explained in Section 1.5. MEMBERS.

[2]The updated list of Member States is available on the website of the World Customs Organization: http://www.wcoomd.org/en/about-us/wco-members/membership.aspx Accessed May 10, 2021.

[3]Data updated as of April 2021.

[4]WCO. World Trade Statistical Review 2019. https://www.wto.org/english/res_e/statis_e/wts2019_e/wts19_toc_e.htm. Accessed May 10, 2021.

H. H. Juárez Allende, *The World Customs Organization*, Law for Professionals,
https://doi.org/10.1007/978-3-030-85296-2_1

by commercial fraud, including false declarations, underinvoicing, overinvoicing, the smuggling of high-tax merchandise, and goods that violate intellectual property laws.

In many underdeveloped or developing countries, import and export duties—as well as other related taxes—represent a significant portion of national income, so the focus of customs control is on revenue collection. For others, particularly developed countries, the emphasis is on controlling import and export restrictions and prohibitions, as well as on the security of their borders.

While the focus placed on one or the other aspect may vary according to the circumstances of each country, depending on economic policies and national priorities, it is necessary and desirable that each Customs Administration preserves its basic or essential functions in order to adequately carry out its responsibilities and be well prepared for the upcoming challenges.

To carry out their multiple tasks and rise to these challenges, Customs Administrations around the world need to operate on a coordinated and harmonized basis, aiming for a standardized and uniform international trade system that ensures the free and agile flow of merchandise.

At this point, we should not forget that every export made by one country has its counterpart in the import by another country. Currently, information technologies enable both states to coordinate their actions and cooperate with each other to facilitate the flow of goods through legal and transparent channels; thus, both parties benefit from the collection and security perspectives. The challenge is to strike a proper balance between security and the facilitation of legitimate trade. An attempt must be made to find a point of equilibrium in which control tasks do not hinder the free movement of goods.

International cooperation and the uniform development of capacities for the adequate exchange of information are essential to contributing to the achievement of an ideal functioning of the customs system. Customs Administrations must apply risk management and assessment techniques, as well as make use of alliances with other customs in a global network and with the business sector in a strategic way.

In this regard, the World Customs Organization, which is perceived as an international model and guide in customs matters, offers its members a platform to reach these goals. It offers a series of instruments that allow for dialogue and the exchange of experiences and agreed multilateral conventions that standardize processes and technical assistance services for least developed countries. The strategic alliance approach sponsored by the WCO is one of the keys for building bridges between Customs Administrations and their partners (customs brokers, transporters, importers, exporters, among others). Promoting the emergence of an honest, transparent, and predictable customs environment contributes directly to the economic and social well-being of its members.

Within the values that guide the operation of the entity, we must highlight the following:

- **Mutual assistance or cooperation**: it is reflected in the joint actions of all customs services for the solution of common problems.
- **Responsibility**: it is observed by responding effectively to the emerging challenges of a dynamic international trade.

- **Democratic attitude**: it is reflected in the consensus required for decision-making.
- **Equity**: it is the fair distribution of operating costs following the contributory capacity of associated states.

Obviously, the problem of corruption is a scourge that could jeopardize the effective action of the Customs Administrations. In order to fight against it, adequate diagnosis and the implementation of the instruments and tools developed by the World Customs Organization (WCO) based on the experience and best practices of its Member States are necessary.

Customs services must integrate, act in real time, operate online, be properly equipped and trained, manage risk, and make informed decisions in collaboration with their counterparts.

On the occasion of the attacks on the Twin Towers (9/11), the USA became aware that it was useless to control in their country possible nuclear weapons that could arrive in a container because the terrorist threat could blow them up right there, at the port of arrival, causing the damage that was intended to be avoided. Under this, it launched the Megaport Program, signing cooperation agreements with its supplying countries and placing scanners at the ports where the cargo is remitted (ports of provenance).

As a result, the WCO began working on a more comprehensive vision of control and, as a result, published the SAFE Regulatory Framework to ensure and facilitate global trade. SAFE includes the Authorized Economic Operators Program, with the final objective of guaranteeing the security of the entire logistics chain of the goods, from the place of shipment to the place of destination.

In this way, a paradigm shift occurred: there is no longer a staggering vision (importing country/exporting country); instead, an effort is made to guarantee security throughout the goods' circulation process, from the exporter's factory to the importer's warehouse.

This paradigm shift, added to the development of information technologies, has produced a substantial transformation in tackling customs challenges, enabling their treatment comprehensively and systemically.

It is within this framework that new developments related to the world's customs network, the global exchange of information, the advance declaration of merchandise, the mutual recognition of certain reliable operators, among others, take place.

During the development of the text, we will see the enormous contributions and benefits provided by the WCO, but we will also examine its weaknesses and limitations.

Regarding the latter, (i) we analyze the issue of **purview**, i.e., those aspects of the international flow of goods that are of the WCO's exclusive jurisdiction and that have been invaded by other international organizations on several occasions.

We will also examine (ii) the lack of *coercive power* of the World Customs Organization, which has led the WCO to be dependent on member states' goodwill to apply its instruments, and take part in its activities (whenever these suit the members' interests and priorities).

Likewise, (iii) we will see the problem of *regional structures*, which play a key role in promoting member participation. In this regard, there is a high level of uncertainty regarding its obligations and responsibilities, which need to be clarified.

The text presented is organized into 18 chapters and contains four complementary annexes.

In the first two chapters, the institutional aspects of the organization are analyzed, and a brief and concise historical review is done. Then we move on to the third chapter, which is of singular importance, where the various types of legal instruments that the Organization produces are discussed and which constitutes the "Output" of its work system.

In Chaps. 4 and 5, the relationship of the WCO with other organizations and with customs brokers is developed.

In Chaps. 6, 7, and 8, the enormous contributions made in the customs technique are described, that is, tariff classification, valuation, and rules of origin of the merchandise.

In Chap. 9, everything related to customs control is analyzed and in Chap. 10 everything related to trade facilitation.

Chapter 11 deals with the training and development of human resources in customs matters and Chap. 12 with aspects related to integrity and the fight against corruption.

Chapter 13 presents the different packages of instruments and tools prepared by the Organization to assist its States Parties.

Chapter 14 brings together other relevant instruments prepared by the Organization, and Chap. 15 has been devoted to an area considered to be of importance for the future growth of the specialty: scientific research on customs issues.

Chapter 16 details the particularities associated with the need to advance in the development of the Organization's performance measurement instruments.

Finally, in Chap. 17, we introduce ourselves to the Agenda for the Future of Customs, analyzing reality, and based on it, we present predictions about the aspects that are considered to be impacted by new technologies. Then we close with a short chapter of final words.

The four annexes include (i) the Agreement establishing the World Customs Organization; (ii) the Protocol to the Agreement between the Kingdom of Belgium and the Customs Cooperation Council regarding the maintenance of the Organization's headquarters in the city of Brussels;[5] (iii) a detailed table of the main agreements drawn up within the WCO, with the signatory States Parties and their accession dates; and (iv) a Customs Self-Assessment Template, which consists of 20 questions that allow evaluating the degree of development of a particular customs.

[5] In French and English.

In the development of the text, special consideration has been given to the relevant instruments in the daily customs work and which constitute the flagship vessels of the WCO (the Harmonized System Convention, the Revised Kyoto Convention, the SAFE Regulatory Framework, among others), as well as those topics that are currently of special interest to the world customs community (cross-border e-commerce, trade facilitation, future customs agenda, among others), trying to reconcile theoretical developments with the practical aspects of customs operations.

The purpose of the work is to analyze and present in a comprehensive, orderly, and synthetic way the enormous contributions that the WCO has been making to the development of control and facilitation of world international trade.

Consequently, it is considered to be of interest to all international trade operators but, in particular, to customs officials, customs brokers, transport agents, and international trade managers of importing and exporting companies, such as those who research and study this specific and exciting area of human knowledge.

1.1 Legal Status

The WCO was established by a multilateral treaty[6] that sets out the provisions that define its functions by determining its objectives, instructing its governing bodies, conferring its jurisdiction, and specifying its decision-making procedures, all of which constitute the so-called "primary law" of the organization.

The constitutional nature of the founding treaty of an organization (its status as primary law) is presented in the preeminence of its provisions over the decisions, resolutions, and other acts of the same organization carried out in the exercise of its powers, i.e. its "secondary law."

This is an open treaty as it can be subsequently acceded by states that have not been part of its negotiation.[7]

In this treaty, we can identify the four essential elements of international organizations: (i) interstate composition; (ii) conventional legal basis; (iii) permanent organizational structure, independent of its members; and (iv) legal autonomy (it establishes its own rules).

The International Court of Justice determined certain requirements to consider an international organization as such. All these conditions have been fulfilled by the WCO:

- International juridical personality for the organization to fulfill its missions
- Organs entrusted with the fulfillment of specific tasks

[6] Available in Annex I of this book.

[7] ARTICLE XVIII (a) The Government of any State which is not a signatory to the present Convention may accede thereto as from April 1, 1951.

- Obligations of members toward the organization, e.g., making financial contributions
- Possession of legal capacity, privileges, and immunities in the members' territory
- Possibility for the organization to enter into agreements with its members

As an international organization, the WCO is a subject of international law and has its own judicial personality (different from that of its members), which confers the capacity to acquire rights and contract obligations.

The Annex to the Convention, titled "Legal Capacities, Privileges and Immunities of the Council, ARTICLE II, Juridical Personality, SECTION 2," expressly states: *The Council shall possess juridical personality. It shall have the capacity: (a) to contract, (b) to acquire and dispose of immovable and movable property, (c) to institute legal proceedings.*

Unlike national states, international organizations are governed by the "principle of specialty." This means that the states that create international organizations invest them with powers of attribution, the limits of which depend on the objectives and functions they have been entrusted with.

To this end, Article III of the founding Convention explicitly established that the functions of the Council are the following:

a. *to study all questions relating to co-operation in Customs matters which the Contracting Parties agree to promote in conformity with the general purposes of the present Convention;*
b. *to examine the technical aspects, as well as the economic factors related thereto, of Customs systems with a view to proposing to its Members practical means of attaining the highest possible degree of harmony and uniformity;*
c. *to prepare draft Conventions and amendments to Conventions and to recommend their adoption by interested parties;*
d. *to make recommendations to ensure the uniform interpretation and application of the Conventions concluded as a result of its work as well as those concerning the Nomenclature for the Classification of Goods in Customs Tariffs and the Valuation of Goods for Customs Purposes prepared by the European Customs Union Study Group and, to this end, to perform such functions as may be expressly assigned to it in those Conventions in accordance with the provisions thereof;*
e. *to make recommendations, in a conciliatory capacity, for the settlement of disputes concerning the interpretation or application of the Conventions referred to in paragraph (d) above in accordance with the provisions of those Conventions; the parties in dispute may agree in advance to accept the recommendations of the Council as binding;*
f. *to ensure the circulation of information regarding Customs regulations and procedures;*
g. *on its own initiative or on request, to furnish to interested Governments information or advice on Customs matters within the general purposes of the present Convention and to make recommendations thereon;*
h. *to co-operate with other inter-governmental organizations as regards matters within its competence.*

1.2 Headquarters

Pursuant to Article VII, subsection (a) of the Convention, "The Headquarters of the Council shall be in Brussels," capital of the Kingdom of Belgium.

Between the years 1953 and 1964, the WCO headquarters was located on Avenue Louise, No. 183-185, (1000 Brussels), which was the location of the European Customs Union Study Group.

From 1964 to 1980, it was located on Rue Washington No. 38-40 (1050 Brussels), which had a large meeting room where the Harmonized System documents, among other texts, were prepared.

From 1980 to 1998, the headquarters relocated to a 14-story building in Rue de l'industrie No. 26-38 (1040 Brussels), which it shared with other Belgian government organizations and departments.

After assessing and considering relocating the WCO headquarters outside of Belgium[8] and following intense negotiations with the Belgium government on December 6, 1996, it was decided that the headquarters would remain in Brussels. Subsequently, on February 7, 1997, a Memorandum of Understanding between the Kingdom of Belgium and the Customs Cooperation Council (CCC) was signed. Through this memorandum, the Kingdom of Belgium granted the CCC long-term lease (*emphytéotique bail*) with an option to buy the physical space (land) for the construction of its own building.[9]

[8] Gómez-Pallete and María (2002), p. 27*: In December 1996, the Council had to once again address the issue of organization's headquarters so that it would be able to accommodate its already 142 contracting parties. On this occasion, circumstances of diverse natures led the WCO to consider the possibility of relocating the headquarters to another Member State. Germany, the Netherlands, Belgium, and Morocco submitted bids for the WCO's headquarters to be situated in Bonn, The Hague, Brussels, and Casablanca, respectively. On December 6th, 1996, the Council held a special session to decide on the organization's new premises. After voting on the various proposals, Belgium's offer obtained the necessary majority and it was agreed that the Organization's headquarters would remain in Brussels.*

[9] At the end of the book, in Annex II, the original version of the Agreement is included. The Agreement roughly states that: 1. The Government of the Kingdom of Belgium offered the CCC the possibility of maintaining its headquarters in Brussels by way of an annual subsidy (BEF 50 million) for as long as the long-term lease and call option between the CCC and BURCO CDP (Limited Liability Company) exists between the years of 1997 and 2024; 2. Should the CCC decide to exercise the call option upon expiry of the contract, it must offer the Kingdom of Belgium the possibility of acquiring 50% of the undivided property, or should it decide not to exercise the call option, it must offer the Kingdom of Belgium 100% of the call option; 3. Whether the Kingdom of Belgium partially or completely acquires the land and property complex, the Kingdom agrees to refrain from any claim for rent from the CCC while the WCO occupies the complex and from any request to abandon the complex without the agreement of the CCC;

In the event that the complex not be available in accordance with the provisions and conditions of the contract mentioned in the first point, the Kingdom of Belgium undertakes to guarantee an adequate space for the Organization until the complex can be made available to it, taking into consideration that the CCC's contribution cannot being greater than the amount that would have been payable, if the complex had been able to be occupied on July 1st, 1998.

Architect M. Jaspers of the *Bureau de Architectes M & C Morijinissen* oversaw the construction of the building, which began in April 1997.[10] The Secretariat relocated there on July 1, 1998.

From that date forward, the WCO has carried out its operations in this comfortable building located in downtown Brussels in Rue du Marché 30 (1210 Brussels). The building consists of a lobby and five upper floors, totaling 7000 m^2 of office space. It also has two underground levels, where the spacious meeting rooms, the kitchen, and the parking area are located. The building exterior harmoniously combines glass, steel, and natural stone, and it faces a well-tended and blooming park that serves as a frame for the flagpoles that surround its structure.

Negotiations on the establishment of the Customs Cooperation Council and related treaties have always been carried out in Brussels, and the World Customs Organization has always chosen Brussels as the center of its international activities and commitments.

Article XVI of the Convention establishing a Customs Cooperation Council stipulates that instruments of ratification shall be deposited with the Belgian Ministry of Foreign Affairs. Article XVIII of the same document stipulates that instruments of accession of governments that are not part of the Convention shall also be deposited with the Belgian Ministry of Foreign Affairs. Article XX subsection (b) provides that any Contracting Party accepting an amendment shall notify all signatory governments and the Secretary-General of the acceptance. The original treaty itself is in the custody of the Belgian government.

1.3 Vision, Mission, Values

1.3.1 WCO Vision[11]

- Bringing Customs together for a safer and more prosperous world
- Borders divide, Customs connects
- To be a dynamic leader in modernization and connectivity in a rapidly changing world

---

[10] Jukka-Pekka Miettinen, who at that moment held a position as Customs Attaché at the Permanent Representation of Finland to the EU before the WCO, recalls that moment: *"Negotiations with the Belgium Government on new premises for the WCO had been completed. The WCO would be given a building in downtown Brussels constructed specifically for its needs. I participated in the laying of the foundation stone of the new building in April 1997. The event was followed by celebratory drinks."* Source: WCO News No. 68, (2012), p 18.

[11] World Customs Organization. http://www.wcoomd.org/en/about-us/what-is-the-wco/vision-mission-values.aspx.

1.3.2 WCO Mission[12]

The World Customs Organization develops international standards, fosters cooperation and builds capacity to facilitate legitimate trade, to secure a fair revenue collection and to protect society, providing leadership, guidance and support to Customs administrations.

1.3.3 WCO Values[13]

- We are a knowledge-based and action-oriented organization.
- We believe in transparent, honest, and auditable governance procedures.
- We are responsive to our Members, stakeholders in trade, and society.
- We capitalize on technology and innovation.
- We believe in inclusiveness, diversity and equitable treatment and opportunities for all.

1.4 Strategic Goals[14]

The WCO has set as its main Strategic Goal to provide leadership, guidance, and support to its members. To this end, the WCO will focus on proposing initiatives that promote more facilitation, improved and fairer revenue collection, and better protection of society. The WCO will continue to create, update, and promote its tools and instruments for modern Customs procedures. The WCO will also continue to provide its members with technical assistance according to their needs and to offer guidance and tools to strengthen cooperation.

From the **MEMBER'S PERSPECTIVE**, it has set three goals:

1. Facilitation
2. Revenue collection
3. Protection of society

The improvement of WCO processes, through the development of international standards, reinforcement of cooperation, and delivery of tailor-made capacity building, aims to provide members with the necessary tools and instruments to provide

[12] World Customs Organization. http://www.wcoomd.org/en/about-us/what-is-the-wco/vision-mission-values.aspx. Accessed May 10 2021.

[13] World Customs Organization. http://www.wcoomd.org/en/about-us/what-is-the-wco/vision-mission-values.aspx. Accessed May 10 2021.

[14] World Customs Organization. http://www.wcoomd.org/en/about-us/what-is-the-wco/strategic-plan/goals.aspx. Accessed May 10 2021.

more facilitation, improve revenue collection, and better protect society. These three Strategic Goals reflect the role customs play in today's world. As a modern and dynamic global organization, the WCO is expected to provide members with various initiatives in order to equip them with instruments as they face current challenges, in addition to preparing them for future challenges.

1.5 Members

Article II of the Convention establishing a Customs Cooperation Council expressly states:

ARTICLE II (a) The Members of the Council shall be:

(i) *the Contracting Parties to the present Convention;*
(ii) *the Government of any separate Customs territory which is proposed by a Contracting Party having responsibility for the formal conduct of its diplomatic relations, which is autonomous in the conduct of its external commercial relations and whose admission as a separate Member is approved by the Council.*

(b) *Any Government of any separate Customs territory, which is a Member of the Council under paragraph (a) (ii) above, shall cease to be a Member on notification to the Council of the withdrawal of its membership by the Contracting Party having responsibility for the formal conduct of its diplomatic relations.*

Therefore, the conditions of admissibility are the following:

a. Government with a separate customs territory
b. Proposed by a Contracting Party
c. Government that conducts its diplomatic relations
d. Autonomous conduct of its foreign trade relations
e. Lastly, and most importantly, approval by the Council

The 183 Member States of the WCO are listed below:[15]

Afghanistan, Albania, Algeria, Andorra, Angola, Antigua and Barbuda, Argentina, Armenia, Australia, Austria, Azerbaijan, Bahamas, Bahrain, Bangladesh, Barbados, Belarus, Belgium, Belize, Benin, Bermuda, Bhutan, Bolivia, Bosnia and Herzegovina, Botswana, Brazil, Brunei Darussalam, Bulgaria, Burkina Faso, Burundi, Cambodia, Cameroon, Canada, Cape Verde, Central African Republic, Chad, Chile, China, Colombia, Comoros, Congo (Republic of the), Costa Rica, Côte d'Ivoire, Croatia, Cuba, Curaçao, Cyprus, Czech Republic, Democratic Republic of the Congo, Denmark, Djibouti, Dominican Republic, Ecuador, Egypt, El Salvador, Eritrea, Estonia, Eswatini, Ethiopia, Fiji, Finland, France, Gabon, Gambia, Georgia, Germany, Ghana, Greece, Guatemala, Guinea, Guinea-Bissau, Guyana, Haiti,

[15] For a more detailed display and access to the dates of accession, see Annex III at the end of the text.

Honduras, Hong Kong, China, Hungary, Iceland, India, Indonesia, Iran (Islamic Republic of), Iraq, Ireland, Israel, Italy, Jamaica, Japan, Jordan, Kazakhstan, Kenya, Korea (Republic of), Kosovo, Kuwait, Kyrgyzstan, Lao People's Democratic Republic, Latvia, Lebanon, Lesotho, Liberia, Libya, Lithuania, Luxembourg, Macau, China, Madagascar, Malawi, Malaysia, Maldives, Mali, Malta, Mauritania, Mauritius, Mexico, Moldova, Mongolia, Montenegro, Morocco, Mozambique, Namibia, Nepal, Netherlands, New Zealand, Nicaragua, Niger, Nigeria, North Macedonia, Norway, Oman, Pakistan, Palestine, Panama, Papua New Guinea, Paraguay, Peru, Philippines, Poland, Portugal, Qatar, Romania, Russian Federation, Rwanda, Saint Lucia, Samoa, Sao Tome and Principe, Saudi Arabia, Senegal, Serbia, Seychelles, Sierra Leone, Singapore, Slovakia, Slovenia, Somalia, South Africa, South Sudan, Spain, Sri Lanka, Sudan, Suriname, Sweden, Switzerland, Syrian Arab Republic, Tajikistan, Tanzania, Thailand, Timor-Leste, Togo, Tonga, Trinidad and Tobago, Tunisia, Turkey, Turkmenistan, Uganda, Ukraine, Union of Myanmar (Republic of the), United Arab Emirates, United Kingdom, United States, Uruguay, Uzbekistan, Vanuatu, Venezuela, Vietnam, Yemen, Zambia, and Zimbabwe.

Separate Customs Territories
A separate customs territory is an autonomous territory or a territory dependent on a sovereign government with a certain degree of independence in foreign trade and customs policy. The governing bodies (or other similarly responsible administrative entities) of the customs territories negotiate and sign trade agreements. A customs territory usually has inspection stations at its borders; there may also be border controls between two parts of the same customs territory.

The following are currently under the status of a separate customs territory before the World Customs Organization—(i) **Hong Kong**, since July 1, 1987; (ii) **Bermuda Islands**, since July 1, 1990; (iii) **Macau**, since July 1, 1993; and (iv) the **Netherlands Antilles**, since July 1, 2001:

i. Hong Kong is a founding member of the World Trade Organization serving under the name of "Hong Kong, China," and has been a member of the General Agreement on Tariffs and Trade (GATT) for some years. It is governed by the Basic Law of Hong Kong (similar to a constitutional rule but temporary), which establishes the principle of "one country, two systems." The people of Hong Kong enjoy a high degree of autonomy and independent executive, legislative, and judicial powers, including that of final adjudication. In accordance with Article 116 of the Basic Law, the Hong Kong Special Administrative Region shall be a separate customs territory. In regard to customs controls, it has a regulated system for imports and exports, with proper control over passengers and cargoes that enter and leave the territory. Hong Kong Customs is using a risk management approach to facilitate the flow of all legitimate trade.
ii. Macau has been considered a separate customs territory since 1993. It has a trade openness rate (measured by the ratio of the sum of exports and imports to the total value of the gross domestic product (GDP)) of 29.94% (2010 data). The

ratio of imports to GDP is 26.99%. These parameters allow us to observe that foreign trade has a small role to play in the territory's economy. According to the Basic Law of the Macao Special Administrative Region, the territory:

1. Shall maintain the status of a free port after China's resumption of the exercise of sovereignty over Macao.
2. Shall be a separate customs territory under the name "Macao, China" and shall participate in relevant international organizations and international trade agreements it adhered to before July 1st, 1999 (continues to be a member of the WTO independently of mainland China). Macao maintains export quotas, tariff preferences and other similar arrangements and any other agreements obtained or made by the territory.
3. The Macao Special Administrative Region may issue its own certificates of origin for locally produced products in accordance with prevailing rules of origin. Macao maintains its autonomy in the commercial field on the same terms until it´s reverted to China.

iii. The **Bermuda Islands** is one of the overseas Non-Self-Governing Territories of the United Kingdom of Great Britain in the Americas. Despite its status, it has chosen not to apply for it from the EU. Therefore, EU legislation (including the extent of its customs territory) does not apply in that territory, in accordance with the Treaty on the Functioning of the European Union.

iv. On the other hand, **the Netherlands Antilles**, specifically **Curaçao**, has the status of an Overseas Country and Territory (OCT). The OCTs are not European countries but territories that have special relations with the European Union (EU) due to their economic and social development. Although Curaçao depends on the Kingdom of the Netherlands, it is not part of the customs territory of the Kingdom of the Netherlands, as stipulated in Article 4.1 of Regulation 952/2013 in the Union Customs Code (UCC): *Article 4.1. The customs territory of the Union shall comprise the following territories, including their territorial waters, internal waters and airspace: - the territory of the Kingdom of the Netherlands in Europe."*

This condition of separate customs territories similarly grants them membership status in accordance with the information *ut supra* and pursuant to Article VIII of the WCO fundamental Convention:

> *ARTICLE VIII (a) Each Member of the Council shall have one vote except that a Member shall not have a vote on any question relating to the interpretation, application or amendment of any of the Conventions referred to in Article III (d) which is in force and which does not apply to that Member.*

This situation favors the countries of origin or those countries that have control over these territories, such as China, the United Kingdom, and the Netherlands. When making a decision within the WCO, they will have another vote, or other votes, favoring their own interests. In conclusion, the condition of having a customs territory that is considered separate before the WCO, but is geopolitically part of the natural territory of a state, implies a broad advantage over policy decisions that might be taken in this organization as it could add a vote before the Council.

Member States of the UN That Are Not a Part of the WCO

1. **North Korea**: the Democratic People's Republic of Korea (DPRK) or North Korea has made tentative attempts to join the international trade arena through its participation in regional organizations in Asia with the support of South Korea. According to statements by government spokespersons, these initiatives are systematically vetoed by the United States due to its socialist republic regime based on the "Juche" ideology (centered on the concept of self-reliance) and its nuclear policies. This country is not a member of the WTO either, nor has not it applied for membership.
2. **Dominica**: this state is not a member of the Caribbean Customs Law Enforcement Council, from which it receives technical assistance. It has not sought to enforce the special and differential treatment provisions of Article 20 of the Customs Valuation Agreement, nor has it responded to the WTO list of issues on customs valuation. Dominica's legislation incorporates the GATT Customs Code of Valuation. According to authorities, customs officials use the valuation methods provided by the Customs Valuation Agreement. As a state, it has notified the WTO of its preferential rules of origin but lacks nonpreferential rules of origin.
3. **Grenada**: this insular country in America, which is part of the Lesser Antilles in the Caribbean Sea, was a Contracting Party of the GATT and has been a member of the WTO since February 22, 1996. It is a founding member of the Organization of Eastern Caribbean States (OECS) and has been a member of the Caribbean Community (CARICOM) since its independence in 1974.

Since 2008, the government undertook a comprehensive reform aimed at, among other issues, modernizing the Customs Division and increasing its efficiency and effectiveness, in addition to improving tax collection, thereby adopting the UNCTAD Automated System for Customs Data (ASYCUDA) World system.[16]

Grenada's legislation on customs valuation is still based on the Brussels Definition of Value, although the Customs Division generally relies on the value declared on the invoices. Grenada's tariff is based on the common external tariff (CET) of the Caribbean Community (CARICOM), and the Harmonized Commodity Description and Coding System (HS) and its rules of origin are also those established by CARICOM.

4. **Equatorial Guinea**: it is a member of the Economic and Monetary Community of Central Africa (CEMAC) and therefore applies a common customs tariff to imports from third countries and allows free trade to other member countries: Cameroon, Chad, Central African Republic, Gabon, and the Democratic Republic of the Congo. In April 2016, the Permanent Secretary of the Action Group against

[16]Software for the control and administration of customs management, developed by the United Nations Conference on Trade and Development (UNCTAD). It is currently used in over 80 countries.

Money Laundering in Central Africa recommended accelerating the process of the country's accession to the World Customs Organization (WCO).

5. **Marshall Islands**: the Marshall Islands is a large group of islands in Micronesia. Its main exports are fish and fish-related products for Thailand, China, the USA, and Japan. It is a member of the Pacific Island Countries Trade Agreement (PICTA) and the South Pacific Regional Trade and Economic Cooperation Agreement (SPARTECA).
6. **Solomon Islands**: Internationally classified as a least developed country (LDC) and a Small Island Developing State (SIDS), its main exports are timber, palm oil, and fish. It has been a member of the WTO since July 26, 1996 (member of GATT since 1994), and is also a member of the Oceania Customs Organisation (OCO). As for trade negotiation groups, it is part of the African, Caribbean and Pacific Group of States (ACP Group); G-90; LDCs; the sponsors of the "W52" document; the group of Pacific countries; Melanesian Spearhead Group (MSG); the Pacific Island Countries Trade Agreement (PICTA); and the South Pacific Economic and Trade Cooperation Agreement (SPARTECA).
7. **Kiribati**: in recent years, customs in Kiribati have contributed approximately 20% of the total government revenue. The country is a member of the Oceania Customs Organisation (OCO); the Commonwealth; the Pacific Islands Forum; the subregional group of Micronesia; the African, Caribbean and Pacific Group of States (ACP); the World Bank; and the International Monetary Fund (IMF).

Kiribati is among the countries that recently acceded to the Revised Kyoto Convention (RKC), demonstrating that the WCO's message of promoting the RKC as a model for modern and effective customs procedures has been well received even outside the WCO membership community.

8. **Liechtenstein**: in 1924, Liechtenstein signed a treaty to form a customs union with Switzerland, which acts on behalf of Liechtenstein in matters related to the customs union, such as trade policy measures affecting imports and agricultural policy. All trade agreements concluded by Switzerland also apply to Liechtenstein.
9. **Micronesia**: the Federated States of Micronesia is an island nation in Micronesia located in the North Pacific Ocean. Its economic activity consists of subsistence agriculture and fishing. Its main exports are fish and fish-related products. It is a member of the Pacific Island Countries Trade Agreement (PICTA) and the South Pacific Regional Trade and Economic Cooperation Agreement (SPARTECA).
10. **Nauru**: the Republic of Nauru is in Micronesia, an island in the South Pacific Ocean, south of the Marshall Islands. It is classified as a Small Island Developing State (SIDS). Its revenues are derived from phosphate exports, which represent over 90% of its total exports mainly to the Republic of Korea, New Zealand, Australia, and India. It is a member of the Pacific Island Countries Trade Agreement (PICTA) and the South Pacific Regional Trade and Economic Cooperation Agreement (SPARTECA).

11. **Monaco**: pursuant to the Customs Convention signed in Paris on May 18, 1963 (*Journal officiel de la République française* of September 27, 1963), the country's customs policy is developed by France (member of the WCO). In addition, this territory is part of the European Union's Customs Territory in accordance with Article 4 of Regulation 952/2013 of the Union Customs Code (UCC).
12. **Palau**: the Republic of Palau is a Micronesian territory located in the western Pacific Ocean. It shares its maritime borders with Indonesia, the Philippines, and the Federated States of Micronesia. This territory's economy depends mainly on tourism. Its main exports are fish and fish-related products. Its main export partners are Japan, the United States, and Mexico. Palau's main imports are oil, fish, machinery, and equipment. Its main import partners are Japan, the United States, Singapore, and the Republic of Korea. It is a member of the Pacific Island Countries Trade Agreement (PICTA).
13. **Saint Kitts and Nevis**: St. Kitts and Nevis' foreign policy is conceived in terms of its membership in international organizations with a universal scope (United Nations (UN); ACP Group; United Nations Conference on Trade and Development (UNCTAD); United Nations Educational, Scientific and Cultural Organization (UNESCO); Organization of American States (OAS); IMF; WTO; World Health Organization (WHO), among others) and regional in nature, such as the Caribbean Community (CARICOM), the Organization of Eastern Caribbean States (OECS), or the Association of Caribbean States (ACS). In December 2014, St. Kitts and Nevis joined the Bolivarian Alliance for the Americas (ALBA).
14. **San Marino**: San Marino is a European microstate in the form of a parliamentary republic and the oldest sovereign state in the world. In 1991, it signed an agreement with the European Union to create a free trade zone, which came into force in 2002. This agreement also constitutes the grounds for cooperation in the development of certain policies, such as support to small and medium-sized enterprises (SMEs) and environmental and tourism policies, among others. In addition, this microstate is part of the European Union's Customs Territory in accordance with Article 4 of Regulation 952/2013 of the Union Customs Code (UCC).
15. **Saint Vincent and the Grenadines**: It is part of the Organization of Eastern Caribbean States, CARICOM, the Commonwealth of Nations, the Bolivarian Alliance for the Americas, and the Community of Latin American and Caribbean States (CELAC). Its small-scale economy is ranked 199th (out of 229) in terms of GDP. It is also a founding member of the WTO. The country made sector-specific commitments in five of the 12 areas under the General Agreement on Trade in Services (GATS) but did not participate in the expanded negotiations on telecommunications or financial services. In addition, it applies the CARICOM common external tariff, with some exceptions provided for by the Council for Trade and Economic Development. The MFN tariff applied in 2013 is based on the 2007 version of the Harmonized System (HS).

16. **Tuvalu**: this Polynesian territory is classified as a least developed country (LDC) and a Small Island Developing State (SIDS). Its main exports are fish and related products, mainly exported to Thailand, Japan, and Australia. It is a member of the Pacific Island Countries Trade Agreement (PICTA) and the South Pacific Regional Trade and Economic Cooperation Agreement (SPARTECA).

Members of the WCO That Are Not Members of the UN the Case of Palestine
On November 29, 2012, the UN General Assembly adopted Resolution 67/19, by which it granted Palestine the status of "Non-Member Observer State" of the organization, thereby confirming the right of the Palestinian people to a territory in accordance with the borders defined before the 1967 War.[17]

During the 121st/122nd WCO Council Sessions (Brussels, August 13, 2013), the president stated that during the previous meetings of the Policy Commission, the delegate of Morocco, in his capacity as Vice President for the North Africa, Near and Middle East region, addressed the issue of Palestinian accession to the WCO in the context of its accession to UNESCO and the need to provide the necessary technical support for its customs.

On that occasion, the delegate of Turkey noted that from his administration's point of view, this accession would facilitate and accelerate technical assistance and capacity-building activities for the Palestinian Customs and that the officials would be able to follow initiatives and developments related to WCO tools with more ease. The delegate proclaimed the full support of his Customs for Palestinian accession to the WCO.

On May 13, 2015, the Belgian Ministry of Foreign Affairs informed the WCO that Palestine had deposited its instrument of accession to the founding Convention, thus becoming the 180th member of the WCO with effect as from March 24, 2015.

The Case of Kosovo
Incorporating Kosovo, a "state" that had not yet been recognized by the UN, generated numerous objections and discussions regarding the hassle of modifying Article XVIII of the Convention establishing the WCO. It was argued that the Belgian Ministry of Foreign Affairs' intervention could have "lightly" allowed this approval.

Regarding the debate on Kosovo's state status, it should be recalled that UN Resolution 1244/99 is in force. This resolution states that this territory remains a province of Serbia.

UNESCO had a similar conflict, and it was solved by establishing the following procedure: when applications for membership come from "states" that do not belong

[17]This resolution does not yet imply the admission of Palestine as a full member of the Organization, as this would require the approval of the UN Security Council in which the United States opposes. On December 17th, 2014, the European Parliament publicly supported the recognition of the State of Palestine. In May 2015 it was also officially recognized by the Holy See, and by early 2018, a total of 136 states recognize Palestine as a sovereign state.

to the UN, they must be filed by the UNESCO Director-General to the plenary body of the Organization for approval.

In the WCO's case, and given the complexity of amending the founding Convention, the Secretariat proposed that the Council adopt a decision recommending the Belgian Ministry of Foreign Affairs to forward any application for membership received from a non-UN member to the WCO Council for guidance. The Secretariat stressed that the application would not be binding for the depository.

Although the proposal was very practical, it met with the reluctance of the Belgian government and its explanation that the accession of non-UN states was the prerogative of the depositary, which is responsible for judging whether it is appropriate to consult WCO members or its Secretariat. This would also introduce an additional mechanism that is not provided for in the founding Convention.

In a previous and similar case (Palestine), the depositary had accepted the accession request of a non-UN member state, and that situation had not been challenged despite the fact that the nation involved (Palestine) was not universally recognized as a state.

It is clear that this is one of the issues pending solution by the WCO. The issue shows a weak point in its empowerment as it depends on the decision of a third party to incorporate new members that are not universally recognized as a state.

The Convention establishing the WCO sets out an exceptionally simple accession process compared to those of other organizations. The problem lies not in the nature of the process but in the definition of what qualifies as a state. The truth of the matter is that states must recognize other states as equals. Some countries recognized Kosovo as a state, but others did not and therefore contested its incorporation. It remains to be defined whether only states recognized by the UN shall be accepted or whether the WCO and the Belgian government will operate according to their own criteria.

Regarding the issue of accession to the WCO, at its July 2017 Sessions, the Council approved the creation of a working group to specifically analyze this issue in the framework of a constructive approach.

Until then, it was decided that Kosovo shall not vote nor seek to become a Contracting Party to any convention where the WCO acts as depositary.

This decision was understandably rejected by Kosovo, which has stated that it seeks to exercise its full rights in the body.

The Case of the European Union

The Convention establishing the Customs Cooperation Council determined that only states can be parties and did not provide for the participation of the customs unions or the economic unions.

On March 19, 2001, the Council of the European Union decided that the European Community should apply for membership to the World Customs Organization and authorized the Commission to negotiate the membership. In April 2001, the European Community submitted a request for accession as a full member to the World Customs Organization.

The issue of accession was addressed at the June 2001 and June 2002 Council Sessions of the World Customs Organization. Several countries opposed the accession of the European Community (the objections were based on the potential voting power of the European Union since it would have a number of votes equivalent to the amount of Member States that constitute the Union, in addition to its own).

In 2002, the World Customs Organization Council put the issue on hold pending a political solution. After a series of political discussions, the request was resubmitted at the June 2006 World Customs Organization Council meeting. This time, the proposal to open negotiations with the European Community for its accession to the organization was approved. The World Customs Organization Council and the Organization's Policy Commission, in December 2006, examined the legal, budgetary, and voting aspects related to the European Community's accession.

Until then, the European Community could only participate in WCO bodies created by other international conventions and agreements, such as the Customs Valuation Agreement, the Harmonized System, or the Revised Kyoto Convention. In all other bodies and commissions, it could only do so as an observer and, in some cases, exclusively by special invitation, for example, in the Policy Commission meetings.

The European Union's interest to become a member of the WCO was based on the desire to have the right to full participation in all WCO bodies open to the general membership, such as the Council, the Permanent Technical Committee, the Executive Committee, among others. Likewise, the European Union sought the right to be elected in organs with restricted participation, such as the Policy Commission, the Finance Committee, and the Audit Committee.

The only exception to this rule is the Convention on the Harmonized System, in which the European Community, along with its Member States, has only one vote as a Contracting Party.

During the 109th/110th Sessions held in June 2007,[18] the WCO submitted the adoption of amendments to Article VIII (a) and the inclusion of a new paragraph (d) in Article XVIII of the Convention[19] for the consideration of the Member States.

Through Council Decision 2007/668/EC, the European Union (at that time the European Community) gave its consent and was appointed an interim member of the WCO on July 1, 2007, thereby obtaining the rights and obligations of a Member

[18]Council Decision No. 318 (2007). In: "Status of the European Communities vis-à-vis the World Customs Organization", doc. SC0081E1a.

[19]At its 109th/110th Sessions, the Council adopted the amendment to the Convention establishing the CCC (Articles VIII and XVIII). This amendment was approved as a Recommendation dated June 30th, 2007 ("Recommendation of the Customs Co-operation Council concerning the amendment of the Convention establishing a Customs Co-operation Council"). To enter into force, this Recommendation, deposited with the Belgian Ministry of Foreign Affairs, must be accepted by all Contracting Parties to the Convention establishing the Customs Cooperation Council. According to the information available on the website of the Ministry of Foreign Affairs of Belgium (last updated on November 13th, 2017), 73 instruments of acceptance have been deposited.

State, including the right to vote and participate in certain committees, as well as the obligation to provide a financial contribution to the WCO.

This financial contribution has always been important and comparable in terms of its contribution to the World Trade Organization, and it reflects the significance and importance of issues related to international trade and customs.

It is worth noting that the Member States of the European Community maintain their status as States Parties in the World Customs Organization.

1.6 Budget

The WCO has an annual budget that covers the period from July 1 to June 30 of the following year. It is set in euros and is modeled on the United Nations scale of assessments. This scale is based on per capita income levels, with maximum and minimum rates to guarantee the independence of the organization vis- à-vis global matters. Currently, a Member State cannot contribute with more than 22% of the organization's regular budget but must contribute with at least 0.15%.[20]

The annual budget is approximately € 6,000,000. The ten main contributions correspond to the following:[21]

United States:	22%
Japan:	7.2%
China:	6.1%

[20]**Maximum contribution rate**. Up to 1963, there was no legal basis regarding a maxi-mum contribution rate. In May 1963, the Council (on its 22nd Session) decided that *"the Council Budget share borne by each Member State cannot, in any case, be higher than 30% of the budgetary income provided by the contributions"* (Council Decision No. 152, May 23, 1963). In June 1970, the Council (on its 35th/36th Sessions) decided that *"the Council budget share borne by each Member State cannot, in any case be higher than 25% of the budgetary income provided by the contributions"* (Council Decision No. 184, June 12th, 1970 which annulled Decision No. 152)

Japan was the largest contributor with a rate of 13.21% before the accession of the United States on November 5, 1970 (according to the scale of contributions adopted in June 1970 - Decision No. 182, June 12, 1970, for the 1970/1971 budget).

After the accession of the United States, the revised scale of contributions for that same 1970/ 1971 budget (Decision No. 186, June 11, 1971) included the United States as the largest contributor with a rate of 25% (Decision No 184).

United States remained the largest contributor with a rate of 25% for 34 years when it requested to level its contribution rate to the WCO with the maximum level of contributions defined by their Department of State (22%) for all the international organizations of which the US is a member.

Council finally approved this request in the 109th/110th Sessions (Decision No. 319, on July 5th, 2007). To this end, there would be a gradual reduction over three years: 24% for the 2007/2008 budget, 23% for the 2008/2009 budget, and 22% for the 2009/2010 budget onwards.

Minimum contribution rate: Since the beginning, the minimum contribution rate has been variable depending on the specific situation of each budget. In June 2018 (Decision No. 351, July 5, 2018), the minimum rate for the 2018/2019 budget was set at 0.161%.

[21]Situation on April 15th, 2019.

Germany:	5.2%
United Kingdom:	3.9%
France:	3.6%
Brazil:	2.9%
Italy:	2.7%
Russia:	2.4%
Canada:	2.3%
Australia:	1.8%
Spain:	1.8%

In addition to regulatory contributions, *voluntary* ones are made; for example, in 2007, Japan made a voluntary contribution of seven million euros and has contributed with a total of 47 million euros over the last 10 years.

Member States that have not fully paid their annual contributions by the date of the Council meeting and have not provided justification for the late admission of payment, shall be deprived of their voting rights in all Council meetings. Furthermore, they shall not be entitled to receive technical assistance by the Organization or be nominated as candidates for positions in the Secretariat or Council or as chairpersons of committees.

The WCO is not a taxable person in the European Union, as stated in Article 9 of Directive 2006/112/EC, and does not have a value-added tax (VAT) register.

As for the minimum contribution rate, it has been variable since the beginning, depending on the specific situation of each budget. In June 2018 (Decision No. 351, July 5, 2018), the minimum rate for the 2018/2019 budget was set at 0.161%.

In community transactions, the WCO is exempt from VAT for the supply of goods and services as established in Article 151.1 (b) of Directive 2006/112/EC. Penalties for late payment can be applied only after the WCO has sent a formal written reminder and should be calculated using the Belgian compensatory interest rates.

The WCO, as an intergovernmental organization, is independent of its Member States, enjoys jurisdictional and judicial process immunities pursuant to international law, and cannot be brought before a national court. Any supplier dispute shall be settled in accordance with its own settlement procedure laid down in Council Decision No. 331/2011.

1.7 Languages

When the Customs Cooperation Council was established, the founding members defined English and French as the official languages.

In the early stage, when there was a strong European influence, these languages were enough to reach the organization's goals. However, with time, it has proved to limit its development for the following reasons:

- Full participation of all Member States is hindered, particularly the participation of technical officers who are deprived of making significant contributions because of language limitations.
- Problems arise with the translation of different instruments, which weakens their consistency.
- In a time of widespread social media, bilingualism becomes an important limit for communicating the activities carried out. This has a negative impact on the international positioning of the Organization.

In this regard, we must take into account that these two official languages do not correspond to the most globally spoken native languages.[22]

This circumstance has contributed to the relegating of the ranking of the WCO in relation to other international organizations that have several official languages, for example, the UN (six official languages: Arabic, Chinese, English, French, Russian, and Spanish), the WTO (three official languages: Spanish, English, and French), and the European Union (24 official languages: Bulgarian, Croatian, Czech, Danish, Dutch, English, Estonian, Finnish, French, German, Greek, Hungarian, Irish, Italian, Latvian, Lithuanian, Maltese, Polish, Portuguese, Romanian, Slovak, Slovenian, Spanish and Swedish), just to name a few.

The cost of multilingualism is undoubtedly high. Just to compare the cost involved, it is worth noting that the European Union spends 1% of its budget on translation.[23]

Notwithstanding, due to the high pressure exerted by the Member States, some options are being considered. The Working Group on the Use of Additional Languages was created in 2017. Subsequently, in March 2018, during the Group's second meeting, delegates unanimously agreed to make a collective effort to translate the documents pertaining to the most important WCO meetings into the additional four selected languages: Arabic,[24] Portuguese, Russian, and Spanish.[25]

The program was launched in September 2018, and now it is in its pilot phase. It is being funded by the WCO equity reserve until additional sources of finance are obtained.

---

[22] Languages with the most native speakers are Mandarin Chinese (917 million speakers), Spanish (460 million), English (379 million), and Hindi (341 million). Ethnologue. Languages of the World: https://www.ethnologue.com/guides/most-spoken-languages.

[23] Information available in http://ec.europa.eu/education/languages/pdf/doc3275_en.pdf.

[24] Arabic is already being used as a partially official language in the Management Committee of the Customs Convention on Containers and as a working language in the Harmonized System Committee.

[25] Spanish is already being used as a partially official language in the Customs Valuation Technical Committee, Rules of Origin Technical Committee, and in the Management Committee of the Customs Convention on Containers, and as a working language in the Harmonized System Committee.

The Group will monitor the attendance at WCO meetings of delegates from the Member States where these additional languages are spoken.[26]

Current affairs, imbued by globalization and multiculturalism, call for making progress in this sense, and the WCO has adequately responded to this challenge.

1.8 Historical Background[27]

The first relevant precedent can be found in the "International Convention relating to the Simplification of Customs Formalities," signed by the League of Nations[28] in Geneva in 1923. We can also find isolated and loose customs matters (with no integral structural frame) in the General Agreement of Trade and Tariffs (GATT) of 1947.

Afterward, among the rebuilding activities of the massive damage of the Second World War, some countries considered the possibility of creating a customs union. To this end, on September 12, 1947, 13 European counties,[29] which in previous years had been involved in an armed conflict, issued a joint declaration, thereby providing the first step toward creating a Customs Union Study Group in Brussels.

In 1948, the Study Group established a Customs Committee to carry out a comparative analysis of customs techniques in several countries with a view to standardizing them. The focus was put on the need for common nomenclature and a common definition of value.

This gave rise to the three conventions signed in Brussels on December 15, 1950:

- Convention establishing a Customs Cooperation Council (entered into force on November 4, 1952)
- Convention on the Valuation of Goods for Customs Purposes (entered into force on July 28, 1953)
- Convention on Nomenclature for the Classification of Goods in Customs Tariffs (entered into force on September 11, 1959)

[26]The first monitoring actions revealed important progress in the participation of Arabic speaking members.

[27]Sources: (i) Customs Cooperation Council Bulletin No. 1, (1995), (Printed in France at the ENCYCLOPEDIE DOUANIERE). (ii) Booklet "Brief introduction" of the Customs Co-operation Council (1990). (iii) World Customs Organization website: www.wcoomd.org.

[28]The League of Nations, officially named Société des Nations (SDN), was an international organization created by the Versailles Treaty on June 28th, 1919, which aimed to establish the bases for peace, and reorganization of international relations after the end of First World War. The SDN was dissolved on April 18th, 1946, after the end of the Second World War, and was succeeded by the United Nations Organization (UN).

[29]Austria, Belgium, Denmark, France, Greece, Ireland, Iceland, Italy, Luxemburg, Netherlands, Portugal, United Kingdom, and Turkey.

Table 1.1 Founding countries and dates of ratification and accession

Countries	Ratification(Art. XVI b of the founding Agreement)
Norway	08/06/1951
Denmark	10/19/1951
Greece	12/10/1951
United Kingdom	09/12/1952
France	10/06/1952
Sweden	10/17/1952
Germany	11/04/1952
Italy	11/19/1952
Belgium	12/11/1952
Netherlands	01/24/1953
Luxemburg	01/24/1953
Portugal	01/26/1953
Countries	**Accession** (Art. XVIII b of the founding Agreement)
Turkey	06/06/1951
Spain	07/13/1952
Ireland	09/23/1952
Switzerland	12/17/1952
Austria	01/21/1953

Source: Author's elaboration based on information from the WCO

- The inaugural session of the Customs Cooperation Council with 17 members, which was held on January 26, 1953,[30] and lasted until Thursday, February 3, 1953.

First Council Meeting

The first Council meeting was presided over by Mr. Meurice, Belgian Minister of Foreign Trade. After opening the session, he detailed the founding countries and the dates of deposit of the instruments of ratification (Table 1.1 shows the founding countries and the dates of ratification and accession).

Pursuant to Articles XVII, XVI (b), and XVIII (b) of the Convention, this came into force on November 4, 1952,[31] when the instruments of ratification and accession were deposited with the Belgian Ministry of Foreign Affairs.

[30] Customs Day is celebrated every year on January 26th in commemoration of this date.

[31] The WCO birth certificate can be seen from two points of view: **legal** or **operational**: (i) from the legal standpoint, the correct date is November 4th, 1952, the moment when Germany deposited its ratification instrument, i.e. the seventh State pursuant to Article XVII (a) of the Conventions establishing the Customs Cooperation Council; and (ii) from the operational point of view, the correct date is January 23rd, 1953. Throughout WCO history, both dates (1952 and 193) have been used to celebrate anniversaries. From the operational point of view (10th anniversary in 1963, 25th anniversary in 1978, 30th anniversary in 1983, and 40th anniversary in 1993). However, since 2002, following a decision made by Secretary-General Michel Danet, the legal point of view has been used (50th anniversary in 2002, 60th anniversary in 2012, 65th anniversary in 2017).

The great merit for the Customs Union Study Group was that it preserved its independent and neutral nature, regardless of economic or political fluctuations, and limited its activities to technical customs matters. It is worth mentioning that the Council started with two specific achievements: the common definition of customs valuation and a harmonized nomenclature for customs tariffs.

Mr. Degois (France) was elected chairperson by acclamation. On the following day, Tuesday, January 27, 1953, the deputy chairpersons were elected as follows:

Dr. Schillinger (Germany)
Mr. Spallazi (Italy)
Mr. Van Den Berge (Netherlands)
Sir William Croft (United Kingdom)

Mr. Wyndhan White, GATT Secretary-General, was present as an observer and recalled that on the fourth session of the GATT, Mr. Degois had given an outstanding report about the work of the Study Group. Any conflict of activities between these two organizations, having similar interests, could be easily overcome as long as there was a mutual spirit of collaboration and cooperation. When the GATT examined the International Chamber of Commerce proposals regarding customs procedures, it sought advice from the Study Group, and they expressed their gratitude to Mr. Edmond Smith and Mr. Roux for the valued assistance provided in Geneva on behalf of the Study Group. The new Council could be of great help to the GATT in the study of customs technical problems. In return, the GATT could assist the Council in its effort to ensure the global adoption of reforms.

Originally, the chairperson suggested forming three working groups. However, after exchanging opinions, only two groups were created:

Group I:	Rules of procedure	Doc. 1082 A Organization of committees	Doc. 1082 B
Group II:	Organization of the Secretariat	Doc. 1082 C/1 Personnel rules	Doc. 1082 C/2
	Financial rules	Doc. 1082 D	
	Budget	Doc. 1082 D	

The *Provisional Committees of Valuation and Nomenclature* would operate temporarily until the entry into force of the two conventions.

On Thursday, February 29, 1953, Working Group I presented its report (Doc. No. II48) on Council rules and the organization of committees. The Group pointed out that although the introductory report showed the Working Group's intentions, it had not been formally approved by all its members. There were discrepancies between the English and French texts. Pursuant to Rule 14 concerning majority voting, the text could be amended after the revision of recommendations made by Group No. 2 regarding the organization of the Secretariat in the financial rules.

With reference to the official languages, it was stated that the Working Group had not adopted the amendment to include Spanish. Notwithstanding, it was argued that if a group of countries with a common language acceded to the Convention, that language would have to be considered an official language; that is, if a group of

Spanish-speaking countries from South America joined the Convention, the Council could amend this premise pursuant to Rule 25.

Mr. Gunver (Turkey) suggested deferring the revision of Rule 14 of the Rules of Procedure until the other rules had been adopted. This proposition was supported by the chairperson and was then approved.

On Friday, January 30, 1953, it was agreed that the Council should appoint the Finance Committee as soon as the Rules of Procedures and the organization of committees had been agreed upon.

With reference to the selection of members for the Financial Committee, it was agreed that every year, the Council would appoint five people from the Council and Permanent Technical Committee delegations to act as the Finance Committee. The Council would have to name one to act as a chairperson of this Committee. As the quorum for the Finance Committee was five, the Council would also nominate five alternates from the same delegations.

On Saturday, January 31, 1953, it was agreed that the Committees would be presided over as follows:

Permanent Technical Committee	United Kingdom
Valuation Internal Committee	Italy
Nomenclature Internal Committee	Belgium
Finance Committee	Spain
	Scandinavian countries
	Greece
	France
	United Kingdom

On Monday, February 2, 1953, the following were nominated and elected as Committee chairpersons:

Permanent Technical Committee	Mr. Owen (United Kingdom)
Valuation Internal Committee	Mr. Calderoni (Italy)
Nomenclature Internal Committee	Mr. Dubois (Belgium)

The chairpersons of these committees remained in office until the session in May 1954. If the Conventions on Nomenclature and Valuation had entered into force before May 1954, the internal committees would have become permanent.

The following members were appointed for the Finance Committee:

	Delegates	Alternates
Denmark	Mr. Korst	Mr. Lottrup Thomsen
France	Mr. Lamic	(to be nominated later)
Germany	Dr. Jancke	(to be nominated later)
Greece	Mr. Frangos	(to be nominated later)
Portugal	Mr. Da Camara Pestana	Mr. Da Costa Rodriguez
Spain	Mr. García Lomas	Mr. Bozzano
United Kingdom	Mr. Ashford	Mr. Hulme

Appointment of the Secretary-General
In agreement with the Government of Belgium, the chairperson proposed appointing Baron François de Selys Longchamps to act as the Secretary-General with a salary and allowance in line with his functions and privileges. As this proposal was accepted, he became the first Secretary-General.

Appointment of Directors
Based on the Council chairperson's proposal, directors were appointed as follows:

Nomenclature Director	Mr. Roux (France)
Valuation Director	Mr. Edmond Smith (United Kingdom)

Budget
Council original expenses were estimated to be 12 million Belgian francs per year, which included the necessary funds for its own building (around 700,000 Belgian francs).

With reference to the furniture purchased by the Study Group and IARA, the chairperson explained that the Council was taking responsibility for housing the Study Group and their furniture, thus subsuming it.

WCO Press Communique (CCC, 1953)

CUSTOMS COOPERATION COUNCIL 1126 E

Brussels, January 26th, 1953 CCD/I/ 3

PRESS COMMUNIQUE

ESTABLISHMENT OF A NEW INTERNATIONAL ORIGANISATION, THE CUSTOMS COOPERATION COUNCIL, IN BRUSSELS

The Customs Cooperation Council, with its headquarters in Brussels, is a new international organization, the aims of which have no connection with either political economy or pure politics. Its sole object is to harmonize, unify and simplify the widely divergent and sometimes complicated Customs practices of the various countries, for the benefit of traders and Administrations.

This was stressed by M. MEURICE, Minister of Foreign Trade, presiding over the Council's first meeting in the Residence Palace on 26 January.

This new Council of technical experts results from the efforts of the European Customs Union Study Group, whose Chairman, Mr. SPIERENBURG, Minister Plenipotentiary, Netherlands Foreign Economic Relations Director General and currently at the head of the High Authority of the European Coal and Steel Community (Schuman Plan) recalled past activities at this inaugural meeting. In 1947 while investigating ways of creating a vast European market, thirteen Western countries decided to create the Study Group, with the Benelux countries acting as sponsoring powers. The Study Group's work threw light on the

> complicated aspects of the plan to unify Customs practice and the technical problems involved. The Study Group still exists and is ready to resume its activities in this field whenever requested to do so.
>
> However, Study Group officials realized that, without waiting for such a request, it was essential to create an international Council on Customs techniques which, with more modest aims, could immediately concentrate on gradually achieving practical improvements. Three conventions were accordingly signed in Brussels, on 15 December 1950, under the aegis of the Study Group. The purpose of the first is to provide a common tariff Nomenclature for the Customs tariffs of participating countries, the second gives a uniform definition of the valuation of goods for Customs purposes, and the third establishes the Customs Cooperation Council responsible for studying these two series of questions and all other issues of the same type for which it seems possible to standardize regulations.
>
> The headquarters of the new organization is located in Brussels, temporarily at 185, Avenue Louise. All the Western European countries are members: Benelux, France, the United Kingdom, Italy, the Federal Republic of Germany, Austria, the Scandinavian countries, Turkey, Greece, Portugal, Switzerland and Spain. The 1950 Convention is, however, open to signature by all States, European or not, whether or not they are members of the United Nations and regardless of geographical or political position. The Customs Cooperation Council works in permanent liaison with the United Nations, GATT, OEEC, the Council of Europe and the International Chamber of Commerce. Its promoters, M. DEGOIS, Director General of French Customs, newly elected Chairman of the Customs Cooperation Council, and Baron de SELYS LONGCHAMPS, currently acting as Secretary General, on the desire not to overlap with the functions of any of these organizations but to cooperate with them while preserving its autonomy regardless of political or other fluctuations, to abstain from academic discussions and to achieve modest but concrete results as soon as possible. We wish the new organization success in its tasks.

There is no doubt that the Customs Cooperation Council was born with a strong European mark: its 17 founding members were all European. Fortunately, the open character of the Organization and the impulse of its founders enabled its global development. On November 16, 1955, Pakistan ratified the Convention, becoming the first non-European member. On October 26, 1956, Egypt, from Africa, also joined the Customs Cooperation Council. The first member from the Americas was Haiti, which deposited its ratification instrument on January 31, 1958. In addition, the first member from Oceania was Australia, which presented the corresponding letter on January 5, 1961. By then, the Customs Cooperation Council already had 26 members distributed in all continents.

The creation of the Customs Cooperation Council is a landmark in the global history of customs. It is the first international organization that has represented

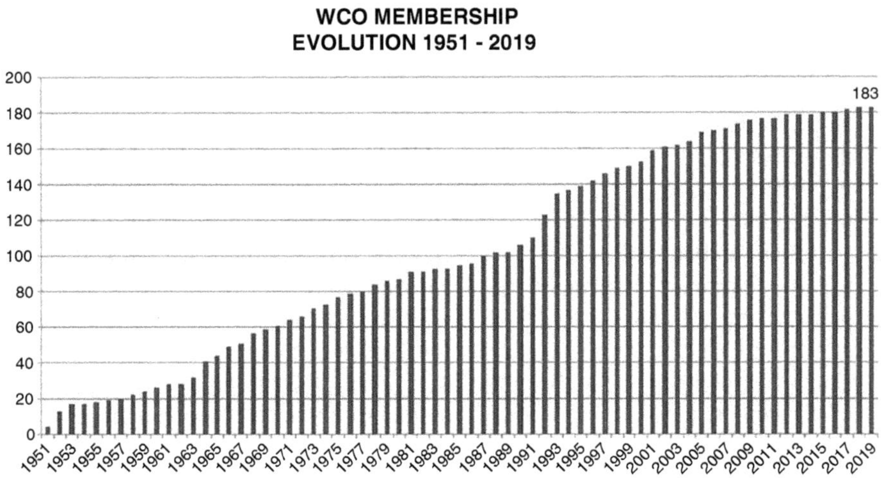

Fig. 1.1 Membership evolution. **Source:** Author's elaboration based on information from the WCO

customs in a direct and specialized way. It projects national actions to a global level in a collaborative way, thus becoming a generator of best customs practices.

Its regulatory propositions have gone from the field of internal administrative law to that of public international law. Its range of regulations, recommendations, technical opinions, and other legal instruments are received with great impact today by customs around the world.

The consolidation of the Organization took place when the United Stated adhered to the Convention on November 5, 1970, overcoming the resentment for its European origin. This was followed by Canada on October 12, 1977, and the rest of the developed countries that accompanied this momentum.

Figure 1.1 shows the evolution of membership from the first member in 1951 to the last one in 2019.

In the 83th/84th Council Sessions (June 20–22, 1994) the name of the Customs Cooperation Council was informally changed to World Customs Organization (WCO), following the footsteps of the World Trade Organization (WTO), which was substituting its previous denomination, GATT, for one more representative of its global nature.

Although its working name has changed, its fundamental convention, the membership system, its privileges and immunities, and its position in international law remain the same. This is because its official name continues to be "Customs Cooperation Council," and the same holds true for its registration as an international organization before the United Nations. Changing the name did not imply any changes in its legal status.[32]

The WCO flag with a white background is the logotype of the Organization. Designed in 1992 and formally adopted in 1993, the WCO logotype represents world countries cradled and gathered by the arms of the Customs Cooperation Council (CCA).[33] The new emblem is royal blue, a color frequently associated with customs worldwide, with a silver metallic border.[34,35]

Reference

Gómez-Pallete Á, María J (2002) The World Custom Organization and its conventions. Centro de Investigación Aduanera y Comercio Internacional, Mexico City, p 27

[32] The official name of the Organization, or its founding Conventions were not changed as the Ministry of Foreign Affairs of the Kingdom of Belgium informed the organization of the possible harmful consequences, particularly, for Belgian officers who would lose tax benefits and prerogatives they hold under the original convention.

[33] Doc. 38. 149 E/REv (1993). In: 29th Session of the Policy Commission, "CCC 40th Anniversary 1953-1993", para 2.

[34] The logotype official colors are "WCO blue" (pantone 3005), and "WCO grey" (pantone 877 – 20% black).

[35] With reference to the previous and current WCO logotype, Don Jorge Enrique Loera, in the prolog of the book "World Customs Organization and its Conventions", by José María ALVAREZ GÓMEZ – PALLETTE: states that "The Council logotype did not survive: that kind of wind rose with an eye in the middle of the world has been swept by the wind of modernity and replaced by a simple design whose meaning is a little complicated to unravel."

Chapter 2
Institutional Structure

2.1 The Council

The Council is the supreme body of the World Customs Organization (WCO) and adopts all final decisions about the Organization's work and activities. Once a year, it elects a Chairperson and at least two Vice-Chairpersons among member delegates (see Fig. 2.1).

The functions of the Council set forth in Article III of the founding Convention are as follows:

a. to study all questions relating to co-operation in Customs matters which the Contracting Parties agree to promote in conformity with the general purposes of the present Convention;
b. to examine the technical aspects, as well as the economic factors related thereto, of Customs systems with a view to proposing to its Members practical means of attaining the highest possible degree of harmony and uniformity;
c. to prepare draft Conventions and amendments to Conventions and to recommend their adoption by interested Governments.
d. to make recommendations to ensure the uniform interpretation and application of the Conventions concluded as a result of its work as well as those concerning the Nomenclature for the Classification of Goods in Customs Tariffs and the Valuation of Goods for Customs Purposes pre- pared by the European Customs Union Study Group and, to this end, to perform such functions as may be expressly assigned to it in those Conventions in accordance with the provisions thereof;
e. to make recommendations, in a conciliatory capacity, for the settlement of disputes concerning the interpretation or application of the Conventions referred to in paragraph (d) above in accordance with the provisions of those Conventions; the parties in dispute may agree in advance to accept the recommendations of the Council as binding;
f. to ensure the circulation of information regarding Customs regulations and procedures;

H. H. Juárez Allende, *The World Customs Organization*, Law for Professionals,
https://doi.org/10.1007/978-3-030-85296-2_2

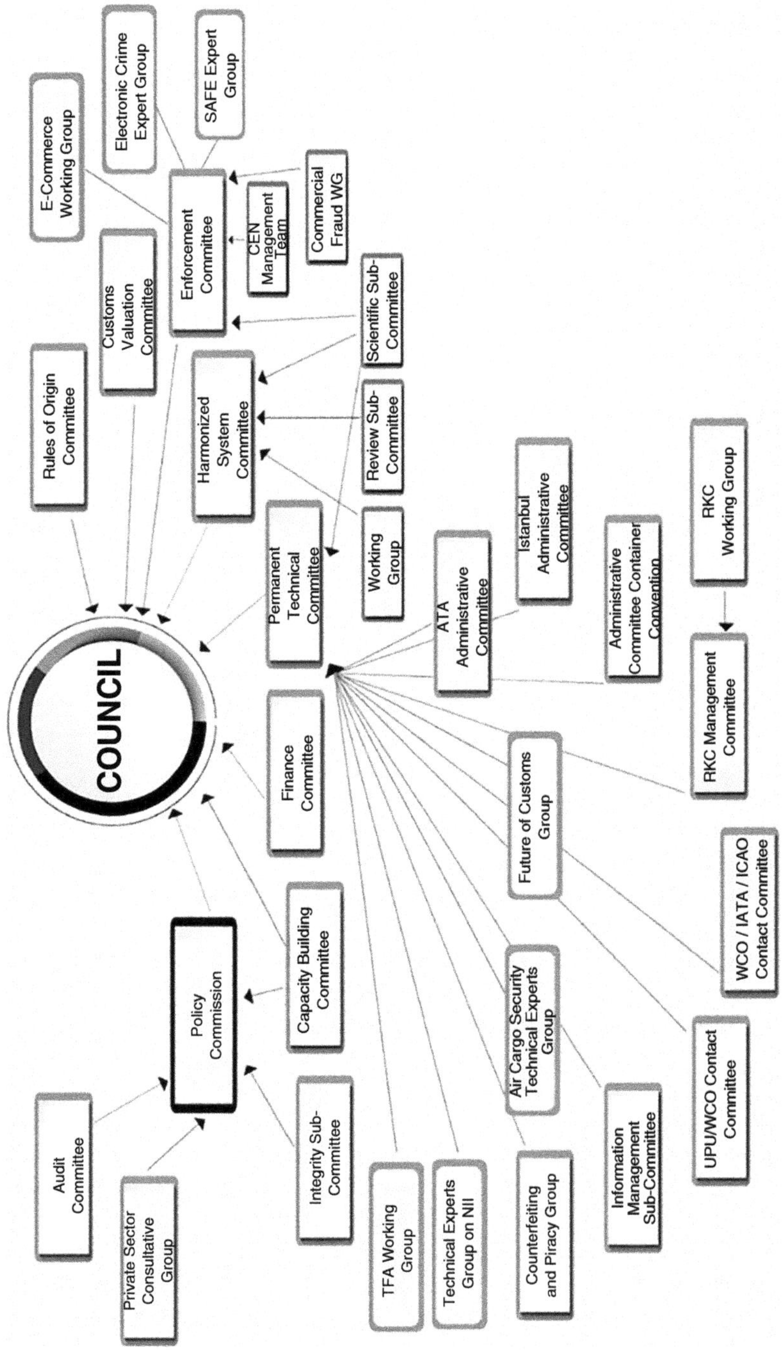

Fig. 2.1 The WCO Council and its main working bodies. **Source:** Author's elaboration based on information from the WCO

g. on its own initiative or on request, to furnish to interested Governments information or advice on Customs matters within the general purposes of the present Convention and to make recommendations thereon;
h. to co-operate with other inter-governmental organizations as regards matters within its competence.

While the functions established in the founding Convention remain broadly relevant, global evolution in trade, transport, and technology have had significant effects on the Organization's activities over the years. Nowadays, the Council's main functions include the following:

- To examine and, where appropriate, to approve the work of the organization's technical bodies, including the preparation or amendment of WCO instruments;
- To review, on the basis of written and oral reports by the Secretary General, the progress made during the previous twelve months with the implementation of the organization's three-year Strategic Plan;
- To direct the future work of the organization, in particular by examining, finalizing and adopting the Strategic Plan. The Strategic Plan, which is prepared each year by the Secretariat and submitted to the Council after preliminary examination by the Policy Commission;
- To examine and decide upon policy issues as may be submitted by the Policy Commission;
- To interpret provisions of the founding Convention;
- To provide a forum for the high-level exchange of information, views, and experiences on current customs issues;
- To make budgetary and financial decisions on the basis of recommendations submitted by the Finance Committee (in particular, acquitting the Secretary General of his financial management responsibilities for the previous financial year, taking note of the Audit Report and follow-up actions, appointing auditors, and adopting a decision concerning budgetary and financial provisions for the forthcoming financial year, including the scale of member contributions);
- To adopt amendments to the Secretariat Staff Regulations and Staff Rules;
- To elect the Council Chairperson and Vice-chairpersons, the members of the Policy Commission, and the Chairperson, Vice-chairperson, and the members of the Finance Committee;
- To appoint the Secretary General and the Deputy Secretary General of the organization, and to nominate the Directors for appointment by the Secretary General;
- To adopt the organization's Calendar of Meetings for the forthcoming year.

Although Article III of the Convention provides that two sessions are to be held per year, since 1966 only one session is held in the month of June in the Brussels premises or where it may be established. In to order to comply with the mandate of the founding regulation, this session is numbered as if the two meetings were held in one, e.g. 133rd/134th Sessions of the Customs Cooperation Council.

The Council is assisted by the Finance Committee and the Policy Commission, which was created in 1979.

It is important to highlight that decisions are made pursuant to Article VIII of the Convention:

> Article VIII
>
> Each Member of the Council shall have one vote except that a Member shall not have a vote on any question relating to the interpretation, application or amendment of any of the Conventions referred to in Article III (d) which is in force and which does not apply to that Member.
>
> Except as provided in Article VI (b), Rules of Procedure, the decisions of the Council shall be taken by a majority of two-thirds of the Members present and entitled to vote. The Council shall not take a decision on any matter unless more than half of the Members entitled to vote on that matter are present.

In the sessions, the Council evaluates the technical issues contained in the reports submitted by the Chairpersons of each Committee and then addresses administrative issues and internal affairs.

Each member of the WCO nominates one delegate[1] and one or more alternates to be its representative on the Council. These representatives may be assisted by advisers (Article II of the Convention). Each active member has one vote, except that a member does not have a vote on any question relating to the interpretation, application, or amendment of any of the WCO Conventions in force that does not apply to that member (Rule 21 of the Rules of Procedure of the Council).

Representatives of nonmember governments or international organizations may be invited to attend Council sessions as observers. They may, at the discretion of the Chairperson, participate in the discussions but not vote.

Representatives of a simple majority of the members of the organization constitute a quorum (Rule 20 of the Rules of Procedure of the Council). Decisions are taken by a majority of not less than two thirds of the members present at the meeting and entitled to vote (Rule 21 of the Rules of Procedure), except in the case of decisions concerning the Rules of Procedure, where a majority of not less than two thirds of all the members is required (Article VI of the Convention).

The WCO Secretariat is responsible for making the arrangements and preparations for the Council sessions; providing professional, administrative, and technical services during the sessions; and performing follow-up tasks after the sessions, including, in particular, the drafting of the minutes.

All members are required to bear the expenses (travel and accommodation) of their own delegations to the Council (Article XII of the Convention).

If the sessions are not held at the WCO Headquarters, at the invitation of a Member State, then that Member State will normally be required to meet the additional costs, which the Organization has incurred by reason of accepting that invitation (e.g., hiring meeting facilities, travel and accommodation expenses of Secretariat officials attending the sessions, and so forth).

[1] Member States usually appoint Customs high-level authorities.

2.1.1 The Policy Commission

The Policy Commission is an auxiliary body of the WCO responsible for submitting policy recommendations and the strategic plan to the Council.[2]

Created in 1979, the Policy Commission is presided over by the Chairperson of the Council. It is a dynamic steering group charged with carrying out studies on all the Organization's important policy issues and providing opinions or recommendations to the Council.

Council Decision No. 334, which repeals Decision No. 284, establishes that membership in the Policy Commission is restricted to a specific number of WCO members, elected by the Council on a regional basis from among the active members in the region. The Policy Commission members are the following:

a. The Chairperson of the Council (as Chairperson of the Commission)
b. The six Vice-Chairpersons of the Council, each representing one of the six WCO regions
c. Former Chairpersons of the Council who are still serving in their national Customs for a maximum of two years immediately after ceasing to hold office as Chairpersons of the Council)
d. Twenty-four members elected by the Council pursuant to the distribution in six regions created by Decision No. 283:

   - two members from East and Southern Africa
   - eight members from Europe
   - five members from the Far East, South and Southeast Asia, Australasia, and the Pacific Islands
   - two members from North Africa and the Near and Middle East
   - five members from South America, North America, Central America, and the Caribbean
   - two members from West and Central Africa

e. The member in whose territory the Council has its headquarters, as an observer
f. The Chairperson of the Audit Committee and the Chairperson of the Finance Committee, as observers
g. Any member that is not a member of the Policy Commission and is to host a session of the Commission away from the headquarters, as an observer

   Some sessions have been held outside of Brussels (Belgium), for example, in Vienna (Austria) in 1971, Kyoto (Japan) in 1973, Buenos Aires (Argentina) in 1975, Nairobi (Kenya) in 1977, Canberra (Australia) in 1979, Varna (Bulgaria) in 1981, Seoul (Republic of Korea) in 1984, Ottawa (Canada) in 1987, and Washington, DC (USA), in 1989.

---

[2] All information related to this internal body can be found on the Organization's official website, under the Terms of Reference of the Policy Commission available at http://www.wcoomd.org/-/media/wco/public/global/pdf/about-us/wco-working-bodies/terms-of-reference-of-wco-working-bodies-august-2019.pdf?db=web. Accessed May 10, 2021.

Purpose and Scope

The objective of the Policy Commission is defined as follows:

> The Commission shall concern itself with broad policy questions relevant to the WCO's activities. The Commission shall act as a dynamic Steering Group to the Council. It shall initiate studies on the policies, practices, and procedures of the WCO with the objective of assisting the Council to achieve the broad aims of its activities.
>
> To this end, the Commission examines questions referred to it by the Council, by individual members of the Policy Commission or Council, or by the Secretary General (either on his own initiative or at the request of one of the WCO's technical Committees or other bodies).
>
> The Commission is entitled, within the limits of its powers, to make recommendations to the Council, or in case or urgency, to ask the Secretary General to take such actions as the Commission deems necessary in the interests of the WCO and to report such decision to the next sessions of the Council.

Main Functions

The main functions of the Policy Commission are as follows:

- To examine questions referred to it by the Council, by individual members of the Policy Commission or Council, by the Finance Committee or by the Secretary General (either on his own initiative or at the request of one of the WCO's technical Committees or other bodies);
- Concerning the questions thus examined, to make recommendations to the Council or the relevant Committee, or provide advice to the Secretary General. The Commission may also instruct the Secretary General to undertake further research or reflection on an issue, on the basis of which the Policy Commission will consider the matter further;
- In case of urgency, the Commission is empowered to ask the Secretary General to take such action as the Commission deems necessary in the interests of the WCO and to report such decision to the next sessions of the Council;
- Each June, to conduct a preliminary examination of the Strategic Plan which is prepared each year by the Secretariat, and is submitted first to the Policy Commission and then to the Council;
- Each December, to examine a Programme Budget for the following financial year and make recommendations to the Finance Committee on the general budgetary orientations (including the total amount of the General Operating Expenses) to be presented to the Council for that year;
- To conduct a mid-year review of WCO activities, based on written and oral reports presented by the Secretary General, as a means of monitoring progress on behalf of the Council;
- Each June, to examine the Audit Report in the light of the comments on it made by the Finance Committee, and make recommendations to the Council according.

Means of Operation

The Policy Commission, under its Chairperson (who is the Chairperson of the Council), examines issues based on documents prepared by the Secretariat or, from time to time, Committee reports or papers submitted by individual members. Although the Policy Commission is a "restricted membership" body, the working documents prepared for the sessions are circulated to all WCO members for information. The Policy Commission's Rules of Procedure specify that the Policy Commission shall hold at least two sessions a year, one of which shall be held in conjunction with the Council sessions. In practice, the Policy Commission holds two three-/four-day sessions each year: one about halfway through the financial year (almost always in December) and the other immediately before the annual Council sessions (almost always in June).

As described above, the members of the Policy Commission are elected by the Council for a two-year term, renewable indefinitely, whereas the Council Chairperson and Vice-Chairpersons are elected for a one-year term, renewable once only unless the Council considers otherwise.

The Rules of Procedure specify that Policy Commission members and observers must be represented by their Heads of Administrations, although exceptionally a Head of Administration may authorize a high-ranking official to represent him/her. Delegates and observers may be accompanied by advisers.

Being a "restricted membership" body, the Policy Commission is not open to observers. Nevertheless, in exceptional circumstances, a WCO member that is not a member of the Policy Commission may be invited to attend part of a Policy Commission session, for example, to present a paper it has submitted or to participate in discussions on a topic that it initiated or to report on a meeting at which it represented the WCO.

Although the Policy Commission is essentially an advisory body for the Council, as opposed to a decision-making body, and normally arrives at its recommendations by a consensus, there are detailed provisions governing voting in the Policy Commission; these are set out in an Appendix to the Policy Commission Rules of Procedure. Essentially, these provisions state that each member of the Policy Commission shall have one vote, the representatives of a simple majority of the Policy Commission's members shall constitute a quorum, and a two-third majority of those present and entitled to vote is needed in order to carry a decision.

Resources Required

The WCO Secretariat is responsible for making the arrangements and preparations for the Policy Commission sessions; providing professional, administrative, and technical services during the sessions; and performing follow-up tasks after the sessions. When the Policy Commission meets immediately before the annual Council sessions, its Report must be drafted during the session and adopted before the close of the session so that it can be circulated to the Council the following day. For the Policy Commission's mid-year session, the Report is prepared and circulated by the Secretariat a few weeks after the session. All members are required to bear the expenses (travel and accommodation) of their own delegations to the Policy Commission.

If a Policy Commission session is held away from the WCO Headquarters at the invitation of a member, then that member will usually be required to meet the additional costs that the Organization has incurred by reason of accepting that invitation (e.g., hiring meeting facilities, travel and accommodation expenses of Secretariat officials attending the session, etc.).[3]

2.1.1.1 The Audit Committee

The Audit Committee, which was established in 2007 (the first session was held on October 22 to 31, 2007), assists the Policy Commission and the Council in reviewing WCO programs, policies, and administrative procedures.

In particular, it oversees the overall implementation of the WCO Strategic Plan, the budget allocation process, and the performance measurement policies and practices of the Organization. Furthermore, it ensures efficient and effective program management and the fulfillment of its objectives.

It acts under the overall direction of the Council and with the administrative support provided by the WCO Secretariat.

All members of the Audit Committee are appointed by the Council and can be removed at its sole discretion. The term of office of the Audit Committee members is three years; however, exceptionally, it may be extended by one year.

The Committee comprises six Directors General from the Council representatives from each of the six regions. The seats on the Committee are allocated ideally on a rotating basis from among the active members in each region. In special circumstances, a lower-ranking official may represent his/her Administration on the Audit Committee, provided that such a representative reports directly to the Director General of the Administration.

As it is a body of restricted membership, the Audit Committee is not open to observers. Although it is essentially an advisory body of the Policy Commission and Council and normally arrives at its recommendations by consensus, in the absence of a consensus, decisions shall be taken by a majority of not less than two thirds of the voting members present at the meeting, as provided for in Rule 21 of the Rules of Procedure of the Customs Cooperation Council.

The Audit Committee issues its reports for necessary actions and seeks to hold, mainly through its Chairperson, a constructive relationship with the Secretary-General and the Chief of Administration and Personnel in all issues of their competence.

[3]The December session is usually held out of Brussels; for example, the 72nd Session was held in Recife, Brazil, on December 8 to 10, 2014; the 74th Session was held in Punta Cana, Dominican Republic, on December 7 to 9, 2015; the 80th Session was held in Bombay, India, on December 3 to 5, 2018; and the 82nd Session was held in Seoul, Republic of Korea, on December 3 to 5, 2019.

The Audit Committee is authorized to work with external auditors, if deemed necessary and if it is within budgetary possibilities.

2.1.1.2 Private Sector Consultative Group

The internal function of the Private Sector Consultative Group (PSCG) was drafted in June 2005 during the Annual Council sessions in Brussels. It was confirmed in June 2015 with the approval of the Terms of Reference (Mandate/Rules).[4,5]

This important and innovative institutional structure was created to inform and advise the WCO Secretary-General, the Policy Commission, and the WCO members on customs and international trade matters from the perspective of the private sector.

The WCO Secretary-General, in consultation with the Council Chairperson and Regional Vice-Chairpersons, appoints all PSCG members, of a diverse membership, taking into account the WCO regions, the business size (including small and medium-sized enterprises), and the industry sector. The PSCG is made up mainly of businesses and associations.

Nowadays, the PSCG has 27 members,[6] which include traders (importers/exporters), producers, international trade chain intermediaries, and people and businesses that provide commercial services.[7] Their prolific experience and knowledge enhance the WCO instruments, standards, and guidelines as they may address the varied activities involved in supply chains and the complex international trade.

A fact that has proved to be controversial in the formation of the group is that some members are individual businesses (e.g., IBM, Huawei, Microsoft, Renault-Nissan-Mitsubishi). Other members, which represent chambers or associations,

[4]The PSCG Terms of reference PSCG are available at: http://www.wcoomd.org/en/topics/key-issues/private-sector-consultative-group/terms-of-reference-for-the-private-sector-consultative-group.aspx. Accessed May 10, 2021.

[5]The latest amendment to the Terms of Reference was made in 2017 (Annex VII of the January 2018 Report of the Policy Commission).

[6]Current Members (2020): American Association of Exporters and Importers (AAEI), Association of Professional Customs Brokers of the Americas (ASAPRA), Baker Hughes Business Alliance for Secure Commerce (BASC), Expeditors, Federation of National Associations of Ship Brokers and Agents (FONASBA), Fonterra, Global Express Association (GEA), GS1 Huawei, International Air Transport Association (IATA), IBM, Indelox International Chamber of Commerce (ICC), International Federation of Customs Brokers Associations (IFCBA), International Federation of Freight Forwarders, Associations (FIATA), International Road Transport Union (IRU), International Trademark Association (INTA), Limited Brands, Michelin, Microsoft, Opora, Pharmaceutical Security Institute (PSI), Procomex, Renault-Nissan-Mitsubishi, South African Association of Freight Forwarders (SAA- FF) y Saudi Basic Industries Corporation. Source: http://www.wcoomd.org/en/to-pics/key-issues/private-sector-consultative-group/membership.aspx. Accessed May 10, 2021.

[7]The Terms of Reference, with its 2017 amendment (Annex VII of the January 2018 Policy Commission Report) provides for up to 27 members.

provide more diverse contributions, vis-à-vis their membership, than the one provided by an individual business with its own particular interests.[8]

Each member is in office for a three-year term and cannot be part of the PSCG for more than two consecutive terms. However, former PSCG members can be reappointed after a one-year hiatus.

In order to be reappointed for a second consecutive term, a member must have had a good level of participation and attendance to meetings, which will be assessed in consultation with the PSCG Chairperson. To promote continuity, the WCO Secretary-General, in consultation with the Council Chairperson and Regional Vice-Chairpersons, will appoint new PSCG members when necessary so that the terms are staggered and the PSCG will have the required number of members.

Every year in January, the WCO Secretary-General will send a letter to the Vice-Chairpersons of the WCO regions, the Chairperson of the Council, and the Chairperson of the PSCG informing them of openings in the PSCG membership. Entities wishing to become members of the PSCG will have to submit a written application to the WCO Secretary-General. Applications can be submitted until the end of March, after which the WCO Secretary-General will consult with the WCO Vice-Chairpersons in April. In May, a notification will be issued, and the WCO Council will be informed about the new constitution of the PSCG at its annual sessions in June. A new PSCG member's term starts in July and ends three years later.

PSCG members will have observer status with the WCO for the duration of their appointment to the PSCG and may be invited to attend official WCO meetings in an individual capacity where the Terms of Reference of such meetings provide for such attendance.

Pursuant to the Terms of Reference, the main functions of the PSCG, aside from informing and advising the WCO Secretary-General, the Policy Commission, and the WCO members on customs and international trade matters from the perspective of the private sector, include the following: (i) to support the adoption and effective implementation of agreed WCO and other relevant international instruments, (ii) to leverage business resources and government relationships to advocate and implement programs developed and adopted by the WCO, and finally (iii) to provide a written report to the Policy Commission and the Secretary-General at the conclusion of each meeting.

During its 15 years, the PSCG has carried out excellent work with its contributions to the customs community on (i) the approach regarding the implementation of the Trade Facilitation Agreement and, in particular, the creation of the Trade Facilitation National Committees; (ii) the development of standards for cross-border e-commerce; (iii) the Authorized Economic Operator (AEO) program; (iv) the

[8] Although there are large multinational businesses whose annual turnover exceeds the gross domestic product of several WCO Member States, it must be highlighted that WCO is an intergovernmental organization that works for the general interests of society and not for private interests, regardless of the size of the businesses or their commercial flow influence.

adoption of SAFE; and (v) the elaboration of the Strategic Plans, providing their vision on global financial and commercial trends, among others.

Although the PSCG began its functions in a limited capacity, with time, it has increased its participation in the WCO working groups. This has enabled and will enable to enhance the data used by the WCO as its standpoint is different from that of governments.

Regarding training, within the PSCG, we find the International Chamber of Commerce (ICC), an organization made up of different companies worldwide that specializes in business training and trade dispute resolutions. Through training and mutual work (ICC-WCO Cooperation Agreement), customs competencies have globally improved, thus generating benefits for both organizations and the public.

2.1.1.3 Integrity Sub-committee

The fight against corruption in customs services has been a major concern for the WCO over the last decades;[9] therefore, integrity, or ethics, was included in the WCO agenda in the eighties. This work culminated in 1993 with the adoption of the "WCO Arusha Declaration," which was later replaced by the "Revised Arusha Declaration" in 2003.[10]

In order to guide the WCO's work on ethics, the Integrity Sub-committee was established in January 2001. The Integrity Sub-committee acts under the overall direction of the WCO Council and Policy Commission, with administrative support provided by the WCO Secretariat. As directed by the Council, the Integrity Sub-committee shall be a small, well-focused yet high-level group having a balanced representation from all the WCO regions. The Sub-committee has a Chairperson and a Vice-Chairperson elected from among its members with a one-year term, who can be reelected.

The decisions and recommendations of the Sub-committee are made through discussions and consensus in their annual meetings or as the Secretary-General deems appropriate. The Secretariat notifies the Sub-committee members of the meeting dates and a draft meeting Agenda is made available 30 days before the scheduled date of the meeting. The Secretariat also provides the working documents before the scheduled meeting date. A report containing the proceedings of the meetings is prepared, and once agreed upon, the report is provided in the next Policy Commission sessions within 30 days of each meeting.

The purpose and main competencies of the Sub-committee are to act as a focal point for the design, development, implementation, and evaluation of the WCO Integrity Action Plan and Integrity-related tools. In addition, it advises the Council,

---

[9]History of the Integrity Sub-Committee: http://www.wcoomd.org/en/topics/integrity/overview.aspx. Accessed May 10, 2021.

[10]Revised Arusha Declaration: http://www.wcoomd.org/-/media/wco/public/global/pdf/about-us/legal-instruments/declarations/revised_arusha_declaration_en.pdf?la=en. Accessed May 10, 2021.

through the Policy Commission, on the appropriateness of WCO strategies and priorities necessary to promote the importance of integrity and ensure the effective implementation of the Revised Arusha Declaration. The Sub-committee also provides a forum for the exchange of views, experiences, and best-practice approaches between member administrations to ensure effective coordination and promotion of integrity-related activities with the private sector and other international organizations. Finally, the objective of the Sub-committee is to ensure the effective integration of integrity principles in all WCO training and technical assistance programs, conventions, and other instruments.

The more tangible contributions or works of the Sub-committee include the "Model Code of Ethics and Conduct" and the integral set of tools. In response to the recommendation made at the Third Global Forum on Fighting Corruption and Safeguarding Integrity in June 2005, the WCO produced the first version of the Compendium on Integrity Best Practices. The Sub-committee also proved to be instrumental in improving the integrity in Customs at national and regional levels, with agreements such as the Maputo Declaration,[11] adopted in March 2002 by the Heads of Customs across the African continent; the Almaty Integrity Resolution[12] (done in Almaty, Kazakhstan, in January 2007); the Nairobi Resolution on Integrity[13] (done in Nairobi, Kenya, in February 2007); and the Transparency and Predictability Guidelines[14] (2017).

2.1.2 The Finance Committee

The Finance Committee is responsible for supporting and advising the Policy Commission and Council in financial and budgetary matters. It acts under the overall direction of the Council, with administrative support provided by the WCO Secretarial. Specific responsibility of the Finance Committee, as described in the Financial Rules adopted by the Council, is to examine the estimates of all of the Organization's resources and usage for the following financial year and to prepare the respective report. The estimates shall include an estimated Profit and Loss Account, a statement on cash flow, and an estimated Balance Sheet. They shall cover all operations envisaged for the financial year concerned.

[11]Maputo Declaration: http://www.wcoomd.org/-/media/wco/public/global/pdf/about-us/legal-instruments/declarations/maputo_declaration_en.pdf?la=en. Accessed May 10, 2021.

[12]Almaty Integrity Resolution: http://www.wcoomd.org/-/media/wco/public/global/pdf/topics/integrity/instruments-and-tools/almaty_resolution.pdf?la=en. Accessed May 10, 2021.

[13]Almaty Integrity Resolution: http://www.wcoomd.org/-/media/wco/public/global/pdf/topics/integrity/instruments-and-tools/almaty_resolution.pdf?la=e. Accessed May 10, 2021.

[14]Transparency and Predictability Guidelines: http://www.wcoomd.org/-/media/wco/pu-blic/es/pdf/topics/facilitation/instruments-and-tools/tools/transparency-and-predictability-guidelines/tp-guide-updated-sp-rev.pdf?la=en. Accessed May 10, 2021.

Membership

The Committee began with only seven members in 1953. Its membership increased to nine in 1967, to 12 in 1971, to 13 in 1977, and to 14 in 1993, and then in 1995, through Decision No. 287 adopted at the 85th/86th Council Sessions, the number of members rose to its 17 current members.

As described in Rule 28 of the Rules of Procedure of the Customs Cooperation Council, the Council annually invites 17 members each to nominate a delegate to serve on the Finance Committee (alternates can also be nominated). The seats are allocated on a regional basis as follows:

- Europe: eight seats
- North Africa and the Near and Middle East: one seat
- East and Southern Africa: one seat
- West and Central Africa: one seat
- South America, North America, Central America, and the Caribbean: three seats
- The Far East, South and Southeast Asia, Australasia, and the Pacific Islands: three seats

As a note to Rule 28, the two members paying the highest contributions to the budget of the Organization shall be members of the Finance Committee.

Purpose and Scope

The purpose of the Finance Committee is to perform the functions assigned to it by the Financial Rules made by the Council, as well as to examine specific financial or budgetary matters referred to it by the Council, by the Policy Commission, or by the Secretary-General. In order to prepare decisions by the Policy Commission and the Council, the Finance Committee presents a financial situation report in respect of the achievement of the Strategic Plan objectives.

Main Functions

The main functions of the Finance Committee are the following:

In respect of the previous financial year:

- Examine the full Audit Report prepared by the WCO's External Financial Auditors, together with the Secretary General's comments thereon and, on the basis of that Report and the audited accounts for the previous financial year, to recommend if appropriate that the Council approve those accounts, accept the Secretary General's proposals for the apportionment of the result of the Profit and Loss Account, and acquit the Secretary General of his financial responsibilities for the previous financial year.

In respect of the financial year in progress:

- Consider the situation with regard to the receipt of Members' contributions and capital subscriptions, the execution of the budget and the cash flow situation for the financial year in progress and, where appropriate, advise the Council of measures to be taken.

- Examine and, where appropriate, endorse any measures already taken during the financial year in order to apply to the WCO's various remuneration scales any changes made in the Co-ordinated Organizations.
- Look into the financial implications of any new tasks assigned to the Secretariat and not included in the budget appropriations approved by the Council, and make recommendations to the Council concerning the financing of those tasks.

In respect of the next financial year:

- Consider a provisional scale of Members' contributions for the next financial year.
- Examine - based on the recommendations made by the Policy Commission with regard to the Program Budget and, as appropriate, recommend to the Council for adoption, total Members' contributions, General Operating Expenses, an estimated Profit and Loss Account and Balance Sheet, and a Staffing Table for the next financial year.

Additional Functions:

- Analyze the financial implications of implementing the Strategic Plan and report the assessment to the Policy Commission and the Council;
- Participate in the process for selecting the External Financial Auditors;
- Participate in the planning of internal audits, and in the selection of areas to be examined in management audits;
- Analyze the WCO's financial and budget situation on a quarterly basis, in addition to the examinations conducted at the annual session of the Committee;
- Examine and, where appropriate, make recommendations to the Council on the medium-term financial perspectives or multi-year budgeting of the Organization; on the Organization's financial investments and income, on the production and sale of WCO publications, on alternative sources of funding for the Organization, on the Annual Report on the Customs Co-operation Fund, and on the position with regard to the Organization's capital expenditure.
- Keep WCO conditions of service under review and, where appropriate, make recommendations to the Council on amendments to the Staff Regulations and Staff Rules.
- Deal with certain specific situations envisaged by the Financial Rules of the Organization, such as: approving requests by the Secretary General to transfer appropriations from one Chapter to another; reviewing supplementary estimates submitted by the Secretary General; scrutinizing reports by the Secretary General on the short- term investment of monies not needed for immediate requirements; if necessary, directing the appointed External Financial Auditors to hold an extraordinary audit of any of the Organization's accounts, and providing for the submission of a report on that audit.

Means of Operation

The Finance Committee, under its Chairperson, examines issues based on the documents prepared by the Secretariat. Although the Finance Committee is a "restricted membership" body, the working documents prepared for the sessions are circulated to all WCO members for information.

The Rules of Procedure of the Customs Cooperation Council establishes that the Finance Committee shall meet at such intervals as may be necessary to execute its functions. In order to deal with decisions taken by the Council without prior costing or where new programs arise during the course of the budget year, the Finance Committee may conduct "virtual" consultations among its members using electronic means organized by the Chairperson of the Finance Committee.

As previously mentioned, the members of the Finance Committee are elected by the Council for a one-year term, renewable indefinitely. Such terms and conditions also apply to the Chairperson and Vice-Chairperson, who are elected from among the members of the Finance Committee.

Being a "restricted membership" body, the Finance Committee is not open to observers. Nevertheless, in exceptional circumstances, a WCO member that is not a member of the Finance Committee may be invited to attend part of a Finance Committee session.

The External Financial Auditors appear before the Finance Committee each year to present their report and answer any questions on it. They may also be invited to participate in the discussions on specific Agenda items relevant to their financial or management audits. In addition, the Organization's portfolio managers may be asked to appear before the Finance Committee to report on their strategy and answer questions about its implementation. From time to time, other specialists (actuaries, investment analysts, etc.) may be invited to attend part of a Finance Committee session to provide information or advice on specific issues.

The Finance Committee is essentially an advisory body and is not responsible for decisions. There are detailed provisions governing voting in the Finance Committee; these are set out in Rule 28 of the Rules of Procedure of the Customs Cooperation Council. Essentially, these provisions state that the quorum of the Committee shall be nine delegates or alternates.

Resources Required

The Finance Committee generally meets at WCO Headquarters with the administrative and technical support of the Secretariat. If necessary, the Chairperson of the Committee may participate in WCO regional meetings.

2.1.3 Permanent Technical Committee

The Permanent Technical Committee (PTC) was created in 1953, simultaneously with the Customs Cooperation Council, and plays an essential role in the Organization. Its functions include analyzing and studying all aspects of customs complex technical matters and making recommendations to the Council thereof.

As stated in Article X of the Convention establishing the WCO, the PTC is composed of representatives of the members of the Council. Each member may nominate one delegate and one or more alternates to be its representatives on the Committee. The representatives should be officials specialized in technical customs matters and may be assisted by experts.

The PTC elects a Chairperson and a Vice-Chairperson each year from among the representatives of its members. The Chairperson and Vice-Chairperson are elected for a period of one year and are eligible for reelection.

Although it is established that the Permanent Technical Committee shall meet not less than four times a year, it actually holds two double annual meetings, usually in the months of June and December.

As it will be shown along this work, the PTC represents one of the medullary structures of the WCO and plays a leading role when tackling complex and specific customs matters.

In its capacity as a general technical body of the World Customs Organization, the Permanent Technical Committee is responsible for carrying out research on the new trends of customs technology and for studying the application of science and modern technology in customs systems.

To this end, the PTC is furnished with the studies and projects that it commissions to the Working Groups at the end of its sessions.

For example, in 2015, the "Virtual Working Group on the Future of Customs" was set up. This Group, consisting of Customs, the private sector, international organizations, and academia, has been working on a document titled "The Future of Customs."

The main subjects under analysis include blockchain, artificial intelligence, the Internet of Things, biometrics, drones, and 3D printing, among the more recent technologies, which are analyzed in the penultimate chapter of this book.

2.1.4 *Technical Committee on Rules of Origin*

The Technical Committee on Rules of Origin (TCRO) was created in 1995. Along with the Technical Committee on Customs Valuation, it is the result of the cooperation between the WCO and the World Trade Organization (WTO).

It was established pursuant to Article III, paragraph (h), of the Convention establishing a Customs Cooperation Council"[15] and the Agreement on Rules of Origin of the WTO, Article 4.2.[16]

[15]Convention Establishing a Customs Cooperation Council: http://www.wcoomd.org/-/media/wco/public/global/pdf/about-us/legal-instruments/conventions-and-agreements/ccc/convccc.pdf?la=en. Accessed May 10, 2021.

[16]WTO, Agreement on Rules of Origin: https://www.wto.org/english/docs_e/legal_e/22-roo_e.htm. Accessed May 10, 2021.

Thus, the Technical Committee on Rules of Origin operates under the auspices of the WCO, as provided for under Article 4.2 of the Origin Agreement, and becomes one of the WCO technical committees.[17]

Aside from this Committee, Article 4.1 of the Agreement created a Committee on Rules of Origin, which works within the scope of the WTO.

The three major responsibilities of the Technical Committee are as follows:

i. to examine specific technical problems arising in the day-to-day administration of the rules of origin of Members and to give advisory opinions on appropriate solutions based upon the facts presented;
ii. to furnish information and advice on any matters concerning the origin determination of goods as may be requested by any Member or the Committee;
iii. to prepare and circulate periodic reports on the technical aspects of the operation and status of this Agreement.

Each WTO member has the right to be represented on the Technical Committee and may be assisted by advisers at the meetings. The WTO Secretariat may also attend such meetings with observer status (Origin Agreement, Annex I, paragraph 4). Members of the WCO that are not members of the WTO may be represented at the meetings of the Technical Committee by one delegate and one or more alternates. Such representatives attend meetings of the Technical Committee as observers (Annex I, paragraph 5). Subject to the approval of the Chairperson of the Technical Committee, the Secretary-General of the WCO may invite representatives of governments that are neither members of the WTO nor members of the WCO and representatives of international governmental and trade organizations to attend the meetings of the Technical Committee as observers (Annex I, paragraph 6).

2.1.5 Capacity Building Committee

The Capacity Building Committee[18] was created in 2010, and its first session was held on October 27 to 29, 2010. It seeks to elaborate training actions, strategies, guidelines, and tools as well as to provide technical assistance. In addition, it is a forum for cooperation and exchange of information regarding organizational development and human resources.

The Capacity Building Committee acts under the overall direction of the WCO Council and Policy Commission, with administrative support provided by the WCO Secretariat.

---

[17] The information included in this paragraph has been extracted from the "Terms of Reference of the Technical Committee on Rules of Origin: http://www.wcoomd.org/en/about-us/wco-working-bodies/tarif_and_trade/technical_committee_on_rules_of_origin.aspx.

[18] World Customs Organization, Capacity Building Committee: http://www.wcoomd.org/en/about-us/wco-structure/wco-working-bodies.aspx. Accessed May 10, 2021.

Members attending the Capacity Building Committee should preferably be officials responsible for the area of human and organizational development, or heads of personnel. A member may nominate one delegate and one or more alternates to be its representative(s) on the Capacity Building Committee. Representatives of members of the Capacity Building Committee may be assisted by advisers. Representatives of international governmental and trade organizations may attend meetings of the Capacity Building Committee as observers.

Every year, the Committee elects a Chairperson and a Vice-Chairperson from among the representatives of its members, which are eligible for reelection.

The Capacity Building Committee shall meet at least once a year at the WCO Headquarters. If appropriate, the Committee's sessions could be held back to back with those of the Integrity Sub-committee and the meetings of the Regional Offices for Capacity Building and Regional Training Centers.

2.1.6 Harmonized System Committee

The Harmonized System Committee[19] was created in 1988,[20] and its first session was held from April 11 to 22, 1988. It is a specialized technical body that carries out the complex management of the Harmonized System (HS). The purpose and scope of HS are to interpret HS legal texts in the most appropriate manner to secure uniform classification of goods, including the settlement of classification disputes between Contracting Parties; besides, it actively participates in the HS amendment process to reflect developments in technology and changes in trade patterns.

It decides on difficult classification matters submitted by the Member States or international organizations and acts as a mediator in their dispute settlements.

It is composed of its own Chairperson, whom the Secretariat is directly dependent on; one or more Vice-Chairpersons; and the delegates of the Member States.

The Committee draws up its own Rules of Procedure through a decision taken by not less than two thirds of the votes attributed to its members. The Rules of Procedure so drawn up shall be approved by the Council.

The Committee normally holds two sessions a year,[21] in which classification issues submitted by the Contracting Parties are discussed and decided upon.

[19] World Customs Organization, Terms of Reference of the Harmonized System Committee: http://www.wcoomd.org/-/media/wco/public/global/pdf/about-us/wco-wor-king-bodies/ter-ms-of-reference-of-wco-working-bodies-august-2019.pdf?db=web. Accessed May 10, 2021.

[20] The first session was held at the then Customs Cooperation Council Headquarters with the participation of 140 delegates and observers of 64 States and Customs territories, and 8 international organizations.

[21] Meetings are usually held at the WCO Headquarters, and the Committee may invite such intergovernmental or other international organizations as it may consider appropriate.

The purpose of these sessions is to discuss the interpretation of the HS texts, including the settlement of classification disputes that have been submitted by the parties. These issues usually refer to the following:

- Classification problems issued via errata sheets
- Issues arising from the harmonization of the official texts in English and French that may lead to a lack of uniformity in the application of the classification
- Creation, removal, or amendment of the Explanatory Notes of the Harmonized System, if necessary
- Issuance of classification criteria in order to improve the classification of goods without amending the Explanatory Notes
- Preparation of the recommendations for HS

The Convention of the Harmonized System empowers the Technical Committee to maintain the classification up to date and to prepare amendments to the basic text pursuant to the technical needs or errors proved in practice that hinder the uniformity required for the classification of goods.

The Committee's activities are supported by the following:

- Review Sub-committee
- Scientific Sub-committee, and
- Working Parties

The Review Sub-committee
This Sub-committee is responsible for keeping HS updated through the creation, removal, or amendment of commodity codes or Explanatory Notes. Once approved by the HS Committee, these reviews are submitted to the WCO Policy Commission for approval and entry into force as Recommendations of Amendments of the HS Convention.

Scientific Sub-committee
This body is composed of a group of professionals appointed by the Contracting Parties to the Convention. The Sub-committee is responsible for studying and proposing solutions of a technical nature referred to by the HS Committee with a view to obtaining suitable reports. These will enable the HS to enhance its efficacy.

Working Parties
These are study groups set up by the HS Committee to tackle specific matters of classification as well as other matters within its competencies.

2.1.7 Enforcement Committee

The Enforcement Committee[22] was created in 1983. It held its first session from December 5 to 9, 1983. It assists the WCO in the fight against smuggling and other customs crimes.[23]

The issues studied and discussed by the Enforcement Committee cover missions and activities provided for in international agreements, such as illicit traffic in narcotic drugs, trade in endangered species, nuclear and chemical materials, money laundering, intellectual property, or transnational organized crime. In addition, the Committee is responsible for studying matters regarding mutual administrative assistance among Customs.

Furthermore, it coordinates the Regional Intelligence Liaison Offices (RILOs) and manages the technical work in the processing of customs intelligence of the WCO Secretariat. The Committee cooperates with a network of partners, including the United Nations Office on Drugs and Crime and the Interpol.

The Enforcement Committee acts under the overall direction of the Policy Commission, with administrative support provided by the WCO Secretariat.

2.1.8 Technical Committee on Customs Valuation

The Technical Committee on Customs Valuation is established in accordance with Article 18 of the Agreement on Implementation of Article VII of the General Agreement on Tariffs and Trade (GATT) 1994. It carries out the responsibilities described in Annex II of the said Agreement.

Its headquarters are in Brussels and works under the auspices of the World Customs Organization with a view to ensuring uniformity in the interpretation and application of the Agreement at a technical level. Therefore, it issues documents such as advisory opinions, commentaries, studies, explanatory notes, and case studies.[24]

[22] In the official WCO documents, there is no authorized translation into Spanish for "ENFORCEMENT COMMITTEE" (English) and "COMITÉ DE LA LUTTE CONTRE LA FRAUDE" (French). As there is no single word in Spanish that actually means "enforcement," the Spanish version of this book has adopted the French translation into Spanish, i.e., "COMMITTEE OF FIGHT AGAINST FRAUD."

[23] The Enforcement Committee was created by a decision adopted by the Council in 1983, whereby the Enforcement Working Group was turned into a committee. Before this change in category, the Group had held 12 sessions, from April 1974 to January 1983.

[24] World Customs Organization, Terms of Reference of the Technical Committee on Customs Valuation: http://www.wcoomd.org/en/about-us/wco-working-bodies/tarif_and_trade/technical_-committee_on_customs_valuation.aspx. Accessed May 10, 2021.

Purpose and Scope

a. Examine specific technical problems arising in the day-to-day administration of the Agreement and to give advisory opinions on appropriate solutions based upon the facts presented;
b. Study, as requested, valuation laws, procedures and practices as they relate to the Agreement and to prepare reports on the results of such studies
c. Prepare and circulate annual reports on the technical aspects of the operation and status of the Agreement;
d. Furnish such information and advice, such as advisory opinions, commentaries, explanatory notes, on any matters concerning customs valuation as may be requested by any Member of the Committee on Customs Valuation;
e. Facilitate, as requested, technical assistance to the Parties with a view to furthering the international acceptance of the Agreement.

   In parallel, within the scope of the WTO, there is another Technical Committee on Customs Valuation with headquarters in Geneva, Switzerland, whose function is to ensure compliance with the trade policy objectives set forth in GATT. It issues decisions regarding the application of the Agreement in matters such as interests, software, and reasonable doubts, among others.

2.1.9 *Working Parties*

In order to accomplish specific goals, Working Groups are created. These may meet face to face, virtually, or in a blended mode. They are made up of experts in the field, who study and prepare proposals. In this book, we shall describe the tasks carried out by some of these groups: the Working Group on Trade Facilitation, the SAFE Working Group (in charge of the SAFE Framework of Standards to Secure and Facilitate Global Trade), the Working Group on the Comprehensive Review of the Revised Kyoto Convention, and the Working Group on the Future of Customs, among others.

2.2 The Secretariat

The Secretariat is in charge of the WCO's day-to-day operation and supplies technical and logistical support to the various working bodies. Together with the WCO's committees, the Secretariat implements the WCO Strategic Plan, as approved by the Council. It is also the governing body of the international customs agreements within the scope of the World Customs Organization.

Its head is the Secretary-General, who along with the Deputy Secretary-General, runs the general management of the Secretariat (see Fig. 2.2).

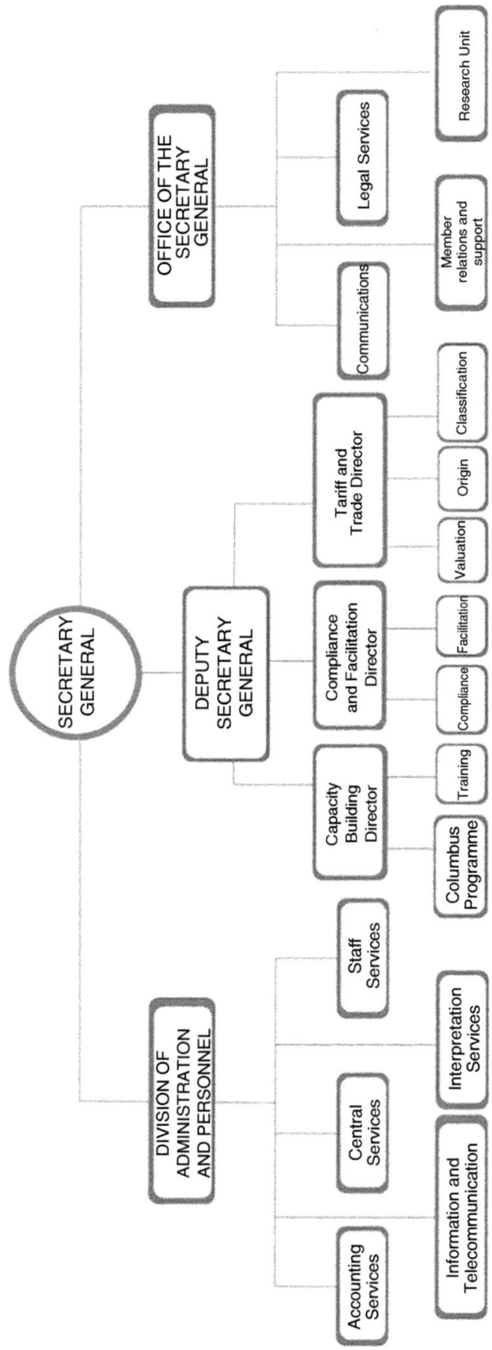

Fig. 2.2 Structure of the WCO Secretariat. **Source:** Author's elaboration based on information from the WCO

Secretary-General

Article XI of the WCO founding Convention provides that the Council shall appoint a Secretary-General, whose functions, duties, conditions of service, and terms of office shall be determined by the Council. Candidates for the position of Secretary-General are nominated by the Member States and must be citizens of said countries. After the definitive vote of the Council, the elected Secretary-General shall hold office for a five-year term.

The Secretary-General is the Executive Director of the Organization, and as such, he runs the Secretariat and undertakes the responsibility of its general work. He is accountable for its actions before the Council.

The Secretary-General acts on behalf of the WCO on a global level when it comes to matters of international law. He is entitled to send representatives to national governments and other international organizations to represent the WCO in customs matters within its jurisdiction. Cooperation between the WCO and WTO and several other international organizations is managed by the Secretary-General as their representatives.

The Secretary-General has labor powers over the Secretariat's staff. The chiefs of the different departments and Secretariat personnel are appointed by the Secretary-General. As employees, they serve as international civil servants; therefore, they are beyond the control of their own governments and are completely within the scope of the staff authority of the Secretary-General.

The Division of Administration and Personnel is responsible for the administrative management of the Secretariat, including budget and human resources.

Over the last years, the Secretariat has carried out its activities with a staff turnover of around 220 officials of over 60 nationalities.[25]

Slightly over half of this total number is composed of permanent staff represented by technical officers Grade A, Grade B, and Grade C.

In addition, the Secretariat has professional associates, who are hired on a temporary basis.

All technical posts are occupied by officials from the Member States' administrations for a period of five years, and the maximum term of office is limited to ten years.

As previously mentioned, the official languages are English and French. Spanish is used as an official language in the Technical Committee on Customs Valuation, the Administrative Committee for the Customs Convention on Containers (along with Russian), and the Harmonized System Committee (Spanish has been a working

[25]During the 133th/134th Council Sessions, which took place in Brussels in June 2019, the Secretary-General reported that the number of Secretariat personnel currently stood at 222, representing 67 nationalities, including 49 technical officers; 40 technical attachés, who had generously been seconded by members at their own expense; and ten professional associates, who had been given the opportunity to obtain international working experience at the WCO, thanks to the funding from Japan under the Career Development Programme: https://www.ifcba.org/sites/default/files/ctd_files/sc0186e%20-%20Draft%20Minutes%20of%20the%20133-134%20Sessions%20of%20the%20Customs%20Co-Ope- ration%20Council_0.pdf. Accessed May 10, 2021.

language since 1999 and Russian since 2000).[26] It is worth mentioning that the Working Group on Trade Facilitation has also incorporated Spanish, and groups and committees created by the WTO consider Spanish as an official language.

The Secretariat employs two full-time interpreters. In addition, it works with 25 to 30 freelance interpreters, who are knowledgeable about customs matters and jargon. They are hired to assist in specific meetings or events throughout the year.

Officials hold the rank of international civil servants, i.e., officials of international organizations such as the United Nations. Their status, including that of the WCO Secretariat, are subject to international principles.

From the moment they are hired, officials of the WCO Secretariat cease to represent the sovereign state they belong to and only work the duty of loyalty to the World Customs Organization. As such, their administrative level, hiring, working conditions, responsibilities, obligations, salary, and benefits respond to the hiring conditions established by the Organization and are unrelated to the officials' country of origin. They enjoy the same privileges and immunities accorded to international civil servants.

In their capacity as international civil servants, WCO personnel benefit from emoluments exempt from, health insurance, education allowance for their children and for qualified officers, expatriation allowance and traveling expenses for the return journey between Brussels and the official's home every two years.

In conformity with Section 17 of the Annex of the founding Convention of the WCO, officials of the Council shall:

a. be immune from legal process in respect of words spoken or written and all acts performed by them in their official capacity and within the limits of their authority;
b. be exempt from taxation in respect of the salaries and emoluments paid to them by the Council;
c. be immune, together with their spouses and relatives dependent on them, from immigration restrictions and aliens' registration;
d. be immune, together with their spouses and relatives dependent on them, from immigration restrictions and aliens' registration;
e. be given, together with their spouses and relatives dependent on them, the same repatriation facilities in time of international crises as officials of comparable rank of diplomatic missions;
f. have the right to import free of duty their furniture and effects at the time of first taking up their post in the country in question, and to return such furniture and effects free of duty to their country of domicile on the termination of their functions.

As mentioned above, technical attachés form part of the group of people who collaborate and work with the Secretariat. They are professionals with a high level of technical qualification who assist in the management of the WCO on behalf of their

[26] Having an official working language means that there is simultaneous interpretation at the expense of the interested countries.

countries. They hold a labor contract with their countries of origin, which bear the cost of their salaries and expenses.[27]

Their work is of a double nature. On the one hand, they work for the WCO; therefore, they shall carry out their labor responsibilities as international experts, in particular when dealing with customs professional and technical affairs; i.e., they shall leave aside their national interests. On the other hand, they work for their own states, which pay their salaries and grant them benefits and administrative levels.

These collaborators, undoubtedly fundamental for the day-to-day work at the WCO, are appointed by their states of origin. The states that can afford the cost of representation by a technical attaché, or more than one, have more level of participation in the decisions made by the WCO Working Groups than those states that, due to budgetary constraints, are unable to take part in the discussions.

The Research Unit produces evidence-based analytical research and policy analysis on customs and international trade topics. It also organizes international research events, such as the Partnership in Customs Academic Research and Development (PICARD) Conference.[28] In light of its relevance, this shall be dealt with in Chap. 15.

The WCO Communications Service is responsible for all public affairs, stakeholder visits, and media engagement. It produces the magazine WCO News, which is issued three times a year and distributed to all WCO members, donor institutions, national development agencies, international organizations, professional associations, and private sector entities.

Secretaries-General in Chronological Order

- February 2 to August 1, 1953
  Barón François de Sélys Longchamps (Belgium)
  (Council Decision No. 3, February 3, 1953)
- August 2, 1953, to August 31, 1978
  Chevalier George Annez de Taboada (Belgium)
  (Council Decision No. 14, May 16, 1953)
- September 1, 1978, to December 31, 1983
  Sir Ronald Radford (United Kingdom)
  Council Decision No. 217, June 16, 1978)[29]
- January 1, 1984, to December 31, 1988
  Mr. Glenn Robert Dickerson (USA)
  (Council Decision No. 234, June 17, 1983)

[27]In June 2019 there were 46 Brussel-based Technical Attachés: Angola, Armenia, Azerbaijan, Bulgaria, China, Democratic Republic of Congo, Dominican Republic, France, Germany, Ghana, Hong Kong China, Japan, Kazakhstan, Korea, Russian Federation, South Africa, Switzerland, Tunisia, Turkey, United Kingdom, United States of America, among others.

[28]The 14th edition of the WCO PICARD Conference was held on October 22 to 24, 2019, in Skopje, North Macedonia. Out of more than 80 proposals, 40 presentations were made by representatives of academia, governments, and the private sector.

[29]Take note that the first three Secretaries-General belonged to the European aristocracy and held noble titles (baron, sir, and chevalier).

- January 1, 1989, to December 31, 1993
  Mr. Thomas P. Hayes (Australia)
  (Council Decision No. 259, June 24, 1988)
- January 1, 1994, to December 31, 1998
  Mr. James W. Shaver (USA)
  (Council Decision No. 278, July 1, 1993)
- January 1, 1999, to December 31, 2008
  Mr. Michel Danet (France)
  (Council Decision No. 296, August 4, 1998)
- January 1, 2008 to date
  Mr. Kunio Mikuriya (Japan)
  (Council Decision No. 323 of July 1, 2008; Council Decision No. 336 of July 2, 2013; and Council Decision No. 352 of July 5, 2018)

Deputy Secretaries-General in Chronological Order

- 1953 to 1971
  Position remained vacant
- January 1, 1972, to December 31, 1976
  Edward Floyd Kilpatrick (USA)
  (Council Decision No. 188, June 11, 1971)
- 1977 to 1981
  Position remained vacant
- January 1, 1982, to December 31, 1991
  Michel Auge (France)
  (Council Decision No. 233, June 19, 1981)
- January 1, 1992, to December 31, 1996
  Pierre Benet (France)
  (Council Decision No. 267, June 26, 1991)
- January 1, 1997, to December 31, 2001
  Leonid Lozbenko (Russia)
  (Council Decision No. 291, July 16, 1996)
- January 1, 2002, to December 31, 2008
  Kunio Mikuriya (Japan)
  (Council Decision No. 304, July 17, 2001)
- January 1, 2010, to July 18, 2017
  Sergio Mujica Montes (Chile)
  (Council Decision No. 326, July 1, 2009, and Council Decision No. 341, July 1, 2014).[30]
- January 1, 2018, to date
  Ricardo Treviño Chapa (México)
  (Council Decision No. 350, December 15, 2017)

[30] After his appointment as Secretary-General of the International Standard Organization (ISO), Sergio Mujica Montes ceased his function as WCO Deputy Secretary-General on July 18th, 2017.

2.2.1 *Tariff and Trade Affairs Directorate*

The Tariff and Trade Affairs Directorate (T&TA) is the most technical area of the Secretariat, and it centers its activities on matters related to commodity classification, valuation, and rules of origin. To that end, it manages the Harmonized System (HS), the WTO Valuation Agreement, and the WTO Agreement on Rules of Origin.

It also promotes the harmonized interpretation and correct application of the WTO Valuation Agreement, including the link between this Agreement and transfer pricing. Additionally, it assists customs administration in the management and application of rules of origin in light of the proliferation of preferential trade agreements.

2.2.2 *Compliance and Facilitation Directorate*

The Compliance and Facilitation Directorate (C&F) is a medullar area in the Organization and centers its work on relevant matters connected with observing customs and international trade legal rules.

Some C&F instruments and tools include the following:

i. The WCO flagship: the Revised Kyoto Convention (RKC)
ii. The instrument that changed the paradigm of the customs treatment of cargo: the SAFE Framework of Standards
iii. The control method that enabled the fluid international traffic of goods: the Customs Risk Management Compendium the Customs Risk Management Compendium
iv. The Customs Enforcement Network (CEN)
v. The Time Release Study (TRS), and
vi. The WCO Data Model

The Compliance and Facilitation Directorate is responsible for the strategies of the WCO in connection with the WTO Trade Facilitation Agreement. The Directorate has been an active and indispensable protagonist in the vertiginous implementation of the agreement.

In addition, it coordinates and leads the Working Group on E-Commerce and all matters related to cross-border e-commerce.

In addition, it coordinates a variety of enforcement operations against illicit trade, such as commercial fraud, drug trafficking, tobacco, intellectual property rights, hazardous goods, and weapons of mass destruction. The C&F Directorate manages the WCO's network of Regional Intelligence Liaison Offices (RILO).

2.2.3 Capacity Building Directorate

The Capacity Building Directorate (CBD) coordinates and delivers technical assistance and training to members. The CBD emphasizes sustainable reform and modernization by sequencing needs assessment, strategic planning, implementation, and monitoring. Its tools include the Customs Capacity Building Diagnostic Framework and the WCO Capacity Building Development Compendium. This Directorate manages the WCO network of regional entities of capacity building, which includes the Regional Offices for Capacity Building (ROCB) and the Regional Training Centers (RTO).

It is worth mentioning that, as stated in the WCO 2019/2020 Report, there are over 830,000 customs officers around the world.

The CBD also develops and implements the WCO's e-learning modules and manages its online portal CLiKC! The CBD participates in the management of the PICARD Programme, which focuses on the relationship between research, development, and human resources.

2.3 Customs Regions

The six WCO regions are as follows:

- North Africa, Near and Middle East, with 18 members representing 10% of the WCO membership
- West and Central Africa, with 23 members representing 13% of the WCO membership
- East and Southern Africa, with 24 members representing 13% of the WCO membership
- South America, North America, Central America, and the Caribbean, with 31 members representing 17% of the WCO membership
- Europe, with 51 members representing 28% of the WCO membership
- Far East, South and Southeast Asia, Australasia and the Pacific Islands, with 33 members representing 18% of the WCO membership

Legal Status

There has been an extensive debate in connection with the legal status of the regional entities. Since 2012, it has been temporarily agreed that these are autonomous initiatives of the regions and not offices dependent on the WCO.

This matter is of utmost importance vis-a-vis the obligations and responsibilities arising from the administrative management, operating costs, financing, audits, staff (do they enjoy diplomatic privileges?) which may have direct impact on the costs and previsibility of the Organization.

Undoubtedly, until this inconsistency is resolved, the decentralization of regional entities by the WCO remains fragile as there is no area entrusted with their coordination and there are several aspects pending regulation.

Furthermore, Vice-Chairpersons, who, among other functions, advise the Secretary-General regarding their respective regions and occasionally act on behalf of the WCO in events or meetings, lack legal status.

This problem is not present in the case of the Regional Offices for Capacity Building (ROCBs), the Regional Training Centers (RTOs), the Regional Dog Training Centers (RDTCs), the Regional Customs Laboratories (RCLs), and the Regional Intelligence Liaison Offices (RILOs). These are financed by the host national governments.

The following are the current active entities:

- Eleven (11) Regional Intelligence Liaison Offices (RILOs), responsible for the collection and analysis of enforcement-related data.
- Six (6) Regional Offices for Capacity Building (ROCBS), which assist WCO members in their capacity-building programs at the regional level, and 29 Regional Training Centers, which provide technical assistance in several fields. In addition, there are 15 Regional Dog Training Centers and four Regional Customs Laboratories.[31]

[31] The geographical distribution: http://www.wcoomd.org/-/media/wco/public/global/pdf/media/annual-reports/annual_report_2019_2020_en.pdf. Accessed May 10, 2021.

Chapter 3
Legal Instruments

The World Customs Organization (WCO) works with six types of legal instruments:

1. International conventions
2. Recommendations
3. Resolutions
4. Declarations
5. Opinions,[1] and
6. Memorandums of understanding

The Convention establishing the WCO only refers to the first two types of instruments in Article III, paragraphs c), d), and e), which were transcribed above.

3.1 International Conventions[2]

The WCO Conventions are legally binding once they have been internalized by the Member States, considering that they are classic multilateral international treaties under the Vienna Convention.

In accordance with the provisions of Article 2 of the Vienna Convention, *"Treaty" means an international agreement concluded between States in written form and governed by international law, whether embodied in a single instrument or in two or more related instruments and whatever its particular designation;*[. . .].

In turn, Article 5 of the Vienna Convention expressly provides: *The present Convention applies to any treaty which is the constituent instrument of an*

[1] In this matter, we take into account the specialized legal doctrine that incorporates Opinions as a legal instrument of the World Customs Organization. See Daillier, Patrick (1976) Le Conseil De Cooperation Douaniere, Annuaire français de droit international.

[2] The International Conventions are available at the following link: http://www.wcoomd.org/en/about-us/legal-instruments/conventions.aspx.

H. H. Juárez Allende, *The World Customs Organization*, Law for Professionals,
https://doi.org/10.1007/978-3-030-85296-2_3

international organization and to any treaty adopted within an international organization without prejudice to any relevant rules of the organization.

Generally, all customs authorities participate in the study and negotiation of international conventions that are drafted within the organism's scope. Once the standard is defined, it is reported to the government's diplomatic department for examination and approval, as well as the subsequent issuance of the applicable credentials. They enter into force after the Letter of Ratification has been delivered (deposited) at the WCO Secretariat.

Two doctrinal positions have been put forward in order to determine whether international law can be applied directly at the states' domestic level or whether it requires a rule of domestic law that integrates it into this legal system and determines the level of hierarchy granted to it in the legal structure:

Dualist theory: it proposes the existence of two totally independent legal orders since it considers that international law and domestic law have different sources (domestic law is based on the will of a single state, while international law is based on the common will of the signatory states), and they regulate different realities (the subjects of domestic law are individuals, and the subjects of international law are states). Therefore, in order for international law to be effective in national systems, the norm must be received and incorporated in such a way that its hierarchical level is similar to the rest of the laws. This could lead to inconsistencies and contradictory norms. In these cases, the prerogative that a *superior law abrogates an inferior law* and the criteria that *a subsequent law abrogates a previous law and a special law prevails over a general law* cannot be applied.

Monist theory: it states that national law and international law form a unique system where the following alterations can occur in regard to the hierarchical position of the norms: (i) the supremacy of international law over national law and (ii) the supremacy of national law over international law.

In this theory, the way in which the national legal systems internalize the Conventions is subject to the legal idiosyncrasies of each signatory state.

Having clarified the above, it is appropriate to highlight the "indirect" level of effectiveness of the Conventions signed within the scope of the WCO. Even if not formally internalized, they "filter" and inspire the national regulations, which then govern certain customs institutes.

It is through these instruments that the WCO fundamentally fulfills its purpose of harmonizing or standardizing the regulation of customs processes in the world.

Below is an inventory and brief description of the Conventions generated within the World Customs Organization, arranged according to their date of entry into force.[3]

[3] Author's note: At the end of the Conventions, the reader will find a statistical analysis of the percentages of incorporation of the Treaties into national legislation. In addition, at the end of the book, Annex III presents the details of the internationalization categorized by country and dates of adhesion.

1. Convention on the Valuation of Goods for Customs Purposes (Entered into Force on July 28, 1953)
This Convention is analyzed in Point **7.1, Valuation of the Goods. Historical Background**. We refer to this point to avoid repetition in its analysis.

2. Customs Convention on ECS Carnets for Commercial Samples (Entered into Force on October 3, 1957)
In 1952, the GATT Contracting Parties adopted an International Agreement to Facilitate the Importation of Commercial Samples and Advertising Material, which entered into force on November 20, 1955. On the basis of this Convention, the Customs Cooperation Council prepared the Customs Convention on the ECS Carnets for Commercial Samples, which entered into force on October 3, 1957. The ECS Carnet, introduced by the Convention, is an optional replacement for national temporary import documents and replaces any suspended import deposits or guarantees and charges if such guarantees are required by customs authorities in a particular case.

The Customs Cooperation Council informed the GATT Executive Secretary that the *satisfactory results obtained by the use of ECS Carnets for the temporary import of commercial samples (in 1960, 15.600 ECS Cards were issued, for a total value of US$ 16,320,000) induced the international trade community to propose that the facilities offered by the ECS Carnet Convention be extended as much as possible.* Accordingly, the Customs Cooperation Council amended this Convention to open it to accession by the government of any member of the United Nations or its specialized agencies, whether a member of the Council or not. This amendment entered into force on July 7, 1961.

At its 47th/48th Sessions in June 1976, the WCO Council recommended that the Contracting Parties denounce this Convention because of duplication with the ATA Convention. Twenty-one instruments of denunciation have been deposited since then, and currently there is only one Contracting Party (Haiti).

3. Convention on Nomenclature for the Classification of Goods in Customs Tariffs (Entered into Force on September 11, 1959)
This Convention is analyzed in Point **6.2**, **Nomenclature and Classification of Goods. Historical Background**. We refer to this point to avoid repetition in its analysis.

4. Customs Convention on the Temporary Importation of Packings (Entered into Force on March 15, 1962)
The Convention entered into force on March 15, 1962, i.e., three months after depositing a third instrument of accession after two signatures without reservation of ratification. For any other government, it will enter into force three months after depositing its instruments of ratification or accession.

The States Parties to this Convention, meeting under the auspices of the World Customs Organization (WCO), must temporarily admit "packings" into the customs territory without paying import duties, provided they are identifiable at reexportation. If they are imported filled, they must be declared empty or filled reexportations; if they are imported empty, they must be declared filled for reexportation. States Parties shall endeavor to waive the requirement for guarantees in favor of a commitment to reexport the containers in question. Filled containers on temporary admission must be reexported within 6 months of the date of import, whereas empty containers must be reexported within 3 months.

The Convention facilitates the export of goods produced in the Member States' territories, and therefore, it promotes national economic development. The Convention on Temporary Admission (Istanbul, June 26, 1990) incorporates the provisions of the 1960 Convention into a single instrument for goods and materials formerly set out in numerous international customs conventions.

The provisions of the Convention do not exclude the application of restrictions and controls imposed under national regulations for reasons of public morality, public security, hygiene, or public health or for veterinary or phytopathological considerations. Each Member State of the United Nations may become a party to this instrument.

Article 13 provides that the Contracting Parties shall meet together when necessary in order to consider the operation of the present Convention and, in particular, to consider measures to secure uniformity in the interpretation and application. Such meetings shall be convened by the Secretary-General of the Customs Cooperation Council at the request of any Contracting Party, and decisions of the Contracting Parties shall be taken by a majority of not less than two thirds of the Contracting Parties present at the meeting and voting.

Any dispute between Contracting Parties concerning the interpretation or application of the present Convention shall in so far as possible be settled by negotiation between them. Any dispute that is not settled by negotiation shall be referred by the disputing Contracting Parties to the other Contracting Parties. The Contracting Parties in dispute may agree in advance to accept the recommendations of the Contracting Parties as binding.

Pursuant to Article 20 of the Convention, the governments of Algeria, Cuba, Israel, South Africa, Spain, Switzerland, and the United Kingdom have made "Reservations" and gave notification that they consider themselves bound only in relation to packings other than those imported on purchase, or under a similar contract, by a person established or resident in the national territory.

5. Customs Convention on the Temporary Importation of Professional Equipment (Entered into Force on July 1, 1962)

In this Convention, the signatory states undertook to admit the temporary importation of professional equipment without levying import duties. Three annexes define the equipment in question, stipulate the conditions for granting temporary admission, and provide illustrative lists—Annex A: Equipment for the Press or for Sound or Television Broadcasting, Annex B: Cinematographic Equipment, Annex C: Other Professional Equipment, including all the material necessary for the exercise of the calling, trade or profession of a person visiting a country to perform a specified task. The ratification of the annexes is at the discretion of the States Parties. The Convention also applies to elements imported for the purpose of repairing temporarily admitted equipment. Equipment granted for temporary admission must be reexported within six months of the date of import.

In cases where a Contracting Party requires security for compliance with the conditions attached to temporary admission, the amount of such security shall not exceed the amount of the import duties chargeable by more than 10%.

The Convention entered into force on July 1, 1962, three months after five states had signed it without reservation of ratification. For any other state, it will enter into force three months after the deposit of the instrument of ratification or accession.

Article 13 provides that the Contracting Parties shall meet together in order to consider the operation of the present Convention and, in particular, in order to consider measures to secure uniformity in interpretation and application. Such meetings shall be convened by the Secretary-General of the Customs Cooperation Council at the request of any Contracting Party, and the decisions of the Contracting Parties shall be taken by a majority of not less than two thirds of the Contracting Parties present at the meeting and voting.

Any dispute between the Contracting Parties concerning the interpretation or application of the present Convention shall so far as possible be settled by negotiation between them. Any dispute that is not settled by negotiation shall be referred by the disputing Contracting Parties to the other Contracting Parties. The Contracting Parties in dispute may agree in advance to accept the recommendations of the Contracting Parties as binding.

The adoption of general rules on the temporary duty-free importation of professional equipment would facilitate the international exchange of specialized skills and techniques.

The provisions of the present Convention shall not preclude the application of prohibitions or restrictions imposed under national laws and regulations on grounds of public morality or order, public security, or public hygiene or health or for veterinary or phytopathological considerations or in relation to the protection of patents, trademarks, and copyrights. All Member States of the United Nations may become members of the Convention.

It should be noted that the Convention on Temporary Admission (Istanbul, June 26, 1990) takes over the provisions of the 1961 Convention. In addition, it incorporates into a single instrument goods and materials formerly set out in numerous international customs conventions.

6. Customs Convention Concerning Facilities for the Importation of Goods for Display or Use at Exhibitions, Fairs, Meetings or Similar Events (Entered into Force on July 13, 1962)

Adopted under the auspices of the Customs Cooperation Council, in consultation with the United Nations Economic Commission for Europe (ECE) and the United Nations Educational, Scientific and Cultural Organization (UNESCO), this Convention regulates the admission in the territory of the Contracting Parties of goods intended for display or demonstration at an event, goods intended for use in connection with the display of foreign products at an event, equipment intended for use at international meetings, conferences, or congresses.

The Contracting Parties undertake to minimize customs formalities regarding these goods. Some items are not subject to generally levied import duties, and this rule applies to small samples; products imported for the sole purpose of displaying them and consuming or destroying them during an event; low-value products used in the construction, furnishing, or decoration of an exhibition stand; and advertising materials. Except for these particular cases, the goods to which temporary admission is granted must be reexported within six months after the day of importation.

Facilities will be granted provided that the following conditions exist:

a. The goods are capable of identification on reexportation.
b. The number or quantity of identical articles is reasonable, having regard to the purpose of importation.
c. The customs authorities of the country of temporary importation are satisfied that the conditions of the present Convention shall be fulfilled.

By adhering to this Convention, the Contracting Parties facilitate the import of products used for trade events and promote trade through the organization of such events.

The provisions of the present Convention shall not preclude the application of prohibitions or restrictions imposed under national laws and regulations on grounds of public morality or order, public security, or public hygiene or health or for veterinary or phytopathological considerations or in relation to the protection of patents, trademarks, and copyrights. All Member States of the United Nations may become members of the Convention.

The Convention entered into force on July 13, 1962, i.e., three months after the deposit of a second instrument of accession after three signatures without reservation of ratification. For any other government, it will enter into force three months after the deposit of its instruments of ratification or accession.

The Convention on Temporary Admission (Istanbul, June 26, 1990) includes the provisions of this Convention.

7. Customs Convention on the ATA Carnet for the Temporary Admission of Goods (Entered into Force on July 30, 1963)

The ATA Carnet system was developed in response to the needs of international trade to transport their products to trade fairs or international exhibitions as samples to potential buyers or simply as their own professional equipment.

In other words, each Contracting Party shall accept, instead of its national Customs documents, the ATA Carnet, valid for its territory, for goods temporarily imported in application of the Customs Convention on the Temporary Importation of Professional Equipment and the Customs Convention concerning facilities for the importation of goods for display or use at exhibitions, fairs, meetings or similar events, as well as for the goods temporarily imported in application of other international agreements related to the temporary import or for the operations of temporary admission carried out in application of their national laws and regulations.

The ATA Carnet is a system that allows the free movement of goods across borders and their temporary admission into a customs territory free of duties and taxes and is guaranteed by an international guarantee system.

Each guaranteeing association shall undertake to pay to the customs authorities of the country in which it is established the amount of the import duties and any other sum payable in the event of noncompliance with the conditions of temporary admission, or of transit, in respect of goods introduced into that country under cover of ATA Carnets issued by a corresponding issuing association.

The term ATA is a combination of the initial letters of the French words "Admission Temporaire" and the English words "Temporary Admission."

The then Customs Cooperation Council adopted the Customs Convention on the ATA Carnet for the temporary admission of goods (ATA Convention) in 1961. This Convention entered into force on July 30, 1963, and currently has 63 Contracting Parties.

This system allowed the international trade community to benefit from the considerable simplification of customs formalities. There are no import duties or taxes to be paid for the temporary importation of products covered by the system since it was established by the national associations that issue ATA Carnets. These national associations must be approved by customs and are affiliated with an international guarantee chain administered by the International Chamber of Commerce (ICC).

The ATA Carnet is now the most widely used document by the international trade community for operations involving the temporary admission of goods.

8. Customs Convention Concerning Welfare Material for Seafarers (Entered into Force on December 11, 1965)

This agreement allows the temporary importation, with a total exemption of import duties, of materials intended for the welfare of seafarers, these being understood as materials for the pursuit of the cultural, educational, recreational, religious, or sporting activities of seafarers, that is, any person carried on board a ship and charged with duties in connection with its work or service at sea. The temporary import of welfare materials for seafarers used onboard ships shall be granted without the requirement of a customs document and without a security deposit.

The importance of this Convention lies in the fact that it exempts the payment of import taxes on materials that are considered necessary so that the people who work onboard ships, that is to say, those considered seafarers, can enjoy the basic necessities that guarantee their well-being while carrying out the typical tasks required in a marine environment.

9. Customs Convention on the Temporary Importation of Scientific Equipment (Entered into Force on September 5, 1969)

This Convention was drawn up under the auspices of the World Customs Organization (WCO) and with the assistance of the United Nations Educational, Scientific and Cultural Organization (UNESCO) in the belief that the development of scientific research and education is a determining factor for economic and social progress.

For this reason, each Contracting Party undertakes to grant temporary admission to scientific equipment that is to be used within its territory solely for the purpose of scientific research or education, free of import duties. The provisions also apply to tools specially designed for the maintenance, checking, gauging, or repair of scientific equipment.

Signatory states shall reduce to a minimum the customs formalities required in connection with the facilities provided for in this Convention whenever it deems it possible not to require security for the amount of import duties and taxes. Scientific equipment granted temporary admission shall be reexported within six months from the date of importation. For valid reasons, the customs authorities may either grant a longer period or extend the initial period.

The temporary admission of scientific equipment, spare parts, and tools may be made subject to the following conditions: (a) they are imported by approved institutions and used under their control and responsibility, (b) they are used for noncommercial purposes within the country of importation, (c) they are imported in reasonable quantities having regard to the purpose of the importation, (d) they are capable of identification on reexportation, and (e) while they are in the country of importation, they remain in the ownership of a natural person resident abroad or a legal person established abroad.

The Convention enables the international exchange of scientific equipment and promotes scientific research and education within the signatory states.

The provisions of this Convention shall not preclude the application of prohibitions or restrictions imposed under national laws and regulations on grounds of public morality or order, public security, and public hygiene or health or in relation to the protection of patents and trademarks. Any Member State of the United Nations may become a Contracting Party to the present Convention.

The Convention entered into force on September 5, 1969, three months after five states had signed it without reservations; the fifth signature was deposited on June 5, 1969. For five other states, it entered into force three months after the deposit of the signature without reservation before June 30, 1969. For any other state, it entered into force three months after the deposit of the instrument of ratification or accession.

The Convention on Temporary Admission (Istanbul, June 26, 1990) takes the provisions of this Convention in its Annex B5 and is therefore repealed (replaced) for the Contracting States that have signed both Conventions.

10. Customs Convention on the Temporary Importation of Pedagogic Material (Entered into Force on September 10, 1971)

The Contracting Parties to the present Convention, established under the auspices of the Customs Cooperation Council in consultation with the United Nations Educational, Scientific and Cultural Organization (UNESCO), seek the temporary duty- and tax-free importation of pedagogic materials for the development of education and vocational training, which are essential foundations for economic and social progress.

The Convention entered into force on September 10, 1971, three months after it was signed without reservation by five states. From that date, it shall enter into force for any state that has signed it without reservation, ratified it, or acceded to it three months after the date of signature without reservation or the deposit of the instrument of ratification or accession.

Each Contracting Party undertakes to grant temporary admission to pedagogic materials that are to be used within its territory solely for the purpose of education or vocational training, spare parts for pedagogic materials, and tools specially designed for the maintenance, checking, gauging, or repair of such materials.

In addition, each Contracting Party undertakes, whenever it deems it possible, not to require security for the amount of import duties and taxes but to be satisfied with a written undertaking. Such undertaking may be required for each importation or on a general basis for a specified period or, where applicable, for the period of approval of the institution.

11. International Convention on the Simplification and Harmonization of Customs Procedures (Kyoto Convention) (Entered into Force on September 25, 1974)

This Convention is specifically analyzed in Points **10.2.1** and **10.2.2**, **Kyoto Convention. Introduction. Historical Background**. We refer to these points to avoid repetition in its analysis.

12. International Convention on Mutual Administrative Assistance for the Prevention, Investigation and Repression of Customs Offences (Nairobi Convention) (Entered into Force on May 21, 1980)

This Convention is analyzed in Point **14.5.1**, **Nairobi Convention**. We refer to this point to avoid repetition in its analysis.

13. International Convention on the Harmonized Commodity Description and Coding System (Entered into Force on January 1, 1988)

This Convention is thoroughly analyzed in Point **6**, **Nomenclature and Classification of Goods**. We refer to this point to avoid repetition in its analysis.

14. Convention on Temporary Admission (Istanbul Convention) (Entered into Force on November 27, 1993)

This Convention is specifically analyzed in Point **10.8**, **The Istanbul Convention**. We refer to this point to avoid repetition in its analysis.

15. International Convention on the Simplification and Harmonization of Customs Procedures (Kyoto Convention) Amendment (Entered into Force on February 3, 2006)

This Convention is specifically and thoroughly analyzed in Point **10.2**, **Revised Kyoto Convention**. We refer to this point to avoid repetition in its analysis.

16. Customs Convention on the International Transit of Goods (ITI Convention) (Acceded to on June 7, 1971, and Has Still Not Entered into Force)

The ITI Convention introduces a customs transit procedure designed to facilitate the international transport of unitized cargoes of goods. It is applicable regardless of the means of transport used and flexible enough to meet the varying requirements of different regions of the world. It regulates the transport of containers, road vehicles, railway wagons, and vessels suitable for use on inland waterways, approved for the transport of goods under customs seal, in the territories of two or more Contracting Parties. It recommends the merging of existing ITI areas and provides for a system of international guarantees.

At the time the Convention was drafted, it was very innovative in nature since all the other active international transport procedures in use were designed to apply to goods transported by a specific means of transport. Since then, in response to the needs and rapid development of the transport business, new and more specific conventions have been proposed to the international community. By 2004, only three states had acceded to the ITI Convention.

17. International Convention on Mutual Administrative Assistance in Customs Matters (Johannesburg Convention) (This Convention Has Still Not Entered into Force)
This Convention is specifically analyzed in Point **14.5.2**, **Johannesburg Convention**. We refer to this point to avoid repetition in its analysis.

Adoption of WCO Conventions
We must clarify that, although the WCO Conventions act as a beacon or guide for the world's customs, states do not always make sufficient efforts to address the formal process of approving an international treaty. This is especially true when it comes to technical issues that are difficult for nonspecialist officials to handle.

Therefore, it is often observed that national standards have allowed the "filtering" of the principles agreed upon in the WCO, but they remain pending formal approval at the international level.

Figure 3.1 shows the level of formal adoption of the 13 main WCO Conventions.

3.2 Recommendations[4]

The Customs' Technical Recommendations are suggestions proposed by the Permanent Technical Committee (PTC) and approved by the Council. They are published in relation to a wide range of topics and constitute an effective practical mechanism to ensure the highest degree of harmonization.

Although they do not have a direct binding effect, it should be emphasized that once they are internalized by the Member States, they entail an implicit commitment to implement their provisions to an extent possible.

There are two modalities for the applicability of the recommendations: (i) when the text does not state so, the classic rule is applied whereby the recommendation is binding on the state that expresses the intention to abide by it and on that state only, and (ii) when the text requires the acceptance of all or some of the Member States for

[4]The content of the different Recommendations: http://www.wcoomd.org/en/about-us/legal-instruments/recommendations.aspx. Accessed May 10, 2021.

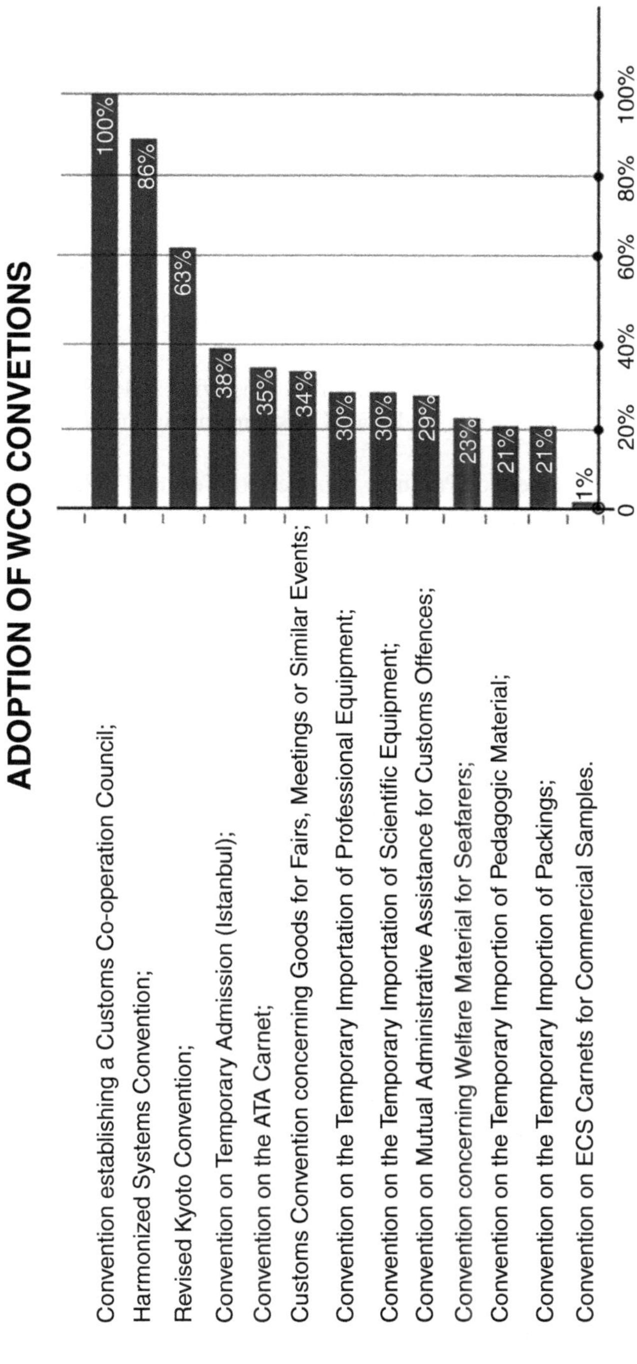

Fig. 3.1 Percentage of accession to the main WCO conventions. Source: Author's elaboration based on information from the WCO

the entry into force of the recommendation, the recommendation is analyzed as a draft Convention.

The WCO has developed nearly 90 Recommendations, among which are the following:

Recommendations to standardize Members' practices regarding duty relief, repayment, remission of customs duties:

Repayment or Remission of Duties on Goods Refused by the Importer as Not Conforming to Contract (1957)

- Tax-Free Shops (1960)
- Repayment or Remission of Import Duties and Taxes on Goods Destroyed or Lost (1962)
- Refund of Import Duties and Taxes on Shortages (1962)
- Reimported Goods (1967)
- Free Admission of Gift Consignments (1968, modified in 1978 and 1983)
- To Expedite the Forwarding of Relief Consignments in the Event of Disasters (1970)
- The Customs Treatment of Products Imported for Testing (1972)

Recommendations to facilitate the international transport of goods and travel and tourism:

- Use of Temporary Importation Papers in Respect of Radio and Television Vans (1955 and 1957)
- Temporary Admission of Radio-Television Production and Broadcasting Equipment (1985)
- Customs Treatment of Provisions Carried in Restaurants Cars, Pullmans Cars, Sleeping Cars and Similar Cars of International Express Trains (1960)
- Customs Treatment of Registered Baggage (1962, modified in 1988)
- Customs Sealing Systems in Connection with International Transport of Goods (1968)
- Measures to Facilitate the Application of the ITI Convention (1973)
- Temporary Admission of Special Equipment Carried in Vehicles Used for or in Connection with the Transport of Radio-Active Materials (1972)
- Links Between Customs Transit System (1982)
- Acceptance of ATA Carnets in Connection with Temporary Admission (1992)
- Advance Passenger Information (API) and Passenger Name Record (PNR) for Efficient and Effective Customs Control (2012 and 2015)
- Recommendation on CSDs (Container Security Devices) (2013)

Recommendations related to information technologies:

- Electronic Transmission and Authentication of Customs and Other Relevant Regulatory Information (1981)
- Codes for the Representation of Data Elements (1984)
- EDIFACT Syntax Rules (1988)
- CCC/IATA Data Interchange Standards (1988)

- Adherence to Standards in Relation to Data Requirements for Advance Passenger Information (API) (1993)
- UN/EDIFACT Rules for Electronic Data Interchange (1995)
- Use of the WCO Data Model (2009)

Recommendations related to compliance and enforcement:

- Illicit Cross-Border Movement of Nuclear and Hazardous Material (Including Their Wastes) (1997)
- Transnational Organized Crime (1997)
- Protocol Against the Illicit Manufacturing of and Trafficking in Firearms, Their Parts and Components and Ammunition, Supplementing the United Nations Convention Against Transnational Organized Crime (2002)
- Global Network of Regional Intelligence Liaison Offices (RILOS) (2003)
- Tackling Money Laundering and in Recovering the Proceeds of Crime (2005)
- Actions Against Customs Commercial Fraud (2006)
- Actions Against Cross-Border Environmental Offences (2008)

Other recommendations:

- Samples Regarded as Being of Negligible Value Within the Meaning of the International Convention to Facilitate the Importation of Commercial Samples and Advertising Material (1956)
- Adoption of a Lay-Out Key for the Goods Declaration (Outwards) (1965)
- Right to Appeal in Customs Matters (1967)
- Standard Form of Certificate of Origin (1973)
- Customs Requirements Regarding Commercial Invoices (1979)
- Single Goods Declaration (1990)
- Use of the Glossary of International Customs Terms (1993)
- Use of Trader Identification Number (TIN) (June 2018)

3.3 Declarations[5]

Declarations express principles (position taking) considered relevant to certain phenomena and are issued for the knowledge of the Member States and the international community. Some of the Declarations of the WCO are as follows:

- Declaration of the Council concerning promotion of Conventions and other international instruments designed to harmonize and standardize customs laws and regulations and technical co-operation—Seoul Declaration (May 1984)
- Declaration of the Customs Cooperation Council concerning its role in the field of customs enforcement—Brussels Declaration June (1986)

[5] Full details and content of the WCO Declarations: http://www.wcoomd.org/en/about-us/legal-instruments/declarations.aspx. Accessed May 10, 2021.

- Declaration of the Council for meeting the challenges of the year 2000—Ottawa Declaration (June 1987);
- Declaration of the Customs Cooperation Council concerning harmonization/computerization of customs procedures and a strategy for the 21st-century—Washington Declaration (July 1989)
- Declaration of the Customs Cooperation Council concerning good governance and integrity in customs—The Revised Arusha Declaration (June 2003)
- Declaration of the World Customs Organization on transnational organized crime—Budapest Declaration (June 1997)
- Declaration of the Customs Cooperation Council on the improvement of customs co-operation and mutual administrative assistance—Cyprus Declaration (June 2000)
- Declaration of the Customs Cooperation Council concerning e-commerce—Baku Declaration (June 2001)
- Declaration of the Customs Cooperation Council on the illicit traffic in drugs—Brussels Declaration (June 2003)
- Declaration of the Customs Cooperation Council on the illegal wildlife trade (June 2014)
- Declaration of the Customs Co-operation Council concerning its role to fight terrorism and strengthen the security—Luxor Declaration (December 2017)
- Declaration of the World Customs Organization on cross-border e-commerce—Beijing Declaration (February 2018)
- Declaration of the Customs Co-operation Council on gender equality and diversity in customs (December 2020)

3.4 Resolutions[6]

Resolutions are regulatory acts issued by the WCO in response to a particular situation. Although they do not have a direct binding effect, it should be clarified that once internalized by the Member States, they entail an implicit commitment to implement their provisions to an extent possible. The following are some of the Resolutions issued by the WCO:

- Resolution of the Customs Co-operation Council on the Role of Customs in Facilitating the Cross-Border Movement of Situationally Critical Medicines and Vaccines (December 2020)
- Resolution of the Customs Co-operation Council on the Role of Customs in Preventing Illicit Trafficking of Cultural Objects (July 2016)
- Punta Cana Resolution of the WCO Policy Commission on the Role of Customs in the Security Context (December 2015)

[6]The list and content of the WCO Resolutions are available at the following link: http://www.wcoomd.org/en/about-us/legal-instruments/resolutions.aspx. Accessed May 10, 2021.

- Dublin Resolution of the Policy Commission on the Conclusion of an Agreement on Trade Facilitation by the World Trade Organization (December 2013)
- Resolution of the Policy Commission on Air Cargo Security (December 2011)
- Resolution of the Customs Co-operation Council on the Role of Customs in Natural Disaster Relief (June 2011)
- Resolution of the Customs Co-operation Council on the Global Economic Downturn (June 2009)
- Resolution of the Customs Co-operation Council on the Role of Customs in the 21st Century (June 2008)
- Resolution of the Customs Co-operation Council on the High Level Strategic Group (June 2005)
- Resolution of the Customs Co-operation Council on the Framework of Standards to Secure and Facilitate Global Trade (June 2005)
- Resolution of the Customs Co-operation Council on Security and Facilitation of the International Trade Supply Chain (June 2002)
- Resolution of the Customs Co-operation Council Concerning the Importance of Intelligence in Supporting Customs Enforcement Activity (June 1992)
- Resolution of the Customs Co-operation Council Concerning the Prevention of Illicit Traffic in Endangered Species of Wild Fauna and Flora (June 1991)
- Resolution of the Customs Co-operation Council on the Introduction of Pre-entry Classification Information Programmes (June 1991)

3.5 Opinions

Opinions are a nonbinding legal instruments and usually provide a criterion for a dispute.

For a better understanding before tackling the subject, it is useful to reestablish a precedent and keep in mind that Article 96 of the Charter of the United Nations establishes "a. The General Assembly or the Security Council may request the International Court of Justice to give an advisory opinion on any legal question. b. Other organs of the United Nations and specialized agencies, which may at any time be so authorized by the General Assembly, may also request advisory opinions of the Court on legal questions arising within the scope of their activities."[7]

In principle, opinions are intended to clarify doubts that may arise.

In the case of the World Customs Organization, advisory opinions mainly correspond to the Technical Committee on Customs Valuation.

[7] UN, Charter of the United Nations: https://www.un.org/en/charter-united-nations. Accessed May 10, 2021.

These instruments are not binding for Customs Administrations, nor do they represent international valuation, but they provide extremely useful guidelines for addressing various technical issues related to customs valuation.

The Technical Committee's decisions play an important and vital role in achieving uniformity in the interpretation and application of the Organization's various Agreements.

An *advisory opinion* answers a question about the modalities of application of an Agreement to a set of existing or theoretical facts. Thus, where the factual elements in a given situation are identical to those described in the advisory opinion, the Customs Administrations will have a clear solution; where the factual elements are not identical, the advisory opinion may not be directly applicable, although it could provide guidance for the solution of the problem.

The character of the interpretation criteria of advisory opinions goes hand in hand with their true nature and purpose, which is none other than to be a complementary instrument for the due application of the Agreements in order to simplify the analysis of the Customs Administration to an effect that it may reach a proper conclusion.

According to the WCO Technical Assessment Committee, these instruments do not constitute an international standard, and none of the provisions of the Agreements imply that the decisions of the Technical Committee are to be legally binding on the signatories. They will be legally binding only after incorporation into their respective legislation.[8]

To exemplify, we believe it is important to note that since 1981, the WCO has issued 42 advisory opinions related to customs valuation, which have referred to the following: Concept of "sale" in the Agreement; Acceptability of a price below prevailing market prices for identical goods; Meaning of "are distinguished" in the Interpretative Note to Article 1 of the Agreement: duties and taxes of the country of importation; Royalties and licence fees under Article 8.1 (c) of the Agreement; Treatment of cash discount under the Agreement; Treatment of barter or compensation deals under the Agreement; Acceptability of test values under Article 1.2 (b) (i) of the Agreement; Treatment under the Agreement of credits in respect of earlier transactions; Treatment of anti-dumping and countervailing duties when applying the deductive method; Treatment of fraudulent documents; Treatment of inadvertent errors and of incomplete documentation; Flexible application of Article 7 of the Agreement; Meaning of the term "restrictions" in Article 1.1 (a) (iii);

[8]For example, for the Republic of Peru, Advisory Opinions (and other documents issued by the Committee) have been incorporated into national legislation. The same situation applies to the other Member Countries of the Andean Community (CAN), which in Decision 571/03 provided that for purposes of customs valuation, the Member Countries of the Andean Community shall be governed by the provisions of the "Agreement on Implementation of Article VII of the General Agreement on Tariffs and Trade 1994" and Article 22 states that for the interpretation and application of the rules, the Decisions of the World Trade Organization (WTO) Committee on Customs Valuation will be taken into account, as well as the Advisory Opinions, Comments, Explanatory Notes, Case Studies and Studies of the World Customs Organization (WCO) Technical Committee on Valuation. In other countries, such as Argentina, this is not the case.

Application of the decision on the valuation of carrier media bearing "software" for data processing equipment; Application of Article 1, paragraph 2; Application of deductive value method; Activities undertaken by the buyer on his own account after purchase of the goods but before importation; Buying commissions; Relationship between Articles 8.1 (b) (ii) and 8.1 (b) (iv); Meaning of the expression "right to reproduce the imported goods" within the meaning of the Interpretative Note to Article 8.1 (c); Warranty charges; Cost of transportation: Free-on-board system of valuation; Meaning of the expression "sold for export to the country of importation" in a series of sales; Examination of the expression "circumstances surrounding the sale" under Article 1.2 (a) in relation to the use of transfer pricing studies; Determination of the value of an assist under Article 8.1(b) of the Agreement and third party royalties and licence fees—General commentary.

In another prolific sector, the WCO issues opinions for the classification of goods, also known as criteria or opinions, which must be taken into account in order to achieve the correct classification of a good, by means of the criteria proposed by the Customs Administrations signatory to the Convention on the Harmonized System. These opinions are found in the Compendium of Classification Opinions, which includes a list of the most important/difficult classification decisions[9] taken by the Harmonized System Committee.

For illustrative purposes, we have listed the classification opinions adopted by the HS Committee at its 62nd meeting (September 2018), which included 36 products, along with their related HS code numbers and, in certain cases, the justification for the classification.

These products include LED panel lights (product C), LED strip lights (product B)—flexible indoor LED strip light, 24V 1.3W—cool white, LED- TP1-12-, dry-bleached earthenware nuts, cough drops, hydraulic cement, 92 octane gasoline engine, heavy distillates, liquid fuels, fuel oil 100, low viscosity liner fuel, etoposide and teniposide (INN List 34), cyclosporine (INN List 46), resin solution, clear liquid, dental zirconia ceramic, and more.

3.6 Memorandums of Understanding

The WCO frequently uses a Memorandum of Understanding (MOU) when it seeks to establish a bilateral or multilateral cooperation agreement with other entities. It expresses a convergence of wills with the intention of undertaking common lines of action.

Most MOUs are written in generic terms and provide a broad legal platform for reciprocal cooperation without specifying the details of the actions to be

[9]Classification opinions (62nd meeting of the HS Committee) http://www.wcoomd.org/-/media/wco/public/global/pdf/topics/nomenclature/instruments-and-tools/classification-rulings/clhs62en.pdf?db=web. Accessed May 10 2021.

implemented. These details will later be established through specific programs or projects.

As of December 31, 2017, the WCO had signed 143 MOUs with various entities, which can be grouped into five categories:

i. Intergovernmental organizations: 52 MOUs (approximately 36% of the total)
ii. Nongovernmental organizations: 38 MOUs (approximately 27% of the total)
iii. Customs Administrations: 42 MOUs (approximately 29% of the total)
iv. Universities and other educational entities: 9 MOU (approximately 6% of the total), and
v. Other entities: two MOUs[10] (approximately 2% of the total)

Although each MOU[11] has its own specific characteristics, it is possible to observe a structure that is generally repeated:

- MOU title.
- Preamble: this is where the vision and mission of the signatory organizations, their mandates, and their areas of common interest are briefly stated.
- Areas and framework of cooperation.
- Cooperation mechanism, information exchange, and contact points.
- Term.
- Management of the MOU (amendments, termination, dispute resolution, languages).
- Legal force: the MOU is not binding. It does not create any legal rights or obligations between the parties. The parties only agree to work together in good faith to achieve the aims set for their mutual benefit. It is like a documented "Gentlemen's Agreement."
- Entry into force: this is usually the date of signature, but a different date can be set.
- Signature of the parties: in the case of the WCO, the Secretary-General signs on its behalf.

At this point and in order to be more precise, we must clarify that although MOUs do not generally have a binding effect on the parties, except for the obligation that is usually established regarding the confidentiality of the exchanged information, its legal force is determined by the autonomy of the parties' will so that if they so wish, they can establish in the MOU that it will be binding and even determine the consequences of its breach.

Having clarified this, it must be said that MOUs are a very valuable instrument in the framework of international cooperation since they allow to express and

[10]One entity with whom a development partnership was signed (TradeMark East Africa (TMEA)) and another entity for monitoring wildlife trade (TRAFFIC).

[11]The complete updated list and the access links to each document are available at http://www.wcoomd.org/en/about-us/partners/mou-new.aspx. Accessed May 10, 2021.

document a convergence of wills without the need to undertake a legal commitment or sign a legally binding agreement.

3.7 Other Agreements Administered and Managed

In addition to the Conventions referred to above, the World Customs Organization is also responsible for the "administration" of three other International Conventions:

1. **The WTO Agreement on Customs Valuation** (see Chap. 7, Point 7.2)
2. **The WTO Agreement on Rules of Origin** (see Chap. 8, Point 8.1)
3. **The "Customs Container Convention" of the International Maritime Organization**

On April 26, 1956, two vessels left the port of Newark, in New York City (United States), carrying two truck boxes specially prepared to be securely fastened to the vessel decks. The first ship to set sail was named "Ideal X." On this day, containers were officially introduced into the world market.

From that moment on, its use as a cargo container has only grown, adopting diverse modalities and forms, along with the construction of specialized cargo vessels.[12] This increased the need to improve security and transportation, as well as the customs regime applicable to them.

On the other hand, since the mid-nineteenth century, with the adoption of some treaties to regulate safety at sea, the need to create an international body to effectively ensure agreements in this area also arose. This demand crystallized shortly after the creation of the UN, and in 1948, the "Intergovernmental Maritime Consultative Organization" (IMCO) was established in Geneva. In 1982, the IMCO changed its name to the International Maritime Organization (IMO).

It was not until 1958 that the Organization effectively entered into force. Among its objectives is to promote cooperation—among governments—in the regulation of international commercial navigation, as well as to facilitate the general adoption of standards of maritime safety, efficient navigation, and the prevention of maritime pollution.

It should be noted that the measures established by the IMO form the pillars on which the sector evolves; approximately 50 of its agreements govern the maritime transport sector, from the construction and equipment of ships to their scrapping or training of personnel working at sea to the customs treatment of containers.

On this last point, the original Customs Convention on Containers was concluded in Geneva on May 18, 1956, and entered into force on August 4, 1959. On December

[12] In July 2019, the Swiss shipping company Mediterranean Shipping Company (MSC) received the largest container ship ever built: 23.000 TEU. https://www.anave.es/prensa/ultimas-noticias/2182-msc-recibe-el-mayor-porta-contenedores-del-mun-do-con-23-000-teu-de-capacidad. Accessed May 10, 2021.

2, 1972, a new Convention was concluded with the provision that when it entered into force, it would replace the 1956 Convention for the parties that had ratified it. The 1972 Convention entered into force on December 6, 1975.

The 1972 Convention has two main objectives. First, it provides for the temporary import of containers, free of import duties and taxes and free of import prohibitions and restrictions, subject to reexport within three months from the date of import. Such temporary admission of containers shall be granted without requiring the presentation of customs documents at the time of import and reexport and without the provision of any security (Articles 3 to 11). In this regard, Annex 2 of the Convention sets out the methods that each administration could use to facilitate the temporary admission procedure.

Second, the Convention provides for the approval of containers for the transport of goods under the Customs seal; containers approved by a Contracting Party that comply with the provisions of the Convention for the transport of goods under the Customs seal shall be accepted by other Contracting Parties for any system of carriage involving such sealing (Article 12). Annex 4 of the Convention prescribes the technical conditions applicable to containers that can be accepted for international transport under the Customs seal. Annex 5 sets out the procedures for the approval of containers that meet the technical conditions prescribed in Annex 4.

The Administrative Committee amends these technical Annexes, whenever necessary, to reflect the updated technical aspects regarding containers.

The Convention allows containers to be transported from a state that has signed and ratified the Convention to another state that complies with the same conditions, with exemption from import duties and taxes (temporary admission) for a period of three months and subsequent reexport, as stated in Article 4.1:[13] *Containers granted temporary admission shall be re-exported within three months from the date of importation.*

The Convention was concluded at the same conference that approved the Customs Convention on the Temporary Importation of Commercial Road Vehicles, the Customs Convention on the Temporary Importation for Private Use of Aircraft and Pleasure Boats, and the CMR Convention.

The WCO administers the technical aspect of this Convention, considering the customs nature that it has, according to the fact that although containers are considered by some as navigation accessories, they contain goods and are used for their transportation. Therefore, establishing a distinct customs treatment cannot be an exclusive task of the IMO, an organization that due to its nature does not specialize in tax matters, much less in customs matters. Thus, the WCO established the **Management Committee for the Customs Convention on Containers**, which is in charge of revising, updating and promoting it, as well as verifying the technical conditions that favor the application of the Convention.

---

[13] Customs Convention on Containers (1972). http://www.wcoomd.org/-/media/wco/public/global/pdf/about-us/legal-instruments/conventions-and-agreements/containers/pf_txt_containers_contract.pdf?la=es-ES. Accessed May 10, 2021.

The most recent amendment to the Convention, made in 2017 during the 16th Meeting of the Committee, includes two of the annexes to the Convention: Annex 1, Provisions concerning the marking of containers, and Annex 4, Regulations on technical conditions applicable to containers which may be accepted for international transport under Customs seal. The amendment to Annex 1 introduces more detailed provisions on the marking of packages and brings Annex 1 of the Convention on the Containers in line with Appendix II of Annex B.3 of the Convention on the Temporary Admission (Istanbul Convention).

The amendment of Annex 4 introduces provisions for the new design of containers, which includes a sliding roof in the form of a sheet or sliding sheets, and conforms to the provisions of Annex 7 of the Convention on the International Transport of Goods Under Cover of TIR Carnets, 1975 (TIR Convention). In accordance with the Convention, the adopted amendments shall be communicated to all Contracting Parties for them to accept these modifications. The Committee also approved an updated version of the Customs Convention on Containers Handbook 1972, which entered into force in February of that year.

This Convention not only is relevant from a tax-customs perspective but also provides a framework for security in the international supply chain as the 1972 Customs Convention on Containers is cited as a minimum level of container security through its provisions, and importers and exporters are encouraged to comply with these. Therefore, the Convention on Containers has an integral role in the effective implementation of the SAFE Framework of Standards.

3.8 Dispute Settlement Mechanisms

International organizations (IOs) arise from the sovereign will of states in the face of the need to address problems posed by global coexistence. They have permanent bodies, with their own will and legal personality distinct from that of the Member States, within the framework of the competencies attributed to them in the founding document.

Among the IOs' main functions, we can find conflict resolution or resolution of differences that may arise among its members based on disparities over unilateral decisions of states that affect or go against the objectives pursued by the Organization.

As we have previously stated in Article III of the WCO's founding Agreement, the functions of the Council are the following:

> (e) to make recommendations, in a conciliatory capacity, for the settlement of disputes concerning the interpretation or application of the Conventions referred to in paragraph (d) above in accordance with the provisions of those Conventions; the parties in dispute may agree in advance to accept the recommendations of the Council as binding;.

On this last point or function, there has been no evidence of its use as an institutional mechanism since the Organization has focused its efforts on negotiation and informal persuasion.

Now, to what extent would the WCO benefit from the implementation of a formal dispute settlement system?

Dispute settlement systems bring a number of advantages to the institutions that implement them on an ongoing basis, such as the WTO with the so-called "Covered Agreements," i.e., subject to the WTO's dispute settlement system (DSS).

In cases of noncompliance with obligations under a covered agreement, the measure is presumed to constitute a case of nullification or impairment. This means that there is normally a presumption that any violation of the rules has adverse effects on other members that are parties to the covered agreement. In such cases, the member against which the complaint has been made must refute the allegation.

Basically, the DSS process has four stages: (i) the consultation stage, which initiates the process, where negotiation and diplomacy prevail (where most of the cases are resolved); (ii) the study of the case by a special technical group, which evaluates the circumstances and proposes a decision to the dispute settlement body; (iii) the appeal stage, which entails a legal analysis of the decision of the technical group; and, lastly, (iv) the compliance stage, which grants the term to comply with the measure, and in case of noncompliance, the appropriate enforcement measures will be applied.

Regarding the coercive action of the WTO Covered Agreements, bear in mind that the decisions issued by the special technical group or the appeal body in the DSS process are of mandatory compliance for the countries linked to the controversy. The compliance in "good faith" by the "condemned" country is expected, and in case of noncompliance, economic coercion mechanisms such as payment of compensation or suspension of concessions (retaliations) may be used.

The dispute settlement procedure is the cornerstone of the multilateral trading system and a unique contribution of the WTO to the stability of the world economy.[14] The WTO process emphasizes the rule of law and provides greater certainty and predictability to the trading system. It is based on clearly defined rules, and deadlines are set for the completion of the procedure. The most important element, however, is not to issue judgments. The idea is to resolve differences, if possible, through consultations.

One of the greatest accomplishments of this system is effective compliance with the adopted recommendations. This is achieved through periodic monitoring of the application of the system's resolutions and by exerting a certain "pressure" on the requested states to comply with them.

This kind of "pressure" exerted by the conflict settlement system would undoubtedly bring more effective results for the WCO. By not formally establishing a

[14]This is without prejudice to the paralysis (since December 10th, 2019) of the WTO Court of Appeals due to the lack of quorum as no agreement on the appointment of the new judges has been reached.

dispute settlement system, Member States have a large "say" in their commitments made to the Organization. This diminishes its effectiveness since compliance with the rules exclusively depends on the goodwill of states.

The importance and greatest advantage that the application of a dispute settlement system would bring to the WCO would come about when, once a verdict is announced, countries focus on complying with the rules, thereby validating the legal relevance that the Organization possesses.

Reference

Daillier P (1976) Le Conseil de Cooperation Douaniere. Annuaire français de droit international

Chapter 4
The WCO's Relationship with Other Organizations

In order to fulfill its mission, the World Customs Organization (WCO) works in close cooperation with other international organizations, private sector entities, as well as academic institutions. This task is all the more relevant since the WCO represents the interests of the international customs community. Therefore, this community will be the subject of special consideration in this text.

4.1 United Nations (UN) Organization

The United Nations (UN) is currently the largest international organization,[1] with a global partnership among governments that allows cooperation on issues such as international law, international peace and security, economic and social development, humanitarian affairs, and human rights. It was founded on October 24, 1945. It is currently structured into various administrative bodies: General Assembly, Security Council, Economic and Social Council, Secretariat, Trusteeship Council, and the International Court of Justice. The main public figure of the UN is the Secretary-General.

The UN and the WCO share common interests of *security, protection of the health and safety of citizens from illicit trade, such as narcotic drugs and fake medicines, trade facilitation as a basis for economic growth, sustainable*

The complete list of Memoranda of Understanding and other Cooperation Agreements: http://www.wcoomd.org/en/about-us/partners.aspx. Accessed May 10, 2021.

[1] 193 Member States.

H. H. Juárez Allende, *The World Customs Organization*, Law for Professionals,
https://doi.org/10.1007/978-3-030-85296-2_4

development and environmental challenges, such as hazardous waste, inter-agency cooperation, and alignment of objectives for maximum impact.[2]

4.1.1 United Nations System

In Articles 57, 58, 59, 63, 64, and 70 of the Charter of the United Nations,[3] the term "Specialized Agencies" is used to refer to intergovernmental organizations that, by means of an agreement or treaty, are associated with the UN. These agreements lay down the conditions for this relation, which must at least include the principles of cooperation and control set out in the Charter. The interaction between these organizations and the UN is mainly carried out by the Economic and Social Council and the United Nations System Chief Executives Board for Coordination (in the case of the Secretariats).

The abovementioned interaction is what is known as the "**United Nations System,**" a group formed by the UN and the specialized agencies. While this is deeply related to the organization, the specialized agencies therein correspond to completely different international governmental organizations (because of their constitution, members, structure, and operation), even though they are not completely independent of the United Nations.

In the United Nations System, the specialized agencies are competent in specific sectors of international cooperation and can therefore enjoy full autonomy in the exercise of the functions and powers conferred on them by the states in their constituent treaties. The specialization and complementary nature of their activities, in relation to those carried out by the UN, are based on budgets that determine the need to coordinate the United Nations System. It should be emphasized that in order to fully obtain effective international cooperation, a true system of coordination that covers all the activities of the specialized agencies is needed as a way to ensure the success of individual or collective efforts.

Currently, 14 agencies that center their activities on fields such as science, technology, communications, transportation, economy, and culture comprise the system. They include organizations such as the World Health Organization (WHO), the International Civil Aviation Organization (ICAO), the International Maritime Organization (IMO), the World Intellectual Property Organization (WIPO), and the United Nations World Tourism Organization (UNWTO). These are autonomous bodies created through intergovernmental agreements and have wide-ranging responsibilities at an international level in economic, social, cultural,

---

[2]See Press Release "WCO and United Nations agree to enhance cooperation and high-level interaction": http://www.wcoomd.org/es-es/media/newsroom/2012/february/wco-and-united-nations-agree-to-enhance-cooperation-and-high-level-interaction.aspx. Accessed May 10, 2021.

[3]See on the UN Official Website, "Charter of the United Nations": https://www.un.org/en/charter-united-nations/index.html. Accessed May 10, 2021.

and educational fields, as well as health and other related fields. Some organizations, such as the International Labour Organization and the Universal Postal Union, were created before the UN.

Below we present a list of the specialized agencies of the United Nations System that closely cooperate with the World Customs Organization to successfully fulfill its functions.

International Atomic Energy Agency (IAEA)
This body works with its Member States and various partners around the world to promote the safe, secure, and peaceful use of nuclear technologies. IAEA's relationship with the United Nations is founded on an agreement signed by both parties in 1957 (INFCIRC/11). The agreement states that the Agency agrees to conduct its activities in accordance with the purposes and principles of the Charter of the United Nations to promote peace and international cooperation, and in conformity with policies of the United Nations furthering the establishment of safeguarded worldwide disarmament and in conformity with any international agreements entered into pursuant to such policies.

By way of a Memorandum of Understanding signed in May 1998,[4] the WCO and the IAEA work together to devise tactics and strategies to combat illicit trafficking in nuclear and radioactive materials, as well as the facilitation of exchange of information. This provides a framework for promoting cooperation at the national level between national customs administrations and regulatory bodies responsible for the control of nuclear and radioactive materials.

International Civil Aviation Organization (ICAO)
The International Civil Aviation Organization (ICAO) is a United Nations agency created in 1944 by the Convention on International Civil Aviation to analyze the problems of air transport and promote regulations and standards in world aviation. It is directed by a Permanent Council based in Montreal, Canada.

The WCO, in collaboration with ICAO and the *International Air Transport Association* (IATA), has been working on revising the WCO/IAA/ICAO Guidelines on Advance Passenger Information (API).

The WCO also cooperates with ICAO in the areas of simplifying customs procedures vis-à-vis air passengers and cargoes. The Council adopted the SAFE Framework of Standards to Secure and Facilitate Global Trade, thus applying a holistic approach to the supply chain in its various modes, including air transport. The WCO also actively contributes to ICAO's work on maintaining and revising Annex 9 to the Convention on International Civil Aviation-Facilitation. This Annex covers many customs procedures. A Memorandum of Understanding between the WCO and ICAO was signed on June 24, 2011.[5]

---

[4] http://www.wcoomd.org/-/media/wco/public/global/pdf/about-us/%20part-ners/%20mou/041_mou.pdf?la=en. Accessed May 10, 2021.

[5] http://www.wcoomd.org/-/media/wco/public/global/pdf/about-us/partners/mou/145_mou.pdf?la=en. Accessed May 10, 2021.

International Maritime Organization (IMO)

In addition to the above regarding the Convention on Containers administered by the WCO, the IMO Facilitation of International Maritime Traffic Committee (FAL) agreed to work on the development of a Single Window, in collaboration with the WCO and other relevant international organizations, as set out in the Memorandum of Understanding signed on July 23, 2002.[6]

The two organizations are considering possible amendments to the IMO instruments to take into account the WCO SAFE Framework.

In 2015, the organizations signed a partnership agreement to maintain, update, publish, and distribute the IMO Compendium on Facilitation and Electronic Commerce. The Compendium contains essential guidelines and standardized forms for the electronic exchange of information on cargoes, passengers and crew of ships, carriers, port authorities, customs services, terminals, consignees, and other parts of the supply chain.[7]

Under the agreement, the WCO is responsible for the technical maintenance of the Compendium,[8] including collaborating with the United Nations Economic Commission for Europe (UNECE), the global focal point for recommendations on trade facilitation and electronic business standards (UNECE-UN). The scope of responsibilities and procedures for maintaining the Compendium are detailed in the annex to the agreement. The Compendium is within the purview of the IMO Maritime Safety Division and the WCO Enforcement and Facilitation Directorate.

International Narcotics Control Board (INCB)

The International Narcotics Control Board (INCB) is an independent control body established in 1986 by the Single Convention on Narcotic Drugs of 1961, currently based in Vienna, with 13 members, each elected by the Economic and Social Council. The INCB works to assist the Member States in the development of their national drug legislation. In addition, its mission is to promote, guide, and recommend actions to the Member States to seize illicit substances and inspect licit ones. At the same time, it must meet with governments to help them fulfill their obligations under international treaties on the subject.

Under the auspices of INCB, two projects, namely "Project Cohesion" and "Project PRISM," have been launched. They are aimed at assisting governments in the fight against the illicit trafficking/diversion of precursor chemicals and synthetic drugs. The WCO is a continuing member of the project's Task Forces. A

[6]http://www.wcoomd.org/-/media/wco/public/global/pdf/about-us/partners/mou/052_mou.pdf?la=en. Accessed May 10, 2021.

[7]https://www.imo.org/en/OurWork/Facilitation/Pages/IMOCompendium.aspx. Accessed May 10, 2021.

[8]http://www.wcoomd.org/en/topics/facilitation/resources/per-manent-technical-committee/~/media/D56C0174852045DE85CF9CA4611DD717.ashx. Accessed May 10, 2021.

Memorandum of Understanding between the WCO and INCB was signed on April 12, 2012.[9]

As a result of the collaboration between the two organizations, in the 2017 Harmonized System, the WCO included new subheadings for the monitoring and control of pharmaceutical preparations containing ephedrine, pseudoephedrine or norephedrine, and alpha-phenylacetoacetonitrile (APAAN), a precursor chemical.

United Nations Conference on Trade and Development (UNCTAD)
The United Nations Conference on Trade and Development (UNCTAD) has been based in Geneva since its foundation on December 30, 1964, by Resolution No. 1995 of the UN General Assembly. UNCTAD supports trade facilitation through, among other things, developing national modernization plans, strengthening national trade facilitation committees, capacity building and customs automation programs.

The WCO has been working with UNCTAD in the area of trade facilitation. UNCTAD launched an assistance program to support developing and least developed countries in the creation of capacity building so that they are to participate more actively in WTO trade facilitation negotiations, with special emphasis on the importance of developmental aspects and the involvement of the private sector.

The organizations signed a Memorandum of Understanding in April 2013 to advance the WCO's performance measurement approach to reform and modernization. They agreed to develop an application on "ASYCUDA Software Global Performance Indicators" to assist WCO members in their operational capacity.

United Nations Counter-Terrorism Committee (UNCTC)
The United Nations Counter-Terrorism Office was established through the adoption of General Assembly Resolution 71/291 on June 15, 2017. It was due to the relocation of the Office of the Counter-Terrorism Implementation Task Force and the United Nations Counter-Terrorism Centre, initially established in the Department of Political Affairs, to a new Counter-Terrorism Office headed by an Under-Secretary-General.

This Committee is charged with assessing country compliance with binding Security Council Resolution 1373. This Resolution requires all UN members to take steps to enhance border security. The WCO has participated in multidisciplinary teams for various country visits since 2005.

The UN envisages a "Global Counter-Terrorism Strategy,"[10] in which the WCO has a key role in providing measures to prevent and combat terrorism and measures to enhance the capacity of states to that end. It aims to work with states to identify any national shortcomings in the area of transport security and to provide assistance to overcome them, if requested.

[9] http://www.wcoomd.org/-/media/wco/public/global/pdf/about-us/partners/mou/151_mou.pdf?la=en. Accessed May 10, 2021.

[10] UN, "United Nations Global Counter-Terrorism Strategy" (2006) https://www.un.org/disarmament/wmdtrashed/counter-terrorism. Accessed May 10, 2021.

United Nations Economic Commission for Europe (UNECE)
The United Nations Economic Commission for Europe (UNECE) was established in 1947 to promote economic cooperation among its Member States. It is one of the five regional commissions under the administrative direction of the United Nations. It has 56 Member States and reports to the United Nations Economic and Social Council (ECOSOC). In addition to the European countries, it includes the United States, Canada, Israel, Turkey, and the Central Asian republics. The UNECE Secretariat is based in Geneva.

Work on trade facilitation activities began in the ECE in 1960, following a 1959 initiative from the Nordic countries, when it was decided that a Group of Experts be set up to explore ways in which export documents could be simplified and standardized. In 1971, the trade facilitation projects were reorganized into the newly established Working Party on the Facilitation of International Trade Procedures, also referred to as Working Party 4 or WP4.

The WCO works closely with the UNECE by contributing to the work of a number of United Nations Centres for Trade Facilitation and Electronic Business (UN/CEFACT) in program development areas (PDAs). The Customs Domain is found in the Trade Facilitation and Transport PDA and in the Regulatory PDA. In particular, the work of the International Trade Procedures Domain (ITPD) and UN/EDIFACT Working Group (EWG) were compelling as regards e-business standardization, as well as UN/CEFACT's activities in the area of trade facilitation.

The principal working partner in this regard is the Customs Domain Group. However, other PDAs and Domains—*Supply Chain, Transport, Business Process Analysis*, and *International Trade Facilitation Domains*—are also becoming important partners. In addition, the WCO contributed to the UNECE Inland Transport Committees Working Group on Customs Questions Affecting Transport (known as WP30).

The UNECE is administering the TIR Convention (Convention on the International Transport of Goods Under Cover of TIR Carnets), and it has been increasingly important to work in a collaborative manner between the administrative bodies of the two Conventions.

United Nations Educational, Scientific and Cultural Organization (UNESCO)
The WCO and UNESCO signed a Memorandum of Understanding on October 26, 2000, to combat the illicit trafficking of cultural property, each within its own area of competence. The MoU foresees the exchange of information between customs authorities and the competent authorities recognized by UNESCO for the protection of cultural heritage. The purpose of the Memorandum is to enhance the effectiveness of fraud investigations and fraud profiles drawn up by inspection services.

For this reason, both organizations produced the "Model Export Certificate for Cultural Objects,"[11] which was designed to be adaptable to the specific nature and needs of the said objects in terms of their protection when transported from one country to another. It thereby constitutes an important tool, whose use has been suggested by both organizations to their member countries.

United Nations Environment Programme (UNEP)
The WCO and the United Nations Environment Programme (UNEP) signed a Memorandum of Understanding on June 2, 2003. Since 2001, the WCO has been a very active partner to the Green Customs Initiatives (GCI), which is a series of collaborative activities by partner organizations, coordinated by UNEP and aimed at raising the awareness of customs officers to trade-related multilateral environmental agreements (MEAs). The two organizations work closely to combat the illegal trade in ozone-depleting substances (ODS); the Regional Intelligence Liaison Offices (RILO) also support the initiatives of UNEP's regional offices.

For this reason, the WCO Harmonized System Committee has identified Harmonized System codes for chemicals or groups of chemicals listed in Annex III of the Rotterdam Convention. The WCO has also developed activities aimed at preventing and combating illegal traffic in chemicals and hazardous wastes under the Basel, Rotterdam, and Stockholm Conventions, for example, through the "Green Customs" initiative,[12] which aims to combat environmental crime and illegal trade in hazardous and other wastes.

United Nations Statistics Division (UNSD)
The United Nations Statistics Division is committed to the advancement of the global statistical system by compiling and disseminating global information, developing standards and norms for these activities, and supporting countries' efforts to strengthen their national statistical systems.

Customs administrations around the world publish trade statistics or play a key role in compiling information that has valuable input for the said task—as customs records are the main source of these statistics. Therefore, the United Nations deems these data vital for monitoring world trade.

In 2010, the United Nations Statistical Commission adopted new recommendations for trade statistics, known as "International Merchandise Trade Statistics: Concepts and Definitions 2010." These recommend that technical specialists use customs records as the main and normally preferred data source.

The main WCO tool to facilitate the collection, comparison, and analysis of statistical data is the *International Convention on the Harmonized Commodity*

[11] UNESCO - WCO Model Export Certificate: http://www.unesco.org/new/es/culture/themes/illicit-trafficking-of-cultural-property/legal-and-practical-instruments/unes-co-wco-model-export-certificate. Accessed May 10, 2021.

[12] World Customs Organization: Polner, Mariya. "Green Customs Initiative, Operation DEMETER". http://www.wcoomd.org/~/media/wco/public/es/pdf/events/2009/picard/presentations/demeter_polner_final_es.pdf?la=en. Accessed May 10, 2021.

Description and Coding System, used by more than 200 countries, territories, and customs or economic unions.

The WCO recommends that the customs administrations of its Member States, as well as the Contracting Parties to the HS Convention, report their import and export trade statistics to the UNDS, being the world's leading repository of global statistics.

The HS classification not only is a fundamental pillar for other product classifications but also provides additional product details for general statistical purposes and wide-ranging socioeconomic and environmental analysis.

Reliable trade statistics are indispensable for good governance since they are the basis for monitoring and evaluating the country's economic performance. Based on this performance, they can formulate suitable economic policies and properly engage in international negotiation processes.

United Nations Office on Drugs and Crime (UNODC)

The partnership between the World Customs Organization (WCO) and the United Nations Office on Drugs and Crime (UNODC) is based on a Memorandum of Understanding (MoU), signed in November 1996. UNODC and WCO have successfully been working together on a number of international activities.

The most recent common project is the UNODC-WCO Container Control Program. This Program seeks to strengthen the structures and processes that allow for the application of sustainable laws for states and selected ports. The aim is to minimize the exploitation of maritime containers for the illicit trafficking of drugs, as well as other transnational organized crime activities.

United Nations Office for the Coordination of Humanitarian Affairs (OCHA)

OCHA is the part of the United Nations Secretariat responsible for bringing together humanitarian actors to ensure a coherent response to emergencies. OCHA promotes and negotiates with disaster-prone countries a customs model agreement that was developed in collaboration with the WCO a few years ago.

UNOCHA and the WCO signed a Memorandum of Understanding on September 27 2010.[13] They also developed a Model Agreement between the United Nations and states/governments on measures to expedite the importation, exportation, and transit of relief consignments and items in the possession of disaster relief personnel in disaster and emergency situations (*Model Agreement on Customs Facilitation in Humanitarian Assistance*)[14] to assist countries in establishing optimal procedures for handling relief consignments in disaster and emergencies. Through the rapid implementation of appropriate measures, countries will thus be able to ensure swift access to their urgent relief assets, including food stocks, personal assistance, and logistical support, to aid survivors in a timely and expeditious manner.

[13] http://www.wcoomd.org/-/media/wco/public/global/pdf/about-us/partners/mou/133_mou.pdf?la=en. Accessed May 10, 2021.

[14] https://vosocc.unocha.org/GetFile.aspx?file=68518_UN_Agreement.pdf. Accessed May 10, 2021.

Universal Postal Union (UPU)
Founded in 1874, the Universal Postal Union is an international intergovernmental body of the United Nations system that specializes in postal services.

The WCO continues to cooperate with the UPU through the WCO/UPU Contact Committee. The items of mutual interest include global security issues, electronic information exchange, implementation and capacity building for the use of CN22 and CN23 forms, and consignment service in the post. An MoU between the WCO and UPU was signed on July 5, 2007.[15]

As we will analyze further on, the collaboration between these organizations has intensified profoundly since the irruption of cross-border e-commerce, which demands immediate and effective actions from both organizations.

World Intellectual Property Organization (WIPO)
The World Intellectual Property Organization is a specialized agency of the United Nations based in Geneva, Switzerland. It was formed as the world forum for services, policies, cooperation, and information on intellectual property rights (IPR) and has 191 Member States.

The WIPO's mission is to lead the development of a balanced and accessible international intellectual property system that allows innovation and creativity for the benefit of all. The mandate, the governing bodies, and the procedures are set out in the WIPO Convention, which established WIPO in 1967.

The WCO and WIPO closely cooperate in promoting the effective use and protection of IP worldwide by strengthening customs administrations' capacity and improving the dialogue between business and customs and border coordination, as well as carrying out interinstitutional control operations.

World Health Organization (WHO)
The World Health Organization (WHO) is a United Nations specialized system that was founded in 1948. Its mission is to achieve for all peoples the highest degree of health, which is defined in its Constitution as a state of complete physical, mental, and social well-being and not merely the absence of disease or infirmity.

The WHO pays particular attention to combating major health problems, especially in developing countries and amid crises. The WCO and the World Health Organization work together on issues such as counterfeiting of pharmaceuticals. In 2011, the WHO Executive Board approved a new resolution that reinforces Directive 2011/62, which aims to establish a mechanism for common action among the Member States for the protection of the legal manufacturing channel. The WCO is an active member of the *International Medical Products Anti-Counterfeiting Taskforce* (IMPACT) project coordinated by the WHO. A Memorandum of Understanding between the WCO and WHO was signed in July 2002.[16]

---

[15] http://www.wcoomd.org/-/media/wco/public/global/pdf/about-us/part-ners/mou/098_mou.pdf?la=en. Accessed May 10, 2021.

[16] http://www.wcoomd.org/-/media/wco/public/global/pdf/about-us/partners/mou/049_mou.pdf?la=en. Accessed May 10, 2021.

4.2 World Trade Organization (WTO)

The World Trade Organization (WTO) is the international organization responsible for promoting world trade and monitoring effective compliance with the agreements that were negotiated and signed by most of the countries participating in global trade and ratified by their respective parliaments.

This organization's mission is to establish a common institutional framework to regulate trade relations among its various members, establish a mechanism for the peaceful settlement of trade disputes based on existing trade agreements, and, ultimately, create an environment conducive to the negotiation of new trade agreements among its members, as it is considered the economic forum par excellence to discuss these issues.

At its heart are the WTO agreements, negotiated and signed by the bulk of the world's trading nations. These documents provide *the legal ground-rules for international commerce. They are essentially contracts, binding governments to keep their trade policies within agreed limits. Although negotiated and signed by governments, the goal is to help producers of goods and services, exporters, and importers conduct their business, while allowing governments to meet social and environmental objectives.*[17]

The WTO requires governments to make their trade policies transparent by notifying the WTO about laws in force and adopted measures, as well as through regular reports by the Secretariat on countries' trade policies.

The WTO currently has 164 members, representing over 95% of total world trade, and 30 observers, who are awaiting accession. The WTO is composed of several bodies. The main ones are the following:

- The Ministerial Conference, the highest body of the organization, composed of the Ministers of Foreign Affairs and Foreign Trade of the members
- The General Council, the body based in Geneva composed of the permanent representatives of the members (technically, the Dispute Settlement Body (DSB) and the Trade Policy Review Body (TPRB) are General Council meetings)
- The Council for Trade in Goods
- The Council for Trade in Services
- The Council for Trade-Related Aspects of Intellectual Property Rights
- The various committees, including the Market Access, Agriculture, and Subsidies Committees, among others; and
- The Secretariat, whose function is to support the organization's activities and which is made up of nearly 700 officials, led by the Director General of the WTO.

Within the framework of cooperation that should exist between the WTO and the WCO, the system of *observers* is the appropriate instrument to guide such participation and mutual cooperation. Although observers who are present at international

[17] Visit the WTO's Official Website, document titled "Understanding the WTO". https://www.wto.org/english/thewto_e/whatis_e/tif_e/understanding_e.pdf. Accessed May 10, 2021.

organizations' meetings do not have the right to vote, they can actively participate in the debates and make recommendations on the issues under discussion. The legal support for such participation should be borne in mind: Article 2 (d) of the Convention establishing the WCO states that "The Council may admit representatives of non-Member Governments or of international organizations in the capacity of observers." Additionally, Article 9 establishes that "The Council shall establish such relations with the United Nations, its principal organs, subsidiary bodies and specialized agencies, and any other inter-governmental organizations, as may best assure collaboration in the achievement of their respective tasks."

The WTO and the WCO have the following common tasks:

- Use of the Harmonized System: the HS was created by the World Customs Organization and implemented in various agreements signed within the scope of the WTO, to delimit the coverage of goods and schedule concessions on goods.
- Rules of origin: the WTO Committee on Rules of Origin and the WCO Technical Committee on Rules of Origin are the two bodies responsible for matters relating to the Agreement on Rules of Origin. In 1999, the Technical Committee completed the technical review of the harmonized rules of origin, and the final results were presented in Geneva for consideration. These results are still being analyzed by the WTO.
- Customs valuation: The WCO Technical Committee on Customs Valuation works to ensure uniformity in the interpretation and application of the WTO Valuation Agreement at the technical level.
- Information Technology Agreement (ITA): it corresponds to a decision of the WTO, where the WCO has a leading role, in that the second sentence of paragraph 5 of the Annex to the Information Technology Agreement establishes: "Participants agree on the common objective of achieving, where appropriate, a common classification for these products within existing HS nomenclature, giving consideration to interpretations and rulings of the Customs Co-operation Council (also known as the World Customs Organization or "WCO"). In any instance in which divergence in classification remains, participants will consider whether a joint suggestion could be made to the WCO with regard to updating existing HS nomenclature or resolving divergence in interpretation of the HS nomenclature."
- Cooperation in technical assistance: it consists of the technical cooperation that both organizations maintain, which has evolved over time. Previously, the cooperation was focused on customs valuation and tariff classification. Now, it is concentrated on negotiations on trade facilitation. Future technical assistance cooperation might be necessary in the area of rules of origin as more and more countries negotiate free trade agreements. The coordination of these activities is managed through contacts between the staff of the respective Secretariats dealing with the relevant subject matter.
- Ensuring trade security: both organizations seek to maximize security standards in the commercial transactions between countries. While the WTO seeks to establish agreements within the framework of the principles of the trading system

where predictability and fair competition are found, the WCO establishes standards to avoid illicit acts affecting commercial transactions.
- Facilitation of trade: considering that the WTO is the forum par excellence for the discussion of agreements on economic matters and the monitoring of their compliance, cooperation in trade facilitation is particularly close and productive. This is evidenced by the regular participation in key meetings where the WCO provides technical advice, the preparation of auxiliary tools, and the broad worldwide technical assistance activities, which result in the generation of facilities for trade transactions between countries. This joint task has been clearly consolidated with the advent of the WTO Trade Facilitation Agreement and its immediate approval and support by the WCO through the Dublin Resolution.

4.3 Other Organizations

4.3.1 Partner Organizations

Commonwealth Secretariat

The Commonwealth is a voluntary association of 54 independent and equal countries. It is home to 2.4 billion people and includes both advanced economies and developing countries. Thirty-one of their members are small states, including many island nations.

The Member States cooperate within a framework of common values and goals, as outlined in the Singapore Declaration of 1971. These include the promotion of democracy, human rights, good governance, the rule of law, individual liberty, egalitarianism, free trade, multilateralism, and world peace.

The CITES Secretariat

The WCO Secretariat has a long working relationship with the Secretariat of the Convention on International Trade in Endangered Species of Wild Fauna and Flora (CITES) to implement this Convention based on the Memorandum of Understanding signed in 1996.[18] Both organizations are part of the International Consortium for Combating Wildlife Crime (ICCWC), which is a collaborative effort of five intergovernmental organizations to provide coordinated support to national wildlife law enforcement agencies and subregional and regional networks that, on a daily basis, act in defense of natural resources.

[18] http://www.wcoomd.org/-/media/wco/public/global/pdf/about-us/partners/ mou/034_mou.pdf?la=en. Accessed May 10, 2021.

4.3.2 International Organizations

International Federation of Red Cross and Red Crescent Societies (IFRC)
Founded in 1919, the International Federation is the world's largest humanitarian organization. This Federation has 187 members of Red Cross and Red Crescent National Societies, a Secretariat in Geneva, and more than 60 strategically located delegations to support activities around the world. In November 2007, the 30th International Conference of the Red Cross and Red Crescent (which brought together States Parties to the Geneva Conventions and components of the International Red Cross and Red Crescent Movement) adopted the Guidelines for the Domestic Facilitation and Regulation of International Disaster Relief and Initial Recovery Assistance (also known as the "IDRL Guidelines"). These guidelines are a set of recommendations to governments on how to prepare their disaster laws and plans for the common regulatory problems in international relief operations. Subsequently, in June 2011, the WCO Council recommended its Members States the implementation of these Guidelines through the adoption of the "Resolution on the Role of Customs in Natural Disaster Relief". The Memorandum of Understanding between the WCO and the International Federation of Red Cross and Red Crescent Societies was signed on June 25, 2012.

Interpol
On the basis of a Memorandum of Understanding signed in 1998,[19] the WCO Secretariat and Interpol (International Criminal Police Organization) have been closely working on a wide range of issues, in particular in combating cross-border criminal activities related to drugs, IPR, cultural heritage, cigarettes, small arms and light weapons (SALW), and the environment.

Cooperation between Interpol and the WCO arises from the fact that the customs services are primarily responsible for the control of cross-border traffic of goods. The operations carried out by these services and the police must be well coordinated in order to avoid needless efforts and ensure synergy between the goals and objectives of each organization. To achieve these objectives, a coordinated approach by all those responsible for border control, both nationally and internationally, is necessary.

International Federation of Freight Forwarders Associations (FIATA)
The International Federation of Freight Forwarders Associations is composed of 112 voting members and more than 5600 individual members. Therefore, it is the perfect body to represent freight forwarders or transportation service providers in the global supply chain. Its members' experience covers all aspects of international transport and logistics and is promoted through an autonomous training program that is implemented in over 100 countries.

[19] http://www.wcoomd.org/-/media/wco/public/global/pdf/about-us/partners/mou/042_mou.pdf?la=en. Accessed May 10, 2021.

Currently, FIATA is the leading nongovernmental organization in the field of transportation and logistics. It represents over 40,000 companies and employs up to ten million people in more than 150 countries. FIATA actively pursues its mandate to define, craft, and promote the role of international forwarders and logistics service providers in international air cargo with strong efforts to improve the professional standards of forwarders in air cargo in regard to facilitation, safety, and security. All these objectives are enshrined in the FIATA statutes, which are publicly available on the FIATA website (www.fiata.com), together with a wealth of additional information on freight forwarding and logistics.

On September 27, 2018, the World Customs Organization signed a Cooperation Agreement with FIATA with the aim of initiating collaboration between the WCO Academy and FIATA in order to offer joint training courses. One of the agreements' priorities is offering WCO virtual courses to the international logistics community through the FIATA network and website.

Financial Action Task Force (FATF)

The Financial Action Task Force (FATF) is an intergovernmental body established in 1989 by the ministers of its member jurisdictions. The objectives of the FATF are to set standards and promote the effective implementation of legal, regulatory, and operational measures for combating money laundering, terrorist financing, and other related threats to the integrity of the international financial system.

As an observer member of this group, the WCO Secretariat maintains close cooperation with FATF and similar regional bodies—such as the Asia/Pacific Group Against Money Laundering (APG) and the Intergovernmental Action Group Against Money Laundering in West Africa (GIABA)—to design and promote the best practices in the fight against money laundering in the customs sector at an international scale. Thereby, they facilitate joint investigations, shared information, and interdiction capacities and promote the timely exchange of experiences and best practices among member countries, through the comprehensive approach of specific actions that constitute a challenge to peace, security, and global development.

Global Facilitation Partnership for Transportation and Trade (GFP)

The aim of the Global Facilitation Partnership for Transportation and Trade (GFP) is to unite all stakeholders, be they public and private, national and international, that want to help achieve significant improvements in transport and trade facilitation worldwide. This Partnership supported the launch of the Mercator Program to help governments implement trade facilitation measures, including the provisions of the WTO Agreement on Trade Facilitation (AFC), in an expeditious and harmonized manner through the use of core WCO instruments and tools, such as the Revised Kyoto Convention (RKC), and tailored technical assistance.

The WCO is a core partner of the GFP, together with the World Bank, the United Nations Conference on Trade and Development, the United Nations Industrial Development Organization (UNIDO), the United Nations Economic Commission for Europe, the International Road Transport Union, the International Air Cargo Association, and the Bulgarian Chamber of Commerce and Industry.

International Centre for Migration Policy Development (ICMDP)
The International Centre for Migration Policy Development, established in 1993, is an international organization working in migration-related fields. The ICMPD was founded to carry out research, projects, and activities on migration-related issues and to provide policy recommendations to state government agencies, as well as to external governmental and intergovernmental agencies. The Centre also has observer status at the United Nations. The WCO cooperates with this institution by ensuring that the transportation of people and goods they carry comply with legal regulatory frameworks.

International Chamber of Commerce (ICC)
The ICC, which is based in Paris, signed the Memorandum of Understanding with the WCO on June 19, 1996. It is the only business organization that has the status of a consultative body to the United Nations and its specialized agencies. The ICC's objective is to act in favor of business interests by promoting trade and investment, opening markets for goods and services, and ensuring the free flow of capital. Through its various commissions, the ICC works in areas such as arbitration, banking, competition, e-commerce, customs and trade facilitation, insurance and financial services, taxation, trade policy, and transport and logistics. In these areas, the ICC conducts research and develops standards and guidelines that can be applied internationally by the private sector. It is one of the world's largest business representation organizations, comprising millions of companies of all sizes and covering all sectors of private enterprise in over 130 countries.

The International Chamber of Commerce, also referred to as the World Business Organization, prepared a set of 54 Customs Guidelines back in 2003 addressing critical areas related to Customs as an institution as well as a border agency. The guidelines were revised in collaboration with the World Customs Organization (WCO) and published again in the 2012 edition. The 2012 edition contains 57 Guidelines that present a comprehensive set of practices that the ICC considers should characterize all modern customs administrations.

Its activities cover a wide spectrum, within which it is appropriate to highlight (i) the Dispute Resolution Services, through which it works toward the resolution of commercial disputes; in addition, it has an International Court of Arbitration in case any problem arises regarding commercial activities, and those involved in a dispute may refer to this court to provide an efficient solution; (ii) the World Federation of Chambers, which is the world's largest network of chambers of commerce and in charge of administering the ATA Card System; and (iii) the International Commercial Terms (Incoterms), which are a series of three-letter trade terms agreed upon by the buyer and seller in regard to the responsibilities and obligations on the terms of delivery of the goods, arising from international commercial practices, which are updated by the ICC every 10 years.[20]

International Council of Museums (ICOM)
To combat the illicit traffic in cultural property, the WCO and ICOM signed a Memorandum of Understanding on January 25, 2000. This agreement allows both organizations to jointly draft and implement, each in its own field of competence, measures to improve cooperation and information exchange.

ICOM is able to carry out its international missions, thanks to international mandates and its collaboration with UNESCO, Interpol, and the WCO. Its main missions centered on the fight against the illicit trafficking of cultural property, risk management, the promotion of culture and knowledge, and the protection of tangible and intangible heritage.

International Trade Centre (ITC)
The International Trade Centre (ITC) is a joint cooperation agency of UNCTAD and WTO for business-related aspects of trade promotion. Initially established in 1964 by the General Agreement on Tariffs and Trade (GATT), it has been jointly administered since 1968 by GATT/WTO and the United Nations, the latter acting through the United Nations Conference on Trade and Development (UNCTAD). It is the center of coordination in the United Nations System for technical cooperation with developing countries and economies in transition in trade promotion and export development.

The WCO works alongside the ITC to promote national developments through international trade emphasizing the relationship between exports and the private sector. The ITC organizes symposiums, which gather participants from legal, academic, and business backgrounds. By participating in these symposiums, the WCO promotes the Revised Kyoto Convention and other WCO instruments to the participants. The ITC has agreed to cover data relating to key WCO instruments on its website, where they also display the countries' adherence status to key treaties related to international trade.[21]

Organisation for Economic Co-operation and Development (OECD)
Founded in 1961, the OECD is an international organization that aims to stimulate economic progress and world trade and has several projects supported by the WCO. Historically, these organizations have been closely associated: in 1948, the Study Group created two committees, one economic and the other customs; the Economic Committee was the predecessor of the Organisation for Economic Co-operation and Development (OECD), and the Customs Committee became the Customs Cooperation Council (CCC).

---

[20]They are a set of internationally recognized rules that determine the responsibilities and conditions involved in the delivery of goods under an international sales contract, the establishment of criteria on the distribution of costs, and the transfer of risks between the buying and selling parties. The latest version corresponds to the Incoterms 2020, which came into force on January 1, 2020.

[21]For more information, visit http://www.intracen.org/default.aspx. Accessed May 10, 2021.

The OECD is a forum of countries committed to democracy and the market economy. It provides a platform for comparing their political experiences, seeking answers to common problems, identifying good practices, and coordinating the domestic and international policies of its members. The WCO works together with the OECD and the World Bank Group to encourage Customs and Tax administrations to establish bilateral lines of communication in order to, where possible, exchange knowledge, practices, and data that would help ensure that each authority has the most detailed information of an activity and its record of compliance which would help the tax administration make informed decisions regarding the right tax responsibility.

Organisation for the Prohibition of Chemical Weapons (OPCW)

The Organisation for the Prohibition of Chemical Weapons (OPCW) is an intergovernmental organization, located in The Hague, Netherlands. The organization promotes and confirms adherence to the Chemical Weapons Convention (CWC), which prohibits the use of chemical weapons and requires their destruction. The verification consists of an evaluation of the declarations of the Members States and on-site inspections. The OPCW issued a recommendation to the WCO to introduce specific subheadings in the Harmonized System for 33 regulated substances subject to greater trade. The approval of the WCO Council Recommendation of June 26, 2009, to add specific subheadings to the statistical nomenclatures for the most widely traded regulated chemicals was an important step for the OPCW. The underlying goal of this Recommendation was to increase the number of States Parties that have effective mechanisms in place to monitor trade in regulated chemicals.

Organization for Security and Co-operation in Europe (OSCE)

The Organization for Security and Co-operation in Europe (OSCE) is the largest regional security agency, created with the aim of preventing conflicts in and around Europe. The OSCE has its origins in the Conference on Security and Cooperation in Europe (CSCE), held in Helsinki in 1975. Currently, the organization groups 57 states in Europe, North America, and Central Asia. The OSCE carries out its activities and adopts its decisions based on the rule of consensus. Its obligations and commitments are of a political nature. Both features give this organization its specific character as it is the most important regional organization after the United Nations. Its relations with other international organizations and institutions are founded on the spirit of cooperation and coordination in an endeavor to avoid needlessly duplicating their respective tasks.

As a result of a cooperation between the WCO and OSCE, held in Vienna, Austria, in July 2005, the OSCE Council has drawn up a Decision in support of the Framework of Standards to Secure and Facilitate Global Trade (SAFE). The OSCE Council agreed to encourage their members, which are also members of the WCO, to sign the Letter of Intent to implement SAFE standards. The OSCE has also offered to assist in capacity-building initiatives related to the same program.

4.3.3 Regional Intergovernmental Organizations

African Union (AU)
Founded in 2002, the African Union is the successor organization of the Organization of African Unity (OAU), and it aims to promote economic development and political stability through greater cooperation among its members. A Memorandum of Understanding between the WCO and the AU was signed on June 25, 2010.[22]

The WCO and AU work together to conduct ethics programs in the Member States regarding the union of customs administrations and to critically examine difficulties in their implementation. In 2014, they produced the "Draft Brazzaville. Customs Declaration on Integrity and Ethics in African Customs Administrations" and a "Conclusions and Recommendations" report.[23]

European Monitoring Centre for Drugs and Drug Addiction (EMCDDA)
Established in 1993, the European Monitoring Centre for Drugs and Drug Addiction (EMCDDA) is a European Union body and agency that provides its member countries with real, objective, reliable, and comparable information within a European scope on drugs, drug addiction, and their consequences, with a view to advising on policy development and guiding initiatives to combat drugs. The WCO and EMCDDA signed a Memorandum of Understanding on January 12, 2007, with the aim of improving international drug control efforts. In addition, the WCO produces reports such as the *Customs and Drugs Report*,[24] which shows drug trafficking status in international trade.

European Free Trade Association (EFTA)
The European Free Trade Association (EFTA) was founded in 1960 on the premise of free trade as a means of achieving growth and prosperity among its Member States, as well as promoting closer economic cooperation between the Western European countries. In addition, the EFTA countries wished to contribute to the expansion of trade in the world at large. The EFTA members are Iceland, Liechtenstein, Norway, and Switzerland.

EFTA is responsible for overseeing the EFTA Convention, the European Economic Area (EEA) Agreement—which allows three of the EFTA states (Iceland, Liechtenstein, and Norway) to participate in the EU Internal Market—and the EFTA Free Trade Agreements with third countries.

---

[22] http://www.wcoomd.org/-/media/wco/public/global/pdf/about-us/partners/mou/128_mou.pdf?la=en. Accessed May 10, 2021.

[23] See WCO Press note African Union Seminar on Integrity and Ethics in Customs Kigali, Rwanda (28-30 May 2014). http://www.wcoomd.org/ru-ru/media/news-room/2014/august/african-union-seminar-on-integrity-and-ethics-in-customs.aspx. Accessed May 10, 2021.

[24] World Customs Organization, "Customs and Drug Report 2009". http://www.wcoomd.org/-/media/wco/public/global/pdf/topics/enforcement-and-compliance/ac-tivi-ties-and-programmes/drugs-and-precursor-chemicals/reports/drugs_2009.pdf?d-b=web Accessed May 10, 2021.

European Union (EU)

The WCO Secretariat cooperates with the relevant bodies of the EU Commission, such as the Directorate General for Taxation and Customs Union (TAXUD) and the European Anti-Fraud Office (OLAF) in order to increase efforts for combating all kinds of fraud that customs encounters.

OLAF (European Anti-Fraud Office), established by the Community institutions of the European Union (EU), is the entity that protects the financial interests of the EU. Its main mission is to fight in an accountable, transparent, and efficient way fraud, corruption, and any other activity that affects the EU's budget, including irregularities within the European institutions. It acts independently, carrying out internal and external investigations. It also organizes cooperation between the competent authorities of the Member States in order to coordinate their activities in the anti-fraud field, and it provides the Member States with the necessary assistance and multidisciplinary technical know-how to support them in their anti-fraud activities.

In the SAFE Regulatory Framework, the European Union implemented the new "Import Control System" (ICS), which aims to ensure the security of merchandise when it enters the EU customs territory. This control system, which is registered in the community system eCUSTOMS, has been in force since January 1, 2011. From this date forward, it became mandatory for operators to lodge an Entry Summary Declaration (ENS) to the EU customs office of first entry before the arrival of goods in the customs territory of the European Union.

Eurasian Economic Community (EurAsEC or EAEC)

The Eurasian Economic Community was created from the Commonwealth of Independent States (CIS) of the Customs Union between Belarus, Russia, and Kazakhstan. It encourages the free movement of goods, services, capital, and labor and ensures that, within the EAEC, there are coordinated, harmonized, and unique policies in the areas determined by the Treaty on the Establishment of the Eurasian Economic Community and international agreements.

It was established with the aim of fostering and improving the competitiveness of national economies in a comprehensive manner, intensifying cooperation among them, and promoting stable development and, thus, improving the quality of life in the Member States. The Treaty on the Establishment of the Eurasian Economic Community was signed in 2000, and common economic space was launched on January 1, 2010. A Memorandum of Understanding between the WCO and EAEC was signed in 2006.[25]

Southeast European Law Enforcement Center (SELEC), Former Regional Center for Combating Trans-Border Crime (SECI Center)

SELEC supports and promotes coordination among the Member States in preventing and combating criminal activities (including organized crime and other serious

[25] http://www.wcoomd.org/-/media/wco/public/global/pdf/about-us/partners/mou/074_mou.pdf?la=en. Accessed May 10, 2021.

crimes) that are, or appear to be, linked to cross-border activities. SELEC's predecessor, the Southeast European Cooperative Initiative (SECI Center) Regional Center for Combating Trans-Border Crime, was established in 1996 to foster regional cooperation among the countries of Southeast Europe. SELEC replaced SECI in 2011. The Centre currently has 17 observer countries, five observer organizations, and two permanent advisors: Interpol and the WCO.

The WCO Secretariat has maintained close cooperation with the SECI Center since the meetings for the establishment of the Center to combat trans-border crimes. The WCO supported this regional initiative to promote combating customs frauds and improving cooperation among the participating countries. An MoU between the WCO and SECI was signed on March 25, 2005.

4.3.4 Donor Organizations

World Bank

The World Bank is a specialized entity of the United Nations (UN). It is often known as the World Bank Group (WBG). This institution, with headquarters based in Washington (United States), was created in 1944 and has 185 member countries. Its main objective is to lower poverty rates through low-interest loans and economic support to developing nations.

The WTO has stated that "Common activities are likely to increase further with both organizations—WCO and WTO—embarking on an extensive needs *and cost assessment program, together with the World Bank and other international partners in the field.*"[26]

The WCO Secretariat participates in the World Bank's Customs modernization and reform projects to increase cooperation programs with other agencies, emphasizing collaboration among border agencies.

For its part, the World Bank also launched a project to help countries improve their participation in the WTO trade facilitation negotiations, with the aim of presenting a wide range of options for establishing coordination mechanisms in a country, introducing effective communication, and supporting its trade facilitation negotiator in Geneva.

African Development Bank

The African Development Bank is a multinational development bank created in 1964, composed of 53 African countries and financed by 24 European, American, and Asian countries. This bank's mission is to promote the economic development and social progress of African countries. Its headquarters are located in Abidjan, in the Ivory Coast, and it is responsible for granting loans to solvent middle-income

[26] World Trade Organization, *"The WTO and World Customs Organization"* available at https://www.wto.org/english/thewto_e/coher_e/wto_wco_e.htm. Accessed May 10, 2021.

countries in slightly more favorable conditions than the market. It also grants credits and guarantees and invests in private sector entities.

The African Development Bank and the World Customs Organization work together to enhance the capacity of customs administrations in Africa. The partnership includes collaboration in identifying, developing, and implementing Customs capacity-building projects by observing internationally agreed best practices and supporting Customs cooperation and regional integration in Africa. A comprehensive Memorandum of Understanding was signed between the two organizations on January 30, 2012.

Canadian International Development Agency (CIDA)
CIDA is Canada's lead agency for development cooperation. Its goal is to manage Canada's support and resources effectively and responsibly to achieve sustainable and meaningful results. It aims to participate in policy formulation in Canada and internationally in order to achieve the goals of sustainable development among various areas of the planet, reduce poverty, and contribute to a safer, more equitable and prosperous world.

This agency focuses on strengthening an environment conducive to economic growth and helping governments and private sector organizations to connect to global markets. This includes harmonizing and standardizing investment policies, fiscal policies, and regulatory frameworks so that the private sector can operate under a common set of rules and regulations. For this reason, the WCO and its guidelines are extremely important to CIDA.

Norwegian Agency for Development Cooperation (NORAD)
The Norwegian Agency for Development Cooperation (NORAD) is an organization subordinate to the Norwegian Ministry of Foreign Affairs. Its primary objective is to provide international aid to developing countries to combat poverty. Since 2004, NORAD has been providing assistance to nongovernmental organizations (NGOs), while official aid is implemented through the Ministry of Foreign Affairs.

Although the organization finances projects in various areas, it particularly focuses on those related to climate change and the environment, health, public administration, and sustainable energy provision. All of these areas are related to the Millennium Goals (MDGs) established by the United Nations (UN). NORAD assures the quality of Norwegian development assistance by means of technical advisory services, the management of concessions, communication, and evaluation.

Swedish International Development Cooperation Agency (SIDA)
The overall objective of the Swedish Development Assistance Agency is to ensure that people living in poverty have the capacity to improve their living conditions. SIDA works broadly across all areas of society in order to carry out its tasks effectively. Through its budget for grassroots organizations, SIDA also distributes grants to NGOs in order to promote a democratic and vibrant civil society in the partner countries and thus contribute to motivating people to lift themselves out of poverty.

The activity is based on close cooperation between Swedish and local organizations in the partner countries, where training and organizational development are important factors. In some cases, cooperation takes place within the framework of different international networks, and the WCO participates in various projects financed by SIDA.

Inter-American Development Bank (IADB)
The Inter-American Development Bank is an international financial organization, created in 1959, with headquarters in Washington, DC. The IDB is the main source of multilateral financing and expertise for sustainable economic, social, and institutional development in Latin America and the Caribbean. The IDB Group is composed of the Inter-American Development Bank, the Inter-American Investment Corporation (IIC), and the Multilateral Investment Fund (MIF). The IIC is centered on the support for small and medium-sized businesses, while the MIF promotes private sector growth through grants and investments, with an emphasis on microenterprise.

The diagnostics of customs administrations and action plans for trade facilitation are the two main components of the IDB-WCO collaborative program. Among the action plans are initiatives in trade security (SAFE Framework) and the promotion of customs-business partnerships. The IDB finances various events where the WCO provides technical assistance, such as symposia and discussions with customs specialists.

4.3.5 Business Organizations

Bureau of International Containers (BIC)
With over 2100 members, the BIC is the only nongovernmental organization linking all groups interested in containerization and intermodal transport, such as carriers, manufacturers, operators, lessors, shippers, and forwarders. Its main objectives are to contribute to the expansion of the use of containers and intermodal transport through professional discussions on all related topics and to obtain and keep specialized documentation for the benefit of its members.

The BIC is an entity that has been officially recognized by the International Organization of Standardization (ISO) and the WCO to assign and protect the ISO 6346 code, which indicates the identification of containers in international trade. A Memorandum of Understanding between the WCO and BIC was signed on June 24, 2006.

Global Express Association (GEA)
The Global Express Association is the global trade association representing express delivery companies (couriers). The GEA promotes the interests of its members and their customers in international regulatory and public affairs forums, in close cooperation with national and regional express delivery associations serving more than

200 countries, carrying more than 30 million packages each day, all guaranteed to be delivered within specified time frames.

This guarantee makes express delivery unique in the transportation industry and enables its customers to operate over broad territories with a high degree of confidence. A Memorandum of Understanding between the WCO and GEA was signed on June 25, 2010.[27] Both work hand in hand to comply with the WTO Agreement on Trade Facilitation (AFC) due to the growing importance of e-commerce for economic growth.

They also coordinate work for the development of the Regulatory Framework aimed at regulating cross-border electronic commerce worldwide.

International Air Transport Association (IATA)

The International Air Transport Association (IATA) is the worldwide organization of scheduled airlines. Its members carry the majority of international air traffic under more than a hundred nations' flags. Its main mission is to ensure that the world's air traffic is carried out with maximum speed, safety, and efficiency under optimal economic conditions.

Due to its structure and activities, IATA maintains close relations with the International Civil Aviation Organization (ICAO), a United Nations agency composed of governments, also created in 1945, which formulates the rules and recommendations governing civil aviation. For governments, IATA is the instrument for the development of industry standards and, where necessary, for the coordination of international rates and freight.

The WCO has been working closely with IATA on several fronts, including Advanced Passenger Information (API), Advanced Cargo Information (ACI), and the IATA E-freight project. The WCO was invited to be involved in the IATA E-freight project, which aims at creating a paperless environment with the goal of removing all papers for all stakeholders from air cargo transportation by 2010. Two Memoranda of Understanding have been signed between the WCO and IATA respectively on June 20, 1988, and June 23, 1986.

IATA and the WCO have been working together toward the integration of Cargo-XML in the WCO Cargo Targeting System (CTS), which allows electronic communication between airlines and customs authorities using the IATA Cargo-XML standard format. This will make communication simpler and more effective, as well as facilitate more accurate risk assessments by customs authorities using the WCO CTS application to capture advance electronic cargo manifest information.

International Air Cargo Association (TIACA)

TIACA is a global not-for-profit trade association that represents all the major segments of the air cargo and air logistics industry—combination and all-cargo airlines, forwarders, airports, ground handlers, road carriers, customs brokers, logistics companies, shippers, information technology (IT) companies, aircraft and

---

[27] http://www.wcoomd.org/-/media/wco/public/global/pdf/about-us/partners/mou/122_mou.pdf?la=en. Accessed May 10, 2021.

equipment manufacturers, trade press, and educational institutions. In pursuit of its mission, TIACA engages in activities that seek to improve industry cooperation, promote innovation, share knowledge, enhance quality and efficiency, and advance education.

TIACA aims to inform both the public and its membership about the role and importance of air cargo, industry developments, and technical trends. It is pledged to support and assist progressive liberalization of the global market and easier, enhanced trade between developing and developed economies. A Memorandum of Understanding between the WCO and TIACA was signed on June 25, 2010.[28]

International Association of Ports and Harbors (IAPH)
IAPH is often referred to as the "United Ports of the World," and it is the entity in which active players in the global port community, namely Port CEOs, Port Directors, and Port Managers are represented to promote and advance their common cause and interests. It strives to achieve the mission of promoting the development of the international port and maritime industry by fostering cooperation among members in order to build a more cohesive partnership among the world's ports and harbors. A Memorandum of Understanding between the WCO and IAPH was signed in 1987.[29]

International Road Transport Union (IRU)
The IRU is a global organization that defends the interests of the road transport industry with the aim of ensuring economic growth and prosperity through the sustainable mobility of people and goods around the world. With a fully global strategy, the IRU effectively influences, on both domestic and international scales, through its network of national road transport associations.

The IRU has been working in a genuine public-private partnership with the UN Economic Commission for Europe (UNECE) to implement the Customs Convention on the International Transport of Goods Under Cover of TIR Cards (TIR Convention).

A Memorandum of Understanding between the WCO and IRU was signed on September 21, 1987.[30] The TIR remote education module was jointly developed by the IRU and WCO.

International Organization for Standardization (ISO)
The International Organization for Standardization (ISO), began in 1946, when 64 delegates from 25 countries met at the Institute of Civil Engineers in London and decided to create an international organization to facilitate the international coordination and unification of industrial standards. It is an independent, nongovernmental organization formed by the standardization organizations of its

---

[28] http://www.wcoomd.org/-/media/wco/public/global/pdf/about-us/partners/mou/123_mou.pdf?la=en. Accessed May 10, 2021.

[29] http://www.wcoomd.org/-/media/wco/public/global/pdf/about-us/partners/mou/003_mou.pdf. Accessed May 10, 2021.

[30] http://www.wcoomd.org/-/media/wco/public/global/pdf/about-us/partners/mou/004_mou.pdf. Accessed May 10, 2021.

163 member countries, with headquarters in Geneva, Switzerland. The ISO is the world's largest developer of voluntary international standards, facilitating global trade by providing common standards between countries.

The Secretariat contributed to the work of the ISO 7372 Maintenance Agency, which is the ISO equivalent of the United Nations Trade Element Directory (UNTDED). The Council approved the ISO 7372 standard, and the United Nations published it as UNTDED 2005 and ISO 7372: 2005 standards. The WCO is a member of the ISO TC 8 Working Group, which is currently working on a set of Publicly Available Specifications (PAS 28001), the precursor to a comprehensive supply chain security standard. PAS 28001 is intended to help an organization establish a minimum level of supply chain security and to meet the applicable WCO requirements for obtaining Authorized Economic Operator (AEO) status. The WCO is seeking to ensure that PAS 28001 is fully compliant with the SAFE program.

4.3.6 Academic Organizations

Centre for Customs and Excise Studies, University of Canberra, Australia

The University of Canberra was established in 1967 as the Canberra College of Advanced Education and then became the University of Canberra with sponsorship from Monash University in 1990. It currently houses the Centre for Customs and Excise Studies and works with the Kenya-based Eastern and Southern Africa Regional Office for Capacity Building. The Memorandum of Understanding between the WCO and the University of Canberra was signed on January 3, 2001,[31] and agrees to explore opportunities for cooperation and to minimize the needless duplication of efforts in training, coaching, and human resource development by articulating training programs.

International Network of Customs Universities (INCU)

The International Network of Customs Universities (INCU) is an international nonprofit organization with more than 200 members and affiliates. Its objective is to raise the academic profile of the customs profession through educational development and promotion by providing academic and applied research in addition to intellectual input for strategic decision-making.

The main objectives of the INCU are to promote the academic standing of the customs profession, to promote academic excellence in customs matters, to support research on customs issues, to organize academic conferences, to generate greater public awareness of the customs profession, to promote the collective interests of its members, to provide the World Customs Organization and other organizations with a single point of contact with universities and research institutes, and to provide a

[31] http://www.wcoomd.org/-/media/wco/public/global/pdf/about-us/partners/mou/089_mou.pdf?la=en. Accessed May 10, 2021.

global resource for governments and the private sector. In short, it is a quality and specialized educational resource for students and professionals wishing to further their knowledge in the field of customs, international trade, and logistics.

The INCU provides a mechanism to progressively establish a knowledge base on various important aspects of customs and allows for a free exchange of ideas and best practices that will not only help countries undertake reform processes but will also serve to build closer links between the government, academia, and the private sector.

In addition, the INCU seeks to achieve the highest visibility of customs and international trade to attract to the industry talented people who can contribute to the sustainability of best practices in customs and international trade law and administration.

Since its creation in 2005, INCU's main aim has been to raise the academic status of the customs profession, which is why it publishes the biannual "World Customs Journal,"[32] which offers the possibility of publishing the results of its studies and experiences in the customs field. The Memorandum of Understanding between the WCO and INCU was signed on September 30, 2009.

Leeds Metropolitan University, United Kingdom
Based in the city of Leeds, this British university is one of the most popular in the country. It is a public university whose origins date back to 1824 with the founding of the Institute of Mechanics in Leeds. Leeds Polytechnic was established in 1970 and was part of the Leeds Local Education Authority until it became an independent Higher Education Corporation on April 1, 1989. In 1992, the institution gained university status, and in 2014, it adopted its current name. With over 29,000 students and 3000 employees, the university's contribution to the region is more than significant. Among its academic offerings are bachelor's and master's degree programs and academic courses for professional training in customs with PICARD certification. The Memorandum of Understanding between the WCO and the University of Leeds was signed on January 24, 2007.[33]

Riga Technical University, Latvia
Riga Technical University is the first technical university in the Baltic countries as its history dates back to 1862, when Riga Polytechnic was founded. It was reestablished in 1958, when the engineering departments of the Latvian State University were divided. The Technical University offers bachelor's degree and master's degree professional programs in Taxes and Customs with PICARD accreditation. The Memorandum of Understanding between WCO and Riga Technical University was signed on September 25, 2005.[34]

[32] Visit the official website "World Customs Journal" at http://worldcustomsjournal.org/.

[33] http://www.wcoomd.org/-/media/wco/public/global/pdf/about-us/partners/mou/094_mou.pdf?la=en. Accessed May 10, 2021.

[34] http://www.wcoomd.org/-/media/wco/public/global/pdf/about-us/partners/mou/086_mou.pdf?la=en. Accessed May 10, 2021.

University of Costa Rica, Costa Rica
The University of Costa Rica is one of the leading research universities within the country as well as Central America. The University offers baccalaureate and master and licentiate diplomas in Customs Administration and Trade. The MOU between the WCO and the University of Costa Rica was signed in 2008.[35]

University of Le Havre, France
The University of Le Havre is situated in the Seine-Maritime department of the Haute-Normandie region in France. Since 1967, it had operated as a Center for University Studies, dependent on the University of Rouen, until its official inauguration in 1984. The university offers various professional training studies, within the programs of the French University Institute of Technology, toward which it is especially oriented and for which it has the support of companies in the Seine Valley. Among its academic offerings is a degree in Customs Operations, which is centered on the management of customs operations and information systems, which is taught in cooperation with French Customs and has PICARD accreditation from the WCO. The Memorandum of Understanding between the WCO and the University of Le Habré was signed in June 2007.

University of Munster, Germany
The University of Munster (in German: *Westfälische Wilhelms-Universität* (WWU) is a public university located in the city of Munster, North Rhine- Westphalia in Germany. It is part of the *Deutsche Forschungsgemeinschaft*, a society of Germany's leading research universities. The University of Munster offers a Master in Customs Administration, Law and Policy. The MoU between the WCO and the University of Muenster was signed in November 2005.[36]

University of Verona, Department of English, Germanic and Slavic Studies, Italy
The University of Verona (Università degli Studi di Verona) is a university located in Verona, Italy. In the 1950s, a group of Catholic historians founded the Free School of Historical Sciences and promoted the project for the creation of a public university for the Veronese. In 1959, the city government initiated the project by creating the Free Faculty of Economics and Commerce and the Consortium for students, which was inaugurated on November 1 of that year. In 1963, the institution became dependent on the University of Padua as a seat of its Faculty of Economics and shortly thereafter opened the faculties of Law, Medicine and Surgery, Art, and Philosophy. Later on, in 1982, it received authorization and became independent from the University of Padua, thereby becoming the University of Verona. Within its academic offer, a master's degree in Customs Administration for operational managers/directors with PICARD accreditation stands out. The Memorandum of

[35] http://10.1.1.181//-/media/wco/public/es/pdf/about-us/partners/mou/101_mou_es.pdf. Accessed May 10, 2021.

[36] http://www.wcoomd.org/-/media/wco/public/global/pdf/about-us/part-ners/mou/087_mou.pdf?la=en. Accessed May 10, 2021.

Understanding between the WCO and the University of Verona was signed on April 29, 2009.[37]

The University of Ss. Cyril and Methodius, Skopje, in the Former Yugoslav Republic of Macedonia
The University of Ss. Cyril and Methodius, based in Skopje, is the largest university in the former Yugoslav Republic of Macedonia. It was founded in 1949 with just three faculties. The university develops programs of study in all scientific fields: natural sciences and mathematics, technical and technological sciences, and medical sciences. The Faculty of Economics of this University is part of the INCU program and actively participates in the academic development of knowledge in the field of customs. The Memorandum of Understanding between the WCO and this institution was signed on May 10, 2007.[38] On June 25, 2009, a Regional Training Center was established at this university (at the Faculty of Economics), in cooperation with the Customs Service of the Republic of Macedonia (see footnote 39).

Zayed University, United Arab Emirates
Zayed University was established in 1998 and is the newest of the three government-sponsored higher educational institutions in the United Arab Emirates. When it received accreditation from the Middle States Commission on Higher Education in the United States, it became the first UAE federal university to be internationally accredited. The Memorandum of Understanding between the WCO and this institution was signed in Abu Dhabi in May 2005.

4.4 Purview: Competence Conflicts

As interstate relations become more complex, we observe a healthy proliferation of international organizations. States create these international organizations with a view to providing effective solutions to the problems that arise from their interactions at a global, continental, or regional scale.

The structure and operation of these entities are fundamentally inspired by the principle of "cooperation" through which the signatory states, by common agreement, transfer their competencies to them.

Hence, each international organization exercises its powers independently or externally from the powers of the state organs that comprise it.

Jurisdiction in the traditional sense corresponds to the power granted to a given body intended to operate within the internal order of the state. Now, in the case of

---

[37] http://www.wcoomd.org/-/media/wco/public/global/pdf/about-us/partners/mou/106_mou.pdf?la=en. Accessed May 10, 2021.

[38] http://www.wcoomd.org/-/media/wco/public/global/pdf/about-us/partners/mou/109_mou.pdf?la=en. Accessed May 10, 2021.

international jurisdiction, it corresponds to the power of judgment granted to a given jurisdictional body. In this sense, Couture[39] defines it as

> a public activity carried out by competent national or international bodies, as required by law, whereby the legal order established for the settlement of conflicts and disputes by means of decisions that may acquire the authority of res judicata and may be enforced, is applied by an act of judgement.

In this regard, it relates it directly to the power-duty attributed to structurally impartial organs to exclude legal dissatisfaction.

Regarding jurisdiction and competence in customs matters, it is up to the World Customs Organization to exercise its power as the sole global body of an intergovernmental nature with the mission to improve the effectiveness and efficiency of member customs.

In accordance with the above, it is quite evident that the term "cooperation" among international organizations should not be confused with interference in matters that are of their own competence (pursuant to the powers granted when these organizations were set up).

Throughout history, the WCO should have resolved certain conflicts that arose. However, these were eventually settled by other international organizations. The following are examples of some of these cases:

- **United States vs European Community** (OMC DS62):[40] in 1996, the United States filed a complaint arguing that the European Community had applied higher tariffs than those provided for in the Community's Schedules to Local Area Network (LAN) equipment and personal computers with multimedia capacity ("PCs with multimedia capacity"). The United States claimed that, by reclassifying LAN adapter cards pursuant to Commission Regulation (EC) 1165/95, the European Community accorded to LAN equipment and/or PCs with multimedia capability a less favorable treatment than that provided for in Part I of Schedule LXXX, thus applying a tariff rate of 3.8 percent to computers "capable of receiving and processing television, telecommunication, audio and video signals" as well as a tariff rate of 10.5 percent to computers "capable of receiving and processing television signals but having no other specific subsidiary functions." Therefore, the United States claimed that this reclassification was incompatible with the obligations under Article II of the GATT.

  Following the respective analysis, the Dispute Settlement Body (DSB) found that the LAN equipment should have been given the tariff treatment provided for automatic data-processing machines in Schedule LXXX and that the European Community has violated Article II:1 of GATT 1994 by failing to accord to

[39] Couture (1960), p. 381; the author has also defined jurisdiction as "the power to judge and enforce what is judged,", Procedure. First Course. Organization of the courts, Montevideo, Medina, s. a., p. 22.

[40] Dispute Settlement Summary. OMC DS62. https://www.wto.org/english/tratop_e/dis-pu_e/cases_e/ds62_e.html. One-page summary (PDF version).

imports of LAN equipment from the United States treatment no less favorable than that provided for in heading 84.71 or 84.73 of Part I of Schedule LXXX.

According to the dispute raised, where a tariff reclassification exists or is requested, the "competent" agency to settle the dispute is the World Customs Organization (WCO). Article 10 of the *International Convention on the Harmonized Commodity Description and Coding System* establishes that "any dispute between Contracting Parties concerning the interpretation or application of this Convention shall, so far as possible, be settled by negotiation between them" and not by the WTO, which resolved the dispute through the Dispute Settlement Body (DSB), alleging its role as a trade facilitator.

- **Brazil, Thailand vs. European Community**: Brazil (2002) and Thailand (2003) had a dispute against the European Community (EC) for the modification of the Community's tariff. First, the classification code on frozen boneless chicken cuts, which these countries commonly exported to the EC, was changed and, consequently, the tariff, thus increasing in customs the amount of about 1.00 euros per kilogram. Brazil and Thailand did not agree with the new classification (02.07) "meat and edible offal, fresh, chilled or frozen," claiming that the previous classification (02.10) "meat and edible meat offal, salted, in brine, dried or smoked" was the correct classification as the chicken rinds were salted. The European Community asserted that the salting to which the cuts were submitted was not sufficient for the purposes of code 02.10 since it allowed the preservation of the cuts for long-term conservation, which did not exist with respect to the aforementioned cuts (as indicated in the 2002 tariff amendment).

In this conflict, we verify again the breach of Article 10 of the International Convention on the Harmonized Commodity Description and Coding System, which gives competence to the WCO. This generated a new responsibility on the part of the WTO, which finally concluded that the products in dispute were covered by the tariff commitment corresponding to classification 02.10 of the EC tariff.

As these cases have shown, on several occasions, there has been an interference with the WCO's functions or exclusive competence in customs matters at a global level. It is important in the field of trade and international law to maintain harmonious relations between the main actors, which is why each member must carry out its work with absolute respect for the assigned scope of competence.

Reference

Couture EJ (1960) Vocabulario jurídico con especial referencia al derecho procesal uruguayo, (Legal vocabulary with special reference to procedural law in Uruguay). Library of Official Publications of the Faculty of Law and Social Sciences of the University of Montevideo, Montevideo, p 381

Chapter 5
WCO Relation with Customs Brokers

Customs brokers[1] are among the foreign trade operators who stand shoulder to shoulder with customs services worldwide. These professionals, who are duly represented within the Private Sector Consultative Group (PSCG), arrange for the clearance of goods before customs on behalf of importers and exporters.

Notwithstanding, the work of these qualified operators, whose competent actions are "essential" for correct and fluid customs clearance, is not uniformly covered by the different national laws.

Thus, in 2014,[2] the World Customs Organization (WCO), exercising its powers of harmonization and technical assistance, carried out a survey. The purpose was to provide a clear understanding in terms of brokers' roles, the institutional framework, and the regulatory/licensing requirements.

To this end, the WCO circulated a detailed questionnaire among all its members requesting, inter alia, information regarding licensing requirements, sanctions or penalties, obligations, restrictions, and cooperation mechanisms.

Ninety-nine countries, representing 55% of the WCO membership at the time, responded with the following result:

TN In Latin America and Spain Customs brokers are named differently. In Brazil, Uruguay, Paraguay, and Argentina, they are called "Despachantes de Aduana"; in Panama, "Corredor de Aduana"; and in Chile, Colombia, Peru, Venezuela, Spain, Central America and other Latin American countries they are just called "Agente de Aduana."

---

[1]The "WCO Glossary of International Customs Terms" defines the Customs clearing agent as the person who carries on the business of arranging for the Customs clearance of goods and who deals directly with the Customs for and on behalf of another person. http://www.wcoomd.org/-/media/wco/public/global/pdf/topics/facilitation/instruments-and-tools/tools/glossary-of-international-customs-terms/glossary-of-international-customs-terms.pdf?db=web. Accessed May 10, 2021.

[2]In its 72nd session which was held in Recife, Brazil, on December 8th to 10th, 2014, the Policy Commission discussed the subject "Customs brokers – Institutional Framework and Agreements".

H. H. Juárez Allende, *The World Customs Organization*, Law for Professionals,
https://doi.org/10.1007/978-3-030-85296-2_5

- Ninety-five administrations declared that their countries have some kind of mechanism for customs brokers, agents, or third parties that act on behalf of traders and customs to handle customs clearance processes and related activities.
- The remaining four countries do not have any requirements for these activities; therefore, they did not provide any framework for this profession.

  The Study Report describes that there is a wide spectrum of models vis-à-vis the activities customs brokers perform. The most relevant include submitting documents for customs release and clearance, paying taxes, providing assistance in postclearance audits, acting on behalf of their clients in the settlement of disputes, and providing consultancy or advisory services to businessmen.

  As there is "no one size fits all" solution, the Study Report suggests an array of considerations that could serve as a reference point for countries wishing to establish or adjust a regime for brokers.

  Once the results of the survey were analyzed, the WCO Policy Commission suggested publishing them as a WCO tool to provide guidance to members. In addition, this tool may be the starting point for further studies to detect and develop best practices based on these experiences.

In October 2017, and based on the abovementioned study, the Permanent Technical Committee (along with the Trade Facilitation Agreement Working Group) approved the Customs Brokers Guidelines with a view to providing reference guidance to the Member States to establish and adjust their regulation in line with the Revised Kyoto Convention (RKC) and the WTO Agreement on Trade Facilitation (TFA).[3]

A summary of the relevant issues of the Study and the Guide is detailed below.

5.1 Optional or Mandatory

The Revised Kyoto Convention states that the usage of customs broker services is *optional.*[4]

Similarly, the Trade Facilitation Agreement (TFA) of the World Trade Organization (WTO) provides that, from the entry into force of the Agreement, members shall not introduce the mandatory use of customs brokers.[5]

[3] http://www.wcoomd.org/-/media/wco/public/global/pdf/topics/facilitation/instruments-and-tools/tools/customs-brokers/customs-brokers-guidelines.pdf?db=web. Accessed May 10, 2021.

[4] Chapter 8 of the RKC (WCO). Standard 8.1: *Persons concerned shall have the choice of transacting business with the Customs either directly or by designating a third party to act on their behalf.*

[5] Article 10.6 of the TFA (WTO). Paragraph 6.1: *Without prejudice to the important policy concerns of some Members that currently maintain a special role for customs brokers, from the entry into force of this Agreement Members shall not introduce the mandatory use of customs brokers.*

Despite the foregoing, the *mandatory* use of customs brokers services still prevails in several parts of the world, e.g., in the Americas and Caribbean region and some parts of Africa.

For this reason, the survey expressly inquired if the use of customs brokers should be *mandatory* or *optional* (following the principles of a free market, as in other professional services).

Of the 99 reporting administrations, 72 declared that the use of customs brokers was optional, nine expressed that their use for customs transactions was compulsory, 14 stated that it was partially compulsory as some specific transactions with a limit of sales and goods were exempt (household articles, used cars, noncommercial samples, and postal items were given asexamples), and four members reported that they allow third parties that are not customs brokers to be used for customs clearance.

As we can see, most of the countries consulted (73%) state as "optional" the use of customs brokers pursuant to the provisions of the Revised Kyoto Convention and the Trade Facilitation Agreement.

However, it is worth noting that in those countries where its activity is completely deregulated, e.g., in the United States of America or Japan, customs brokers are used in 98% of customs releases of goods. This evidences that their intervention is necessary and convenient, regardless of the legal obligation.

5.2 Fees and Charges

This section analyzes whether fees and charges should be fixed and regulated by an authority or if they should be determined by a free market. Eighty-one administrations noted that free-market principles apply in their countries. Only 12 countries reported that fees are fixed or monitored in some way (e.g., setting minimum fees or flat rates) by a government authority, mainly the Customs department and, in some instances, by Customs together with a private sector body. Said practices may have been adopted to avoid overcharging or to prevent monopoly situations.

In light of the foregoing, customs brokers' fees and charges should be guided by free-market principles that ensure free competition but uphold the principle of adequate compensation for customs brokerage services. Invoices issued for their services should provide a breakdown of their fees and any charges paid to Customs and other government agencies for services provided by them, in addition to any amount of duty, tax, or other charge paid on the client's behalf.

5.3 License

Customs Administrations were asked if they should be the regulating agency for customs brokers licenses.

In response, members identified a combination of models and criteria: 53 members reported that a key aspect in their regulation is the issuance of a license if certain requirements are met, 39 answered that they also issued licenses as a regulating factor but with a specific term of validity and renewal formalities, 48 countries said that periodic audits and inspections have been used as part of the regulation of customs brokers to ensure permanent compliance, and 58 members also established sanctions or penalties for licenses.

The research reveals that the requirements for issuing a license should be objective, public, transparent, nondiscriminatory, and measurable.

In this respect, Standard 8.2 of the General Annex of the RKC provides that national legislation shall set out the conditions under which a person may act for and on behalf of another person in dealing with Customs and shall lay down the liability of third parties to the Customs for duties and taxes and for any irregularities. In addition, Article 10.6 of the TFA provides that members shall apply transparent and objective rules for licensing.

5.4 Natural and Legal Persons

The study examined if both individuals (natural persons) and companies (legal persons) should be permitted to become licensed brokers in cases where licensing is required.

The results showed that in 42 countries, both natural and legal persons can become licensed customs brokers; in 24 countries, only companies or legal persons; and in 15 countries, only natural persons.

The above showed that most of the countries that replied have corporate entities as customs brokers.

5.5 Examination

Sixty-five participating administrations declared that they have a testing system in place to evaluate brokers' knowledge of customs, laws, and the regulations of international trade before the issuance of a license. Twenty-two did not have an examination requirement. Ten countries, including some that do not have an examination system, employ additional means to evaluate brokers' knowledge on customs matters.

Some of the methods used to assess customs knowledge include interviews (Australia and the Democratic Republic of Congo), completing an approved course of studies (Australia), a customs diploma program (Fiji), a specific training program (Malta), five years' experience in customs matters (Mexico), and "fit and proper person assessment" based on education, work experience, and industrial knowledge (Seychelles).

An additional aspect reported is that 71 members require that authorized customs brokers have sound knowledge of customs laws and related legislation, while 34 members also demand knowledge of transport and trade finance as important criteria for the issuance of licenses.

An examination (oral and/or written) as part of the customs broker licensing requirements is useful to assess the level of knowledge and ensure adequate professional performance.

The examination can also be developed in collaboration with associations representing customs brokers in the jurisdiction where the candidate will exercise their duties. Notice of the time and place of the examination should be posted on the website and in public areas of customs checkpoints no less than 60 days before the date of the examination.

5.6 Cooperation

Customs Administrations and customs brokers collaborate in several ways. Bilateral consultation, even though the Customs Brokers Association, is the most prevalent mechanism declared by 76 members (76%). In addition, 66 members reported having a broad consultation process, which comprises all international trade stakeholders, including customs brokers. Only 17 members stated that they consult customs brokers as part of their National Committee on Trade Facilitation created under the Trade Facilitation Agreement (TFA) of the World Trade Organization (WTO) or any other similar existing body. Just three members informed that their administrations do not consult and do not involve customs brokers.

Some cooperation areas mentioned are as follows:

i. Customs modernization and trade facilitation initiatives, including new policies and programs such as automation, authorized economic operators (AEOs), coordinated border management (CBM), and the implementation of a Single Window (SW)
ii. Ensuring compliance with Customs and other government agencies, including due diligence and data quality
iii. Effective and efficient implementation of bilateral and multilateral agreements
iv. Development of joint training
v. Assessment of performance, and
vi. Regular meetings to discuss procedure general matters and mutual interest issues

5.7 Relation of the WCO with the International Federation of Customs Brokers Associations (IFCBA)

Within the work carried out between Customs and the Private Sector Consultative Group (PSCG), we find the recommendations and contributions made by the International Federation of Customs Brokers Associations (IFCBA), especially those related to best practices by the World Customs Organization (WCO). In this respect, the IFCBA created a document named "Best Practices,"[6] which deals with an important gap between Customs Administrations and the private sector on an issue of mutual interest, i.e., granting licenses to act on behalf of importers and exporters.

The general principle is that it is the government's responsibility to enact legislation for the licensing of customs brokers. It is recognized that regulation may be for individuals and/or business entities (sole proprietorships, partnerships, or corporations). IFCBA recommendations to the WCO include the following:

1. Economic operators can only use customs brokers as third parties to transact business with Customs.
2. Economic operators operating on their own behalf to transact business with Customs must meet the same knowledge standard as customs brokers.
3. Licensed customs brokers may direct and supervise the work of employees performing release and accounting functions.
4. Customs brokers may wish to assume joint and several liability with their clients for the payment of duties and taxes.

The model of best practices recommends that an individual, or at least one partner of a partnership or at least one officer of a corporation, applying for a customs brokerage license must have the following qualifications:

1. Be a citizen or permanent resident where such legislation exists
2. Have reached the legislated age of majority
3. Provide records demonstrating (a) the minimum experience requirements, usually 3–5 years in a customs brokerage environment, or (b) the successful completion of a training program as required by legislation or regulation
4. Have successfully completed a licensing examination or equivalent procedure
5. Have passed a credit history check, and
6. Have no violations of a serious nature related to imports/exports

Additionally, the document states that business entities operating as customs brokers must provide evidence of financial stability (e.g., with past and current financial statements).

[6] "Best Practices" (2009) IFCBA. https://www.ifcba.org/sites/default/files/ctd_files/BestPracticesModel_LicensingCustomsBrokersENGLISH.pdf. Accessed May 10, 2021.

Chapter 6
Nomenclature and Classification of Goods

6.1 Introduction

The International Convention on the Harmonized Commodity Description and Coding System, generally known as "Harmonized System" or just HS, is an international nomenclature of goods.

Since the beginning of 1970, a group of World Customs Organization (WCO) experts has developed this multipurpose tool. The HS is a nomenclature system of goods that enables countries to individualize and control goods that cross their borders. Without it, several national regulations and international conventions could not be enforced, and there could be doubt about the certainty of each bilateral and multilateral negotiation. Any country that aims to enhance the efficacy of its Customs Administration will find the HS a fundamental aid. The Harmonized System comprises 5000 commodity groups,[1] each identified by a six-digit code, arranged in a legal and logical structure. In addition, it is supported by well-defined rules to achieve uniform classification.

On January 1, 2017, the WCO published a new edition of the Harmonized System. It is worth mentioning that to create it, there was a five-year revision cycle. Since the adoption of this renewed tool, all Customs Administrations supervise and control the trade of goods, especially those with social and environmental impacts. The fact of considering these issues led to new associations between the WCO and different international organizations, such as the Food and Agriculture Organization of the United Nations. More revisions are expected in the future as new situations, which demand new answers, arise.

The HS is used in more than 200 countries and customs territories, including some that have not formally adhered to the Convention as a basis for their customs

[1] World Customs Organization, complete version of the Harmonized System available at http://www.wcoomd.org/en/topics/nomenclature/instrument-and-tools/hs-nomenclatu-re-2017-edition/hs-nomenclature-2017-edition.aspx. Accessed May 10, 2021.

H. H. Juárez Allende, *The World Customs Organization*, Law for Professionals,
https://doi.org/10.1007/978-3-030-85296-2_6

tariffs for international trade statistics and for carrying out international negotiations. Over 98% of the merchandise in international trade is classified in terms of the Harmonized System. Thus, the HS contributes not only to joint customs methods and to the exchange of nondocumentary trade-data-related customs procedures but also to reducing operating costs.

Governments, the private sector, and international organizations implement the HS to accomplish objectives such as establishing internal taxes, creating trade policies, monitoring of controlled goods, setting up rules of origin, establishing freight tariffs, collection of transport statistics, price monitoring, quota controls, compilation of national accounts, and economic research and analysis. Therefore, it may be assured that the HS is, on the one hand, a universal economic language and, on the other, an indispensable tool for the development of international trade.

The WCO publishes the official version of the "International Convention on the Harmonized Commodity Description and Coding System" and its official interpretation in the Explanatory Notes (five volumes in English and French). These Notes are also available online, and on CD-ROM, as part of the HS Database which groups all the available HS Tools, including the information on the HS Nomenclature, the Compendium of Classification Opinions, the Explanatory Notes, the Alphabetical Index, and the Brochure on Classification Decisions taken by the Harmonized System Committee.

On January 1, 2018, the Harmonized System commemorated its 30th anniversary. During its successful existence, it has incorporated the necessary mechanisms to adapt to the challenges of the permanent flow of international trade. It is now on its Sixth Edition, with its Seventh Edition due in 2022.[2] In these 30 years, 60 meetings of the Harmonized System Committee (HSC) have been held; 4144 agenda items have been discussed; ten recommendations on the application of the Conventions have been drawn up; 2280 classification decisions have been made; and 871 Classification Opinions have been adopted. Additionally, 53 meetings of the Review Subcommittee and 32 meetings of the Scientific Subcommittee have been held.

6.2 Historical Background

The efforts to produce a global common nomenclature to facilitate international trade lasted more than a century. Between 1853 and 1908, several international economic conferences were held to prepare an international statistical nomenclature. The first, held in Brussels in 1853, promoted the creation of a uniform international tariff nomenclature as a prior requisite for the development of international statistics.

The Second Statistical Congress, held in Brussels in 1913, approved the first global Nomenclature, which comprised 186 articles organized in five groups:

[2]The Seventh Edition of the Harmonized System (HS) nomenclature has been approved by all Contracting Parties of the Convention and will enter into force on January 1st, 2022.

livestock, food and beverages, raw materials or simply manufactured materials, manufactured products, and gold and silver. This Nomenclature was the basis of the first compiled trade statistics of the International Office of Trade Statistics in 1922. It was also used for tariffs in around 30 countries.

The World Economic Conference, held in May 1927 under the auspices of the League of Nations, recommended a common framework for customs tariffs. Afterward, a Committee of Experts drafted a Customs Nomenclature, whose first edition was commonly referred to as the "Geneva Nomenclature." This Nomenclature had 991 four-digit headings, organized into 86 chapters grouped into 21 sections; in addition to the basic headings, there were secondary, tertiary, and, in some cases, quaternary subheadings.

In 1949, the European Customs Union project was created as a draft Nomenclature. Thus, the need for an international common nomenclature was acknowledged once more. The work carried out by the European Customs Union Study Group in the preparation of common customs tariffs was based on the Geneva Nomenclature. At that time, the Geneva Nomenclature was the only standard framework of its kind. Nevertheless, considerable amendments were made to the Geneva text partly to reflect technical progress and partly because of shortcomings revealed by the experience of countries that had already adopted Geneva-type tariffs.

First, a preliminary draft containing headings and subheadings was produced. However, by the end of 1949, the Study Group decided that irrespective of the progress that might be made on the European Customs Union project, the very valuable results already attained in the field of nomenclature should be turned to advantage. Therefore, it was decided that the headings of the preliminary draft Nomenclature (other than the subheadings that were left to the initiative of individual countries) should be established by a convention.

On December 15, 1950, the "Convention on Nomenclature for the Classification of Goods in Customs Tariffs" was subscribed in Brussels. A "Tariff Nomenclature" was published as an appendix, named "Appendix to the Convention on Nomenclature for the Classification of Goods in Customs Tariffs." Nevertheless, this Nomenclature was never implemented as such. It was heavily modified on July 1, 1955, by the Protocol of Amendment to the Convention. The Customs Cooperation Council published a text named "Nomenclature for the Classification of Goods in Customs Tariffs," commonly referred to as the "Brussels Tariff Nomenclature" (BTN).[3,4]

[3]In 1974 it was renamed the "Customs Cooperation Council Nomenclature" (CCCN) to avoid any confusion as to the international organization in charge of it.

[4]Chronologic sequence of the entry into force: December 15th, 1950. The Convention on Nomenclature for the Classification of Goods in Customs Tariffs is done in Brussels and includes, as Appendix, the tariff nomenclature. The Convention provides that it is open for signature until March 31st, 1951 (Article X), and that three months after the date on which the Belgian Ministry of Foreign Affairs has received the instruments of ratification of seven Governments, the Convention shall come into force (Article XII (a)).

1951. In parallel with the ratification process already initiated, the European Customs Union Study Group began the work to write the Explanatory Notes of the 1950 Nomenclature.

By 1960, the Customs Cooperation Council Nomenclature was widely used by several countries. There was a growing awareness of the need to further rationalize and harmonize data, not only from a strict customs standpoint (customs tariffs) but also from all the information involved: transport and insurance statistics, etc. Fundamentally, goods should have a harmonized designation and coding, which is as broad and detailed as possible, to avoid situations in which, for instance, a commodity could be designated up to 17 times in the course of a single international transaction. Data transmission and processing offered a solution to this problem but only if an internationally recognized code was available for identifying goods.

Later on, the UN Economic Commission for Europe, through its Working Party on Facilitation of International Trade Procedures and a Group of Experts on data requirements and documentation, began studies on this matter. In 1970, it was decided that the Customs Cooperation Council would be the organization responsible for coordinating and managing the pending work for the elaboration of a multifunctional international nomenclature. To this end, the Council set up a study group to examine the possibility of preparing a system capable of meeting the principal requirements of customs authorities, statisticians, carriers, and producers.

At that time, around 150 countries and territories, which represented 80% of international trade, used the Customs Cooperation Council Nomenclature (CCCN) as the basis for their customs tariffs. All of them used four-digit headings. These headings were subsequently divided at the national level, depending on their own tariff or statistics needs. Consequently, customs tariffs and trade statistics were standardized internationally on a four-digit level for the signatories to the Convention.

On January 1, 1972, pursuant to Article XVI of the Convention, a series of amendments to the Nomenclature entered into force in accordance with the Recommendation of the Customs Cooperation Council regarding the amendment of the Nomenclature for the classification of goods in customs tariffs (June 9, 1970). In addition, the bilingual publication (loose-page format) was reprinted with the cover sheet "Fourth Edition (1972)."

In 1973, in its final Report, the Study Group, which had been set up by the Customs Cooperation Council, concluded that the creation of a Harmonized

---

1951–1955. During the process of writing the Explanatory Notes, the need to promote amendments to the legal text of the Nomenclature arises ("legal" because it is the Appendix to the Convention) in order to maintain coherence between this legal text and the Explanatory Notes.

1955. As month after month the list of proposed amendments increased, by 1955 the Explanatory Notes' writers conclude that the voluminous group of amendments represent a new version of the original Nomenclature. Therefore, it is decided to halt the process of ratification and to add a Protocol of Amendment to the 1950 Convention (its specific Appendix).

July 1st, 1955. The Protocol of Amendment to the 1950 Convention is done in Brussels and it incorporates the adopted amendments to its Annex. Therefore, it annuls the ratification process, which had not yet been finalized, to initiate a new process of subscription and ratification.

June 1st, 1959. Norway deposited the 7th instrument of ratification of the Amendment Protocol.

September 11th, 1959. Pursuant to Article XII (a), the "Convention on Nomenclature for the Classification of Goods in Customs Tariffs" entered into force with a revised Annex.

Commodity Description and Coding System was necessary.[5] The System should be viable and make up for the need for international trade facilitation. Therefore, it should be developed from the CCCN (as the core of the system) and the Standard International Trade Classification (SITC) and taking into account the existing nomenclatures, which represented customs, statistics, and transport requirements. Lastly, it should be developed under the auspices of the Customs Cooperation Council.

In 1977, the Customs Cooperation Council set up a committee to prepare the Harmonized System. The Deputy Secretary-General, Juan José A. Sortheix, was in charge of the Technical Team and became the Chairman of the **Harmonized System Committee**. To carry out the technical work, the Committee was assisted by a working party, which was made up of members of the Committee itself, together with representatives of other countries (some of them not members of the Council). It was important that both the Committee and the Working Party should be representative of all the interests involved; consequently, they were made up of delegates from the Customs Administrations and representatives of national and international organizations. The latter could attend Council plenary sessions as observers; however, in the Working Party, they enjoy the same voting rights as Committee members. This was extremely important when the Committee agreed that decisions adopted by a simple majority would be considered Committee decisions and would not be revised unless a delegation would declare a formal reservation.

Almost 60 countries and more than 20 international and national organizations took part in the activities of the Harmonized System Committee and its Working Party. There were representatives from the United Nations Statistical Office, the United Nations Conference on Trade and Development (UNCTAD), the General Agreement on Tariffs and Trade (GATT), the International Organization for Standardization (ISO), the International Chamber of Commerce (ICC), the International Chamber of Shipping (ICS), the International Air Transport Association (IATA), and the International Union of Railways (UIC), who took part in the development.

Both the Committee and the Working Party observed the recommendations of the Annual Report of the Study Group set up by the Customs Cooperation Council in 1973. Therefore, although the System was developed from the CCCN and SITC, it also considered other classification systems, such as the Customs Tariff of Japan, the Tariff Nomenclature for the Latin American Free Trade Association (NABALALC), the Nomenclature of Goods for the External Trade Statistics of the European Community and Statistics of Trade Between Member States (NIMEXE), the Customs Tariff of Canada, and the Customs Tariff of the United States. It also took into account transport nomenclatures: railways (NUM), air cargoes (WACCC),

[5]Between 1970 and 1973, the feasibility study for the Harmonized System was carried out by a Study Group called (in French) "Groupe d'étude sur l'élaboration d'un système harmonisé de désignation et de codification des marchandises pour les besoins du commerce international" (There was a preparatory meeting in October 1970, and eight more meetings between December 1970 and March 1973).

trans-Atlantic steamship (WIFT), and the Standard Transportation Commodity Code (STCC).

In 1981, the Committee completed the preparatory work, and the System revealed itself with its full importance and implications. Toward June 1983 (deadline set by the Customs Cooperation Council to submit the system for approval), work intensified. The Harmonized System Committee, along with the Nomenclature Committee, carried out a complete revision of the provisionally approved texts in order to finalize all remaining technical issues. Meanwhile, delegates also took part in difficult negotiations—at different levels—which resulted in agreed terms for the provisions that would govern the Harmonized System. One of the most important Committee achievements was offering developing countries the opportunity to implement the Harmonized System at a level below six digits, as long as their international trade patterns or administrative resources could justify such partial application.

The implementation of the System demanded the analysis of legal repercussions; hence, in May 1983, the Harmonized System Committee and its Working Party held their 31st and last session jointly with the Nomenclature Committee in order to finalize agreed terms, which all are remaining technical issues of legal standing common to both Committees (particularly the Explanatory Notes). It was also agreed to recommend some measures to the Council. One measure was the establishment by the Council of a Provisional Harmonized System Committee for the management and care of the HS and its interests until the new Convention and its Committee entered into force, and the other measure was the creation by this Provisional Committee and by the Nomenclature Committee of a Joint Working Party to complete the Explanatory Notes.

Since the creation of the Harmonized System Committee up to 1983, the preparation of the Harmonized System included a critical and detailed analysis of the CCCN. Not only did it consider the changes in technology and trade patterns, but it also recognized the needs of the different regions worldwide. The HS underwent a genuine restructuring; several headings and complete chapters were cut out, and seemingly overloaded headings were divided to achieve a more rational distribution or to simplify classification.

During its plenary session on June 14, 1983, the Customs Cooperation Council adopted the **International Convention on the Harmonized Commodity Description and Coding System,** which included, as an annex, the HS Nomenclature, commonly referred to as HS (managed by the then Customs Cooperation Council). However, the Convention entered into force in 1988.[6]

The first bilingual HS publication (loose-page format) was printed in 1987, with a cover page that read "First Edition (1987)." Until 1987, 52 countries were

[6]Since October 1983 and up to November 1987, while the International Harmonized System Convention was expected to enter into force, technical work continued to elaborate complementary instruments, mainly the Explanatory Notes and the Alphabetical Index. This was carried out by the HS Provisional Committee in nine sessions.

Contracting Parties to the Nomenclature Convention, and over 150 countries and territories used the Customs Cooperation Council Nomenclature (CCCN) as a basis for their national customs tariffs. Most of the countries that were Contracting Parties to the Nomenclature Convention have adopted the Harmonized System for their national tariffs.

On January 1, 1992, a set of Article 16 amendments to the Nomenclature enclosed in the Convention entered into force (accepted pursuant to the Customs Cooperation Council's Recommendation of July 5, 1989). This is commonly referred to as the "1992 HS" or the "1992 HS version." This version was not reprinted, and the amended supplement was inserted into the first edition, printed in 1987.

On January 1, 1996, another set of amendments to the Nomenclature, enclosed in the Convention, entered into force. On this opportunity, the bilingual version (loose-page format) was completely reprinted with a cover page that read "Second Edition (1996)."

In 2007, on the occasion of the fourth set of amendments to the Harmonized System, the evolution of techniques was discussed, precisions for their uniform application were incorporated, trade realities were adapted, and the supervision and control of issues related to social, environmental, and technological progress were facilitated.

The fifth set of amendments to the HS Nomenclature was prepared in 2012. Two hundred twenty amendments were made in response to the need to enhance precision in the Nomenclature texts to guarantee its complete application and to consider environmental issues that had become a priority. The amendments were mainly focused on Chapter 3, in the individual identification of certain fish, crustaceans, mollusks, and other aquatic invertebrate species. They aimed at improving the quality and precision of the trade-related data of these goods. Similarly, new subheadings were created to identify some vegetables, fruits, nuts, cereals, etc.

The sixth set of amendments to the Harmonized System took place in 2017. This edition includes 5386 six-digit subheadings (in comparison to the 5205 subheadings of the 2012 edition). These amendments reflect more than statistical needs or tariff fixing; they allow the trade of goods, especially those that have social and environmental impacts, to be monitored and controlled.

Due to the importance of the HS in collecting trade statistics, the 2017 HS has incorporated amendments for fish and fishery products to further enhance the coverage of species and product forms that need to be monitored for food security purposes and for better management of resources. The split for more detailed product forms for crustaceans, mollusks, and invertebrates is motivated by the importance of the trade and consumption of these species in the various product forms. The subdivisions enable a better correspondence between the HS and the United Nations Central Product Classification (CPC).

The amendment for forestry products aims at one main area: the enhancement of the coverage of wood species in order to get a better picture of trade patterns, including endangered species. The HS 2017 amendments also include the creation of new subheadings for the monitoring and control of certain products of bamboo and rattan, requested by the International Network for Bamboo and Rattan (INBAR).

In 2018, for the 62nd meeting of the Harmonized Committee System, Portuguese and Arabic were adopted as languages of the Committee for the first time. In addition, the project "Harmonizing the classification of goods based on WCO standards to enhance African trade" was discussed. This project was initiated and financed by the European Union, and it is implemented by the WCO to contribute to the establishment of the African Continental Free Trade Area (AfCFTA), launched in March 2018.

Moreover, during this meeting, delegates discussed 43 classification decisions related to products covered by the HS Nomenclature, including a new tobacco product, several petroleum products, and a quadrocopter. In addition, three sets of amendments to the current Explanatory Notes were adopted, and 21 new Classification Opinions were approved.

Regarding the 2022 version, several important changes[7] to the Harmonized System have already been made, with a total of 351 sets of amendments that cover a wide array of transborder products, such as light-emitting diode (LED), solar energy, electronic waste, drones, and Montreal Protocol gasses.

6.3 Structure of the Harmonized System

The Harmonized System (2017 VI Amendment) has the following logical structure:

- Rules (six general interpretative rules)
- 21 sections
- 97 chapters[8]
- 1226 headings (four digits)
- 5386 subheadings (six to ten digits)
- Legal notes

  The 21 sections are subdivided into 97 chapters. Goods are arranged in the order of their degree of manufacture, from the simplest to the most complex. The headings are represented in Roman numbers and have two digits placed right next

[7] The WCO Council in its 133th/134th Sessions in June 2019 approved the amendments prepared and recommended by the Harmonized System Committee.

[8] In fact, the Harmonized System has 96 effective chapters as Chapter 77 was left blank. This chapter consists of a blank page with the following expression (in French) "(Réservé pour une utilisation future éventuelle dans le Système harmonisé)". The reason for mentioning "a possible future use" is found in the first years of the process of writing the HS when it was thought of new materials and metals yet to be discovered (in particular as a result of space exploration). In the end, the reservation of a specific chapter proved to be unnecessary. Blank Chapter 77 could have been eliminated, and all subsequent chapters could have been renumbered; however, it was considered that this renumbering would be confusing as future HS users would have already acquired well-established chapter/content references.

to the chapter they correspond to. Headings are subdivided into subheadings and are identified with six to ten digits.

This Nomenclature is governed by six general rules and eight complementary rules and by Explanatory Notes[9] in each chapter, which guide the user to make correct classifications of goods.

6.4 Classification Opinions

The Compendium of Classification Opinions includes a list of some of the most significant and/or difficult classification decisions taken by the Harmonized System Committee that were approved by the WCO Council. Although the Compendium does not form an integral part of the Harmonized System Convention, it is a useful tool to assist with classification.

6.5 Amendment Process

Ever-changing technology constantly creates new goods or transforms their uses. Therefore, a goods nomenclature for technological commodities cannot be rigid and must be kept abreast of transformations. This is particularly relevant with the HS Nomenclature, as it organizes its classifications based on the lower or higher complexity (or degree of manufacture) of products.

Amendment proposals may be submitted by any Contracting Party to the Convention or by the technical bodies of the World Customs Organization.[10]

Article 16 of the Convention provides that once the amendment is accepted, the Secretary-General of the Council shall notify the Contracting Parties, which have six months to indicate any objections to the amendment. If no objections are outstanding at the end of this period, the amendment is deemed to have been accepted.

However, states need time to finalize all the legal and regulatory procedures for the amendment of their own tariffs or statistical nomenclatures. Therefore, it has been established that accepted amendments enter into force within at least 30 months after the notification of the recommended amendments to Administrations.

To recap, the amendment process can be summarized in the following flowchart (see Fig. 6.1).

[9]They do not form an integral part of the HS Convention; however, they are interpretative elements of the scope and content of the heading and subheading texts. They have the importance and legal value that the parties may grant them.

[10]Article 7.1.a) of the HS Convention specifically provides this function of the Harmonized System Committee, as it was mentioned when describing it.

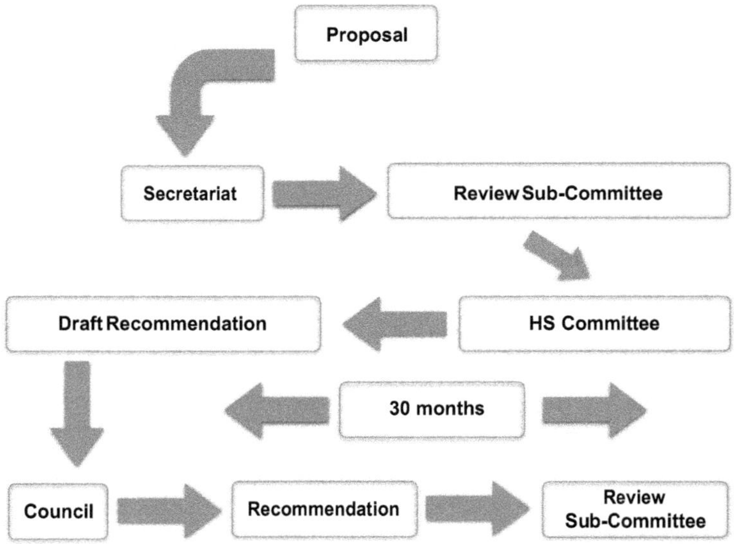

Fig 6.1 Harmonized System amendment process. **Source:** Author's elaboration based on information from the WCO

In addition to the five-year-term amendments, the WCO technical officers are evaluating the need to change and modernize the HS structure in order to capture the new international trade environment, in particular (i) the growing trade of spare parts and components as a consequence of the increase of chain values, (ii) the growing complexity of traded goods (a telephone that takes pictures, controls blood pressure and pulse, also reproduces a sound and can be used to make payments, etc.), (iii) the increase of operators[11] and transactions with the evolution of transborder electronic trade, and (iv) the increase in classificatory lawsuits and controversies related to the subjective "essential character" used by the current rules of classification.

6.6 Dispute Settlement

Article 10 of the HS Convention establishes the applicable procedure for the settlement of disputes between two or more Contracting Parties in connection with the interpretation or application of the Nomenclature. In the first instance, the parties concerned should strive to reach an agreement among themselves. However, disputes that cannot be settled by direct negotiation are referred to the Harmonized System Committee for its intervention, analysis, and solution. If the Committee is

[11]End consumers who must classify goods at the moment of purchasing products.

unable to settle a dispute, it shall refer the matter to the Council for a recommendation on the issue.

Parties to a dispute may agree in advance to accept the recommendations of the Committee or the Council.

Chapter 7
Valuation of Good

To allocate "ad valorem" customs duties, rules criteria have been harmonized to uniformly determine the value of goods, i.e., its tax base. Additionally, valuation is an essential element to collect trade statistics, follow up quantitative restrictions, apply preferential tariffs, and collect national taxes.

Nowadays, almost all Customs Administrations value imported goods pursuant to the provisions of the WTO Agreement on Customs Valuation (1994). However, in order to reach this point, a process is briefly described below.

7.1 Historical Background

In 1947, a set of general principles for customs valuation was agreed upon at the United Nations Conference on Trade and Employment. These principles were incorporated into Article VII of the General Agreement on Tariffs and Trade (GATT).

In 1949, the European Customs Union Study Group (with headquarters in Brussels) drafted a definition of value for use within a customs union framework based on the principles set out in Article VII.

On December 15, 1950, the **Brussels Definition of Value** (BVD) was signed in Brussels. It was based on *the price that a good would fetch in an open market between a buyer and seller independent of each other*, and it entered into force on July 28, 1953.

The specialist in customs valuation, Miguel E. Bueno, has defined it in the following terms: *The Brussels Definition of Value is based on a theoretical concept, as it established the selling and buying of a good under certain circumstances, having to assimilate to it all trade transactions effectively carried out between a*

H. H. Juárez Allende, *The World Customs Organization*, Law for Professionals,
https://doi.org/10.1007/978-3-030-85296-2_7

buyer and a seller, thus making the corresponding adjustments to reach this theoretical value.[1]

The first session of the BVD "Valuation Committee" was held from November 3 to 12, 1953.

Specialist Germán Pardo Carrero states: *The Theoretical Concept of Value (or Brussels Definition) method was widely accepted in Europe and South America, especially by customs authorities who welcomed its ease of application and control, for Customs determined what the normal price under normal conditions was.* Notwithstanding, he points out the following: *However, not all countries accepted the Brussels Definition of Value, and even countries such as the United States continued to use the method known as the "American Selling Price".* As a coinciding point for the different systems, it offered to respect the price of the trade invoice.[2]

Likewise, José María Álvarez Gómez Pallete expresses that "The serious inconvenient of the Brussels definition was that, among the counties that were not applying it, there were several countries with specific importance, inter alia, the United States, Canada, Australia, South Africa and New Zealand."[3]

Between 1973 and 1979, the so-called *"Tokyo Round" GATT Multilateral Trade Negotiations took place. These aimed to "achieve the expansion and ever-greater liberalization of world trade, inter alia, through the progressive dismantling of obstacles to trade".* The "Agreement on Implementation of Article VII of the GATT," commonly referred to as the GATT Valuation Code, was signed on April 12, 1979. It was based on the *price actually paid or payable* for the imported goods.

On January 1, 1981, the GATT Valuation Code came into effect with 25 Contracting Parties.

Between March 9 and 13, 1981, the "Tokyo Round" Technical Committee on Customs Valuation met for the first time.

Between 1986 and 1994, the "Uruguay Round" Multilateral Trade Negotiations took place, and on April 15, 1994, the "Agreement on Implementation of Article VII of the GATT, 1994," was signed in Marrakech.

On January 1, 1995, the World Trade Organization (WTO) was created with the requirement that all WTO signatories accept all GATT instruments, including the WTO Valuation Agreement, as it then became known.

Between October 2 and 6, 1995, the "Tokyo Round" Technical Committee on Customs Valuation (comprising 44 members) formally concluded its activities, giving rise to the "Uruguay Round" Technical Committee on Customs Valuation (comprising 109 members), which held its first session.

---

[1] Bueno (2007), p. 9.

[2] Pardo Carrero (2015), p. 121.

[3] Álvarez Gómez Pallete (2002), p. 46.

7.2 WTO Valuation Agreement

The WTO Valuation Agreement, known as the *Agreement on Implementation of Article VII of the General Agreement on Tariffs and Trade (GATT)*[4] 1994, substituted the GATT Valuation Code as a result of the Uruguay Round Multilateral Trade Negotiations.[5]

This Agreement sets forth a customs valuation system based on transaction value, i.e., the price actually paid or payable for the goods when sold for export to the country of importation, with certain adjustments.[6]

It is worth noting that, currently, more than 90% of world trade is valued based on the transaction value method, which provides more predictability, uniformity, and transparency to the business community.

The Agreement has created two committees: (i) the Committee on Customs Valuation (WTO), tasked with monitoring the application of the Agreement and offering members the opportunity to consult on matters relating to the administration of the Agreement, and (ii) the Technical Committee on Customs Valuation (WCO), which we have referred to in the preceding Sect. 2.1.8.

The WTO Trade Facilitation Agreement (see Sect. 10.12), which entered into force on February 22, 2017, sets forth a series of guidelines to strengthen the implementation of the Valuation Agreement, such as the publication of customs laws and rules for valuation, the requirement of consultation with the private sector prior to the adoption of measures, advanced rulings (method or criteria to be used), guarantees for the release of goods, postclearance audits of valuation, cooperation, and exchange of information, among others.

---

[4]World Customs Organization, WTO Valuate Agreement. http://www.wcoomd.org/en/topics/valuation/overview/wto-valuation-agreement.aspx. Accessed May 10, 2021.

[5]World Trade Organization, The Uruguay Round. https://www.wto.org/english/thewto_e/whatis_e/tif_e/fact5_e.htm. Accessed May 10, 2021.

[6]WTO Valuation Agreement. Article 1.1 The customs value of imported goods shall be the transaction value, that is the price actually paid or payable for the goods when sold for export to the country of importation adjusted in accordance with the provisions of Article 8, provided: a. that there are no restrictions as to the disposition or use of the goods by the buyer other than restrictions which: i. are imposed or required by law or by the public authorities in the country of importation; ii. limit the geographical area in which the goods may be resold, or iii. do not substantially affect the value of the goods; b. that the sale or price is not subject to some condition or consideration for which a value cannot be determined with respect to the goods being valued; c. that no part of the proceeds of any subsequent resale, disposal or use of the goods by the buyer will accrue directly or indirectly to the seller, unless an appropriate adjustment can be made in accordance with the provisions of Article 8; and d. that the buyer and seller are not related, or where the buyer and seller are related, that the transaction value is acceptable for customs purposes under the provisions of paragraph 2.

7.3 Benefits of the Agreement

The Agreement essentially aims to provide a unique, fair, uniform, and neutral system for the valuation of goods for customs purposes—a system that conforms to commercial realities and that outlaws the use of arbitrary or fictitious customs values. The Agreement asserts that valuation for customs purposes should be based, to an extent possible, on the actual price of the goods to be valued.

With the implementation of the Agreement, more transparency and security in international trade have undoubtedly been achieved.

7.4 Methods

7.4.1 Method 1—Transaction Value

The Agreement stipulates that customs valuation shall, except in specified circumstances, be based on the actual price of the goods to be valued, which is generally shown on the invoice. This price, plus adjustments for certain elements listed in Article 8, equals the transaction value, which constitutes the first and most important method in the Agreement.

For cases in which there is no transaction value or where the transaction value is not acceptable as customs value because the price has been distorted as a result of certain conditions, the Agreement lays down five other methods of customs valuation,[7] to be applied in the following order.

7.4.2 Methods 2—Transaction Value of Identical Goods

The transaction value is calculated in the same manner on identical goods if the goods are as follows:

- The same in all respects, including their physical characteristics, quality, and reputation
- Produced in the same country as the goods being valued, and
- Produced by the producer of the goods being valued

[7] World Customs Organization, Brief Guide to the Customs Valuation Code, 3rd Edition, WCO, Brussels, 1996. http://www.wcoomd.org/-/media/wco/public/global/pdf/topics/valuation/instruments-and-tools/gatt/brief-guide-to-the-customs-valuation-code.pdf?db=web. Accessed May 10, 2021.

For this method to be used, the goods must be sold for export to the same country of importation as the goods being valued. The goods must also be exported at or about the same time as the goods being valued.

7.4.3 Method 3—Transaction Value of Similar Goods

The transaction value is calculated in the same manner on similar goods in the following cases:

- The goods closely resemble the goods being valued in terms of component materials and characteristics.
- The goods are capable of performing the same functions and are commercially interchangeable with the goods being valued.
- The goods are produced in the same country as and by the same producer of the goods being valued.

To use this method, the goods must be sold to the same country of importation as the goods being valued. The goods must be exported at or about the same time as the goods being valued.

7.4.4 Method 4—Deductive Value

When customs value cannot be determined based on the transaction value of the imported goods or identical or similar goods, it will be determined on the basis of the unit price at which the imported goods or identical or similar goods are sold to an unrelated buyer in the greatest aggregate quantity in the country of importation. The buyer and the seller in the importing country must not be related, and the sale must take place at or about the time of importation of the goods being valued. If no sale took place at or about the time of importation, it is permitted to use sales up to 90 days after the importation of the goods being valued.

7.4.5 Method 5—Computed Value

Computed value, the most difficult and rarely used method, determines the customs value on the basis of the cost of production of the goods being valued, plus an amount for profit and general expenses usually reflected in sales from the country of exportation to the country of importation of goods of the same class or kind.

7.4.6 Method 6—Fallback Method

Customs value determination is based on "reasonable means consistent with the principles and general provisions of the Agreement, Article VII GATT and on the basis of available data." When the customs value cannot be determined under any of the previous methods, it may be determined using reasonable means consistent with the principles and general provisions of the Agreement and of Article VII of GATT 1994 and on the basis of data available in the country of importation. This method should, to the greatest extent possible, be based on previously determined values and methods with a reasonable degree of flexibility in their application.

7.5 Customs Valuation and Transfer Pricing

Multinational enterprises carry out a significant portion of international trade. They transfer goods, tangible assets, and services. This is why transfer price setting and international taxation represent two fundamental issues.

Transfer prices involve price setting and other conditions for the transfer of goods, services, and assets among related companies in accordance with their situation in the different tax jurisdictions. Naturally, regarding tax effects, the different members of a multinational enterprise group distribute benefits among themselves.

Transactions between independent parties are subject to market rules. However, with transactions between two branches of a multinational enterprise, the status is different. Overpricing may affect the tax base in the different jurisdictions where the multinational enterprise operates. By shifting profits from one jurisdiction to another, through distorted transfer prices, governments may be deprived of fair revenue. Additionally, transfer prices may expose multinational enterprises to double taxation if two jurisdictions that are involved in a cross-border transaction claim duty over the same profit. For this reason, so many developed, developing, and emerging countries have realized that transfer price setting is critical as it protects the tax base and provides certainty to foreign investors—a value that respects international rules.

The Organisation for Economic Co-operation and Development (OECD) and the World Customs Organization (WCO) have carried out multiple activities and have held multiple conferences together, striving for a "meeting point" between the criteria for determining internal taxes in transfer prices and those used in customs valuation, thus avoiding different tax assessments for the same economic reality.

In 2015, the WCO published the Guide to Customs Valuation and Transfer Pricing.[8] It was designed primarily to assist customs officials responsible for the

[8] http://www.wcoomd.org/en/topics/valuation/instruments-and-tools/guide-to-customs-valuation-and-transfer-pricing.aspx. Accessed May 10, 2021.

analysis of merchandise valuation or who conduct audits on multinational enterprises. It is also recommended for the private sector and tax administrations that have an interest in this topic.

Although the Guide (updated in 2018) does not provide a definite approach to dealing with "divergence" (which the Technical Committee of Valuation continues to discuss), it does deliver technical background, offers possible solutions on the way forward, and shares ideas and national practices, including the point of view of trade.

References

Álvarez Gómez Pallete JM (2002) La Organización Mundial de Aduanas y sus Convenios. In: Customs and International Trade Research Center (CIACI, for its acronym in Spanish). p 46

Bueno ME (2007) El valor en Aduana de las mercaderías. IARA S.A, Buenos Aires, 7th updated edition, p 9

Pardo Carrero G (2015) Relevancia Tributaria del Valor en Aduana de la mercancía importada. In: Colombian Institute of Tax Law (ICDT for its acronym in Spanish), Bogota, Colombia. p 121

Chapter 8
Origin of Goods

Determining the "origin" of goods is of vital interest in international trade, either for meeting tax collection needs or for the eventual application of measures beyond such scope.

From a tax collection standpoint, the origin of goods is relevant to assess customs duties as there may be preferential trade agreements in force that offer benefits depending on the origin of these goods. Origin may also lead to the application of antidumping duties or other selective tariff measures.

From a tax noncollection standpoint, we must take into account that trade policies are usually based on measures regarding the origin of goods, thus allowing, restricting, or prohibiting the circulation of these goods if these come from a specific country or region. Examples are sanitary policies that establish stricter controls to merchandise originated in specific countries or geographical zones or, oppositely, a regional development policy that facilitates the circulation of these goods based on rules of origin.

These circumstances have given rise to trade deflections that aim to obtain a tariff benefit that would not be applicable otherwise or to elude the aforementioned restrictions.

The concepts "country of origin" and "country of last departure" should not be confused; the latter refers to the last country where the goods went through before arriving at a specific customs territory.

In connection with the generic concept of origin and pursuant to the forenamed, there are two clearly defined systems: "**preferential origin,**" which focuses on the benefits granted by bilateral or multilateral agreements, and "**nonpreferential origin,**" which depends on the rules and trade policies applied by each country or union of countries.

The scheme of requirements and conditions regarding origin set forth by these rules aims to avoid any type of traffic deviation, thus clearly assigning a concrete origin to each product.

In the International Convention on the Simplification and Harmonization of Customs Procedures, the World Customs Organization (WCO) defines rules of

H. H. Juárez Allende, *The World Customs Organization*, Law for Professionals,
https://doi.org/10.1007/978-3-030-85296-2_8

origin as *the specific provisions, developed from principles established by national legislation or international agreements ("origin criteria"), applied by a country to determine the origin of goods (Annex D, currently Annex K of the Revised Kyoto Convention).*

The fundamental goal of the rules of origin is to define the "nationality" of a given good. The three essential factors to determine the tax base for customs duties and the related corresponding taxes are (i) the country of origin, (ii) the classification code, and (iii) customs valuation.

The origin of goods will also lead to the application, if appropriate, of trade policy measures (quotas, antidumping duties, commercial seizures, etc.).

With a view to preventing obstacles to international trade, the World Trade Organization (WTO) members entered into an Agreement in 1994 (Uruguay Round). The Agreement states that rules of origin must not be used as instruments to pursue trade policies and must not themselves have restrictive, distorting, or disruptive effects on international trade. In addition, it establishes the harmonization of nonpreferential rules of origin. By securing transparency in trade policy, this harmonization is expected to facilitate international trade.

The WTO Committee on Rules of Origin (CRO) and the Technical Committee on Rules of Origin (TCRO) are the two bodies responsible for the full development of this Agreement.

In 1999, the Technical Committee on Rules of Origin (TCRO) concluded the technical review of the Harmonized Rules of Origin, and these final results were forwarded to the CRO in Geneva for consideration. These results remain under examination by the WTO.[1]

8.1 Agreement on Rules of Origin

Article 1 of the Agreement defines rules of origin as those laws, regulations, and administrative determinations of general application applied to identify the country of origin of goods, except for those related to the granting of tariff preferences.

Therefore, the Agreement only covers rules of origin in nonpreferential trade policy instruments used in the application of the following:

- Most-favored-nation treatment (MFN)
- Antidumping and countervailing duties
- Safeguard measures
- Origin marking requirements
- Discriminatory quantitative restrictions or tariff quotas
- Trade statistics; and
- Government procurement

[1]The unresolved issues are related to agriculture, chemical, textile, and footwear. The sensitiveness of these products for developing countries should be taken into account.

Most-Favored-Nation Treatment (MFN)
In the WTO, each member country shall treat its fellow members equally. A member country shall grant the same favors to all WTO members. "Non- discrimination" is one of the most important principles of the WTO trading system, and it is included in Article 1 of the General Agreement on Tariffs and Trade (GATT) 1994. Nevertheless, some exceptions are allowed. For example, countries within a region can set up a free trade agreement that does not apply to goods from outside the group. In addition, a country can raise barriers against products from specific countries if these goods are considered to be traded in an unfair manner.

Antidumping and Countervailing Duties
Article VI of the GATT ensures the right of Contracting Parties to apply dumping measures, i.e., measures against imports at an export price below its normal value (usually below the price in the domestic market of the exporting country), if such dumped imports cause injury to a domestic industry of the importing country.

In the territory of the Contracting Party of import and in order to offset or prevent dumping, a Contracting Party may levy on any dumped product an antidumping duty not greater in amount than the actual margin of dumping.

The term "countervailing duty" is a special duty levied for offsetting any bounty or subsidy bestowed, directly or indirectly, upon the manufacture, production, or export of any merchandise.

Safeguard Measures
Article XIX of the GATT 1994 allows members to take a safeguard action to protect a specific domestic industry from an unforeseen increase in imports of any product that is causing, or that is likely to cause, serious injury to the industry. The safeguard measure should be applied only to the extent necessary to prevent or remedy serious injury and to facilitate adjustments. Contrary to dumping, these imports are not defined as "unfair trade," but they are nevertheless causing injury to local industry.

Origin Marking Requirements
Article IX of GATT 1994 stipulates that Contracting Parties shall cooperate with each other to prevent the use of trade names in such manner as to misrepresent the true origin of a product, to the detriment of such distinctive regional or geographical names of products of the territory of a Contracting Party as are protected by its legislation. Whenever it is administratively possible, Contracting Parties should allow marks of origin to be affixed at the time of importation.

Discriminatory Quantitative Restrictions or Tariff Quotas
Quantitative restrictions imposed as a result of safeguard measures should normally not reduce the quantities of imports below the annual average of the last three representative years for which statistics are available.

In principle, safeguard measures must be applied to the imported product regardless of its source. In cases where a quota is allocated among supplying countries, the member applying restrictions may seek agreement with other members having a substantial interest in supplying the product concerned.

Trade Statistics
In the field of international trade, there are close links between customs and statistical aspects. It is for this reason that in most countries, the primary data used for the preparation of international trade statistics are taken from customs import or export documents, which means that the data are based on the national tariff classification system or the Harmonized System. The harmonized rules of origin that are devised on the premises of the Harmonized System provide further detailed information in complying with trade statistics.

Government Procurement
The procurement of products and services by government agencies for their own purposes represents an important share of the total government expenditure and, thus, has a significant role in domestic economies. It is estimated that government procurement typically represents 10–15% of the gross domestic product (GDP). The Agreement on Government Procurement (1994) establishes an agreed framework of rights and obligations among its parties with respect to their national laws, regulations, procedures, and practices in the area of government procurement. Foreign suppliers and foreign goods and services must be given no less favorable treatment in government procurement than national suppliers and goods and services.

Disciplines to Govern the Application of Rules of Origin
Under the Agreement, members are obliged to adhere to the following disciplines:

- Not to use rules of origin as instruments to pursue trade policy objectives
- Not to create restrictive, distorting, or disruptive effects on international trade
- Not to discriminate against imports and exports or between members
- To administer rules of origin in a consistent, uniform, impartial, and reasonable manner
- To base rules of origin on a positive standard
- To publish laws, regulations, judicial decisions, and administrative rulings relating to rules of origin
- To provide origin assessments upon request
- Not to apply changes in rules of origin retroactively
- To treat confidential information confidentially

Articles 2(b) and 9(d) of the WTO Rules of Origin Agreement clearly establish that rules of origin shall not be used as instruments to pursue trade objectives directly or indirectly; neither should they create restrictive, distorting, or disruptive effects on international trade.

Moreover, when the harmonized rules of origin enter into force, they will be applied by current members of the WTO and new members wishing to join this organization. It is evident that determining the origin of a product and the conditions of its application can be carried out with uniformity.

The objectives and principles of the Agreement on Rules of Origin are as follows:

- To develop clear and predictable rules of origin
- To facilitate the flow of international trade

- Not to create unnecessary obstacles to trade
- Not to nullify nor impair the rights of members under GATT 1994
- To provide transparency of laws, regulations, and practices regarding rules of origin
- To ensure that rules of origin are prepared and applied in an impartial, transparent, predictable, consistent, and neutral manner
- To make available a consultation mechanism and procedures for the speedy, effective, and equitable resolution of disputes arising under the Agreement
- To harmonize and clarify nonpreferential rules of origin

  The nonpreferential rules of origin are not related to contractual or autonomous trade regimes that lead to the granting of tariff preferences.

8.2 Preferential Rules of Origin

Nondiscrimination among trading partners is one of the core principles of the free trade system encouraged by the WTO. Members have committed, in general, not to favor one trading partner over another. This is a general principle; however, regional trade agreements (RTA)[2] constitute one of the exceptions to this rule. RTAs, by their nature, are discriminatory as only their signatories enjoy more favorable market access conditions. WTO members recognize the legitimate role of RTAs, which aim at facilitating trade between its parties but which do not raise trade barriers vis-à-vis third parties.

Preferential rules of origin are set out under the preferential trade arrangements, which facilitate trade from developing countries (within the frames of the Generalized System of Preferences (GSP)) or between Contracting Parties (e.g., RTA) by offering a reduced or zero rate of duty to goods exported from beneficiary countries or Contracting Parties. To benefit from the preferential trade arrangements, the goods exported must be originating in the beneficiary country or the Contracting Party.

Preferential trade arrangements include *autonomous trade regimes*, e.g., Generalized System of Preferences (GSP), and *contractual trade regimes*, e.g., the North American Free Trade Agreement (NAFTA), currently the "United Sates-Mexico--Canada Agreement" (USMCA).

Preferential rules of origin are more restrictive than nonpreferential ones. The theoretical reason for this is to prevent *trade deflection*. Trade deflection involves the transshipment of a good via a preference-holding country in order for the good upon import to obtain the preferential treatment available under a preferential trade agreement.

In addition, preferential rules of origin may act as nontariff instruments of protection from domestic production requirements that are difficult to meet.

[2]There are currently over 300 Trade Agreements are in force. http://rtais.wto.org/UI/PublicAllRTAList.aspx. Accessed May 10, 2021.

Structure of the Preferential Rules of Origin

To determine the country of origin of products, the following two criteria are used:

- Wholly obtained goods definitions, and
- Substantial/sufficient transformation

Wholly obtained goods are goods found in nature or live animals born and raised in a given country or plants harvested in a given country or minerals extracted or taken in a single country. The definition of "wholly obtained" also extends to goods produced from wholly obtained goods or scrap and waste derived from manufacturing or processing operations or from consumption.

There are three major criteria to express a substantial/sufficient transformation:

a. A criterion of change in tariff classification—a good is considered substantially transformed when the good is classified in a heading or subheading (depending on the exact rule) different from all nonoriginating materials used.
b. A criterion of value added ("ad valorem" percentages)—regardless of a change in its classification, a good is considered substantially transformed when its value added increases to a specified level expressed by "ad valorem" percentage. The value-added criterion can be expressed in either two ways: (i) a maximum allowance for nonoriginating materials or (ii) a minimum requirement for domestic content.
c. A criterion of manufacturing or processing operations (technical requirement)—regardless of a change in its classification, a good is considered substantially transformed when the good has undergone specified manufacturing or processing operations.

Some exceptions to substantial transformation criteria exist as well in the area of preferential origin:

- Several operations or processes are identified as "minimal operations or processes" and do not by themselves confer origin.
- The *de minimis* or tolerance rule permits a specific share of the value or volume of the final product to be nonoriginating without the final product losing its originating status.

Under "cumulation" rules, Contracting Parties to a preferential trade agreement or beneficiary countries under the GSP regimes may source nonoriginating raw materials or components from specified countries and count them as originating. There are three types of cumulation:

- Bilateral cumulation—where only raw material or components in the preference-granting country can be counted in this way
- Diagonal cumulation—where raw materials or components from the preference-granting country and a list of other designated countries to which the same rules of origin apply can be counted; and
- Full cumulation—where raw materials from all countries to which the same rules of origin apply can be counted

Different types of cumulation can appear in one and the same preferential trade agreement, where each type would then apply to different countries.

Direct Consignment Rule

For a product to be eligible for origin treatment, it must be transported directly from the place of production to its preferential destination. The purpose of such a rule is, on the one hand, to ensure that the imported goods, in particular bulk cargoes (whose identity is difficult to establish), are identical to the goods that left the exporting country and, on the other hand, to reduce the risk of eligible goods being mixed with noneligible goods.

However, provisions are made in most rules of origin that goods may be transported through different territories as long as this is justified for geographical reasons. In this case, the goods in question must remain under customs surveillance and must not have entered, under any circumstance, into the commerce of the transit country.

Documentary Evidence

Documentary evidence of origin is required for a good to benefit from the preferential regimes. The evidence can be a certificate of origin issued by the competent authorities, a certified declaration of origin certified by a competent authority, or an origin declaration made on a commercial document (e.g., invoice) by the manufacturer, producer, supplier, exporter, importer, or other competent persons.

The definition of the competent authority or person is clearly stipulated in the free trade agreements, as well as the general requirements, the procedure for the issue, the validity of the proof of origin, and the possible exemptions from proof of origin.

In June 2020, the WCO Secretariat published an updated version of the Comparative Study on Certification of Origin (the previous version had been published in 2014). The study captures the present state of affairs regarding certification of origin, in the areas of both nonpreferential origin and preferential origin (209 free trade agreements were analyzed). In this study, new developments have been added regarding a "self-certification" of origin by the exporter, electronic certificates of origin (e-Cos), and the impact of blockchain technology.[3]

Prohibition of Duty Drawback

Rules of origin in preferential trade agreements are always accompanied by more or less restrictive administrative conditions. A frequent condition is a prohibition on beneficiary countries to provide their exporters with remission or exemption of import duties (duty drawback) on nonoriginating raw materials or components where these are applied to products benefiting from a preferential treatment when the final product is exported.

---

[3]http://www.wcoomd.org/-/media/wco/public/global/pdf/topics/origin/instruments-and-tools/comparative-study/related-documents/comparative-study-on-certification-of-origin_2020.pdf?db=web. Accessed May 10, 2021.

8.3 Committees on Origin (WTO and WCO)

In connection with the role of international organizations in the Harmonization Work Programme, we should highlight the work of the WTO **Committee on Rules of Origin** (CRO), which reports to the WTO Council for Trade in Goods, and the **Technical Committee on Rules of Origin** (TCRO), established under the auspices of the WCO, to undertake the technical work related to harmonization. The membership of both Committees is limited to members of the WTO. However, the TCRO admits, as observers,

WCO members that are not WTO members, as well as some international organizations, including the Organisation for Economic Co-operation and Development (OECD), the United Nations Conference on Trade and Development (UNCTAD), the UN Statistical Division, the UN Law of the Sea Convention Secretariat, and the International Chamber of Commerce.

The WTO Agreement on Rules of Origin indicated that the Harmonization Work Programme (HWP) to harmonize nonpreferential rules of origin would finish within three years of its initiation on July 20, 1998. However, due to the complexity of many issues raised during the work, the intended time schedule in the agreement has been extended several times.

Article 9 of the Agreement sets forth the principles for the Harmonized Rules of Origin (HRO) as follows:

- HRO should be applied equally for all purposes as set out in Article 1;
- The country to be determined as the origin of a particular good is: (a) either the country where the good has been fully obtained, or (b) when more than one country is concerned in the production of the good, the country where the last substantial transformation has been carried out;
- HRO should be objective, understandable and predictable;
- HRO should not be used as instruments to pursue trade objectives directly or indirectly;
- HRO should not themselves create restrictive, distorting or disruptive effects on international trade;
- HRO should be administrable in a consistent, uniform, impartial and reasonable manner;
- HRO should be coherent and be based on a positive standard.

The architecture and content of the Agreement on Rules of Origin are as follows:

- Definitions
- General Rule 1—Harmonized System (is the basis for the product specific rules);
- General Rule 2—Determination of origin;
- General Rule 3—Neutral elements;
- General Rule 4—Packing and packaging materials and containers;
- General Rule 5—Accessories and spare parts and tools;
- General Rule 6—Minimal operations and processes.

Appendix 1: Wholly Obtained Goods:

- Rule 1: Scope of application;
- Definitions 1(a) to (i) and 2.

Appendix 2: Product Specific Rules of Origin (Rules for determining the country of origin when the origin of the good is not determined under Appendix 1:

- Rule 1: Determination of Origin (Provisions of this Rule applied in sequence, taking into account Rule 2 where applicable);
- Rule 1 (a): The country of origin is the country in which the good is produced exclusively from originating materials;
- Rules 1 (b) and (c): Primary Rules;
- Rules 1 (d) to (g): Residual Rules;
- Rules 2 (a) to (g): Application of the Rules;
- Terminology Guide;
- Origin Criteria for HS Chapters 1–97 in matrices.

Recently, the ITC-WCO Rules of Origin Facilitator has been launched,[4] which is a joint initiative of the World Customs Organization and the International Trade Centre (ITC) to improve the transparency and knowledge of rules of origin. It contains product-specific duties and requirements of origin under different regional trade agreements.

Ricardo Xavier Basaldúa, in his work "El Régimen de Origen de las Mercaderías" (The Origin of Goods Regime),[5] comments: *Beyond efforts spread out, in particular, in connection with the Kyoto Convention, the WCO has not been able to establish or capture a single international system to determine origin. Instead, it has only limited to specify different issues and make distinct recommendations. Therefore, without removing the merit of its objective, this constitutes only a valuable first step that should be continued with additional work leading to a more compulsory regulation.*

It seems that more progress has not been achieved in this field because the USA and other developed countries (e.g., Canada) have preferred the issue of rules of origin to be discussed and analyzed within the GATT—today the WTO—with all the political implications at stake, rather than within the more aseptic and technical WCO. For this reason, the subject of rules of origin was included in the agenda of the Uruguay Round Negotiating Group on Non-Tariff Measures. The result was the Agreement on Rules of Origin.

However, it is evident that the possibilities of advancement within the WTO—an organization that discusses trade policies—are less likely than within the WCO which deals with this issue from an essentially technical standpoint that is not contaminated by the trade interests at stake. It is therefore a pity that the WCO has abandoned its competence over this subject as it has done with many others."

[4] www.findrulesoforigin.org. Accessed May 10, 2021.

[5] Basaldúa and Sumcheski (2019), p. 116.

Reference

Basaldúa RX, Sumcheski AL (2019) El Régimen de Origen de las Mercaderías. Publisher "Guía Práctica y Ediciones IARA S.A.". p 116

Chapter 9
Enforcement

9.1 Customs Fraud

Commercial customs fraud (customs crimes) is not only a concern for the developing countries, it affects developed countries as well. Perpetrators take advantage of every opportunity in international trade flows to execute a variety of fraudulent schemes causing significant damage, not only in the form of leakage of government revenues or threatening population safety, but also inhibiting economic competitiveness of compliant traders.

Customs enforcement teams engage in actions, such as: fighting against counterfeiting and commercial fraud; the smuggling of drugs, precursor chemicals, and highly taxed goods (such as cigarettes, alcohol, and spirits), weapons and nuclear materials; combating electronic crime, wildlife trafficking, ozone depleting substances, toxic waste, weapons of mass destruction, trafficking cultural property, to name just a few.

In addition, some aspects of Customs commercial fraud, particularly over- valuation of goods, are allegedly linked to money laundering. Such illegal capital outflows could provide criminal groups with funds to fuel other criminal activities such as purchasing/selling weapons, drug smuggling, among others.

To effectively prevent and combat commercial fraud, Customs must act together and employ a strategic, collaborative, multi-faceted, and holistic approach which includes capacity building and international cooperation.

Therefore, to provide its members with support, the WCO offers a wide array of legal instruments (Recommendations, Guidelines, Guides, Model Cooperation Agreements, etc.), networks, databases, technical materials, guidance documents, and fundamentally, a "platform" where customs around the world can jointly work on prevention and combat strategies.

To address these risks in a structured manner and provide members with a forum to discuss and exchange best practices, the **Working Group on Revenue Compliance and Fraud** was established in November 2014. It was set on the foundation of

H. H. Juárez Allende, *The World Customs Organization*, Law for Professionals,
https://doi.org/10.1007/978-3-030-85296-2_9

the previous **Working Group on Commercial Fraud**, which had been set up in 2005. This group operates under the overall direction of the Enforcement Committee and receives administrative support from the WCO Secretariat.

According to the proposal that the Working Group submitted to the 11th Enforcement Committee, and which was approved by this Committee and adopted by the WCO Council, "Commercial Fraud" means:

> Any offence against statutory or regulatory provisions which Customs is responsible for enforcing, committed in order to: 1. evade, or attempt to evade, payment of duties/levies/taxes on movements of commercial goods; and/or 2. evade, or attempt to evade, any prohibition or restrictions applicable to commercial goods; and/or 3. receive, or attempt to receive, any repayments, subsidies or other disbursements to which there is no proper entitlement; and/or 4. obtain, or attempt to obtain, illicit commercial advantage injurious to principle and practice of legitimate business competition.[1]

This fraud can be committed at various times or stages, namely, (i) prior, (ii) during, or (iii) after dispatching the goods. (i) Prior fraud precedes declaring before Customs the intention of importing / exporting goods, for example, in valuation-related matters (over or under-invoicing), in inaccurate declarations of goods quantities, in incorrect tariff classifications, among others. (ii) Fraud during the release process can take place, for instance, when the goods are delivered without the authorization of Customs. Lastly, (iii) post-release fraud occurs when, for example, there is failure to comply with the obligation arising from the requested and applied customs regime.

This Working Group is made up of representatives from three-member administrations from each WCO region and are nominated through the Regional Vice-Chairpersons. The tenure of members is usually of two years with no bar to their re-election.

The members of the Working Group elect the Chairperson from among them.

The purpose and scope of this Group are: to study the nature and extent of commercial fraud and analyze its linkages with money laundering, organized crime and terrorist financing; to assist in ascertaining perceived needs of member administrations in the area of commercial fraud; to propose strategies and methods of international cooperation to combat commercial fraud; to develop appropriate tools—such as Guidelines and Recommendations—regarding commercial fraud for member administrations' approval; and to consider any other issues of relevance to commercial fraud.

The Working Group on Commercial Fraud reports to the Enforcement Committee on the Agenda items it has examined and presents its findings in the form of recommendations or options for the Enforcement Committee to consider. The Working Group works on a continuous basis using e-mails and the WCO members' website. Information on the activities and progress of the Working Group and the

---

[1]This definition was agreed by the Working Group to the 11th Enforcement Committee (Doc. 36.540), approved by the Enforcement Committee and adopted by the Council. http://www.wcoomd.org/en/wco-working-bodies/enforcement_and_compliance/working_group_on_commercial_fraud. Accessed May 10, 2021.

papers and reports it generates are made available on the WCO members' website. Members of the Working Group meet at least once a year for no more than three days. Meetings are held at WCO Headquarters, unless participants agree otherwise.

A particular aspect of this Working Group is that it does not receive any funding from the WCO. Its members finance their activities and bear travel and accommodation costs. The Secretariat only provides the necessary support for meetings when they are held in Brussels.

The Working Group and the WCO have developed several tools to counteract commercial fraud, among them we find the **I2C or Information and Intelligence Center** which emerged in the spirit of the *Globally Networked Customs* initiative. Its main objective is to facilitate communication and coordination on Customs compliance and law enforcement-related matters. I2C operates under the auspices of the WCO Compliance and Enforcement Sub- Directorate and promotes four key goals:

i. Enable better operational law enforcement coordination at the international level
ii. Provide members with a help desk function/interface for international law enforcement issues
iii. Collect and distribute open-source intelligence and other non-restricted Customs-related intelligence to members on regular basis
iv. Support/co-host WCO law enforcement operations, providing intelligence and operational coordination support for WCO global operations across the five key Customs risk areas which will be discussed further on (Drugs and Precursors, Environment, Intelligence and Risk Management, Health, Finance and Safety)

The **Customs Enforcement Network (CEN)**, which began operating in 2000, is also underway, essentially as an analytical tool. Its functions allow users to extract data (all information related to customs offenses, their participants, modalities and seizures, among other data) which are crucial to define strategies, prepare risk indicators and identify trends. Collected data are recorded in a MS Access database that can be downloaded. Additionally, its built-in statistics function facilitates their conversion into tangible results. Intelligence is a vital element of the CEN software which enables all WCO members to access the critical mass of information that forms the basis of customs intelligence actions.[2]

Since then, the **CEN Suite** has grown to include several independent applications, such as: **nCEN**, a database for collection and storage of law enforcement information at the national level; and **CENcomm**, a secure (encrypted) communication platform permitting a closed user group (with a WCO-issued ID and password) to exchange and use data in a timely, reliable and secure manner, with direct access 24 hours a day. Several operations have been organized with CENcomm since its creation.

[2]The CEN system electronically links all customs administrations through the WCO network of Regional Intelligence Liaison Offices (RILO). These RILOs contribute to the CEN by the collection of national information and data input.

The World Customs Organization frequently provides and updates documents such as the **Customs-Police Cooperation Handbook** that aims to foster increased cooperation between the two types of agencies at a national level. This document highlights the need for customs–police cooperation and offers professional insight on how to strengthen the collaboration between these institutions that are so important to a country's national security. In addition, the WCO has developed the **WCO Strategic Trade Control Enforcement Implementation Guide**.

This guide responds to requests from World Customs Organization (WCO) members for practical assistance related to enforcing strategic trade controls. It should serve as a guide for WCO members when developing and reviewing their Strategic Trade Control Enforcement (STCE) processes and procedures, and provide a framework for training in those aspects.

Additionally, the WCO provides member states with a series of compendiums. The Compendium of Customs Operational Practices to Combat Fraud and Seizures (COPES) to improve knowledge sharing. The practices outlined in this Compendium raise awareness for Customs administrations to seriously examine their procedures and possibly take steps towards improving their current systems, notably enhancing their legal foundation (enabling powers) and the operational options on which their procedures and practices are based. The Compendium, to which only WCO members have access due to the sensitive nature of its content, is available in English, French, Spanish, and Arabic. The WCO Customs Risk Management Compendium is composed of two separate but interlinked volumes: Volume 1 sets out the organizational framework for risk management and outlines the risk management process. Volume 2, available only to members, addresses risk assessment, profiling and targeting tools which are the basis for the selection criteria to identify high-risk consignments, passengers and means of transport for Customs intervention.

Regional Intelligence Liaison Offices (RILO) emerged as it was evident that this contribution was necessary to further protect society, public health, and safety. Therefore, in 1987, the first Regional Intelligence Liaison Office (RILO) was established with the intention of creating a Global Intelligence Network. Today, the RILO network has grown to 1 offices and provides effective coverage throughout all six WCO regions. The unique nature of the RILO network offers an added layer of information exchange to the already existing intelligence exchange taking place between the Secretariat and member administrations at the strategic level. In addition to responding to intelligence-related requests, the RILO network supports its WCO member administrations by providing them with operational support, designing and implementing target-oriented intelligence analysis projects and regional intelligence-led operations, facilitating mutual administrative assistance, and promoting and maintaining regional cooperation with other law enforcement agencies and organizations.

Among the WCO tools that the RILO network uses are the aforementioned WCO Customs Enforcement Network (CEN), which has a global database containing customs seizures information, and the CEN-based secure communications platform for closed user groups, CENcomm.

In addition to the above, the WCO periodically presents the **Commercial Fraud Typologies Summary** to provide member countries with updated information on new criminal methodologies that have been detected. The annual typology reports on money laundering are produced by organizations with which the WCO jointly works with, such as the Financial Action Task Force and some regional bodies. These reports are prepared based on the information provided by its members and relevant stakeholders to get a better understanding of money laundering methods, techniques, and trends.

The opacity of international finance (tax havens, shell companies, and the anonymity of international transactions) offers criminals a wide range of options. Therefore, customs administrations play an essential role enforcing activities against money laundering due to their presence at the borders, their legal powers, their knowledge of trade and their experience.

In the international field, the United Nations (UN) has promoted a series of treaties that seek to promote the fight against money laundering and the financing of terrorism, such as the International Convention for the Suppression of the Financing of Terrorism, approved in 2002.

The WCO has actively championed anti-money laundering programs and boosted its members' capacities to combat money laundering by raising awareness, elaborating training programs, developing legal instruments, promoting the CEN suite, including its seizures database, and promoting best practices.

In 2001, the WCO issued a comprehensive anti-money laundering recommendation entitled "Recommendation of the Customs Co-operation Council on the Need to Develop and Strengthen the Role of Customs Administrations in Tackling Money Laundering and in Recovering the Proceeds of Crime."

In 2005, the WCO revised that recommendation[3] to include references to relevant United Nations Security Council Resolutions and new Financial Action Task Force (FATF) Recommendations.

In 2018, the WCO issued the Study Report **Illicit Financial Flows via Trade Mis-invoicing**[4] which reaffirms the role of Customs in the fight against money laundering and expands the scope of the recommendation to cover the financing of terrorism. It seeks to ensure that Customs have sufficient mandate to address: improperly invoiced imports intended to evade customs duties; over-invoiced imports intended to disguise capital flight as a form of trade payment; exports invoiced with the intention of concealing trade profit abroad such as tax havens; and over-invoiced exports or counterfeited imports intended to bring illicit proceeds

[3] Recommendation of the Customs Cooperation Council on the Need to Develop and Strengthen the Role of the Customs Administrations in Combating Money Laundering and Recovering the Proceeds of Crime. Revised edition 2005. http://www.wcoomd.org/en/about-us/legal-instruments/recommendations/~/media/FEE94FB75264494FBAC781B84D70D1D6.ashx. Accessed May 10, 2021.

[4] Illicit Financial Flows via Trade Mis-invoicing Study Report 2018. http://www.wcoomd.org/-/media/wco/public/global/pdf/media/newsroom/reports/2018/wco-study-report-on-iffs_tm.pdf?la=en. Accessed May 10, 2021.

into to the domestic legal financial system. Additionally, the study states that Customs should be allowed to access the database of foreign currency transactions and should have the powers to examine whether "financial transactions" between traders correspond to the "value of the traded goods."

For its part, the Financial Action Task Force (FATF) recommendation requires the different jurisdictions to implement measures to detect and prevent the physical cross-border transportation of currency and bearer negotiable instruments, which is one of the main methods used for the movement of illicit funds, money laundering and financing of terrorism.

Today, customs and other law enforcement agencies around the world are facing the phenomenon of the globalization of crime. Identifying and stopping illicit capital flows at the border is an effective way to cut the financial life of criminal and terrorist groups. Partnerships with other international organizations are key components in the fight against illicit financial flows. Therefore, the WCO actively contributes in forums and initiatives of the FATF, INTERPOL, Europol, and other relevant agencies.

The WCO Secretariat and INTERPOL have been closely collaborating on a wide range of issues. In particular, they have focused on combating transnational criminal activities such as drugs, intellectual property rights, trafficking in stolen cultural objects, cigarettes, small arms and light weapons, and environmental crime. In 2003, the highest authorities of both organizations signed a Memorandum of Understanding.

The WCO also closely cooperates with the World Intellectual Property Organization (WIPO) in promoting the proper use and effective protection of intellectual property worldwide.

Furthermore, the WCO collaborates with the United Nations Office on Drugs and Crime (ONODC) within the framework of a Memorandum of Understanding, signed in November 1996. Both entities have conducted numerous activities together, the most influential one is the so-called "UNODC-WCO Container Control Programme," launched in 2010.

The World Customs Organization faces modern day challenges with a new approach. Currently, the effort is thematically divided into six programs that cover the following areas: Drugs and Precursors, Environment, Intelligence and Risk Management, Health, Finance and Security. Other risk areas such as electronic crime and the trafficking of stolen cultural objects are also covered.

9.2 Drugs and Precursor Chemicals

For years, drug trafficking has become a scourge for society. Not only does it seriously damage people's health, but it also impacts states' security and economic development. Enormous amounts of money derived from this market are used in illegal activities by organized criminal groups and terrorists.

The current situation is severe: drug markets continue to grow, and drug trafficking patterns are constantly changing. Furthermore, new psychoactive substances (NSPs) have been added to "classic" drugs such as opiates, cocaine, and cannabis. The WCO Illicit Trade Report annually identifies and exposes trends and patterns of analysis in this area.[5]

The WCO works closely with other partner agencies in the cooperative fight against drug trafficking such as the Central Asian Regional Information and Coordination Centre for Combating Illicit Trafficking of Narcotic Drugs, Psychotropic Substances and their Precursors (CARICC), the European Monitoring Centre for Drugs and Drug Addiction (EMCDDA), INTERPOL, the International Narcotics Control Board (INCB), the South East Europe Law Enforcement Centre (SELEC) and the United Nations Office on Drugs and Crime (UNODC), to name a few.

The WCO Drugs Programme is aimed at countering global illegal trade covering the cultivation, manufacturing, distribution, and sale of substances which are subject to drug restriction and prohibition laws. The Programme consists of several major components:

- UNODC-WCO Container Control Programme (CCP)
- Project AIRCOP
- EU-WCO COLIBRI Project
- Global Forum on Combating Illicit Drug Trafficking and Related Threats,
- Global Canine Fora
- Operational activities
- UNODC-WCO Container Control Programme (CCP)
- Project AIRCOP
- EU-WCO COLIBRI Project
- Global Forum on Combating Illicit Drug Trafficking and Related Threats,
- Global Canine Fora
- Operational activities

UNODC-WCO Container Control Programme (CCP)

In 2003, the World Customs Organization (WCO) and the United Nations Office on Drugs and Crime (UNODC) launched the Container Control Programme to improve port surveillance in developing countries so that they could minimize the risk of sea containers being used for illicit drug trafficking, transnational organized crime, and other forms of fraudulent activity.

The program covers over twenty (20) countries with Port Control Units[6] in operational ports. Countries participating in the CCP are trained to profile, target and examine containers that are used to transport illicit goods. This includes

[5]http://www.wcoomd.org/en/topics/enforcement-and-compliance/resources/publications.aspx. Accessed May 10, 2021.

[6]Countries and Joint Port Control Units. Official Source of the UNODC-WCO Global Container Control Programme. https://www.unodc.org/ropan/en/BorderControl/container-control/ccp.html. Accessed May 10, 2021.

narcotics;[7] strategic and dual use goods; forest products and wildlife crime; and goods that infringe intellectual property rights.

The WCO and its members prioritize combating drug trafficking by training their agents and improving the information exchange system among the global trade administrations of each country. They use CENcomm to speed up port processes and to confront illegal actions.

The program's most important task is to target high-risk containers for committing crimes, but allowing the smooth movement of containers belonging to serious companies with adequate safety and traceability standards. Although there is illicit traffic through open sea, shipping drugs by containers remains a very active method and, therefore, it is necessary to increase controls in all ports.

The program uses the ContainerComm System, the WCO's real-time communication tool for information exchange and cooperation that facilitates container targeting between Port Control Units (PCUs). The System is a user-friendly, multi-functional web-based program that facilitates the encrypted exchange of confidential information between authorized users in participating countries, including alerts[8] of potential high-risk container shipments.

It has also taken the lead in tackling integration from a gender perspective by launching the CCP Women's Network. This Network contributes to promote professionalism and leadership and to increase women's participation in the program (approximately 12% of PCU Programme staff).[9]

The program covers theoretical and practical training, as well as more specialized training, including the Compendium of Customs Operational Practices for Enforcement and Seizures (COPES) which introduces investigative and evidence management techniques and training on Intellectual Property Rights (IPR) and the Convention on International Trade in Endangered Species of Wild Fauna and Flora (CITES). The Programme also incorporates training in the use of non-intrusive tools for container control.

In addition, the cooperation with the private sector—particularly, with terminal operators and shipping lines—resulted in improved access to data and information on port operations and in the PCU's enhanced ability to target high-risk cargoes.

---

[7] A very widespread modality of transporting illegal drugs in containers is called "Rip-Off" in the customs jargon. It is a concealment mechanism that is carried out in the country of origin or in the port of transshipment before the container arrives in the country of destination. In cases of "Rip-Off," neither the sender nor the recipient is aware that the shipment is being used for the traffic of illicit goods. For this method to be successful, there will always be local conspiracy both in the country of origin or the transshipment port as well as in the destination country. Bags or backpacks containing narcotics are usually used and surreptitiously placed in the containers.

[8] There are two types of alerts, the first is communicated to the country of origin of the cargo, with the purpose of seizing illicit goods before the container leaves, and the second is sent to the country of destination of the cargo to facilitate seizures on arrival.

[9] Women in the CCP - CCP Annual Report – WCO UNODC. Available at: https://www.unodc.org/documents/Container-control-programme/CCP_Annual_Report_2018_FINAL.pdf. Accessed May 10, 2021.

Thus, advanced, more coordinated and swifter inspections have given way to trade facilitation and security.

By 2018, PCUs had seized 51,341 kg of cocaine, 969 kg of heroin, 76,737 kg of precursor chemicals, in addition to seizing many other drugs, including marijuana and synthetics. The CCP has seized goods that infringe intellectual property rights, cigarettes and endangered forest and wildlife species as noted in the CCP Annual Report.[10]

Given the program's success and having confirmed the benefits of joining forces in combating the criminal scourges that are constantly seeking weak entry points, the CCP extended its focus to air cargo and invited the International Civil Aviation Organization (ICAO) to join the partnership in 2015. In 2018, the UNODC and ICAO signed a Memorandum of Understanding.

By employing the same methodology developed by CCP for establishing and maintaining PCUs in land and seaports, CCP-Air aims to prevent the misuse of the international air transport system by establishing inter-agency units at CCP-Air airports.

Project AIRCOP

In 2008, in response to the emerging threat posed by the opening of the new trafficking route for cocaine from South America to Europe via West Africa, the WCO carried out the first Operation COCAIR.

Project AIRCOP was launched in 2011.[11] It is funded by the European Commission and Canada, managed by the UNODC and implemented by the WCO and INTERPOL in close cooperation with the WCO members and other law enforcement agencies in the field of illicit substance trafficking.

Its main objective is to combat illicit cocaine trafficking by air from South America, via Africa, to Europe, as well as fighting airport crime. It is primarily focused on West and Central African airports, where the first multidisciplinary Joint Air Interdiction Task Force (JAITF) units, comprising officers from Customs, Police, the Gendarmerie, and other law enforcement agencies, were established.[12]

AIRCOP task forces participate in multiple joint operations during which controls are intensified for a special type of product or concealment method, for a limited period at selected airports.[13]

---

[10]CCP Annual Report – WCO UNODC. Available at: http://www.wcoomd.org/-/media/wco/public/global/pdf/topics/enforcement-and-compliance/activities-and-programmes/illicit-trade-report/itr_2018_en.pdf?db=web. Accessed May 10, 2021.

[11]More information: http://www.wcoomd.org/en/topics/enforcement-and-compliance/activities-and-programmes/drugs-programme/project-aircop.aspx. Accessed May 10, 2021.

[12]The project has expanded its geographic coverage by adding airports in Africa, Latin America, the Caribbean, and the Middle East.

[13]As of February 2019, seizures reached 8 tons of cocaine; 422 kg of heroin; 6 tons of cannabis; more than 2 tons of methamphetamine; nearly 10 tons of cigarettes and other tobacco products; more than 13 tons of counterfeit medicines; 1.2 tons of pangolin scales; $14.5 million in undeclared earnings; and 1.4 tons of precursors (ephedrine, phenacetin, etc.). Source (in Spanish): https://www.

Project AIRCOP's annual program includes operational activities; therefore, Operation COCAIR was conducted within its framework to test the operational capabilities of JAITF in real time. In 2014, the Project began to expand to supplier countries in South America and the Caribbean by establishing JAITFs at key airports in the region. Liaison officers and JAITF officials use the CENcomm or the WCO Customs Network Communication Platform as a means of communication.

Additionally, Project partner countries in other regions, such as Europe and North Africa, have also benefited from participation in CENcomm and INTERPOL's I-24/7 database that is also used to enable secure information exchange between airports and to access passenger's criminal records.

EU-WCO COLIBRI Project

During 2018, the WCO and the European Union (EU) launched the "COLIBRI" Project, with the aim of combating cocaine trafficking in Latin America and the Caribbean, and West and Central Africa, on one of the weak sides of customs control: airfields and non-commercial flights.

This project reinforces the Cocaine Route Programme (CRP), financed by the European Union. It is being implemented as part of Goal 3 of the WCO Strategic Plan (2016/2019), "Protect society, public health and safety, and contribute to combating crime and terrorism" (Compliance and Enforcement Package), and is in line with the role of Customs in achieving the Sustainable Development Goals adopted by the United Nations in 2015.

The purpose of the COLIBRI Project is to monitor and control "general aviation," that is, all civil aviation operations for purposes other than commercial transport. Although most civil airports are open to general aviation, many secondary airports are not subject to the same police and customs inspection mechanisms as commercial flights. This means that general aviation represents an opportunity for organized crime and offers a series of advantages to traffickers. This is a discreet, fast mode of transport, which can use smaller airports that law enforcement agencies often overlook.

There are three main components to COLIBRI: (i) Capacity building for Customs officials and the staff of the administrations concerned; (ii) The creation of a new specialist database with relevant information on the control and monitoring of general aviation and using CENcomm; (iii) The promotion and strengthening of international operational and intelligence cooperation through joint operations in the field.

Global Forum on Combating Illicit Drug Trafficking and Related Threats

The WCO Secretariat held the first Global Forum on Combating Illicit Drug Trafficking and Related Threats from the 25th to 27th of January 2012. It brought together over 170 delegates from 65 Customs administrations as well as some 10 international and regional organizations. The WCO prioritized the fight against

interpol.int/es/Noticias-y-acontecimientos/Noticias/2019/La-6a-Reunion-Mundial-del-Proyecto-Aircop-aborda-el-tema-de-la-deteccion-del-trafico-ilicito-por-via-aerea.

trafficking in drugs and precursor chemicals including money laundering and corruption, thus responding to the concerns of its members and partners.

The forum featured an exhibition that provided the private sector an opportunity to display a range of equipment and technical aids available to officials responsible for combating the traffic in drugs and precursor chemicals, such as drug tests, urine drug screens, ionscan, and endoscopes.

Global Canine Fora

Dog and handler programs were originally aimed at enhancing Customs anti-drug trafficking activities. This traditional role has grown to encompass other areas such as fighting terrorism, especially through the detection of weapons and explosives, and more recently to combating trafficking in currency, CD-ROMs, cigarettes, or even pharmaceuticals and CITES protected species. Dog and handler teams now form a key component of global risk management programs established by Customs administrations.

In 2011, the WCO organized the first Global Canine Forum, specifically focused on the potential of using detector dog and their team of handlers.[14] Given the success of this first Forum, the WCO made the event a permanent fixture to be convened every two years, with a view to creating the conditions needed for experts to share experiences and pool best practices. The second Forum was held from May 28th to 30th, 2013 in Moscow, Russia, and the Third Global Canine Forum was held from June 24th to 26th, 2015 in the city of Buenos Aires, Argentina. About 90 experts from 28 countries attended the forum where they actively exchanged knowledge and experience on various aspects of canine programs, such as the design and management of training detector dogs and handlers, dog breeding, veterinary issues, and the overall operation of dog centers.

From October 2 to 4, 2017, around 120 delegates representing 44 Customs administrations and international organizations attended the fourth edition of this event in Prague, which was organized with the support of the Czech Customs administration and funded by Japan Customs. From October 1 to 3, 2019, the Fifth Global Canine Forum was held in the city of Melbourne, Australia. The Conference brought together over 100 participants from around 30 countries across five continents to share best practices for implementing and enhancing Canine Programmes.

In relation to the Global Canine Force, we must also mention the **WCO Regional Dog Training Centers**, which emerged when the Customs Control Committee (Ministry of Finance of the Republic of Kazakhstan) and the Customs Administration of the Czech Republic signed a Memorandum of Understanding with the WCO, thereby establishing the first training centers in Almaty, Republic of Kazakhstan, and Hermanice, Czech Republic. There are currently fifteen of these centers located in Azerbaijan, Canada, China, Czech Republic, Germany (Bleckede and

[14] In some English-speaking countries, detector dogs are known as "K-9" or "K9," a homophone of the term "canine."

Neuendettelsau), Hungary, Kazakhstan, Russian Federation, Saudi Arabia, Turkey, Ukraine, United States (Texas and Virginia) and Uzbekistan.[15]

Operational Activity
To support its members, the WCO has implemented the Training of Customs Officers. Students acquire knowledge on the latest risk management techniques, concealment methods and previously detected drug routes; in addition, they learn how to use the various WCO tools and instruments. Regional Intelligence Liaison Offices (RILO) also play a key role in supporting capacity building and operational activities. Furthermore, over the last decade, the WCO has been continuously providing its Brussels-based facilities to host the Operational Coordination Unit.

9.3 Environment

Currently, one of the most difficult problems humankind is facing are the disastrous consequences of environmental crime. Our planet is suffering from air, water and land pollution, extinction of wildlife and depletion of natural resources.

The international community has concluded a number of the Multilateral Environmental Agreements (MEAs) with international trade-related provisions, such as the Convention on Trade in Endangered Species of Wild Fauna and Flora (CITES); the Montreal Protocol on Substances that Deplete the Ozone Layer (ODS); the Basel Convention on the Control of Trans-Boundary Movements of Hazardous Wastes and Their Disposal; the Stockholm Convention on Persistent Organic Pollutions (POPs); the Rotterdam Convention on the Prior Informed Consent Procedure for Certain Hazardous Chemicals and Pesticides in International Trade and the Cartagena Protocol on Biosafety.

Customs play a crucial role when implementing these MEAs and in the fight against environmental crime.

Some of the most important allies that work jointly with the WCO is the Secretariat of CITES (Convention on International Trade in Endangered Species of Wild Fauna and Flora), based on the Memorandum of Understanding signed by both Organizations in 1996, which among other arrangements establishes:

(i) the WCO Secretariat and the CITES Secretariat will send each other any general information of common interest; (ii) the two Secretariats will invite each other as observers to meetings of common interest that they organize and (iii) measures to improve cooperation and information exchange between customs authorities and CITES Management bodies; particularly for the purpose of detecting consignments likely to contain protected species whose trade is regulated.

Since 2001, the WCO has been an active Partner to the Green Customs Initiative (GCI), a series of collaborative activities by partner organizations, coordinated by

[15] http://www.wcoomd.org/-/media/wco/public/global/pdf/media/annual-reports/annual-report-2018_2019.pdf. Accessed May 10, 2021.

the UNEP (United Nations Environment Programme) and aimed at raising the awareness of Customs officers to trade-related MEAs. In 2008, the WCO Council adopted a Recommendation concerning Actions Against Cross-Border Environmental Offences, outlining steps to be taken by Customs administrations to improve their skills in this area. In November 2010, five international organizations, the WCO, the CITES Secretariat, INTERPOL, the UNODC and the World Bank founded the International Consortium on Combating Wildlife Crime (ICCWC) to provide the national wildlife law enforcement agencies more support, as well to assist regional and subregional networks combating against illegal trade in natural resources. In addition, in July 2012, the ICCWC launched the Wildlife and Forest Crime Analytic Toolkit, which was developed to provide a comprehensive overview on issues related to wildlife and forest crimes and was aimed at government officials in wildlife and forestry authorities, as well as customs and other relevant agencies.

In March 2012, the WCO launched the Environment Programme to contribute to the fight against environmental crime, particularly illegal wildlife trade, illegal trade in hazardous and other waste, ozone depleting substances (ODSs), and illegal trade in timber. The Illicit Trade Report provides further information on every component of the Programme on the annual basis.

ENVIRONET, a real-time communication tool for information exchange among all competent national authorities, international organizations and regional networks, and CLiKC!, WCO e-learning facility containing courses on environmental crime, should be particularly highlighted.

In 2014, the WCO started implementing the activities of the Inama ("inama" means wild animals in the language of the Zambian Bemba tribe) Project, a multi-donor funded endeavor to strengthen Customs enforcement capacity related to CITES in selected countries of the Sub-Saharan Africa.

On the other hand, the WCO constantly works on broadening the scope of partnerships with other organizations fighting against environmental crime. Throughout the past years, the WCO signed Memoranda of Understanding with the CITES Secretariat, Secretariat of the Basel Convention, United Nations Environment Programme, Lusaka Agreement Task Force and TRAFFIC, an NGO that works in plants and wild animals trade in the context of sustainable development and biodiversity conservation.

Lastly, in June 2014, the WCO Council approved the WCO Declaration on the Illegal Wildlife Trade that clearly states the world customs community's commitment to address these crimes in a timely, consistent, and coordinated manner.[16]

[16]By way of example, OPERATION THUNDER 2020 coordinated by the World Customs Organization (WCO) and INTERPOL brought together 103 countries in the fight against wildlife and forest crimes. The operation lasted one month (from September 14th to October 11th, 2020) and seized more than 2000 specimens and protected forest and wildlife products (pangolins, turtles, birds, reptiles, plants, ivory, etc.), and 699 offenders were apprehended. More information available at: https://www.interpol.int/en/News-and-Events/News/2020/Wildlife-and-forestry-crime-Worldwide-seizures-in-global-INTERPOL-WCO-operation.

9.4 Intelligence and Risk Management

Customs administrations must face the challenges of the accelerated growth of international goods flows in this twenty-first century, and try to minimize risks anywhere in the world with the speed these issues require in the most structured and systematic way possible. For this, they use an enormous wealth of information (known as "Big Data") and develop information technology (data mining). Today, risk management[17] is considered one of the guiding principles associated with modern customs administration.

To this end, the WCO developed the Customs Risk Management Compendium[18] to enable customs administrations around the world to identify and address potential risks. The methodology described in the Compendium establishes a common framework, but at the same time remains flexible enough to meet its members' individual conditions.

The Compendium is composed of two separate but interlinked volumes. Volume 1 sets out the organizational framework for risk management and outlines the risk management process. Volume 2, available only to member states, addresses risk assessment, profiling and targeting tools which are the basis for the selection criteria to identify high-risk consignments, passengers and means of transport for customs intervention.

In the Handbook for Customs Modernization published by the World Bank in 2005, David Widdowson states: "The concept of organizational risk refers to the possibility of events and activities occurring that may prevent an organization from achieving its objectives. Customs authorities are required to achieve two primary objectives-provide the international trading community with an appropriate level of facilitation, and ensure compliance with regulatory requirements [. . .] Sound risk management is fundamental to effective customs operations, and it would be true to say that all administrations apply some form of risk management, either formal or informal. Drawing on intelligence, information, and experience, customs has always adopted procedures designed to identify illegal activity in an effort to reduce its risks."

In addition, and as specified in the following section, the WCO has considered the value of exchanging information and disseminating intelligence among its member Customs administrations. For this reason, it created the Global Network of Regional Intelligence Liaison Offices (RILO) with its various tasks; established Customs Enforcement Network (CEN) applications; and implemented tools that help members exchange information.

---

[17] The 2018 edition of the Glossary of Customs Terms incorporated the concept of "Risk management," defining it as: "Coordinated activities by administrations to direct and control risk." In addition, it defined "Risk analysis" as: "Systematic use of available information to determine how often defined risks may occur and the magnitude of their likely consequences."

[18] http://www.wcoomd.org/en/topics/enforcement-and-compliance/instruments-and-tools/compendiums/rmc.aspx. Accessed May 10, 2021.

It is important to note that the Technology Network (TeN), is the only communication platform for Customs and other border agencies, technology companies, international organizations and relevant stakeholders to exchange experiences and information on technologies related to border management. TeN also includes a wide range of products related to risk management and intelligence systems.

9.4.1 Regional Intelligence Liaison Offices

The WCO, recognizing the strategic value of developing a system for regional and international information exchange that would lead to more effective enforcement and controls, created the first Regional Intelligence Liaison Office (RILO) in 1987. This RILO was set up with the intention develop a Global Intelligence Network. Today, the RILO network has 1 offices that provide effective coverage to all six WCO regions.[19]

Each RILO office covers several member states within its respective region and is staffed by personnel from those affiliated member states (who function as Liaison Officers), as well as from the Customs Administration of the regional office's host country.

At the operational level, the RILO network supports its member Customs administrations by responding to intelligence-related requests, providing operational assistance, designing, and implementing targeted-oriented intelligence analysis projects, and regional intelligence-led operations, facilitating mutual administrative assistance, and promoting and maintaining regional cooperation.

Each RILO is a regional center for collecting and analyzing data. It also disseminates information on trends, modus operandi, transit routes and significant cases of fraud.

National Contact Points (NCPs) collect information on significant seizures, or new and unusual concealment methods regarding customs offences in their jurisdiction, including photos and other relevant details. Then, they electronically input this information into the CEN network (which uses encryption technologies to protect communication and data transfers) so that other jurisdictions can access it or to trigger monitoring alerts.

In practice, the RILO network has proven to be a powerful and effective intelligence and information exchange tool. It enables data exchange in an accurate and expeditious manner. The purpose is to identify and disrupt complex transnational crime such as origin trade deflection, over or under-invoicing maneuvers or the detection of simulated or false operations.

[19]The RILO network covers all six WCO regions and has offices in the following 1 countries: Cameroon, Chile, Republic of Korea, Germany, Morocco, Poland, Russia, Saudi Arabia, St. Lucia, Senegal, and Zimbabwe.

Table 9.1 Customs contribution to tax revenue

	South America, North America, Central America	West and Central Africa and the Caribbean	East and South Africa	Middle East and North Africa	Europe	Far East, South and South-east Asia, Australasia and Pacific Islands
Customs contributions to tax revenue	30%	41.4%	31.9%	36.7%	25%	20.5%

Source: WCO Annual Report for 2019/2020

9.5 Health and Safety

Illegal medicine trade is the greatest risk to public health worldwide. There are numerous cases of counterfeit medicine, or pharmaceutical products and prescription medicines manufactured from poisonous or inferior constituents or without the active ingredients they claim to offer, or medicines that attempt to enter the country with no proper authorization.

These products may cause anything from light injuries to profoundly serious consequences locally, regionally, and even globally. The WCO IPR, Health and Safety Program, is based on the premise that nothing can be achieved in isolation. Therefore, the Organization is active in delivering extensive effort coordination activities among its members and related international organizations, working with the private sector and developing various enforcement and capacity building tools.

Within this framework and as we have previously stated, the WCO and its members closely work with organizations such as GS1, the Union of Manufacturers (UNIFAB), the Federation of the European Sporting Goods Industry (FESI), the National Association for the Defense of the Brand (ANDEMA), the French Pharmaceutical Industry Association (LEEM), the Customs Intellectual Property Information Center (CIPIC), and the Office for Harmonization in the Internal Market (OHIM), among others.

9.6 Finance and Safety

Customs revenue, which was once the core revenue of countries, has gradually been displaced by a collection of excises as the main revenue stream for the fiscal coffers. However, it still plays a vital role in tax collection.

Table 9.1 was extracted from the WCO Annual Report for 2019/2020:[20]

[20]Complete content is available at: http://www.wcoomd.org/en/about-us/what-is-the-wco/annual-reports.aspx. Accessed May 10, 2021.

Revenue risks in Customs include not only evasion through smuggling of highly taxed goods, such as tobacco and alcohol, but also through other modalities of commercial fraud which are more complex and difficult to detect, such as undervaluation, misclassification, misuse of origin and preferential duties, among others.

The smuggling of tobacco and tobacco-related products is one of the crimes that affects tax collection; additionally, it is extremely harmful to public health. According to WCO Illicit Trade Reports,[21] there are numerous cases of large-scale smuggling leading to the subsequent seizure of millions of cigarettes. There is growing concern in the international community in relation to this type of illegal trafficking, as it appears to be carried out by organized criminal groups that handle large amounts of money. These funds are most likely being used to finance the activities of international terrorism organizations.

Cigarette smuggling is destined to certain countries. The WCO has been working with other regional and international organizations to identify the best possible enforcement strategies to counter this problem, including collaborative projects between Customs and other law enforcement agencies.

In connection with the combat of more complex types of fraud (usually referred to as "white collar" fraud), the WCO began working on the **Post-Clearance Audit** (PCA) or audit-based controls. This audit is a structured analysis of a business' relevant commercial systems, sales contracts, financial and non-financial, physical stock, and other assets to evaluate and improve compliance.

Although physical control at the border is especially important, few import documents are often required; thus, hindering the complete vision and context of the commercial transaction. For example, documents may not evidence how customs value or tariff classification were determined, or if the goods benefited from a preferential regime in terms of origin.

The PCA is the most effective tool for many aspects of these complex customs controls. By applying this technique and a risk-based approach, Customs are also able to target their resources more effectively and work in partnership with the business community to improve compliance levels and facilitate trade.

The WCO Council recognized the importance of the PCA as a tool to improve the multi-layered risk management approach. Therefore, in 2012, it adopted **PCA Guidelines**, which serve as a fundamental tool for members.

To complement the Guidelines, the WCO has developed other tools such as an e-learning module, a Diagnostic Tool on Post-Clearance Audit and Infrastructure, an Implementation Guidance on PCA and a PCA Typology "How to Audit."

The transition between physical border inspections to post-clearance audits is not immediate; rather, it requires an extensive period of preparation, i.e., the time to develop new processes, establish the new procedures and acquire new skills.

First, it is necessary to implement a national regulatory framework which provides Customs with the legal basis to conduct an audit and sets out the rights and

[21] http://www.wcoomd.org/en/topics/enforcement-and-compliance/resources/publications.aspx. Accessed May 10, 2021.

obligations of the auditee. This regulatory framework must include: (i) the definition of the scope of application of PCA (persons/ companies subject to PCA); (ii) powers of the Customs officers/auditors who conduct the; (iii) rights and obligations of auditees; (iv) penalty regime in case of non-compliance, and (v) right to appeal, among other aspects.

9.7 Security

Customs play a key role at international border crossings. Among other responsibilities, they are in charge of mitigating the threats to global security and human safety posed by the presence of terrorism, weapons of mass destruction, and trafficking of explosives. Customs manage the cross-border flows of goods, people and means of transport to ensure that they comply with the law. They also detect and prevent the traffic of dangerous, restricted, and prohibited goods.

The **WCO Security Programme** focuses its efforts on the need for Customs administrations to address all these issues which threaten security at the national and international levels.

The activities of the WCO's Security Programme are aimed at achieving border security outcomes in strategic areas that include:

- Policy setting and foresight
- Providing guidance and good practices on Customs controls in relation to security
- Coordination of security related Customs law enforcement programs and operations
- International cooperation
- Technology
- Technical assistance and capacity-building

At the operational level, the Programme has Commodity-Based Projects. These include:

- Passenger controls
- Improvised Explosive Device (IED) Programme Global Shield
- Strategic Trade Control Programme (STCE)
- Small Arms and Light Weapons Project (SALW)
- Terrorist Financing
- Border Security Initiative

Passenger Controls

Given the growth in international passenger traffic, Customs administrations have used various instruments (scanners, merchandise detectors, dogs, traffic lights, etc.) to facilitate their circulation without neglecting their control. Among these measures, we can highlight the passenger control initiative focused on the use of "Advance Passenger Information" (API) and "Passenger Name Records" (PNR) as part of their risk assessment processes and which was implemented by the World Customs Organization and the International Air Transport Association (IATA) in 1993.

Ten years later, the WCO, in cooperation with IATA and the International Civil Aviation Organization (ICAO), revised the Guidelines to consider the developments in communications, the aviation industry and Customs, and published the 2003 Edition of the IPA Guidelines. These developments include elements such as security, data protection and mutual administrative assistance. In February 2011, WCO, IATA, and ICAO formally adopted these Guidelines in their respective organizations.

Today, passenger control in Customs has been undoubtedly strengthened by managing information prior to the arrival of the means of transport (and even before its departure abroad), and passengers' relevant data which gives way to applying risk control techniques very effectively.

Programme Global Shield

Improvised explosive devices (IEDs) are the most prevalent form of explosives used by terrorists around the world, especially since the precursor chemicals needed to manufacture them are cheap and widely available.

In a unique initiative to secure global supply chains and enhance public safety, the WCO partnered with INTERPOL and the United Nations Office on Drugs and Crime (UNODC) and launched the Global Shield Programme. This program aims at preventing the smuggling and illicit diversion of precursor chemicals that could be used to build IEDs.

It started in November 2010 as a six-month project; however, its achievements and prominence led the WCO to support it as a long-term endeavor. Customs administrations in over ninety countries are now sharing information on 14 precursor chemicals used for IEDs. Through this unprecedented effort by the international community, the threat posed by these dangerous precursor chemicals is being seriously addressed.

Along with training, technical assistance, real-time information and intelligence sharing, the Global Shield Programme makes its participants and partners to be better equipped to intercept the illicit diversion of these precursor chemicals. Information on the latest seizures of precursor chemicals can be found in the annual Illicit Trade Report.

Strategic Trade Control Programme (STCE)

Strategic goods include weapons of mass destruction (WMD), conventional weapons, and related items involved in the development, production, or use of such weapons and their delivery systems.

United Nations Security Council Resolution 1540 (UNSCR 1540) adopted in 2004 to prevent illicit trafficking using weapons of mass destruction and their means of delivery, and related items, focuses on the need to develop and maintain adequate border control systems.

Customs are faced with two strategic threat scenarios: the possibility that the supply chain will be used as a system to deliver weapons of mass destruction (WMD) (the "bomb in a box" situation), and the possibility that the supply chain will be used to transport materials, equipment and components needed to produce a weapon. The former threat scenario is addressed through supply chain security initiatives such as the SAFE Framework of Standards, while the latter is addressed through the Strategic Trade Control (STCE).

In March 2013, the WCO launched the Strategic Trade Control Implementation Project (STCE) focused on providing technical assistance. This document was designed as a resource for WCO members to establish or review their national STEC programs.

In 2016, this project became a long-term STCE Programme that now focuses on six core areas:

- Organizing training workshops for STCE trainers to certify experts
- Delivering STCE trainings
- Operating the communication platform STRATComm 24/7/365 and developing the system
- Organizing other operational control exercises related to STCE
- Improving the scope of activity at global and national level
- Development of STCE seizure reports in the CEN system

Small Arms and Light Weapons Project (SALW)

"Small arms" are, broadly speaking, weapons designed for individual use. They include revolvers and self-loading pistols, rifles and carbines, machine guns, assault rifles and light machine guns among others.

"Light weapons" are generally weapons designed to be used by two or three people, although some can be carried and used by one person. They include, but are not limited to, general purpose or universal machine guns, medium machine guns, heavy machine guns, rifle grenades, under-barrel grenade launchers and mounted grenade launchers, portable anti-aircraft guns, portable anti-tank guns, recoilless rifles, portable launchers of anti-tank missile and rocket systems, portable launchers of anti-aircraft missile systems, and mortars of less than 100 mm.

The illicit and global trade in small arms and light weapons has been a growing cause of insecurity, violence, and death around the world. In response to this growing threat, the WCO initiated the Small Arms and Light Weapons Project (SALW) in March 2015, which aims to detect and prevent the illicit trade in these items.

Terrorism Financing

UN Security Council Resolutions 1373 (2001) and 2178 (2014) called on Member States to strengthen their controls over financial flows and ensure that these flows do not end up in the hands of extremist groups.

In this regard, please refer to the information provided in Sect. 9.6—Finance and Security.

Border Security Initiative

The objective of the initiative is to facilitate members' activities to implement measures, whether standards, guidance, IT tools, operations, or specialized training, to improve the members' overall border security and country management capabilities. The main contributions of the Border Security Initiative are diagnostic missions, training, and various forms of technical assistance.

9.8 Trademark Counterfeiting

The economic weight of the current strength of a recognized brand means that this is often considered to be a company's most valuable asset. One of the most serious problems the global economy currently faces is related to counterfeiting and piracy.

The proliferation of counterfeit goods generates a substantial loss of revenue for governments, damages the market of legitimate products. The consequent impact on the member's economic stability leads to the loss of business profit and jobs; in addition, it inhibits creativity and technological development. More importantly, since the quality of counterfeit goods is generally inferior to the original, they pose a threat to public safety.

The main purposes for protecting Intellectual Property Rights (IPR) include to encourage and reward investment in creative work and technological innovation, to create an incentive to finance research and development, to stimulate and ensure fair competition, and to protect consumers from unsafe and misleading products.

There is an additional social impact of counterfeiting. Trading counterfeit goods may: lead to increased levels of corruption and increased budgets for public safety, endanger public security and health, pose social and environmental problems, and violate criminal or administrative law such as in cases of tax and customs evasion or fraud. This reality and the high profitability of trademark fraud are the pillars on which the business is based. In the hands of perfectly structured criminal organizations, this business brings substantial benefits to its authors, but damages the image and results in undoubted economic harm to the right owners of the pirated trademarks.

In response, the WCO has adopted a strategy based on growing cooperation with rights holders to raise awareness and strengthen detection through targeting techniques.

The international commitment to protect trademark rights reached its peak with the regulatory harmonization achieved under the Agreement on Trade-Related Aspects of Intellectual Property Rights (TRIPS) within the World Trade Organization (WTO). In 2007, the WCO launched the SECURE (Standards Employed by Customs for Uniform Rights Enforcement) Programme, which provides measures that its members can incorporate into domestic law to enforce intellectual property rights in Customs. The SECURE Programme became the organization's first documented action to face this issue.

In 2009, the WCO took part in the Global Congress on Combating Counterfeit and Piracy, a public-private initiative with the International Chamber of Commerce (ICC-BASCAP21), INTERPOL, the OECD, and WIPO to "work together and with governments to improve enforcement, strengthen legislation, and educate and protect consumers from the dangers of counterfeiting."[22]

However, it was not until 2010 that the WCO made its most important contribution and progress in this area by developing the Interface Public Members (IPM), an online and mobile anti-counterfeit application that works as a secure, real-time communication hub between customs officials and the private sector[23] that helps exchange information to intercept counterfeit products.

From the basic functionality of a genuine and fake database, with photos and product descriptions, it has developed to a more complex system that offers additional options, including the function to send alerts to Customs officers, an e-learning feature and a mobile application. Late 2018, the IPM halted operation due to financial issues. In 2020, the WCO created a new Intellectual Property Rights (IPR) information exchange channel to replace the IPM. This is the CENcomm IPR Group that facilitates the use and timely exchange of data under reliable and secure conditions. This online communication system will help a closed group of Customs officers exchange messages and alerts through encrypted channels.

Another aspect to consider is the partnership with the private sector. Legitimate companies benefit from this partnership because by providing trade data and strategic information to Customs offices, these can detect counterfeit products in real time. Additionally, Customs administrations obtain information about companies and get a better perspective to successfully facilitate legitimate trade.

In relation to anti-counterfeiting statistics, the WCO has reported that it has faced challenges when requesting its members to submit data for various reasons: data delivery is optional, resources are limited in many member countries, some Customs administrations may not be responsible for IPR infringements, and some countries do not even have their own data to submit. For example, out of the 70 countries that provided information in 2010, 40 were developing countries. Moreover, the voluntary nature of this activity means that more detailed reports cannot be edited for publication until all members agree on what is sensitive data, which is no easy task.

The WCO recognizes and defends that international cooperation against trademark counterfeiting should include information exchange between Customs, promotion of effective control practices, a strong legal framework of cross-border measures, criminal and civil proceedings, suspension of imported goods due to IPR infringement which should be seized and destroyed rather than channeled to the market by other means. Hence, the importance of the Global Customs Network (GCN) which is a standardized way for Customs authorities to exchange information (data comes from commercial sources). This mechanism uses generic templates and blueprints and presents a series of protocols, standards, and guidelines. One of its

[22] World Commerce Review, The Fifth Global Congress on Combating Counterfeit and Piracy, December 1st–3rd 2009. https://www.worldcommercereview.com/publications/article_pdf/15. Accessed May 10, 2021.

[23] Some of the first companies to register at IPM were: Sony, Diageo, Pfizer, HP, Louis Vuitton, Hewlet Packard, Lacoste, Procter & Gamble, Glaxo Smith Kline, Beiersdorf, Burberry, Nike, Puma, Servier, Longchamp, Philips, just to name a few.

main objectives is to speed up the drafting and implementation of information exchange agreements with a view to facilitating interconnections among Customs and detecting smuggling or fraud.

9.9 Electronic Crime

By profiting from the anonymity and advantages by modern technologies, criminals also exploit technological innovations to commit a wide range of criminal activities. Cybercrime is one of the fastest growing crime areas. It has been defined as a crime committed through electronic storage devices, computer systems and networks.

Computer crimes have some specific characteristics that must be mentioned: (i) Cross-border: they can be committed remotely from anywhere in the world, (ii) Evidentiary volatility: the mechanisms used allow crime tracks to disappear, (iii) Timeless: crime can be programmed to run automatically at a certain date and time, (iv) Anonymity: there are virtual environments that are difficult to access (Deep Web) and, (v) Electronic payment: secure payment methods have been developed that are difficult to track (Bitcoin).[24]

Customs administrations must meet the challenge of being prepared to deal with complex crimes committed in cyberspace, which pose major obstacles, especially in terms of identification and tracking. Acknowledging this, in 2000, the 3rd Cybercrime Working Group recommended forming a group of specialized experts to examine a wide range of issues related to electronic crime. The Electronic Crime Experts Group (ECEG) was created in 2001 and endorsed by the WCO Council in June 2003; it reports to the Anti-Fraud Committee.

The ECEG provides the WCO with a group of qualified and updated specialists who can provide Customs Administrations with strategic and practical advice. This network of specialists meets once a year and develops guidance materials on technological developments, relevant to modern Customs administrations and their operational activities. Its activities cover a wide range of issues, from computer forensics, preconditions for establishing a cybercrime unit, to software analysis and data mining products.

Among the subjects covered by the ECEG, some are preventive such as encryption and security in storing Customs information, and others are more operational such as pursuing payments with bitcoins for money laundry, seizing bitcoins, using e-commerce for the traffic of prohibited merchandise, artificial intelligence and its

[24]To fully understand the full extent of this danger, the book "AMERICAN KINGPIN, The Epic Hunt for the Criminal Mastermind Behind the Silk Road" by Nick Bilton (Ed. Portfolio/Penguin) is a good read. It tells the story of the young American student Ross Ulbricht who, when he was only 26 years old, and from a distance (through the "Deep Web"), created a virtual drug trade network, which moved more than 1.2 billion dollars, using the following elements (available to everyone): (i) the Tor browser, which allowed him to explore the Deep Web from anonymity, (ii) Bitcoins, a secure and difficult-to-trace virtual currency, and (iii) the use of cross-border mail as a distributor.

use in the recognition of X-ray images, Big Data analysis to apply Rights of Intellectual Property (IPR), just to name a few.

9.10 Trafficking Cultural Property

Culture is a fundamental element in peoples' identity. A civilization where there is no vestige of representations relative to itself, of past (or present) life which identifies the place or people that are part of what is known as society would be inconceivable. The term culture is directly related to "Cultural Heritage," which according to Askerud and Clément corresponds to "a great range of objects or artifacts that constitute the expression of a specific culture and that stand out either because there are not many of them, or because of the craftsmanship with which they were made, or because they possess unique characteristics of such culture."[25]

The importance attached to cultural property and the protection of cultural heritage is not a recent phenomenon. Hugo Grotius, in his masterpiece "On the Law of War and Peace," quotes the famous historian Polybius (c. 203 B.C. - 120 B. C.), who refers to the unnecessary destruction of objects such as porticoes, temples, statues and all other elegant works and art monuments, even in times of war, as "brutal rage" and "madness to destroy things."

Until the nineteenth century, legal tools related to cultural property were limited to isolated bilateral or regional multilateral agreements. However, in the twentieth century, specifically since 1972, UNESCO in its "Convention on the Means of Prohibiting and Preventing the Illicit Import, Export and Transfer of Ownership of Cultural Property,"[26] generated an extraordinary global shift, clarifying concepts and adopting the term "Cultural Heritage" to refer to property that for each state, based on religious or secular motives, has archaeological, pre-historic, literary, artistic or scientific value, for example: rare specimens and collections of zoology, botany, mineralogy or anatomy, objects of paleontological interest, goods related to history, antiques that are over 100 years old, ethnological material, goods of artistic interest (paintings and drawings made entirely by hand on any support and in any material, sculpture, engravings, prints and original lithographs, rare manuscripts and incunabula, books, documents and antique publications, objects of furniture that are over a hundred years old and antique musical instruments), also buildings, monuments and elaborated art.

In addition, Article 3 of the UNESCO Convention is particularly important. It states that the import, export, or transfer of ownership of cultural property effected contrary to the provisions adopted under this Convention by the States Parties thereto, shall be illicit.

---

[25] Askerud and Clément (1999).

[26] UNESCO, Convention concerning the Protection of the World Cultural and Natural Heritage. Adopted by the General Conference at its 17th session in Paris on November 16th, 1972.

In this way, it not only criminalizes the exporter's conduct (the trafficker who usually steals the goods), but also the persons who seek to legally import the goods when they cannot prove their legitimate origin, thus providing an additional control for the receiving countries.

In this regard, the Convention provides for and encourages States Parties to establish an "Export Certificate" that must accompany cultural property when it exits the country of origin.

In 1995, the "UNIDROIT Convention on Stolen or Illegally Exported Cultural Objects" was created and it constituted another major step at the international level. It was produced to promote the harmonization and unification of private law at the international level. In this Convention, states focus on uniform management of the restitution of stolen or illicitly exported cultural objects and allow claims to proceed directly through national courts. Furthermore, this Convention concerns all cultural property, not just those inventoried, and states that all stolen cultural property must be returned. UNIDROIT recognizes the importance of private trade in the trafficking of cultural property and establishes the fundamental obligation for buyers to act with "due diligence" and take such steps as are reasonably available to them to determine the lawful provenance of the objects they acquire.

Notwithstanding the established prevention measures, and due to the particularities of these objects, there is a large black market (currently favored by the various dissemination and marketing options offered by information technologies)[27] where these goods are traded illegally.

Every year, thousands of artifacts disappear from museums, monuments, religious temples, etc.; these rage from ancient weapons, paintings, coins, clocks, religious objects to archaeological findings, the latter being a significant percentage of the objects stolen.

The looting of these goods is one of the oldest forms of transnational organized crime widespread worldwide. It is high on the list of priority concerns for international bodies such as the United Nations Organization, the United Nations Educational, Scientific and Cultural Organization (UNESCO), INTERPOL, the United Nations Office on Drugs and Crime (UNODC), the International Institute for the Unification of Private Law (UNIDROIT), the International Council of Museums (ICOM) and the World Customs Organization.

Within the framework of the 1977 Nairobi Convention on Mutual Administrative Assistance for the Prevention, Investigation and Repression of Customs Offences, Annex 11 Assistance in action against the smuggling of works of art, antiques, and other cultural property) establishes measures to prevent and suppress the fraudulent export of works of art, antiques, and other cultural property.

The WCO is particularly concerned and engaged in this issue, as international borders have become ideal settings for intercepting stolen cultural objects, and

[27] K. Paul (2018) Ancient Artifacts vs. Digital Artifacts: New Tools for Unmasking the Sale of Illicit Antiquities on the Dark Web, Vol. 7, No. 2, p. 12 https://www.mdpi.com/2076-0752/7/2/12/html. Accessed May 10, 2021.

Customs play a leading role in combating the unauthorized export of these items. It has clearly and carefully observed the obvious links that exist between illicit trafficking of cultural property, organized crime, tax evasion and money laundering.

This is a consequence of the existing profitability of black markets in looted, stolen, or smuggled works of art, where there are art buyers and collectors eager for works and new objects for their collections.

To face this issue, the WCO seeks to generate cooperation and partnership actions with other international and national organizations. For this purpose, it uses tools such as the Regional Intelligence Liaison Offices or RILO network, where member Customs share information on possible illegal activities. It has also created the electronic exchange platform based on CENcomm whose code name is ARCHEO with the aim of preventing fraud in cultural heritage. Information sent through this network is encrypted and protected. The platform aims to enable the exchange of experiences, provide training materials, manuals, guides to identify stolen goods and objects that are being looked for, as well as additional information related to seizures.

In July 2016, the Council issued the "Resolution of the Customs Co-operation Council on the Role of Customs in Preventing Illicit Trafficking of Cultural Objects."[28] which contains concrete measures to counteract the illicit traffic of these objects in the global Customs community and urges countries to conduct an analysis and take action to unify criteria of legislation and current techniques, such as using Export Certificates or revising existing certificates in line with the Model Export Certificate of the United Nations Educational, Scientific and Cultural Organization (UNESCO). With these efforts, the WCO seeks to prevent criminals from destroying the past to guarantee future generations the fundamental components of their heritage and history.

Reference

Askerud P, Clément E (1999) Means of prohibiting and preventing the illicit import: a UNESCO handbook for the implementation of the 1970 Convention. UNESCO Division of Cultural Heritage, Mexico

[28]World Customs Organization (2016) RESOLUTION OF THE CUSTOMS CO-OPERATION COUNCIL ON THE ROLE OF CUSTOMS IN PREVENTING ILLICIT TRAFFICKING OF CULTURAL OBJECTS. http://www.wcoomd.org/-/media/wco/public/global/pdf/about-us/legal-instruments/resolutions/resolution_cultural-objects.pdf?la=en. Accessed May 10, 2021.

Chapter 10
Procedures and Facilitation

10.1 Legitimate Global Trade Facilitation

Since its creation, the WCO has tried to simplify and standardize customs processes. To achieve this, it has focused on the development of programs and rules that lead to trade facilitation without neglecting the due control of customs operations. Undoubtedly, these two factors are in permanent tension: the correct balance of "facilitation" and "control" is essential for the economic growth of WCO members.

Customs administrations play a critical role in the development of global trade and in the economic competitiveness of nations. Applying effective Customs controls guarantees correct collection of revenue and the protection of society.

In this context, the facilitation of legitimate global trade tends to avoid unnecessary obstacles or restrictions to the international flow of goods. It is evident that the business community has benefited from the reduction of delays and costs and is able to enjoy an efficient cross-border flow of cargo.

10.2 The Revised Kyoto Convention

10.2.1 Introduction

Since its creation, in the middle of the past century, the WCO has sought, with success, the harmonization and standardization of customs systems. To accomplish this, several instruments and development areas have been employed, among which the Permanent Technical Committee (PTC) stands out. One of the functions entrusted to this Committee was the design of a globally acknowledged legal instrument that would encompass all detected advancements in the international flow of goods and that could be applied in a standardized and voluntary way by interested countries.

H. H. Juárez Allende, *The World Customs Organization*, Law for Professionals,
https://doi.org/10.1007/978-3-030-85296-2_10

In the past, international trade operators who conducted business in more than one country had to deal with different rules and regulations that entailed additional costs to global trade and transport systems. The amount and complexity of customs requirements discouraged small and medium enterprises to expand their business to foreign markets. Therefore, there was a growing and urgent need to apply simplified and harmonized customs systems at a global level.

In 1969, with the active participation of the United Nations Conference on Trade and Development, the proposal to analyze and prepare an international instrument regarding the harmonization of customs techniques was formally presented. The acceptance of this proposal gave rise to the analysis of comparative law and the systematization of the so-called "best practices." On May 18th, 1973, the draft was adopted as the International Convention on the Simplification and Harmonization of Customs Procedures at the 41st/42nd Council Sessions that were held in Kyoto, Japan. This Convention entered into force on September 25th, 1974.

From then on, this instrument injected the spirit of the international trade of goods, and most customs services worldwide tried to follow its proposals and recommendations whether they had adhered to it or not. Not only were these proposals and recommendations effectively rooted in customs practices, they also showed a logical and systemic structure that was difficult to elude.

Given the increase in global trade and technologic development (particularly in communication) and the need to reduce costs with more modern and efficient Customs, the possibility of revising and updating the Convention began to be analyzed. Five years later the Revised Kyoto Convention (RKC) was announced in Brussels on June 26th, 1999. The RKC incorporates modern principles and concepts designed to enhance the efficiency of the release of goods without neglecting Customs control.

By October 30th, 2020, 124 Contracting Parties[1] have adhered to the Convention among which we find developed and developing countries with socialist and capitalist political systems. Among them we can mention the USA, all European Union Members States (and the EU as a block), Cuba, Japan, China, and Russia, just to name a few.

By joining the Convention, signatories become Contracting Parties and acquire the right to actively participate in the Management Committee where customs recommendations, standards and guidelines are discussed. In addition, signatories undertake the obligation to promote simplification and harmonization of customs procedures and practices and to comply with the Convention's provisions, standards, transitional standards, and recommended practices. However, this does not hinder the sovereign application of national legislation vis-à-vis prohibitions or restrictions of goods subject to Customs control.

When the WTO started their trade facilitation negotiations as part of the Doha Round in 2001, it used the RKC as an important source for the potential agreement.

[1] The updated list is available at: http://www.wcoomd.org/Topics/Facilitation/Instrument%20and%20Tools/Conventions/pf_revised_kyoto_conv/Instruments. Accessed May 10, 2021.

In December 2013, the so-called Trade Facilitation Agreement or Bali Agreement that is specifically discussed in Sect. 10.12 of this chapter was approved.

10.2.2 Historical Background

As aforementioned, since its creation, the Permanent Technical Committee, which had been entrusted with (a) studying customs cooperation-related matters and (b) examining the technical aspects of customs systems, sought the creation of a legal instrument that could uniformly regulate customs matters.

After several years of trials, in 1969 the PTC changed its strategy and proposed analyzing and drafting a structured, logical, and systematic “guide.”

The secret of its success lies here. The “directing” methodology through which hegemonic countries had sought to impose their criteria was abandoned, and the model of “best practices” was adopted, i.e., a rational model based on the comparative analysis of successful experiences. Interested parties could either totally accept this new model or make “reservations” regarding those aspects which disfavored them.

This draft was created under the auspices of the United Nations Conference on Trade and Development.

At this point, the working document of the 41st/42nd Sessions of the Customs Co-operation Council, held from May 15th to 24th, 1973 is worth noting. The Argentine delegation was made up of Attorney Juan J. Sortheix, National Director of Taxes, as principal delegate and Engineer Felipe Manzano, Chief of the National Customs Administration, as deputy delegate.

These sessions were attended by delegates from the following Council Members: Algeria, Argentina, Australia, Austria, Belgium, Cameroon, Canada, Cyprus, Czecho-Slovakia, Denmark, England, Finland, France, Germany, Ghana, India, Indonesia, Iran, Ireland, Israel, Italy, Ivory Coast, Japan, Kenia, Korea, Luxembourg, Malaysia, Mauritius, Morocco, New Zealand, Nigeria, Norway, Saudi Arabia, South Africa, Spain, Tunisia, Turkey, United States, Uganda, Yugoslavia, and Zaire. Bangladesh, Philippines, Khmer Republic, Singapore, and the International Organization of European Communities attended as observers.

Mr. H. Hutter from Germany was the Council Chairperson and Mr. J.J.A. Sortheix from Argentina was the Deputy Chairperson.

The Chairperson of the Permanent Technical Committee, Mr. J. Queloz (Switzerland) presented the reports of the 77th/78th and 79th/80th Sessions and submitted the Draft International Convention for the Simplification and Harmonization of Customs Procedures and the Annexes regarding customs warehouses, temporary importation, and drawback.

It was established that the Convention would be administered by the Council, but its adhesion would be open to any Member State of the United Nations Organization or any of its Specialized Agencies with a view to incorporating the highest possible number of Contracting Parties and, thus, advance on its implementation at a global scale. Contracting Parties could make reservations to all provisions and concepts contained in the annexes. In return, Contracting Parties undertook the obligation of amending their legislation to align it with the provisions therein.

The Draft was then presented at the 41st/42nd Council Sessions held in Kyoto, Japan and was approved as the "International Convention on the Simplification and Harmonization of Customs Procedures." It entered into force on September 25th, 1974.

Amendment

The justification for the Convention's revision is found in the vertiginous changes in global trade practices, communication, transport, and management administrative techniques; in the lack of significant advances in harmonization and simplification of customs practices at a global level; in the reduced number of contracting parties that had accepted its annexes; and in the large number of parties that had made reservations.

The amendment was designed to keep the Convention updated, facilitate its understanding and adhesion, avoid its non-compliance, and set longer terms to comply with its provisions.

The main changes of content and form in the structure of the Convention are the following:

- amendment of the preamble
- obligatory acceptance of the General Annex
- revision of the Specific Annexes
- simplification of the amendment procedures
- incorporation of guidelines to support provisions implementation
- establishment of transitional standards for the implementation of certain rules
- adoption of risk management methods, audit-based controls, advanced information, information technology, joint interventions, among others
- inclusion of definitions of new concepts and clarification of existing ones
- creation of a Management Committee to revise and update the Convention

In addition, the Revised Convention includes not only "customs procedures," but also "customs practices." "Customs procedures" refer to the treatment applied by Customs to goods which are subject to their control, whereas "customs practices" cover other standards that do not directly apply to goods but are, nonetheless, related to customs tasks such as venues licensed for the arrival of means of transport at a country's customs territory, appeals in customs matters, use of information, rights and obligations of persons involved in the release of goods, just to name a few.

10.2.3 General Aspects

Scope

The Revised Kyoto Convention applies to the Contracting Parties' sovereign territories.

Each Contracting Party undertakes to promote the simplification and harmonization of Customs procedures and practices, and to comply with Standards, Transitional Standards and Recommended Practices. However, states may grant greater facilities than those provided for in the Convention.

The provisions of the Convention shall not preclude the application of national legislation regarding either prohibitions or restrictions on goods which are subject to Customs control.

Structure

The Convention comprises a Body, a General Annex, and 10 Specific Annexes. Annexes are divided into chapters and include detailed guidelines that explain how the provisions shall be applied.

The binding Body is made up of a preamble with objectives and principles and the provisions related to scope, structure, management, accession, and amendment of the Convention.

Contracting Parties are also bound by the General Annex. This includes the base principles that are not repeated in the Specific Annexes and consists of 10 Chapters with Standards and Transitional Standards.

The non-binding Specific Annexes cover several aspects of Customs procedures. They consist of Chapters with Standards and Recommended Practices. Contracting Parties may accede to one or several complete annexes or to one or more chapters of an annex. Non-observed Standards and Recommended Practices become binding upon accession to a Specific Annex or Chapter.

All annexes and chapters are accompanied by guidelines that do not form part of the legal text and are not obligatory. They are guiding best practices which are under permanent revision.

Management Committee

The Management Committee is the Body charged with monitoring the implementation of the Convention, and with considering measures that secure uniformity in the interpretation and application.

This Committee is made up of Contracting Parties and its main functions include recommending new incorporations or amendments to the Body, General Annex or Specific Annexes of this Convention. The Management Committee shall inform the Permanent Technical Committee and the Council of its decisions.

The Management Committee shall meet at least once each year. Where a decision cannot be arrived at by consensus, matters before the Management Committee shall be decided by the vote of the Contracting Parties present.

Article 14 provides that upon request of the Contracting Parties involved in a dispute, these parties shall refer the dispute to the Management Committee for its settlement.

Participants
The following may become Contracting Parties to the Convention: (a) any member of the WCO Council, (b) any member of the United Nations or its specialized Agencies, and (c) any Customs or Economic Union.

Acceptance and Reservations
The Body and General Annex are obligatory for joining the Convention. However, each Contracting Party is free to accept all Specific Annexes or just some Specific Annexes or Chapters according to its needs.

To achieve better harmonization of Customs legislation worldwide, reservations regarding definitions or other General Annex's provisions are not accepted. Neither are accepted reservations in connection with definitions and Standards of the Specific Annexes that a Contracting Party had agreed on.

Implementation of the Provisions
Pursuant to the Convention's Article 13, paragraph 1, each Contracting Party shall implement the Standards in the General Annex and in the Specific Annex(es) or Chapter(s) therein that it has accepted within 36 months after such Annex(es) or Chapter(s) have entered into force for that Contracting Party. Additionally, paragraph 2 provides that each Contracting Party shall implement the Transitional Standards in the General Annex within 60 months of the date that the General Annex has entered into force for that Contracting Party.

Paragraph 4 (a) of said Article states that "Where the periods provided for in paragraph 1 or 2 of this Article would, in practice, be insufficient for any Contracting Party to implement the provisions of the General Annex, that Contracting Party may request the Management Committee, before the end of the period referred to in paragraph 1 or 2 of this Article, to provide an extension of that period. In making the request, the Contracting Party shall state the provision(s) of the General Annex with regard to which an extension of the period is required and the reasons for such request."

Paragraph 4 (b) sets forth that the grant of such extension may occur in exceptional circumstances, justifying the decision, and for only one year.

> In exceptional circumstances, the Management Committee may decide to grant such an extension. Any decision by the Management Committee granting such an extension shall state the exceptional circumstances justifying the decision and the extension shall in no case be more than one year. At the expiry of the period of extension, the Contracting Party shall notify the depositary of the implementation of the provisions with regard to which the extension was granted.

Amendments
With a view to granting dynamism to the Convention's amendment process, Article 15 regulates the amendments procedure. Amendments to the Body of the

Convention recommended by the Management Committee shall enter into force for all Contracting Parties twelve months after deposit of the instruments of acceptance by those Contracting Parties present at Management Committee's Session during which the amendments were recommended; therefore, here we find the importance of taking part of this Committee.

Any recommended amendment to the General Annex or the Specific Annexes shall be deemed to have been accepted six months after the date the recommended amendment was communicated to Contracting Parties and shall enter into force six months after the date on which it was deemed to be accepted.

Duration and Entry into Force

Article 17 states that the Convention is of unlimited duration. Nevertheless, the Convention may be denounced at any time. The denunciation shall take effect six months after the receipt of the instrument of denunciation by the depositary. Acceptance of the Specific Annexes or Chapters may be withdrawn at any time, however, the withdrawal of acceptance of the General Annex implies the denunciation of the Convention.

Main Principles of the General Annex

The RKC General Principles state that Definitions, Standards and Transitional Standards shall be included in a "simple" way in the Contracting States' national legislation that regulates Customs Procedures.

The concept of "simplicity" referred to by the RKC is related to the need of simple operative rules that can be understood by all global trade operators, both local and foreign, who conduct business in each country and who need to understand their obligations and the procedures to be observed.

Lastly, the RKC provides that Customs shall institute and maintain formal consultative relationships with the trade to increase cooperation and facilitate participation in establishing the most effective methods of work.

This rule has been broadened by the SAFE Framework of Standards where we find the need to strengthen the Customs-to-Business pillar. To this end, an in important drive is found in Customs Consultative Councils, Customs Rules Councils, and other general discussion forums.

Definitions

The Convention includes a chapter on Definitions that details the scope of its concepts and marks their denotations in depth. The reason for this is that the Convention shall be uniformly interpreted by different signatory states with different languages and cultures.

This chapter is meant to avoid common inconvenient produced by the ambiguity and vagueness of the natural language employed in the wording of this type of instruments.

Thus, 27 fundamental concepts are defined. These, along with the Standards and Transitional Standards shall apply to Customs procedures and practices as provided for in Paragraph 1.1 of the General Annex.

Customs Formalities

This chapter is of key importance as it covers the formalities to be complied with by Customs administration and agents from the arrival of goods at the customs territory up to their release.

In broad terms, we may state that obligations are related to: presenting the goods and the means of transport before Customs, lodging the goods declaration and its supporting documents (trade invoice, import license, certificate of origin, etc.), or presenting securities in their absence if legislation allows it. In addition, the chapter includes standards regarding setting up customs offices and their hours of business, the verification of the goods declaration, the examination of goods, the assessment and collection of duties and taxes and the clearance of goods.

Competent Customs Offices

Customs shall designate the Customs offices at which goods may be produced or cleared. Additionally, it shall determine the competence and the days and hours of business of these offices.

Customs offices in the main ports, airports or border land roads shall usually be responsible for complying with all Customs procedures and may be open 24 h a day for goods to be produced or declared.

The competence of certain customs offices may be restricted in terms of the kinds of transport, e.g., only trains, airplanes, or private vehicles; or in terms of the type of goods, e.g., oil terminals, or bulk goods.

Furthermore, a provision is made for Customs procedures and practices to be performed outside the designated hours of business with costs chargeable by Customs that shall be limited to the approximate cost of the services rendered.

Juxtaposed Customs

It is established that at a common border crossing, the Customs administrations concerned shall operate joint controls, correlating the business hours of those offices.

The advantage of these joint controls is given by the greater cooperation that exists between neighboring officers and their customs territories. Joint customs activities lead to faster and more fluid exchange of information, more efficient control of documents, goods and transport, and lower building and operative costs.

The Declarant

Any person having the right to dispose of the goods shall be entitled to act as a declarant and shall be held responsible to the Customs for the accuracy of the information given in the Goods declaration and the payment of the duties and taxes.

With a view to facilitating customs management, this Standard should not be taken as referring solely to the owner of the goods, but should be interpreted as broadly as possible, in accordance with national legislation, to include the carrier, the consignee, a forwarding agent or Customs broker, and third parties acting on behalf of the owner.

Customs may require any representative acting on behalf of another person to produce evidence for such representation. In case a representative fails to do so, he will be deemed to be acting on his own behalf.

To avoid lack of accuracy the declarant shall be allowed to inspect the goods and to draw samples before lodging the Goods declaration.

The Goods Declaration

Customs shall prescribe the contents of the Goods declaration that may be lodged in paper form or electronically. The data required shall be limited to only such particulars that are deemed necessary for the assessment and collection of duties and taxes, the compilation of statistics, and the application of Customs law.

In support of the Goods declaration the Customs shall require only those documents necessary to permit control of the operation and to ensure that all requirements relating to the application of Customs law have been complied with.

National legislation shall make provision for the lodging and registering or checking of the Goods declaration and supporting documents prior to the arrival of the goods.

The Customs shall permit the declarant to amend the Goods declaration that has already been lodged, provided that when the request is received the Customs have not begun to check the Goods declaration (except upon valid reasons) or to examine the goods.

Special Procedures for Authorized Persons

For authorized persons who meet criteria specified by the Customs, including having an appropriate record of compliance with Customs requirements and a satisfactory system for managing their commercial records, the Customs shall provide for:

- release of the goods on the provision of the minimum information necessary to identify the goods and permit the subsequent completion of the final Goods declaration
- clearance of the goods at the declarant's premises or another place authorized by the Customs

In addition, to the extent possible, other special procedures such as:

- allowing a single Goods declaration for all imports or exports at a given period where goods are imported or exported frequently by the same person
- use of the authorized persons' commercial records to self-assess their duty and tax liability and, where appropriate, to ensure compliance with other Customs requirements
- allowing the lodgment of the Goods declaration by means of an entry in the records of the authorized person to be supported subsequently by a supplementary Goods declaration

Examination of Goods

When the Customs decide that the goods declared shall be examined, this examination shall take place as soon as possible after the Goods declaration has been registered giving priority of live animals and perishable goods.

If the Customs deem it useful, they shall require the declarant to be present or to be represented at the examination of the goods to give them any assistance necessary to facilitate the examination.

Samples shall be taken only where deemed necessary by the Customs to establish the tariff description and/or value of goods declared or to ensure the application of other provisions of national legislation.

Release of Goods

Goods declared shall be released as soon as the Customs have examined them or decided not to examine them, provided that:

- no offense has been found
- the import or export license or any other documents required have been acquired
- all permits relating to the procedure concerned have been acquired; and
- any duties and taxes have been paid or that appropriate action has been taken to ensure their collection.

Lastly, the goods may be released furnishing a security to ensure collection of any applicable duties and taxes in cases where documents or laboratory results are pending or a customs offense has been committed, on condition that the goods are not prohibited or restricted or subject to seizure.

Abandonment or Destruction of Goods

It is stated that repayment or remission of duties and taxes may be granted when goods are destroyed or irrecoverably lost by accident or force majeure while under Customs control (including goods in Customs transit, in bonded warehouse or under temporary admission procedures). In all cases, the repayment or remission may be subject to the satisfaction of the Customs that the destroyed or lost goods had been legally imported and that, up to the time of their destruction or loss, any customs conditions imposed on those goods had been complied with.

In other words, when goods have not yet been released for home use or when they have been placed under another Customs procedure, and provided that no offense had been detected, the person concerned shall not be required to pay the duties and taxes or shall be entitled to repayment when:

- at their request and with the Customs' authorization such goods are abandoned to the National State
- such goods are destroyed or irrecoverably lost by accident or force majeure, provided that such destruction or loss is duly established to the satisfaction of the Customs
- on shortages due to the nature of the goods when such shortages are duly established to the satisfaction of the Customs

Any waste or scrap remaining after destruction shall be liable, if taken into home use or exported, to the duties and taxes that would be applicable to such waste or scrap imported or exported in that state.

The proceeds of the sale, after deduction of any duties and taxes and all other charges and expenses incurred, shall be made over to those persons entitled to receive them or, when this is not possible, held at their disposal for a specified period.

Duties and Taxes

The release of goods and their inclusion in the national economic circulation usually involves the lodgment of a Goods declaration regarding its quality, quantity, and value as well as the payment of the applicable duties and taxes.

National legislation shall determine what duties and taxes have, as taxable event, the importation for home use; the conditions and circumstances when liability is incurred; and the point in time to be considered in determining the exchange rate, the beginning of the liability, and its due date.

The assessment (definition of the amount) of duties and taxes to be paid must be done as soon as possible after the Goods declaration is lodged or the liability is otherwise incurred.

Requirement of Securities

National legislation shall contain provisions that enable the Customs to require a security, as facilitating instrument for the release of goods, to ensure that the obligations arising from a Customs procedure will be fulfilled. The primary aim of a security is to secure the payment of duties and taxes. In other instances, a security may also be required to secure the fulfilment of any other obligations that the declarant or operator may have about a Customs procedure or practice or any other requirements that may be specified by the Customs.

When Customs require a security to assure payment of duties and taxes and any other obligations, the security is generally provided by the person who is liable or may become liable for these obligations. This is usually the declarant. However, in many circumstances Customs will allow the security to be provided by another person, such as a third party who is authorized to deal with the Customs on behalf of the declarant.

The form in which security is usually provided is the deposit of cash or negotiable securities, or given by an approved surety (generally a bank or an insurance company). The Customs may also accept other forms of security, if these provide equal assurance that the obligations to Customs will be discharged.

The Customs shall accept a general security instead of a separate security in each instance to reduce the declarant's costs and to enable Customs to monitor the securities in a more centralized and efficient manner.

Customs Control

"Customs Control" is defined in the WCO Glossary of Customs terms as "measures applied to ensure compliance with the laws and regulation which Customs are responsible for enforcing."

To ensure that Customs can appropriately apply these laws and regulations, all the declared international movements must have a Customs-approved treatment or use.

Customs administrations must apply efficient and effective controls by implementing risk management techniques to simultaneously fulfill the responsibility to collect revenue, implement trade policy, safeguard the public manage the increase in world trade and tourism, reduce Customs personnel, and offer trade facilitation to legitimate traders, travelers, and carriers.

Principles of Customs control promoted in the RKC:

- Implementation of audit-based controls
- Use of risk management techniques
- Compliance measurement and the execution of control programs
- Customs – Trade cooperation
- Staff who are sufficiently trained, motivated, and paid
- Adequate legislation, organization, and procedures
- Mutual assistance among Customs administrations
- Intensive use of information technology

Application of Information Technology

Customs shall employ information technology to support Customs operations, where it is cost-effective and efficient for the Customs and trade. The Customs shall specify its conditions in agreement with trade and these shall be internationally accepted.

With a view to achieving a Customs with less paper, all new or revised national legislation shall provide for:

- electronic commerce methods as an alternative to paper-based documentary requirements
- electronic as wells as and paper-based authentication methods
- the right of the Customs to retain information for their own use and, as appropriate, to exchange such information with other Customs administrations and all other legally approved parties by means of electronic commerce techniques

Relation Between the Customs and Third Parties

A third party is defined in the Kyoto Convention as "any person who deals directly with the Customs, for and on behalf of another person, in connection with the importation, exportation, movement or storage of goods."

The exporter or importer can choose between dealing with the Customs directly or appointing a third party to act on their behalf.

Availability of Information, Decisions, and Rulings

The Customs shall ensure that all relevant information of general application pertaining to Customs law is readily available to any interested person.

At the request of the interested person, the Customs shall provide, as quickly and as accurately as possible, information relating to the specific matters raised by the interested person and pertaining to Customs law. The Customs shall ensure that they do not divulge details of a private or confidential nature affecting the Customs or third parties.

Decisions and Rulings on Customs Matters

At the written request of the person concerned, the Customs shall notify their decision in writing within a period specified in national legislation. Where the decision is unfavorable to the person concerned, the reasons shall be given, and the right of appeal advised.

The right of appeal is a fundamental element of rule-of-law-based legal systems, whereby actions carried out by the state and its executive bodies must be based on existing laws and regulations (Principle of Legality).

The appeal system consists of four levels of escalation:

- right to request the reason for the decision or omission
- right of an initial appeal to the Customs
- right of further appeal to an authority independent of the Customs
- right of appeal to a judicial authority

The right of appeal in Customs matters combined with the obligation to publish all Customs laws and regulations contribute to the predictable and transparent environment that must prevail between the Customs and trade.

The Specific Annexes

The RKC has ten Specific Annexes, each regulates a different Customs procedure. Acceptance of the annexes is not obligatory, and the Contracting Parties may accede to them at their discretion. A Contracting Party which accepts a Specific Annex or Chapter(s) therein shall be bound by all the Recommended Practices, unless it enters reservations.

The Specific Annexes regulate:

- The arrival of goods in a Customs territory
- Importation
- Exportation
- Customs warehouses and free zones
- Transit
- Processing
- Temporary admission
- Offenses
- Special Procedures
- Origin

Guidelines

All the annexes and their chapters are accompanied by guidelines. These guidelines contain detailed information regarding the implementation of the:

- provisions in the annexes
- simplified procedures
- methods of application

Guidelines do not form part of the legal texts; therefore, they must be revised and updated to reflect modern practices.

The Kyoto Convention is one of the most important and influential WCO Agreements. However, although the main Body and General Annex have a high-level of adhesion, reticence to adopt all the Specific Annexes remains. Therefore, work related to its integral adoption must continue, as well as its update for twenty years have gone by since its latest revision.

10.2.4 New Review

During the most recent meetings of the Revised Kyoto Convention Management Committee (RKC/MC), particularly during meetings 16, 17, and 18, a comprehensive review of the RKC was discussed and unanimously approved. Based on the strong arguments during these discussions, the Council approved the setting up of a Working Group for a comprehensive review of the RKC and its Functioning Rules.

The comprehensive review will cover both the structure and content of the Body of the Convention, General Annex, Specific Annexes and Guidelines.

The Working Group on the Comprehensive Review of the Revised Kyoto Convention (WGRKC) is open to all interested WCO members. In addition, the WGRKC may invite partner international governmental and non-governmental organizations, and representatives of the Private Sector Consultative Group, Academia, and other external stakeholders, to attend the meetings as necessary.

Aware that the RKC is the WCO flagship Convention, this review seeks to incorporate latest developments such as: multilateral agreements for the coordination of actions, the creation of globally networked Customs, information technologies, traceability of supply chains, advanced electronic declarations, data standardization, systems interconnectivity and interoperability, electronic signature, big data, blockchain, artificial intelligence, monitoring and follow-up of implementation processes, cross-border electronic commerce, just to name a few.

The RKC update seeks to achieve the following benefits:

i. Keep the preeminence of the Convention as a guide for Customs work worldwide.
ii. Support the compliance with the WTO TFA and other relevant developments (e.g., Integration Agreements with Customs Chapters) suggested after the previous revision.
iii. Adopt efficient amendments mechanisms.
iv. Guarantee the efficiency of Customs procedures to global trade.

10.3 SAFE Framework of Standards

10.3.1 The Paradigm Shift

On February 2nd, 2004, during the 50th Session of the Policy Commission a decision was made to create a High-Level Group to carry on with, and consolidate the excellent work of the "Working Group on Supply Chain Security." This

High-Level Group should incorporate into their work trade facilitation-related matters, modern customs procedures, information and communication technology and risk management techniques.

The Group would be made of a limited number of Customs Directors General of the member states who were committed to the development of instruments and practices to secure the international trade supply chain.

This Group would meet at least once a year, or more frequently, if needed, and would count with the support of specialized Secretariat's staff.

At this point it is worth noting—because it was the key to its success—the High-Level Group's will to maintain its predecessor Working Group's initiative of involving business and other intergovernmental organizations. This guaranteed capturing the correct operative reality from its multiple perspectives. Furthermore, it enabled a holistic and systemic vision of all the factors that impact on the supply chain security.

The private sector[2] requested new rules and standards to replace the great quantity of national rules and requirements that triggered conflict and that were of difficult compliance. Additionally, it requested the coordination of the already adopted international maritime and aviation security measures designed to strengthen the supply chain security.

After thorough preparation and methodic organization, the draft was submitted to the WCO Council which approved it as a Resolution in June 2005, thus giving rise to the "SAFE Framework of Standards to Secure and Facilitate Global Trade," or SAFE Framework of Standards as it is usually referred to.

This unique international instrument was the starting point of modern rules regarding supply chain security, and marked the beginning of a novel, integral and holistic approach for the control of goods. This approach takes care of the entire supply chain, from the exporter sending the merchandise to the importer receiving it. Additionally, it acknowledges the importance of a closer relation between Customs and Business.[3]

---

[2]The weak point in the development of the SAFE Framework of Standards was the lack of participation of SMEs. Multinational enterprises had been represented all along, therefore they had the opportunity of expressing their opinions and needs; however, SMEs had not been able to do for there was no international organization which could act on their behalf other than the International Chamber of Commerce was already part of the Consultative Group.

[3]The analysis of delays in logistics carried out by the renowned cargo transport company "Maersk" in 2014 evidenced a huge opportunity for improvement which led the shipping company to establish a strategic partnership with IMB (International Business Machines Corp). The result was "TradeLens," a blockchain-enabled supply chain digital platform that allows the follow-up in real time of cargo and documents. "TradeLens" seeks to become the traceability standard of the maritime logistics chain. TradeLens Ecosystems currently operate in six continents and include more than 92 operators in ports and terminals worldwide (this represents around 234 seaports). Five of the six largest maritime shippers have already joined TradeLens. In addition, Customs authorities in Canada, Saudi Arabia, Azerbaijan, United Arab Emirates, Singapore, The Netherlands, Bahrein, Russia, Ghana, and Peru are exploring the benefits of this platform. Its efficiency has already been proven by the millions of operations carried out through this technological framework. Furthermore, the possibility of its adoption as an international standard has risen following the decision of transforming it into an open platform in which big players are already participating.

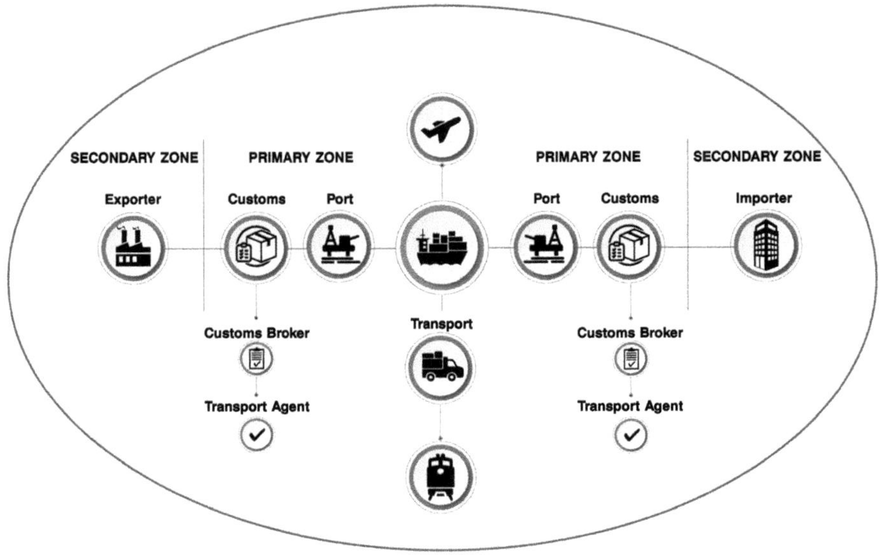

Fig. 10.1 Supply chain. **Source:** Author's elaboration

It represents a true **"paradigm shift"** whereby the vision ceases to be stepped (importer country/exporter country) to become holistic. This approach seeks to secure the entire process from the exporter's factory to the importer's warehouse (see Fig. 10.1).

This paradigm shift produced a substantial turn regarding the approach of customs challenges enabling dealing with these issues in a more holistic and systematic way.

The Systemic Method

At this point, and to have a better understanding of the issue under analysis, we shall resort to the methodology proposed by Dr. Mario Bunge, an expert in research and scientific research methods. He has developed a useful methodology to understand complex systems like the one we discuss here (supply chain and its traceability) which is related to the so-called General System Theory.

In his masterpiece, Treatise on Basic Philosophy, volume II, Ontology, A World of Systems,[4] the Argentinian epistemologist and philosopher Dr. Mario Bunge explains that everything (material and immaterial) is either a system or a component of a system (excluding the Universe which is the only system that does not form part of any other system but comprises all other systems). Dr. Bunge defines a system as a set of interrelated and structured elements which has its own functioning mechanism. Each system has peculiar (emergent) properties in which the whole is not equal to the sum of its parts.

[4]Treatise on Basic Philosophy. Vol. 4: Ontology II: A World of Systems. (1979) D. Reidel Publishing Company.

Research into a concrete system requires building a **CESM** model, i.e., the description of its **C**omposition (its parts or elements), the **E**nvironment (external elements that modify the components of a system or that are modified by them), the **S**tructure (relations among the components), and lastly the **M**echanism (processes that occur within a system).

With this conceptual argument, CESM, Dr. Bunge analyzes everything, from a simple atom (system made up of a set of elements—electrons, protons, etc.—that are interrelated in a structured manner and that interact with their environment), to the most complex biological structure (Man, who as an individual is a system in itself—set of atoms and molecules (mainly H2O and Carbon) that related among themselves and through sub-systems—digestive, respiratory, nervous, etc.—and that form a whole different from the parts that compose it).

In addition, he analyzes social phenomena, from a family (primary social system made up of elements—father, mother, children, grandparents, aunts, and uncles, etc.—who are interrelated through blood and/or legal bonds, and interact with their environment; and its own functioning mechanism), to a large city or a country.

The huge benefit of this method is that it allows us to see the "relations" among the elements comprising the system,[5] its internal organization, hierarchical levels, and environment. This leads us to accomplish a higher level of understanding (of the systems' parts and components) than with the analytical method.[6] We do not give up the analytical method, however, we incorporate the analysis of relations.

Systemic analysis is extremely useful for understanding complex phenomena such as global trade. Global trade presupposes the existence of systemic levels, i.e., a system forms or may form part of a larger system that we can call meta-system or be made up of sub-systems, which may also be made up of smaller systems, and we could continue like this until we reach the most basic components.

With this powerful instrument based on the extended General System Theory, we can analyze each of the aforementioned operations, end-to-end. Thus, we can identify the different components of the supply chain, their relations, the environment that holds them, and their functioning mechanism and can detect possible interference or obstacles in their flow.

Each of these end-to-end operations shall sub-systems of a given country's international trade system which, in turn, shall be sub-systems of the global trade meta-system.

[5]The General System Theory has been widely applied in the field of Natural Sciences (mainly Physics and Biology), in Social Sciences, and fundamentally in specialties such as cybernetic, theory of information, theory of games, theory of chaos or the theory of catastrophes.

[6]The analytical approach has enabled the great development of natural sciences (physics, chemistry, biology, etc.). It remains valuable when the variables at stake are not many or their relations are simple. However, it is not sufficient for addressing complex issues.

This vision is clearly in line with Article 23 of the World Trade Organization Trade Facilitation Agreement that provides the creation of an International Facilitation Committee to monitor the agile and expeditious functioning of trade flows.[7]

10.3.2 Brief Historical Background

Since 2005, work has progressed, at intervals, to update and improve the SAFE Framework of Standards.

The main updates have been:

- 2007: Incorporation of detailed guidelines about the conditions and requirements of users and Economic Authorized Operators (AEO), developed initially in a separate document.
- 2010: Publication of the SAFE Package including all WCO instruments and guidelines supporting the application of the SAFE Framework. The SAFE Package has been regularly updated.
- 2012: Incorporation of new parts 5 and 6 regarding Coordinated Border Management and Trade Continuity and Resumption, and the definition of "high-risk cargo."
- 2015: Inclusion, inter alia, of Pillar 3 to encourage closer cooperation between Customs and other Government and Inter-Government Agencies, ensuring efficient responses to the challenges of the supply chain security. It also incorporates preloading "Advance Cargo Information" (ACI) for air cargo to carry out a first layer of risk assessment; the definition of "container" for the SAFE Framework of Standards; and the update of the relevant text vis-à-vis the evolution of the WCO Risk Management Volumes 1 and 2.
- 2018: Augments the objectives of the SAFE Framework of Standards with respect to strengthening cooperation between and among Customs administrations, for example through the exchange of information, mutual recognition of controls, mutual recognition of AEOs, and mutual administrative assistance.
- In addition, it calls for enhanced cooperation with enforcement government agencies entrusted (e.g., food, medicine, weapons, hazardous materials) and passengers, as well as entities responsible for postal issues. The Framework

[7] More about this subject can be found in the following articles by the author available at: https://www.researchgate.net/publication/339715631 "TRAZABILIDAD DE LA CADENA LOGISTICA"; at https://www.academia.edu/38234604/Trazabilidad_de_la_Cadena_Log%C3%ADstica TRAZABILIDAD DE LA CADENA LOGÍSTICA. In addition, watching the following educational video is suggested: OMC - UN ENFOQUE SISTEMICO PARA EL COMERCIO INTERNACIONAL available at https://youtube/Ugj9PC8nAKY. TN: Both articles are in Spanish and relate to the traceability of the supply chain. The educational video is also in Spanish, and it is called "WTO – A SYSTEMIC APPROACH FOR INTERNATIONAL TRADE."

now also includes certain minimum guaranteed benefits to AEOs, while providing a comprehensive list of AEO benefits.[8]

The SAFE Package has also been updated to include new tools such as: Pillar 1. Practical Guide; updated Guidelines for the Procurement and Deployment of Scanning/NII Equipment,[9] including the Threats and Technology Solutions Orientation Guide and the WCO Recommendation concerning Customs Formalities in connection with the Temporary Admission of Container Security Devices (CSDs);[10] Pillar 2. Strategy Guide for AEO Mutual Recognition; Pillar 3. Coordinated Management Compendium, Single Window Compendium, Joint WCO/ICAO Brochure; other guidelines such as the Data Manual or the CCC Recommendation on the Guiding Principles for Data Quality, among others.

The updated SAFE Framework offers new opportunities for Customs, relevant government agencies and economic operators to work towards the common goal of enhancing supply chain security and efficiency, based on mutual trust and transparency.

Objectives of the SAFE Framework

The SAFE Framework aims to:

- Establish standards that provide supply chain security and facilitation at a global level to promote certainty and predictability.
- Enable integrated and harmonized supply chain management for all modes of transport.
- Enhance the role, functions, and capabilities of Customs to meet the challenges and opportunities of the twenty-first century.
- Strengthen cooperation between Customs administrations to improve their capability to detect high-risk consignments.

[8] World Customs Organization, all versions of the SAFE Framework of Standards are available at: http://www.wcoomd.org/en/topics/facilitation/instrument-and-tools/frameworks-of-standards/ecommerce.aspx. Accessed May 10, 2021.

[9] To illustrate we can mention the following non-intrusive inspection equipment: • Mobile scanners are big machines where trucks with containers enter for imaging control. The truck's and container's interior are observed, and the products are identified without opening the carrier. Different colors are assigned to organic and inorganic materials or narcotic drugs. Only when Customs officials do find something that calls their attention, the truck or its unloaded cargo is physically inspected. In addition, scanning enables the detection of false bottoms designed for concealing goods. • Cabinet or backpack scanners are smaller and allow the observation of baggage or the contents of small packages. They are usually employed at airports. • Fiberscopes are flexible instruments that use fiber optics technology to examine the interior of areas through small openings. They are like modern periscopes but flexible and with a light to illuminate the field of observation. • Busters are pieces of equipment that work measuring the density of materials. It can be placed on surfaces such the pumps, drums, panels, or wheels of a vehicle. It shows densities in a graded scale.

[10] World Customs Organization Guides, Guidelines, and other instruments of the SAFE Framework of Standards: http://www.wcoomd.org/en/topics/facilitation/instrument-and-tools/frameworks-of-standards/safe_package.aspx. Accessed May 10, 2021.

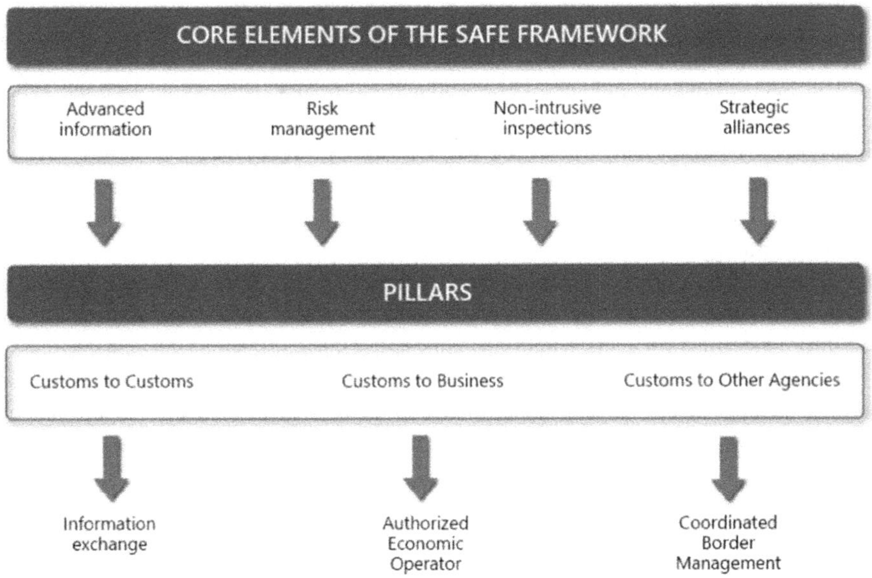

Fig. 10.2 Structure of the SAFE framework of standards. **Source:** Author's elaboration based on information from the WCO

- Strengthen cooperation between Customs administrations, for example through exchange of information, mutual recognition of controls, mutual recognition of Authorized Economic Operators (AEOs), and mutual administrative assistance.
- Strengthen cooperation between Customs administrations and other government agencies involved in international trade and security such as through Single Window.
- Strengthen Customs/Business cooperation.
- Promote the seamless movement of goods through secure international trade supply chains.

10.3.3 Structure

Four Core Elements of the SAFE Framework

The SAFE Framework consists of four core elements (see Fig. 10.2). First, it harmonizes the advance electronic cargo information requirements on inbound, outbound and transit shipments.[11] Second, each country that joins the SAFE

[11] As background, it is worth noting the Standard 3.25 of the Kyoto Convention establishing that "national legislation shall make provision for the lodging and registering or checking of the Goods declaration and supporting documents prior to the arrival of the goods."

Framework commits to employing a consistent risk management approach to address security threats. Third, it requires that at the reasonable request of the receiving nation, based upon a comparable risk targeting methodology, the sending nation's Customs administration will perform an outbound inspection of high-risk cargo and/or transport conveyances, preferably using non-intrusive detection equipment such as large-scale X-ray machines and radiation detectors. Fourth, the SAFE Framework suggests benefits that Customs will provide to businesses that meet minimal supply chain security standards and best practices.

Three Pillars of the SAFE Framework

The SAFE Framework, based on the previously described four core elements, rests on the three pillars of Customs-to-Customs network arrangements, Customs-to-Business partnerships, and Customs-to-other Government Agencies cooperation. The three-pillar strategy has many advantages. The pillars involve a set of standards that are consolidated to guarantee ease of understanding and rapid international implementation. Moreover, this instrument draws directly from existing WCO security and facilitation measures and programs developed by member administrations.

- **Customs-to-Customs**: Customs administrations must work cooperatively with common and accepted standards to maximize the security and facilitation of the international trade supply chain as cargo shipments and transport conveyances move along the nodes of the global trading system.

  The Customs-to-Customs Pillar achieves this objective. It provides an effective mechanism for securing the international trade supply chain against the effects of terrorism and other forms of transnational crime.

  Traditionally, Customs administrations inspect cargo and transport conveyances once it has arrived at their domestic ports. Today, the aim is to incorporate the ability to inspect and screen cargo and transport conveyances before their arrival into the customs territory.

  The central tenet of this pillar is the use of advance electronic information to identify high-risk cargo and transport conveyances. Using automated targeting tools, Customs administrations identify shipments that are high-risk as early as possible in the supply chain, at or before the port of departure.

  Provision should be made for the automated exchange of information. Systems should therefore be based on harmonized messages and be interoperable to be effective and to ensure that the process does not slow down the movement of trade. Customs administrations should use modern technology to inspect high-risk shipments including large-scale X-ray and gamma-ray machines among others. Maintaining cargo and container integrity by facilitating the use of modern technology is also a vital component of this pillar.
- **Customs-to-Business**: Each Customs administration will establish a partnership with the private sector to involve it in ensuring the safety and security of the international trade supply chain. The focus of this pillar is the creation of an international system for identifying private businesses that offer a high degree of security guarantees in the supply chain (Authorized Economic Operators). These

business partners should receive tangible benefits in such partnerships in the form of expedited processing and other measures.

- The following statement from the "High Level Guidelines for Cooperative Arrangements between WCO Members and Private Industry to Increase Supply Chain Security and Facilitate the Flow of International Trade" sums up the necessary relationship between Customs and Business in adding another layer to the protection of international trade: "To the extent that Customs can rely on its partners in the trade community to evaluate and address threats to their own supply chain, the risk confronting Customs is reduced. Therefore, companies that demonstrate a verifiable willingness to enhance supply chain security will benefit. Minimizing risk in this way helps Customs in performing their security functions, and in facilitating legitimate trade."[12]

  Such programs (AEO) push assessments on supply chain security further back into the supply chain by involving the private sector and by requiring increased security at the point of origin, e.g., through video recorder cameras that register the entire boarding process or through satellite tracking of containers.

  This SAFE Framework sets forth the criteria by which businesses in the supply chain can obtain authorized status as a security partner. Such criteria address issues such as threat assessment, a security plan adapted to the assessed threats, a communication plan, and procedural measures to prevent irregular or undocumented goods entering the international supply chain, physical security of buildings and premises used as loading or warehousing sites, security of cargo, means of transport, personnel vetting, and protection of information systems.

- **Customs-to-Other Government and Inter-Government Agencies:** Since the development of the SAFE Framework of Standards in 2005, the importance of cooperation between Customs and other government and inter-government agencies involved in international trade and supply chain security has increased. The WCO has recognized this and has introduced several key tools and instruments especially the Coordinated Border Management and Single Window Compendiums that impact on and guide cooperation between Customs and other government agencies and inter-government agencies.

  The main objective of this cooperation is to ensure that the government response to the challenges of supply chain security is both efficient and effective, by avoiding duplication of requirements and inspections, streamlining processes, and ultimately working toward global standards that secure the movements of goods in a manner that facilitates trade.

  There are a variety of potential forms of cooperation: agencies may share common facilities, equipment, databases, exchange information, and jointly conduct targeting/risk assessment, program validations or inspections. It may

[12]High Level Guidelines for Co-operative Arrangements between WCO Members and Private Industry to Increase Supply Chain Security and Facilitate the Flow of International Trade http://www.wcoomd.org/-/media/wco/public/global/pdf/media/newsroom/communiques/2005/wco-_-framework-of-standards--april-05-def.pdf?la=en. Accessed May 10, 2021.

also include aligning the various agencies' security programs and control measures.

To assist with the implementation of this Pillar, members are referred to the tools and instruments of WCO including but not limited to the Revised Kyoto Convention, Coordinated Border Management Compendium, Single Window Compendium, AEO Compendium and Risk Management Compendium.

10.3.4 Implementation

For this instrument to be implemented, not only will human resources training be necessary (for which there is an assistance program in place), but also an understanding that a phased approach will be required. It is unreasonable to expect that every administration will be able to implement the SAFE Framework immediately.

While the SAFE Framework is considered a minimum set of standards, it will be implemented at various stages in accordance with each administration's capacity and the necessary legislative authority. To this end, it has been structured in a flexible manner to enable Customs administrations to move at different speeds and to implement it in line with their own unique levels of development and conditions.

10.3.5 Benefits

This SAFE Framework provides a consolidated platform which will enhance world trade, ensure better security against terrorism and other forms of transnational crime, and increase the contribution of Customs and trade partners to the economic and social wellbeing of nations. It will improve the ability of Customs to detect and deal with high-risk consignments and increase efficiencies in the clearance and release of goods.

As aforementioned (in a footnote of this chapter), there are important private open platform initiatives that are making the effective traceability of the supply chain real (more than 50% of the containerized maritime transactions are carried out through them). These platforms incorporate all operators in a blockchain that ensures the traceability of all maritime cargo enabling them to see, in real-time, the status of their cargo and to know the estimated date of delivery.[13]

Courier companies behave in a similar way vis-à-vis air cargo. The company receiving a parcel in the exporting country (usually a multinational enterprise), identifies it through a mechanism that allows real-time traceability, automatic

[13] https://www.academia.edu/38234604/Trazabilidad_de_la_Cadena_Log%C3%ADstica, y https://youtu.be/0O2E9bCpKDk. Accessed May 10, 2021.

communication to the consignee regarding the status of the cargo, and the estimated time of arrival at the address of the importing country.[14]

In addition, the following sector benefits are observed:

- Governments

One of the main objectives of the SAFE Framework is to secure global trade against the threat of global terrorism and, other forms of transnational crime. In addition, the SAFE Framework seeks to facilitate global trade to contribute to economic growth and the development of society. This will, in turn, improve revenue collection and the proper application of national laws and regulations.

The SAFE Framework also encourages the establishment of cooperative arrangements between Customs and other government agencies to ensure coordinated border management and control. By putting the necessary measures in place, the SAFE Framework also empowers governments to expand the mandate and responsibilities of Customs administrations in this area.

- Customs

One of the main thrusts of the SAFE Framework is to establish and enhance Customs-to-Customs network arrangements to promote the movement of goods through secure international trade supply chains. These cooperative "networks" will result, inter alia, in the exchange of timely and accurate information that will place Customs administrations in the position of managing risk on a more effective basis. Not only will this improve the ability of Customs to detect high-risk consignments, it will also enable Customs administrations to improve their controls along the international trade supply chain and make for better and more efficient allocation of Customs resources.

These network arrangements will strengthen cooperation between Customs administrations and enable them to carry out controls earlier in the supply chain.

The SAFE Framework also provides for the mutual recognition of controls under certain circumstances. The application of this instrument will enable Customs to eliminate duplication and multiple reporting requirements.

- Business

The SAFE Framework makes it easier for buyers and sellers to move goods across borders as it takes account of modern international production and distribution models.

Authorized Economic Operators (AEO) will reap benefits, such as faster processing of goods by Customs such as reduced examination of goods. This, in turn, translates into time and cost savings. In this regard, entering international AEO mutual recognition agreements, at bilateral, regional, and international level prevents the duplication of security controls and may contribute to achieve facilitation and control of goods in the international supply chain.

[14] https://youtu.be/5K2heb-NFXc and at: https://youtu.be/3vvrxgfMZQw. Accessed May 10, 2021.

These processes ensure AEOs to see a benefit of their investment in good security systems and practices, including fewer documentary examination and physical inspections, and expedited release/clearance of their goods.

10.4 Authorized Economic Operator

In connection with this last section (Customs-to-Business partnership), all economic operators engaged in the transnational movements of goods may request the condition of Authorized Economic Operators (AEO). To this end, they shall comply with several requirements that mark the difference between high-risk and low-risk operators.

The AEO enables enterprises that show the intention of improving the security of the supply chain to obtain benefits in the clearance/release of goods. These benefits are granted because through businesses' collaboration the objectives of risk reduction and facilitation of legal trade are achieved.

Therefore, the Authorized Economic Operator (Qualified or Trusted Economic Operator),[15] , is a "special condition" granted to persons who take part in international trade such as manufacturers, importers, exporters, brokers, carriers, intermediaries, port, airport or terminal operators, integrated operators, warehouses, etc., regarding several criteria such as good demonstrated compliance with Customs requirements, proven commitment with security in the supply chain, and a satisfactory system for management of commercial records.

The AEO originates in Chapter 3, Clearance and other Customs formalities, of General Annex of the Revised Kyoto Convention. Part 7, Special procedures for authorized persons, enumerates special or "speedy" procedures that call for little intervention of the Customs. These procedures apply to operators that regularly import or export goods. However, they are not mandatory as they are designed only for those who meet the qualifications authorized.

The objectives of AEO international initiative aim basically to:

a. Provide more security to the international supply chain.
b. Concentrate the efforts and resources of Customs administrations on those operators that pose higher risk of carrying out illicit activities.
c. Facilitate the negotiation and conclusion of trade transactions of those operators with AEO certification.
d. Facilitate the international flow of goods and with it, the competitiveness and development of society.

[15] Doctrine uses different terms such as "Trusted Economic Operator," "Authorized Economic Operator," or "Qualified Economic Operator." The MERCOSUR Customs Code has adopted the latter as the status reflects the special "qualification" of the operator that meets certain differential requirements in relation to the rest of economic operators.

To be certified as AEO involves the possibility of receiving the benefits of Mutual Recognition Arrangements (MRA). MRAs are established by the Customs or governments of two or more countries (bilateral and multilateral agreements) that formally recognize the legal and operative compatibility of their Authorized Economic Operators programs, thus granting benefits to enterprises that belong to two or more programs. MRAs advantages include, inter alia, fewer inspections of goods, lower costs, reduced time of release or the implementation of simplified procedures to comply with administrative requirements through simplified Customs declarations.

Paragraph 7.3 of Article 7 of the WTO Trade Facilitation Agreement provides that at least three of the following measures shall be granted.[16]

10.5 Single Window

Over the last years, Customs administrations have been developing automated systems with a view to improving trade facilitation and to pursuing effectively their objectives of revenue collection, social protection, and the provision of data and intelligence to government. Evidently, new developments in IT have led to new possibilities to help bring transformational change to the regulatory environment of international trade. These developments have also been about new operative philosophies and architectures that have enhanced convenience and efficiency for the trading community. A clear example of such development is the emergence of the *Single Window* concept.

Through this new tool citizens and businesses receive government services through a single interface. It is visible that through a single window the complex organizational arrangements that go into service delivery are made transparent to the consumers of those services, resulting in increased efficiencies and a reduction in transaction costs.

The distinct characteristic of a single window is that business and transport actors can submit the data required by the different enforcement agencies for the

[16]According to the 2020 edition of the AEO Compendium prepared by the WCO (we suggest its download and study at this link: http://www.wcoomd.org/-/media/wco/public/global/pdf/topics/facilitation/instruments-and-tools/tools/safe-package/aeo-compendium.pdf?db=web), there are currently 97 operational AEO programs low documentary and data requirements: a. low rate of physical inspections and examinations; b. rapid release time; c. deferred payment of duties, taxes, fees, and charges; d. use of comprehensive guarantees or reduced guarantees; e. a single customs declaration for all imports or exports in a given period; and f. clearance of goods at the premises of the authorized operator or another place authorized by the Customs.

From a commercial standpoint, the AEO certification represents a quality seal or mark that enables an operator to be perceived as safe and trusted in customs and financial terms. Moreover, by complying with protection and security standards an enterprise is considered secure, i.e., a globally trusted commercial partner.

application of cross-border controls (importation, exportation and transit of goods, people and means of transport) only once.

The *single delivery of data* seeks to avoid supplying the same information to different government agencies. However, it does not imply the complete submission at once. Traders may add new data at different stages following the operative processes involved in customs clearance.

Certainly, it will take time for Customs administrations worldwide to implement this transformation. In the same way as the single window is being employed by different government areas, it can be used for the complex official processes regulating the cross-border circulation of goods, people and means of transport. The trade community strongly supports a single window approach because it will dramatically simplify the interaction with all border enforcement agencies whereby the entire government apparatus that deals with the movement of goods across borders is re-engineered to meet the specific needs of business.

To support capacity building efforts, the WCO has developed a Compendium on "Building a Single Window Environment." The Compendium has two volumes, and "Executive Guide" and a "Professional Practical Guide."

The United Nations Centre for Trade Facilitation and Electronic Business (UN/CEFACT) issued Recommendation No. 33. This important piece of work explains the single window in terms of data flow between the private and public sectors involved in an international trade operation.

Pursuant Recommendation No. 33 a Single Window is defined as "a facility that allows parties involved in trade and transport to lodge standardized information and documents with a single entry point to fulfil all import, export, and transit-related regulatory requirements. If information is electronic, then individual data elements should only be submitted once."

The WCO members prefer the term "Single Window Environment,"[17] as it highlights the systemic nature of the Single Window as a network of independent facilities of cross-border regulatory agencies and other stakeholders.

In Latin America it is commonly referred to as international trade single window (VUCE, for its acronym in Spanish), a similar name to the one employed by SITPRO, a British non-department public body which carried out the first analytical studies in the field.[18]

To develop an understanding, we can compare it with a virtual company with which we interact through Internet and interfaces that connect to a group of collaborative systems. All this mechanism needs a coordinator or operator and is backed up by solid technical and legal bases.

---

[17] The WCO website offers the following non-official definition: A "Single Window Environment" is a cross border, "intelligent," facility that allows parties involved in trade and transport to lodge standardized information, mainly electronic, with a single entry point to fulfill all import, export and transit related regulatory requirements. This definition almost coincides with that of Recommendation No. 33 of UN/SEFACT.

[18] Davis et al. (2009).

In Volume I of its Compendium the WCO explains that: "The Single Window concept, however, examines regulatory controls through the eyes of the trader and views all interactions between trade and cross-border regulatory agencies without regard to internal separations within government. This approach brings out all the procedural redundancies, any duplication in the filing of information, and the wastefulness involved in the overall effort to move goods across borders. This analytical approach gives rise to a set of solutions that significantly simplify the government-trade interface by reorienting procedures and reorganizing regulatory data requirements."

In its 2019/2020 Annual Report, the WCO informed that 49% of Customs administration members use Single Window systems.

Benefits

- Submission of electronic data at single point of entry. All information related to the process of importation, exportation or transit of goods is lodged online only once and through a single point of entry.
- Round-the-clock service accessed from anywhere. Data can be submitted any time, any day of the year and from any place in the world.
- Less time and lower cost. As a result of the simplification and harmonization of management processes, time and cost are reduced, both for the Customs and for the global trade operators.
- Better logistics. Paperless formalities speed up the release of goods and the supply chain becomes more efficient.
- Increased transparency. Automated global trade processes prevent arbitrary decisions by civil servants and provide better risk control.
- Enhanced legal certainty. Standardization and clarity of requirements for the compliance with international trade obligations gives legal certainty.
- Elimination of paper formats. Digital information replaces the use of paper.
- Information security improves. Using IT technologies, we avoid data damage or loss, even in cases of catastrophes.

International Experience

The guidelines included in UN/CEFACT Recommendation No. 33 describe the most common models for a single window: (i) **A Single Authority** coordinates the activities of all participating agencies to prevent undue hindrance in the logistical chain. (ii) **A Single Automated System**, i.e., an IT system that processes information or coordinates a group of systems that process data to be received or sent; this system may be categorized as an integrated system that operates as a centralized processing unit for the users of each agency, or as an interfaced system that connects with the systems of other agencies; a hybrid system that combines the integrated and interfaced systems could also exist (iii) **An automated Information Transaction System** that acts as a transactions centralizing system (integrated with all authorities) through which declarations and authorizations are received electronically and without fragmentation in a single application. Declarations and requests are processed by the corresponding authority and the replies are submitted electronically to the declarant.

The guidelines in Recommendation No. 33 point out the need of a lead agency to coordinate all stakeholders; describe the rules and instruments that can be used; provide preliminary orientation in connection with practical measures to design and implement a single window; and list key factors in establishing a successful single window.

The functions of modern Customs imply intense and diverse collaboration with other government agencies involved in international trade; and the Single Window is a valuable aid for this.

10.6 Time Release Study

Customs administrations have been making efforts to harmonize and simplify their procedures through international standards such as the Revised Kyoto Convention, the WCO Data Model, and the widespread use of information and communications technology (ICT). More recently, heightened dialog has been established between the trading community and Customs who are working in partnership to deliver common solutions in response to these critically important trade facilitation objectives.[19]

With a view to ensuring that trade facilitation measures are effectively applied, the WCO not only establishes global standards regarding simplification and harmonization for Customs, it also provides operative tools to guarantee secure and fast cross-border trade flows.

One of these tools is the Time Release Study (TRS). The TRS is a strategic and internationally recognized tool to measure the actual time required for the release and/or clearance of goods, from the time of arrival until the physical release of cargo. Its main objectives are: to find bottlenecks or constraints that affect the fluid clearance of goods; to assess new procedures; to estimate the approximate position of a country as a comparative tool.

Specifically, it allows to measure the average time between the arrival of goods and their clearance, the time required for each intervening event between the arrival and release of the goods: by Customs, by country, by region and by type of traffic. This diagnostic tool enables the monitoring and improvement of cargo flow-related processes.

[19] World Customs Journal. The Time Release Study as a performance measurement tool for a supply chain and an international corridor. Shingo Matsuda. http://worldcustomsjournal.org/Archives/Volume%206%2C%20Number%201%20(Mar%202012)/06%20Matsuda.pdf. Accessed May 10, 2021.

The WCO TRS is specifically referenced in Article 7.6 of the WTO Trade Facilitation Agreement (TFA) as a tool for members to measure and publish the average release time of goods.

The WCO developed the original TRS Guide in 2001 to advise its member customs administrations that wished to undertake measurement and comparison of their times of release. Increasingly, the TRS has been considered a useful tool to identify obstructions and it is one of the key performance indicators for measuring effectiveness in border management.

In March 2010, the WCO members shared the view that there was scope for updating the original TRS Guide and decided to commence work to that effect, in response to the procedures and practices currently in place in many countries. As a result, the TRS Guide was updated and relaunched in October 2011 as the WCO TRS Guide Version 2.

In 2018, the WCO published the third updated edition of the TRS Guide,[20] With its new features, the TRS Guide is designed to provide integral support to Customs administrations, other relevant government agencies, and stakeholders of the private sector in their collective search to measure the time of release/clearance at the border and to adopt appropriate policies and to improve facilitation of trade even more.

Among the innovations of this version, we find detailed information on the use of TRS in the implementation, monitoring and evaluation of the TFA. The Guide sets out a concrete approach, including in the context of strategic planning to foster the implementation of the TFA measure by National Committees on Trade Facilitation (NCTFs). In addition, it provides an explanation of the possibility of conducting, as a first step, a simplified TRS, mapping out only that part of the clearance process that directly relates to Customs, and suggests appropriate measures to quickly address shortcomings.

It also includes illustrations of different approaches to conducting TRS (for example, a consecutive or simultaneous TRS at all identified border points), and detailed information on the use of modern technologies in data collection, and analysis for improving the TRS process (e.g., electronic processing systems, Single Window, and GPS-enabled track and trace). This approach endeavors to exploit the growing use of ICT by Customs, other government agencies and private sector stakeholders.

Moreover, it provides guidance on business process planning, and on performance measurement of entry/exit points and related trade lanes, including the development of model business processes with associated flows. The Guide has a future-oriented approach to conducting a Joint TRS in a bilateral and multilateral context, and practical guidance on carrying out a TRS for performance management of regional trade corridors.

In the Annual 2019/2020 Report, the WCO informed that approximately 42% of member Customs administrations have carried out a TRS.

[20] World Customs Organization. http://www.wcoomd.org/en/topics/facilitation/instrument-and-tools/tools/time-release-study.aspx. Accessed May 10, 2021.

This instrument provides benefits to national governments. First, it improves the efficiency of Customs administrations and other government agencies involved in the flow process of cargo related to the importation, exportation, or transit of goods. It also allows Customs and other stakeholders to explore synergies, and to work together in addressing national obstacles which represent a source of delay or problems in the movement of cargo.

In addition, it creates better conditions for accelerating the international movement of cargo thereby reducing transaction costs for traders and encouraging domestic and international investment; it enhances opportunities for expansion of national productivity, leading to the improvement of the country's international competitiveness in the global market; and supports the government's macroeconomic initiatives through growth and development by strengthening efficiency and effectiveness of cross-border agencies.

Furthermore, it offers benefits from the processes' standpoint and their internal regulatory legislation as their efficiency can be diagnosed considering concrete data. Consequently, Customs may adopt measures to enhance their performance, simplification, automation, or amendment of relevant legislation.

The TRS also improves transparency and predictability for the business community about the release or clearance process, thus leading to better inventory management and just-in-time deliveries; and it enables private terminals and warehouse operators, freight forwarders and others to operate and improve their businesses in a dynamically efficient environment.

However, the time release study is not only covered by the WCO. Other international organizations such as the World Bank have produced similar tools or instruments, e.g., Doing Business analyzes the regulations applied to an economy's companies through their life cycle, including starting up, operations, trading across borders and paying taxes.

In the transnational arena, Doing Business registers the time and cost associated to the logistics of goods exportations, measuring the total time and cost (excluding duties) in connection with three sets of procedures: documents, border inspections and domestic transport.

In this regard, expert Yotaro Okazaki from the WCO Research Unit explains that the main problems with Doing Business is that it collects data from contributors through "surveys." Such data are not reliable enough to be used for the scoring and ranking exercises and for the classification of companies presented in the annual report,[21] The gathered information depends exclusively on what is submitted by importers and exporters,[22] Therefore, the methodology of *Doing Business* across

[21] Doing Business Economy rankings https://www.doingbusiness.org/en/rankings. Accessed May 10, 2021.

[22] WCO Research Paper No. 44. Doing Business and its Customs-related issues: A Study on the Trading across Borders Indicators (May 2018). http://www.wcoomd.org/-/media/wco/public/global/pdf/topics/research/research-paper-series/44_doing_business_en.pdf?la=en. Accessed May 10, 2021.

borders (available online)[23] does not make any reference to how each contributor can obtain experimental figures.

In contrast, the TRS Guide establishes more effective methods to accomplish the objective related to measurements, e.g., it states that sampling should be used in cases where it is difficult to capture all the relevant transactions in a defined period, Furthermore, the TRS establishes that measurement of concrete operations should be carried out in four phases:

1. Preparation of the Study
2. Collection and recording of data
3. Analysis of data and conclusions
4. Monitoring and evaluation

In this way, we ensure that the gathered information does not only depend on the primary source that carried out the transaction, but that other actors, such as the Customs authority, are also involved.

To reduce the discrepancies in methodology and results of these tools, in February 2018, the World Bank and the WCO discussed *Doing Business*.

Both organizations addressed issues such as the quality and source of data; the methodology, including how best to convey information on process changes: the measurement of the use of means of transport (land, sea, and air); the treatment of commodities (agricultural and industrial); and the impact of intra-member trade by Customs Unions. The purpose was for Customs to take a more active role. The WCO agreed to provide contact points through whom issues may be raised and comments provided regarding *Doing Business.*[24] It recommended members to look beyond the actual ranking and study the impact of their modernization programs on the underlying score given that such programs often result in enhanced performance that is not necessarily reflected in the comparative ranking.

10.7 Coordinated Border Management

Border control posts are centers of concentration of cargo and people in which several national and international sectors and interests come together. Any initiative seeking to speed up global trade should pay priority attention.

As far as border controls around the world are concerned, all Customs administrations must face increasing volumes of people, goods and means of transport without any corresponding increase in resources for dealing with physical flows of goods and information, In addition, traders and travelers have greater expectations

[23] https://doingbusiness.org. Accessed May 10, 2021.

[24] WCO visits World Bank for discussion on "Doing Business." http://www.wcoomd.org/en/media/newsroom/2018/february/wco-visits-world-bank-for-discussions-on-doing-business.aspx. Accessed May 10, 2021.

for speedier processing and clearance times while governments and society expect border authorities to rigorously apply the law to protect their interests, safeguard the health and safety of their citizens, and ensure national security.

This means balancing trade facilitation with border security to allow legitimate goods and travelers to pass through borders without unnecessary delays.

Coordinated Border Management (CBM) is a possible solution. It was included in the strategic policy of the WCO Council in June 2008 as one of the 10 fundamental pillars for border management in current environment. This approach is based on the coordination of border enforcement, in the context of seeking greater efficiencies in managing trade and travel flows, while maintaining a balance with security requirements.

An essential part of CBM involves dialog between Customs and other agencies at the border as well as between Customs and the business community. Therefore, the World Customs Organization organized the first Inter-Agency Forum on Coordinated Border Management during July 2009. The Forum raised awareness about the CBM concept and its benefits and encouraged governments and individual border agencies to engage one another more actively to ensure better and smarter management of national borders.

On February 22nd, 2017, the Trade Facilitation Agreement (TFA) entered into force. The first paragraph of Article 8, Border Agency Cooperation, expressly provides that authorities and agencies responsible for border controls shall ensure to cooperate with one another and coordinate their activities to facilitate trade. In addition, the second paragraph sets forth that to the extent possible and practicable, each member shall cooperate, on mutually agreed terms, with other members with whom it shares a common border with a view to coordinating procedures at border crossings to facilitate cross-border trade (alignment of working days and hours, alignment of procedures and formalities, common facilities, joint controls, etc.)

As we can see, the first part establishes an "obligation" to coordinate internal agencies, whereas the second part sets forth a "recommendation" or "suggestion" to be carried out with neighboring countries.

In this regard, we must not forget that the World Customs Organization approved the Dublin Resolution in 2013 whereby it absolutely supports the agreement and emphasizes its commitment to the efficient implementation of the Trade Facilitation Agreement. The Resolution further specified that the WCO will assist its members when needed, thus creating the Trade Facilitation Agreement Working Group (TFAWG). The WCO also made available several specific tools for the TFA customs-related provisions (approximately 98%).

Among the WCO instruments related to the TFA Article 8, we should specifically highlight, the *Coordinated Border Management Compendium* which includes the best practices, provisions and principles globally agreed in connection with this issue.

Agencies Involved

There are multiple activities and responsibilities related flows of people and goods at the frontiers. In addition to Customs, we find agencies charged with migration controls, phytosanitary and quality inspections, transport, security border agencies, to mention just a few. Agencies' involvement at the border vis-à-vis their level of intervention or physical presence vary from country to country due to factors such as priorities, geography, and national resources. Consequently, goods and travelers must undergo multiple controls and comply with numerous regulations that may lead to inefficiencies, bottlenecks at the border, and the frustration of trade operators and travelers.

Operative Compatibility
The Trade Facilitation Agreement provides that all border enforcement authorities and agencies should cooperate with one another and coordinate cross-border controls and trade facilitation procedures. This cooperation and coordination may include the alignment of working days and hours, the alignment of procedures and formalities, the development and sharing of common facilities, joint controls, and the establishment of one stop border post control.

Standard 3.25 of the Revised Kyoto Convention provides that the inspection of goods carried out by the Customs should be coordinated with the other competent authorities. The SAFE Framework of Standards follows the same approach of the TFA.

In particular, the TFA sets forth that:

1. Each member shall ensure that its authorities and agencies responsible for border controls and procedures dealing with the importation, exportation, and transit of goods cooperate with one another and coordinate their activities to facilitate trade.
2. Each member shall, to the extent possible and practicable, cooperate on mutually agreed terms with other members with whom it shares a common border with a view to coordinating procedures at border crossings to facilitate cross-border trade. Such cooperation and coordination may include:

   a. alignment of working days and hours
   b. alignment of procedures and formalities
   c. development and sharing of common facilities
   d. joint controls
   e. establishment of one stop border post control

Joint Controls: Simultaneous and Consecutive
There are several models for coordinated border customs controls, however, the international experience reveals mainly two large groups: (i) controls carried out simultaneously, i.e., with actual presence and performance of the competent authorities at the same time, and (ii) consecutive controls, i.e., controls that are first carried out by officers of one country, and then by the officers of the other country, even if they share an integrated common space.

10.8 The Istanbul Convention

Between 1950 and 1970, there was a proliferation in the number of international Conventions, Recommendations, Agreements, and other instruments on temporary admission, creating confusion for the international business community and complicating the work of Customs. In the early 1990s, the WCO decided to draft a worldwide Convention on temporary admission to combine, into a single international instrument, 13 existing temporary admission agreements.

The Convention on Temporary Admission was adopted in Istanbul in 1990 and became known as the "Istanbul Convention." Its objectives and principles are:

- To devise a single instrument for the simplification and harmonization of temporary admission formalities, replacing all the existing Conventions or Recommendations dealing solely or principally with temporary admission. The subjects covered by the former Conventions are now covered by the annexes to the Istanbul Convention.
- Each annex authorizes the temporary admission of goods imported for a specific purpose, e.g., Annex B.1. covers goods for display or use at fairs or exhibitions.
- Goods imported duty-free cannot remain indefinitely in the country of temporary importation. The period fixed for re-exportation is laid down in each annex.
- The goods must be reexported in the same state. They must not undergo any change during their stay in the country of temporary importation, except normal depreciation due to the use made of them.
- Economic prohibitions or restrictions at importation are not applied since they generally relate to goods cleared for home use, thus serving as a national protection measure.

The Convention details the rules applicable to:

- Temporary admission papers (ATA Carnet and CPD Carnet)[25]
- Goods for display or use at exhibitions, fairs, meetings, or similar events
- Professional equipment
- Containers, pallets, packings, samples, and other goods imported in connection with a commercial operation
- Goods imported in connection with a manufacturing operation
- Goods imported for educational scientific and cultural purposes
- Travelers' personal effects and goods imported for sports purposes
- Tourist publicity material

[25] **CPD Carnet**: It is an international customs document which covers the temporary admission of motor vehicles (private and commercial road motor vehicles) in countries where required. The CPD Carnet or **Carnet de Passages en Douanes** is like a passport for a vehicle to enter multiple countries for temporary importation without having to pay the duty and taxes. It serves as a customs declaration identifying the vehicle to be imported and constitutes an international guarantee for the Customs authorities of the payment of any customs duties and import taxes chargeable should the vehicles not be re-exported.

- Goods imported as frontier traffic
- Goods imported for humanitarian purposes
- Means of transport
- Animals
- Goods imported with partial relief from import duties and taxes

Article 4 of the Convention expressly states that unless otherwise provided for in an annex, each Contracting Party shall have the right to make the temporary admission of goods (including means of transport) subject to the production of a Customs document and provision of security.

The Convention creates an Administrative Committee (Article 22) within the scope of the WCO. This Committee shall consider the implementation of the Convention, study any measures to secure uniformity in the interpretation, and any amendment proposed.[26]

The Istanbul Convention entered into force on November 27th, 1993.

10.9 The ATA System

The ATA Carnets System[27] (ATA Convention) replaces the national Customs formalities for temporary admission or transit, thus reducing clearing at each frontier.

Any duties and taxes that may come due are guaranteed merely by the presentation of the carnet and its acceptance by Customs offices. There is therefore no need to furnish a cash deposit or other forms of security.

The ATA carnet covers the transport of goods in Customs transit while en route to or returning from a country of temporary importation and, where applicable, within that country.

For the period of validity of the ATA carnet (normally one year), the goods can be temporarily imported under the same carnet in the Customs territories of as many Contracting Parties, and as often, as the carnet holder wishes.

The seals affixed or the identification of the goods by a Customs office can be recognized by the Customs offices of other Contracting Parties where the goods subsequently pass. This facilitates Customs controls and saves the carnet holder time when the goods cross frontiers.

---

[26] The Istanbul Convention is applied by 71 Contracting Parties on April 16th, 2019. The list of Contracting Parties and the dates of ratification are available at: http://www.wcoomd.org/-/media/wco/public/global/pdf/about-us/legal-instruments/conventions-and-agreements/conventions/pg0289e1.pdf?la=en. Accessed May 10, 2021.

[27] The term "ATA" is a combination of the initial letters of the French words "Admission Temporaire" and the English words "Temporary Admission."

Each country has its own characteristics. Not only the surety may vary, but also the demanded security (25%, 50%, 75%, or 100% of the value of goods) and the types of articles which may be admitted temporarily.

The practical advantages of this system are evidenced in the increasing number of Contracting Parties,[28] and in the number of carnets issued by the International Chamber of Commerce.[29]

The International Chamber of Commerce has been working on the digitalization of the ATA Carnet.[30] The advantages of this modernization include the simplification of customs and border formalities, enhanced security in data transmission, fewer mistakes and claims and less paper.

10.10 Cross-Border E-Commerce

10.10.1 Introduction

The global growth of Cross-Border Electronic Commerce (Cross-Border E-Commerce) has surpassed regular international trade transactions, posed profound challenges to governments, and generated enormous opportunities for global economy operators.

The best "empirical" evidence of this phenomenon is the recent arrival (July 2017) of Mr. Jeff Bezos to the podium of the "Riches Man in the World" (Forbes Magazine). He is the main shareholder (17%) of the e-commerce company AMAZON and has removed Mr. Bill Gates, owner of Microsoft (Window, Office, X Box, etc.), who had been considered the richest person since 2013.

Likewise, we may refer to Mr. Jack Ma, a visionary teacher of English who in 1995 realized that there were no Chinese products on the internet and decided to set up Alibaba, an e-commerce company that processes today more products that eBay and Amazon together. This gives us an idea of how thriving the sector is.

The expectations for these markets to continue skyrocketing are supported by the following contributory factors:

1. Technological advance (broadband, optic fiber, etc.) 5G network (fifth generation of Internet) is expected to expand as from 2020.

[28] The ATA Convention is applied by 63 Contracting Parties on October 23rd, 2013. The list and dates of ratification are available at: http://www.wcoomd.org/-/media/wco/public/global/pdf/about-us/legal-instruments/conventions-and-agreements/ata/pg0233e1.pdf?la=en. Accessed May 10, 2021.

[29] According to the International Chamber of Commerce (ICC) in 2017 over 185,000 ATA Carnets were issued which equals an importation of goods worth 26 billion dollars. Information available at: https://iccwbo.org/resources-for-business/ata-carnet. Accessed May 10, 2021.

[30] https://iccwbo.org/media-wall/news-speeches/at-carnet-ad-vances-towards-digitisation. Accessed May 10, 2021.

2. Growing number of Internet users (from 10,000 in 1987 to 4.1 billion people connected in 2018).
3. Efforts of e-commerce companies to continually improve their processes and products. eBay, Amazon, Walmart, Alibaba, Mercado Libre, and others are permanently offering better after-sale service, product warranty, timely delivery, insurance to protect deliveries, return programs, more secure platforms, promotions, discounts, and other strategies to invite purchasers to come back.
4. The approval of legal frameworks such as the Trade Facilitation Agreement (TAF) that reduces transaction costs between 10% and 15%.
5. Progress in the logistics and transport of parcels (own air fleets, tracking technologies, post-delivery studies with drones, etc.).
6. Diversity and security on online payment. Companies such as PayPal have guaranteed the security of transactions, therefore, guaranteeing consumers' trust.
7. More offers, i.e., more goods. More and more traders are currently operating on the Internet.
8. Other factors of psychological or sociological characteristics (maybe the most important ones, but that exceed the purpose of this book), the maturity time of this form trade, etc.

This commercial environment in constant growth is receiving a rapid, integral, and correct response from the World Customs Organization. In two years the WCO went from the creation of a Working Group to the approval of a guide that was agreed and drafted with contributions of the public sector and the main actors of the private sector: cargo carriers (DHL, UPS, Federal Express, etc.), commercial platforms (Amazon, Alibaba, eBay, etc.), Financial Intermediaries (PayPal, Alipay, Payoneer, etc.), service providers and universities, among others.

The development of a Framework of Standards on E-Commerce concentrates the expectations to offer a globally harmonized approach to ensure the fast delivery of packages across borders while complying with security requirements and fair tax collection.

The main work of the WCO is focused on matters related to the growth of cross-border transactions B2C (Business-to-Consumer) and C2C (Consumer-to-Consumer), excluding of its core concern the B2B (Business-to-Business) and of B2G (Business to Government) transactions. These last two are more important regarding their value but usually take place within the framework of international trade.

Consequently, we could define cross-border electronic commerce as: *A set of purchase/sale of goods carried out through electronic means between a trader and a consumer (B2C) or between consumers (C2C) who reside in different customs territories and which involves the move of products through postal or courier parcels.*

We use the term "cross-border," defined by the Spanish Royal Academy as "that operates beyond the borders. Cross-border trade," as it is a more accurate term than "international" that has different meanings and is, therefore, more ambiguous.

To better restrict the issue under analysis, we point out that we refer to purchase/sale transactions, i.e., bilateral, onerous, and voluntary agreements, whereby two parties undertake the exchange of physical goods (therefore, "services" are exempt) that can be classified by the harmonized system for a price. We exclude from the material universe donations, transfer of office goods, moves, mail, etc. that usually employ these channels (postal or courier parcels).

It is also necessary to consider that these transactions are conducted through electronic means, specifically, on the Internet. The parties involved must reside in different customs territories (for an exportation and importation to exist) and the transport of merchandise must be done through on these means: (a) mail procedure or (b) courier procedure, detailed below:

10.10.2 Classification. Postal System. Courier System

For a better understanding of this issue, we will resort again to the methodology proposed by Dr. Mario Bunge that is related to the General System Theory and that was explained in Sect. 10.3.1 (The Paradigm Shift) of this text.

Research into a concrete system requires building a **CESM** model, that consists of the description of its **C**omposition (its parts or elements), the **E**nvironment (external elements that modify the components of a system or that are modified by them), the **S**tructure (relations among the components), and lastly the **M**echanism (processes that occur within a system).

We should be aware that the systemic analysis is completely useful for understanding complex phenomena such as electronic cross-border trade as it presupposes the existence of systemic levels, i.e., that a system forms or may form part of a larger system that we may call meta-system or be made up of sub-systems, which may also be made up of smaller systems. We could continue like this until we reach the most basic components.

The object under study, cross-border electronic trade, is evidently made up of two sub-systems: The postal sub-system and the courier sub-system. These differ in their composition (government official posts are part of the postal sub-system whereas not officially licensed private companies are part of the courier sub-system); Environment (the Universal Postal Union intervenes in the postal sub-system whereas the Global Express Association does so in the courier sub-system); Structure (in the postal sub-system one entity receives the package at the origin, and a different one receives it at the destination, whereas in the courier sub-system the same multinational enterprise receives the goods at the origin and at destination); and a Mechanism (for a long time the postal sub-system has been regulated by the agreements entered into by the Universal Postal Union whereas the courier sub-system is not harmonized or standardized).[31]

[31] To complement this, we suggest watching the presentations by the author available at: https://youtu.be/3vvrxgfMZQw and https://youtu.be/5K2heb-NFXc. Accessed May 10, 2021.

Postal System

This system comprises the postal companies licensed (official) by the Universal Postal Union (UPU), sellers/exporters (on their own or through virtual platforms), enforcement agencies placed on exit and entrance frontiers (Customs, Sanitary, Electrical Security Agencies, etc.) and purchasers/importers of products. This system is externally influenced by the World Customs Organization (WCO) and by the Universal Postal Union (UPU) that establish provisions and guidelines for their functioning and the development of the industry.

To know the origin of the postal service we must go back to the seventeenth and eighteenth centuries when the exchange of mail was regulated by agreements—mostly bilateral agreements—between nations. By the nineteenth century, this network of agreement became so complex that it prevented fast delivery. For this reason, several projects were implemented among which Sir Rowlands Hill's stood out. He introduced a system to standardize letter sizes. He is also known for the creation of stamps. In 1863 at a conference, delegates from fifteen European and American countries gathered to agree on the main postal treaties. However, as they were unable to collect some individual agreements, they failed to establish a universal postal system.

A new conference was convened in Bern on September 15th, 1874, in which it the creation of an organization for global postal regulation was proposed. Thus, on October 9th, 1874, the General Postal Union was established when the Treaty of Bern was signed. Nowadays, World Post Day is celebrated on October 9th. The organization became a specialized Agency of the United Nations by virtue of an agreement that entered into force on July 1st, 1948. Later, in 1978 the name was changed to Universal Postal Union.

The WCO and the Universal Postal Union (UPU)

The WCO cooperates with UPU through the "WCO–UPU Contact Committee" that coordinates the elaboration of rules and initiatives of common interest for Customs and Posts. Mutual interest issues include, among others, postal security, electronic exchange of information, the implementation of forms CN22 and CN23 and capacity building for their use, and the service of postal deliveries.

We point out two precepts of the UPU Convention, Article 23 and Regulations Article 20-001 (exoneration provisions) that have a huge impact on customs policies:

> 3. Member countries and designated operators shall accept no liability for customs declarations in whatever form these are made or for decisions taken by the Customs on examination of items submitted to customs control.

> 1. Designated operators shall accept no liability for the customs declarations. Completion of customs declarations shall be the responsibility of the sender alone. However, designated operators shall take all reasonable steps to inform their customers on how to comply with customs formalities, and specifically to ensure that CN 22 and CN 23 customs declarations are completed in full, in order to facilitate rapid clearance of items.

We find here that the role of Customs worldwide is limited by a Multilateral Treaty (with "Constitutional" rank in several countries) that states that Official Posts are not liable for the customs declarations that are lodged, and that these are of the exclusive responsibility of the sender/exporter who, being abroad, is not liable in the countries receiving the goods and before whom the customs declaration is filed (e.g., the Argentinian State cannot act against the Chinese seller that fixed a lower price/value than corresponding or who declared goods different to the ones sent).

This differential note is "substantial" vis-à-vis Customs in relation to the other sub-system (courier) that lacks this regulatory benefit.

Notwithstanding, the World Customs Organization (WCO), in addition to the joint work with UPU, has issued provisions suggesting improvements for Customs worldwide through different instruments, for instance:

- Revised Kyoto Convention (RKC). Annex J, Chapter 2
- Baku Declaration concerning E-Commerce (2001)
- Immediate Release Guidelines (2014)
- SAFE Framework of Standards (2005)
- Advance cargo information
- WCO Data Mode

Courier System

In this system parcel delivery is carried out by private companies (e.g., DHL, UPS, FEDEX, among many others) that move more than 500 million small parcels every year and that oversee the entire logistics of packages tracking delivery in real time and advancing information for the controls upon arrival at the destination.

Its origin is very recent and dates from the 60s and 70s of the past 20th century when air cargo was deregulated in the United States. Courier emerged to satisfy the need of fast and guaranteed deliveries that could not be made by postal services.

The Global Express Association (GEA) is the international trade association of the express delivery industry (couriers). The GEA promotes the interests of its members and their customers in international regulatory and public affairs arenas, in close cooperation with national and regional express delivery associations. They serve 215 countries and delivery more than 30 million parcels a day guaranteeing their delivery within the specified period.

This guarantee is unique in the transport industry and enables its customers to operate in wide territories with a high degree of trust. The WCO and the GEA signed a Memorandum of Understanding on June 25th, 2010. The World Customs Organization and the Express Association work hand in hand to comply with the Trade Facilitation Agreement (WTO) given the growing importance of electronic trade for economic growth.

Treatment in the WCO and in the WTO

While the postal system's procedures are usually globally harmonized and standardized, the courier system has not been regulated by international provisions or guidelines so far. Each country regulates their activities on an individual basis and not necessarily in the same way.

Therefore, on February 4th, 2005, the Government of the United Sates (US), through Note TN/TF/W/15, submitted to the WTO Negotiating Group on Trade

Facilitation a proposal to provide specific expedited procedures for expedited shipments (a special procedure). The US expressed the importance of its implementation vis-à-vis the growth of this trading mode.

The United States envisioned a significant enhancement of certainty and consistency for treatment of express shipments through a commitment to provide separate expediting procedures, including individual elements such as providing for import data being submitted in advance of arrival of goods, an absence of weight or value restrictions on what is considered "express," the availability under normal circumstances to secure rapid release, and the availability of "de minimis" procedures for low value shipments.

This proposal (remarkably similar to the rule established by the US in all its Free Trade Agreements, e.g., with Chile, Ecuador, Peru, etc.) was slightly amended by the rest of the WTO member states and later approved as follows:

Trade Facilitation Agreement (AFC)
The TFA entered into force at international level on February 22nd, 2017, and up to now has been ratified by 153 states.[32]

Article 7.8 of said Agreement regulates the procedure of Expedited Shipments:

> 7.8.1 Each Member shall adopt or maintain procedures allowing for the expedited release of at least those goods entered through air cargo facilities to persons who apply for such treatment, while maintaining customs control.
>
> 8.1.b) Submit in advance of the arrival of an expedited shipment the information necessary for the release;
>
> 8.1.f) Assume liability for payment of all customs duties, taxes, fees, and charges to the customs authority for the goods;
>
> 8.2.d) provide, to the extent possible, for a de minimis shipment value or dutiable amount for which customs duties and taxes will not be collected.

As we can see, the first paragraph establishes a direct mandate to be complied with ("hard law") whereas the following paragraphs set forth recommendations or suggestions to be implemented ("soft law").

The Trade Facilitation Agreement is not currently in the state of global implementation. However, through the Trade Facilitation Committee (Article 23.1 of the Agreement) compliance with the agreed terms will eventually be monitored.

10.10.3 Challenges and Creation of Working Group

Now that we know about the two sub-systems involved in Cross-Border Electronic Trade, their differences, and regulatory frameworks, we need to move on to the

[32]The TFA updated ratification status is available at: https://www.tfafacility.org. Accessed May 10, 2021.

"challenges" reported by Customs administrations and that have given rise to a specific approach.

In July 2016, the WCO Council created an ad hoc mixed working group (public and private sectors), open to all stakeholders to address the issue of cross-border electronic trade granting it two years to yield results.

The Working Group was tasked with addressing cross-cutting issues in relation to the growing e-commerce and proposing practical solutions for the clearance of low-value shipments, including appropriate duty/tax collection mechanisms and control procedures that will facilitate and encourage the growth of e-commerce for the benefit of economic and social development.

In a "paradigmatic" and avant-garde manner, this collaborative Working Group (Working Group on E-Commerce—WGEC) gathered all sectors related to cross-border electronic trade:

Customs administrations, international organizations (WTO, UPU, OECD, UNCTAD, UNCITRAL, ICC, etc.), courier companies (DHL, UPS, Federal Express, etc.), trade platforms (Amazon, Alibaba, eBay, etc.) financial intermediaries (PayPal, etc.), universities (UBP, Katholieke Universiteit Leuven), among others.

Four sub-groups were made to face the "challenges" or core problems of this issue:

I. Trade Facilitation and Simplification of Procedures

- Definitions
- Legislation
- Automated systems—Single window
- Advance exchange of electronic data (interoperability, minimum data set, data quality, data privacy)
- Trusted Trader Programme/AEO for electronic sellers, markets, and intermediaries—improvement of facilitation
- Framework/guidelines/rules—harmonization and support to MSME
- Return processes/reimbursement (return)
- Implementation and revision/update of WCO Immediate Release Guide and other related tools

II. Safety and Security

- Product safety
- Illicit trade
- Quarantine/biosecurity
- Dark web/cybernetic security network
- Illicit financial flows—follow-up of financial paths
- Cooperation and exchange of information among Customs administrations
- Smuggling of high-value articles and sensitive environmental goods
- Non-intrusive inspection technologies (NII)
- Revision/update of relevant tools
- Case studies

III. Revenue Collection

- De minimis
- Simplified threshold entry
- Classification, value, and origin-related matters
- Harmonized system, integrated tariffs databases
- Transactional approach versus account-based approach
- Alternative revenue collection models (including impact analysis for industry and government)
- Tariffs and charges
- Cooperation among authorities (Customs and Taxes)

IV. Measurement and Analysis

- Big Data
- Storing and analysis of the work currently carried out by international organizations
- Research and analysis of several e-commerce business models
- E-commerce flow and economic benefits measurement
- Capacity building, awareness-raising and technical assistance in the implementation.

The first meeting of WGEC was held in Brussels from September 21st to 23rd, 2016 and more than 175 delegates on behalf of the industries attended. The second meeting was held in the same city from October 10th to 13th, 2017 with the participation of over 100 delegates. In addition, a permanent virtual working space was created to present and discuss initiatives, under the efficient guidance of the former Director of Facilitation and Enforcement, Ms. Ana Hinojosa.

During the last meeting, the final touches of the document approved in Luxor and presented in Buenos Aires were given. The work related to a Recommendation or Guide of Best Practices remained pending for June 2018.

Luxor Resolution

Before addressing the current Regulatory Framework, we shall point out an important precedent of its development: the abovementioned "Luxor Resolution" that was named in honor of the Egyptian city where the WCO Policy Commission held its session between December 4th and 6th, 2017 and where the Resolution was unanimously approved.

The principles agreed on in the Luxor Resolution are the following:

PRINCIPLE I—Advance Electronic Data and Risk Management

Regulatory frameworks for the timely and accurate exchange of advance electronic data between e-trade operators and Customs shall be established. These frameworks are meant to secure effective risk management and therefore, Customs control.

PRINCIPLE II—Facilitation and Simplification

Simplified clearance procedures for dealing with the increasing volumes of low-value small shipments/parcels shall be adopted.

PRINCIPLE III—Safety and Security
Government and business should work in partnership in the use of IT, the implementation of non-intrusive inspections and the analysis of risk profiles based on advance electronic data (pre-loading/pre-arrival) to identify and intercept dangerous shipments.

Unfortunately, news shows that several customs offenses are carried out through this form of trade. In the digital world, through the so-called "deep web" countless number of absolutely prohibited goods (narcotic drugs, organs, persons, weapons, etc.) are secretively traded. In addition, modern technologies facilitate their trading; therefore, data analysis and risk management techniques should be improved for early detection.

In this sense, and as aforementioned (Sect. 9.9—Electronic Crime) the story of Ross Ulbricht is paradigmatic. This American university student, aged 26, in less than two years became the leader of a drug dealing digital network that moved over USD 1.2 billion[33] until he was detected, arrested, and sentenced to life in prison in 2015.

The striking characteristic of this case is that he sold narcotic drugs worldwide without moving from the State of San Francisco in the United States. He used the "Deep Web" for his business and to this end he had created the online marketplace Silk Road whereby he sold hallucinogenic mushrooms, heroin, cocaine, LSD, and ecstasy, among other substances and objects. He made the shipments from Holland and exploited the advantages of cross-border electronic trade, mainly the TOR browser (that prevented the identification of his IP) and the cryptocurrencies BITCOIN to achieve the anonymity of his transactions.[34]

PRINCIPLE IV—Revenue Collection
E-commerce operators shall supply advance relevant and necessary electronic data for adequate revenue collection. Governments shall evaluate alternative models of revenue collection to facilitate accurate and efficient revenue collection with minimum intervention (simplified and automated) while enforcing customs controls.

PRINCIPLE V—Measurement and Analysis
Reliable mechanisms to accurately measure and analyze cross-border e-commerce shall be established in close cooperation with international organizations and business stakeholders. In addition, trade statistics shall be facilitated for evidence-based decision making.

PRINCIPLE VI—Partnerships
All stakeholders shall work in partnership to develop trade solutions that satisfy individual and collective needs of all participants of the supply chain.

---

[33] https://www.semana.com/gente/articulo/ross-ulbricht-el-estudiante-que-paso-a-vender-drogas-en-al-red/528711. Accessed May 10, 2021.

[34] For those who would like further information about this passionate and cinematographic story, we recommend the best seller "American Kingpin: The Epic Hunt for the Criminal Mastermind behind the Silk Road Drugs Empire" in which the author investigates Nick Bilton and tells his story.

PRINCIPLE VII—Public Awareness, Outreach, and Capacity Building
Public awareness and communication programs, and appropriate capacity building mechanisms shall be implemented. Thus, ensuring that all stakeholders understand their obligations to com- ply with Customs requirements and other regulations.

PRINCIPLE VIII—Legislative Frameworks
National legislation shall be amended, as appropriate, as a supplement of international instruments, conventions, agreements, and WCO tools and guidelines in order to facilitate cross-border e-commerce, collect revenue and protect society while ensuring high-level work for all economic operators.

As we can see, the agreed principles clearly evidence that studying cross-border e-commerce calls for a holistic and systemic approach that sums up the complexity of this issue an includes participation of all stakeholders.

10.10.4 Framework of Standards on Cross-Border E-Commerce

As aforementioned, we shall now refer to the WCO Session in June 2018 in Brussels (Belgium) where the Council finally approved the draft **Framework of Standards**[35] that had been finalized and presented to several WCO bodies, such as the Enforcement Committee, the Permanent Technical Committee, and the Policy Commission immediately preceding this Council Session.

The Framework of Standards aims to provide reference standards, technical specifications, and global guidelines.

Although the basic Framework of Standards had been developed, there remain much to be done. Hence, the rules were approved but the WGEC's work was extended one more year (until June 2019) to further enrich the Framework and, mainly, to finish the technical specifications and other supplementary items such as case studies and innovations shared by members.

The expectations focused on having an integral Framework of Standards to assist WCO members in developing e-commerce strategic and operational frameworks working in partnership with stakeholders

The Framework shall be supplemented by action plans and timelines to help government develop e-commerce operative programs ensuring a harmonized and fast implementation based on national and regional needs and demands.

Broadly speaking the Framework of Standards promotes:

- A standardized framework for the exchange of advance electronic data between e-trade operators, Customs, and other government agencies to facilitate legitimate

[35] http://www.wcoomd.org/-/media/wco/public/es/pdf/topics/facilitation/instruments-and-tools/ecommerce/wco-framework-of-standards-on-cross_border-e_commerce_es.pdf?db=web. Accessed May 10, 2021.

shipments using risk management dynamic techniques and non-intrusive inspections.
- Cooperation among cross-border e-trade actors, Customs administrations, government agencies and business.
- Simplified clearance procedures and expansion of the concept of Authorized Economic Operator (AEO) to cross-border e-commerce.
- Global standards to provide certainty, predictability, transparency, security, and efficiency to cross-border e-commerce.
- A harmonized approach for risk assessment, clearance, release, revenue collection and border cooperation vis-à-vis e-commerce.
- Transparent and reliable gathering, measurement, analysis, and publication of cross-border e-trade statistics in accordance with international statistic rules and national policy to make informed decisions.

10.10.5 Summary of the Work Carried Out by the WCO

- **Risk indicators for express and postal shipments—Year 2010**

The WCO Risk Management Compendium, volume 2 has incorporated Risk Indicators for Postal and Express Shipments. The indicators listed in the Compendium are used to inspect high-risk shipments that could entail customs offenses (revenue protection, narcotic drugs, security, intellectual property rights, etc.). To protect these controls, access to the document is restricted to members.

- **Joint WCO–UPU Guidelines on the exchange of electronic advanced data—Year 2014**

The WCO and the Universal Postal Union (UPU) have collaborated to jointly develop electronic messages, to permit the pre-advice and pre-clearance of postal items (part of the WCO *Data Model Declaration Derived Information Package*) Moreover, the UPU's Postal Technology Centre has developed an electronic Customs Declaration System (CDS) based on the Joint WCO/UPU Customs-Post EDI message.

- **Pre-Loading Advance Cargo Information (PLACI) for air and postal shipments—Year 2015**

In the 2015 edition of the SAFE Framework of Standards the PLACI (Pre-Loading Advance Cargo Information) rules were included. These rules aim to strengthen air cargo security. The use of PLACI in civil aviation is addressed by the WCO – ICAO Joint Working Group Advance Cargo Information (JWGACI). This joint group with ICAO (International Civil Aviation Organization) was established in 2014. The JWGACI followed a two-phased approach:

Phase I, involved drafting a report on the concept of PLACI, its benefits and implementation cost; Phase II, included a provisional report regarding the practical and technical ways of implementation.

- **Revision of Forms CN22/23 with additional data elements—Year 2016**

Amendments in the shipment forms CN22 and CN23 were included in 2016 with a view to helping Customs adjust risk profiles, obtain more efficient collection of tariffs and taxes when appropriate, and offer better services. The changes included: additional columns in CN22 for the Harmonized System (HS) and country of origin, boxes for "sale of goods" and "returned goods," "reason for export," telephone number or the sender and addressee, and an option S10 bar code; harmonization and alignment of these documents.

Form CN22 corresponds to parcels with weight under two kilos or worth less than 300 special drawing rights (SDR—1 SDR is worth USD 1.43—the rate is daily updated on IMF web). Form CN23 is used for parcels worth over 300 SDR or that weigh more than two kilos.

- **Analysis of alternative models for revenue collection—Year 2016**

Joint work with the Organization for Economic Cooperation and Development (OECD) regarding the exploration of alternative methods for revenue collection (duties and taxes) of low-value shipments. The results were published last year as part of an OECD report called "Addressing the tax challenges of the digital economy."

- **Study Report on E-Commerce—Year 2016**[36]

The WCO circulated a survey to gather information regarding current practices of their members. To identify the present situation based on the results of the survey a Study Report was published. The Study addresses five topics: facilitation; risk management; data exchange/cooperation with e-commerce operators; control and enforcement; and revenue collection.

- **Luxor Resolution on the guiding principles for cross-border e-commerce—Year 2017**

It aims to assist Customs, other government agencies, companies, and stakeholders in the supply chain of cross-border e-commerce, in understanding, coordinating, and better responding to the current situation, and to face the emerging challenges. It describes the guiding principles of cross-border e-commerce and addresses eight key aspects: Advance Electronic Data and Risk Management; Facilitation and Simplification; Safety and Security; Revenue Collection; Measurement and Analysis; Partnerships; Public Awareness, Outreach and Capacity Building; and Legislative Frameworks.

---

[36]We suggest supplementing this text watching the author's lecture available at: https://youtu.be/3vvrxgfMZQw. Accessed May 10, 2021.

- **Communiqué at the Eleventh WTO Ministerial Conference—Year 2017**

The Communiqué strongly reaffirms the WCO's leadership in providing policy and operational frameworks for the effective management of cross-border e-commerce, clearly demonstrates its strong commitment to supporting the WTO's Work Programme on E-Commerce, moving forward.

- **Approval of the Cross-Border E-Commerce Framework of Standards—Year 2018**

It was approved at the WCO Council Session in June 2018 in Brussels. It aims to provide reference standards, technical specifications, and global guidelines and to be an integral.

Instrument to assist WCO member in the development of e-commerce strategic and operative frameworks.

Since June 2018, the Working Group held several virtual and face-to-face meetings to finalize the "E-Commerce Package" that was approved by the Council in mid-2019 and is already in its implementation stage The Package includes technical specifications, definitions, flow charts, data elements, business models, stakeholders roles and responsibilities, revenue collection approaches, implementation strategy, an action plan and capacity building mechanism, case studies of several WCO members as background.

10.10.6 Current Status

Now that the Cross-Border E-Commerce Framework of Standards has been approved, and considering that certain aspects may need to be refined, revised, and amended in the future—as e-commerce evolves dynamically—a permanent amendment mechanism is being evaluated. All WCO members have been requested to contribute with their experiences to enhance the case studies.

Regarding the institutional aspect, in its August 2019 meeting the WCO Council, among other measures, (i) Recognized the need to place electronic commerce the future agendas of the Permanent Technical Committee and the Enforcement Directorate; (ii) Approved the E-Commerce Package with the exception of three annexes (Annex B "Reference Data Set for E-Commerce"; Annex E "Revenue Collection Approaches"; and Annex F "E-Commerce Stakeholders: Roles and Responsibilities"; (iii) Extended the mandate of the E-Commerce Working Group (WGEC) virtually (not face-to-face) until June 2020 (mainly to work on the aforementioned annexes); (iv) Adopted the WCO-UPU Guidelines on the exchange of electronic advance data.

10.11 Globally Networked Customs

In 2008, the WCO Council approved the document "Customs in the 21st Century" based on the strategic vision of the new century. The purpose was to ensure that their members were well positioned to deal with the challenges and opportunities of global trade. Of the ten building blocks of this document, Globally Networked Customs (GNC) is the first one. Moreover, to ensure the GNC success the WCO created an ad hoc Working Group to undertake a comprehensive analysis of the potential to rationalize, harmonize and standardize the secure and efficient exchange of information between WCO members.

Between 2009 and 2012 WCO members have reinforced the ad hoc Group's work in connection with the importance of "connectivity." Furthermore, it has been confirmed that maximum benefits of Customs-to-Customs cooperation can be accomplished more efficiently through the exchange of information, a process which may also benefit other stakeholders.

The standard method involves the use of generic templates that facilitate and improve these processes speeding up the development and application of exchange of information agreements.

This technological interaction must be applied following a regulatory framework; therefore, the subscription of bilateral and multilateral agreements is fundamental.

GNC, which is underlined by enhanced Customs cooperation, provides an overarching framework through which WCO members can apply a common, disciplined and coordinated methodology to develop and perfect strategic and operational blueprints based on WCO tools and instruments.

The "connectivity" between individual WCO members through automated systems at the technical level, in the international realm, can be significantly enhanced through this common and global approach.

Using GNC is voluntary. WCO members may continue to negotiate, develop an agree one-off arrangements. This also applies even if partner countries are using GNC for other exchange of information agreements.

An administration must have national laws which allow for the exchange of information and which protect the information shared with others. Customs must also be prepared to share information electronically using GNC standards.

Obstacles to the implementation usually refer to legal issues, data security and protection concerns, lack of trust, the need to have an organization responsible for the system, the complexity of setting up and financing such a system, and the absence of initial investment funds.

10.12 Trade Facilitation Agreement (WTO)

In December 2013, during the Ministerial Conference in Bali, WTO members concluded the negotiations related to the Trade Facilitation Agreement that is part of the broader "Bali Package." Later, after a detailed legal analysis, on November 27th, 2014, members accepted the Protocol Amendment to insert to the WTO Trade Facilitation Agreement into Annex 1A of the WTO Agreement. This landmark agreement that fosters the growth of global trade entered into force on February 22nd, 2017, and because of its characteristics it will specially addressed in this book.

10.12.1 Historical Background: Evolution

On October 30th, 1947, the General Agreement on Tariffs and Trade (GATT) was signed. This gave rise to a series of multilateral meetings to promote international trade among which we should point out the so-called Uruguay Round. This Round began in 1986 and concluded in 1996 in Marrakech (Morocco) when the World Trade Organization was formally established.

Within the framework of these multilateral meetings, on occasion of the Ministerial Meeting held in Singapore in December 1996 some WTO members requested undertaking exploratory and analytical work on the simplification of trade procedures (paragraph 21 of the declaration).

In 2001, the Doha (Qatar) Round began with the aim to achieve major reform on the international trading system through the introduction of lower trade barriers. Therefore, in July 2004 WTO members were requested to clarify and improve **Article V of the GATT** (Freedom of Transit), **Article VIII** (Fees and Formalities Connected with Importation and Exploration), and **Article X** (Publication and Administration of Trade Regulations). On October 12th, 2004, the Trade Negotiations Committee set up the Negotiating Group on Trade Facilitation (NGTF) that was the body charged with receiving and organizing multiple proposals.

During the first year more than 50 written proposals were received. The first ones were related to Article X of the GATT that was considered the "easiest" of the three as the majority agreed on the importance of "transparency." Proposals concerning Article VIII of the GATT followed some months later. The last issue to be dealt with was Article V on freedom of transit.[37]

The first WTO "Draft Consolidated Negotiating Text" on trade facilitation was distributed in December 2009. It had around 1700 square brackets which evidenced the numerous areas of disagreement. This number continued to rise during the first round of the text negotiations to reach a zenith of 2200 brackets. Afterwards the

[37] See on the WTO Official website the working document: "The long and winding road: How WTO Members finally reached a Trade Facilitation Agreement" by Nora Neufeld available at: https://www.wto.org/spanish/res_s/reser_s/ersd201406_s.htm. Accessed May 10, 2021.

trend reverted, and the numbers started to decrease. To speed up the process, the NGTF Chairperson appointed several facilitators—all were technical experts of the different delegations—to address specific parts of the text and who worked in parallel. Hence, work notably intensified and the results improved.[38]

Days before the Bali Conference there remained 70 brackets to be defined. These were agreed on after intense negotiations leading to the adoption of the so-called "Bali Package" in December 2013. This Package was the first important agreement among WTO members since the creation of the Organization in 1995.

The Package's most important part for global trade concerns trade facilitation. This part deals with streamlining red tape and speeding up customs clearance. The rest of the package addresses related to least-developed countries, food security, cotton, and the political commitment to reduce export subsidies in agriculture.

In broad terms (depending on the country) there are four stages for the agreement to enter into force: (i) first, members submit national notifications, for this they revise their national legislation to ensure compatibility with the agreement and determine according to which category they will join the agreement; (ii) second, according to their internal organizational structure, members draft the ratification instrument to be approved by their National Parliament and later be endorsed by the Executive Power (subscription by the Chief of State, the Chief of Government or the Minister of Foreign Affairs); (iii) third, member states officially submit to the WTO the ratification notification; and (iv) lastly, as the Agreement entered into force at a global level on February 22nd, 2017, members who submit their ratification after such date will receive individual treatment; in these cases the entry into force of the TFA shall be thirty days after the deposit of the ratification instrument.

10.12.2 Main Aspects

The Trade Facilitation Agreement is divided into three sections:

Section I, distributed in 12 articles, includes provisions to speed up customs clearance and the international flow of goods, and customs cooperation.

Section II contains provisions for developing and least-developed countries providing them more favorable treatment and capacity building for the implementation of the Agreement in connection with the category they choose. Category A: contains provisions that members designate for implementation upon entry into force of the Agreement (or in the case of least-developed members within one year after its entry into force); Category B: contains provisions that members will apply after a transitional period of time following the entry into force of the Agreement; Category C: contains provisions that members will apply on a date after a transitional

[38] See on the WTO Official website the working document: "The long and winding road: How WTO Members finally reached a Trade Facilitation Agreement" by Nora Neufeld, available at: https://www.wto.org/spanish/res_s/reser_s/ersd201406_s.htm. Accessed May 10, 2021.

period following the entry into force of the Agreement and requiring the assistance and support for capacity building.

Finally, Section III states the creation of a Committee on Trade Facilitation (Article 23.1) that will be charged with monitoring and managing the Agreement and for the establishment of National Committees (Article 23.2).

The Trade Facilitation Agreement is one of the WTO agreements subject to the Dispute Settlement Body (DSB).

As we mentioned in Sect. 3.8 (Dispute Settlement Mechanisms) of this text, we should remember that failure to comply with the obligations included in any of the annexes to the Agreement establishing the WTO is understood as a case for annulment or damage. Therefore, it is usually presupposed that all rule violations entail unfavorable effects for other members that are parties to any of the agreements covered by these annexes, and that it would be the member against whom the claim had been made who would have to refute the accusation.

Basically, the DSB follows four phases: (i) the request for consultation that initiates the process and where negotiation and diplomacy prevail (most disputes are solved at this phase): (ii) the establishment of a dispute panel that examines the circumstances and submits their decision to the Dispute Settlement Body, (iii) the appeal which involves the legal analysis of the decision made by the panel, and lastly (iv) the phase of compliance whereby a period is given to comply with the measure, and, in case of non-compliance, sanctions are adopted.

We shall bear in mind that the Panel's or Appellate Body's decisions are of obligatory compliance by the countries involved in a dispute. The "loser" is expected to comply in "good faith," however, when this does not occur the complainant may request the DSB to authorize economic retaliation, e.g., compensation or the suspension of subsidies.

10.12.3 The Role of Customs in Its Development and Implementation

Rapidly, and soon after the approval of the "Bali Package," the WCO Policy Commission approved the Dublin Resolution whereby the WCO committed to back up the TFA and to efficiently cooperate in its successful implementation. The WCO further resolved to assist its members in all necessary aspects, and thus, established a Working Group on the WTO Trade Facilitation Agreement

(TFAWG)[39] developed an online orientation tool for the implementation of the TFA[40] and launched the Mercator Programme.[41]

Evidently, the WCO rather than being jealous for the WTO's interference in affairs of its exclusive competence saw the agreement approval as an opportunity to carry out its programs and initiatives.

Just the WCO orientation website for the TFA implementation evidences that most of the customs initiatives contained in this Agreement had already been developed by the different WCO instruments (more than 40).

In addition, the fact that customs delegations took part in the TFA negotiations shows that customs contents had already been agreed upon and harmoniously received at a global level.

For instance, we can mention the Revised Kyoto Convention (RKC) which had already covered most of the aspects regulated by the TFA,[42] The main difference resides in the biding nature of the WTO's Agreements that the RKC lacks.

This is precisely how the WCO will benefit for many of its standards could be "demanded." Moreover, most WCO members who adhere to the TFA will not face inconvenience to adhere to the RKC later.

Other WCO tools designed to facilitate trade and whose contents have been included in the TFA are, inter alia: The Coordinated Border Management Compendium, the WCO Data Model, the Single Window Compendium, the Revised Arusha Declaration, the Customs Valuation Compendium, the Risk Management Compendium, the Customs Laboratories Guide, the SAFE Framework of Standards.

We can see that although the huge incorporation of customs content into the TFA facilitates its adoption and implementation at a global level, it also involves the need

[39] The Working Group (TFAWG) began in March 2014 and holds regular meetings with delegates from Customs administrations, other border agencies, trade ministries, international organizations (including the WTO), business and Academia.

[40] The WCO included in its website a Guide for implementing the WTO FTA to assist its members. http://www.wcoomd.org/en/topics/wco-implementing-the-wto-atf.aspx. Accessed May 10, 2021.

[41] The Mercator Programme was launched in June 2014 and includes awareness-raising activities at global, regional, and national levels. In addition, it includes personalized support to requesting members which uses the WCO's traditional approach: diagnostic/needs assessment and strategic planning/implementation/follow-up and evaluation.

[42] For example, Standard 9.1 of the RKC General Annex provides that Customs shall ensure that all relevant information of general application pertaining to Customs law is readily available to any interested person. This is consistent with the publication requirement in Article 6.1., paragraph 1.2. The Guidelines in Chapter 9 of the RKC General Annex contain sufficient information to facilitate the implementation of the TFA Article 1.1 regarding the publication of information and of Article 6.1., such as orientation of where the information should be. Published and made available, quality and clarity of information, update and publication, etc. The RKC also provides for consultation with the trade sector and for information related to changes in Customs law to be readily available sufficiently in advance of the entry into force, "unless advance notice is precluded" (Standard 9.2 of General Annex), just to name a few (see the WCO vs TFA comparison at http://www.Wcoomd.org/en/topics/wco-implementing-the-wto-atf/~/media/WCO/Public/Global/PDF/Topics/WTO%20ATF/Analysis%20of%20Section%20I/Analysis%20of%20Section%20I%20November%202014_EN.ashx. Accessed May 10, 2021.

to coordinate efforts to avoid problems of competence and implementation. We should bear in mind that these rules and provisions are the result of international customs cooperation aged in the WCO oak barrels (the Kyoto Convention goes back to 1973.

The best evidence of this is found in Article 23, paragraph 1 of the TFA itself that provides for the creation a WTO Committee on Trade Facilitation and in paragraph 1.5 states that "The Committee shall maintain close contact with other international organizations in the field of trade facilitation, such as the WCO, with the objective of securing the best available advice for the implementation and administration of this Agreement and in order to ensure that unnecessary duplication of effort is avoided. To this end, the Committee may invite representatives of such organizations or their subsidiary bodies to: (a) attend meetings of the Committee; and (b) discuss specific matters related to the implementation of this Agreement."

If this "unnecessary duplication of effort" did not exist, this provision would not have been made.

In connection with the establishment of National Committees of Trade Facilitation provided for in Article 23, paragraph 2 of the Agreement, the WCO approved a Guide[43] ("National Committees on Trade Facilitation. A WCO Guidance") whose standard[44] would be advisable to observe as they are the result of a technical comparative analysis among the different countries that submitted their best practices. This guide was approved within the Mercator Programme by the World Customs Organization during the 4th meeting of the TFAWG, held in October 2015.

The results of the survey published in the NCTF Guide, updated in January 2016 show that out of 78 members that answered the survey, 33 reported that they already set up a NCTF. In at least 19 of these 33, the Customs either chairs or vicechairs the NCTF.

In this regard, Customs are encouraged to play a key role in the NCTF as they are responsible for ensuring compliance with international trade agreements and with national legislation and rules directly linked to multilateral trade rules. Furthermore, as the technical provisions of TFA (Section I, Articles 1 to 12) are mainly customs-related (applying completely or partially 98% of the provisions), the Customs are placed at the core of the national efforts to implement the Agreement.

References

Davis et al (2009) International trade single window: a new conceptual model. SITPRO, London

Treatise on basic philosophy. Vol. 4: Ontology II: a world of systems. (1979) D. Reidel Publishing Company

[43] http://www.wcoomd.org/-/media/wco/public/global/pdf/topics/wto-atf/national-commit-tees-on-trade-facilitation/guidance/nctf.PDF?db=web. Accessed May 10, 2021.

[44] It includes the establishment of: a Focal Point, Terms of Reference for the NCTF, a national roadmap to TFA implementation and an Action Plan to establish said Roadmap.

Chapter 11
Capacity Building

As we have stated throughout this text, the evolution of modern technologies, especially the evolution of information technologies, has drastically and shakily impacted the international trade flow. This constant evolution makes it difficult for unprepared institutions to adapt to this continuous change.

Institutions are a reflection of their human resources: the higher the qualification of their staff, the better their organization performs.

Digitalization, advance information, risk analysis, "big data," interconnectivity between the world Customs, the proliferation of trade agreements and their consequent reforms and normative adaptations, and the evolution of computer systems in all the fields of action, along with many other factors, demand customs officials around the world to be strongly prepared. These elements also demand customs officials to strive for constant training with a well-balanced combination of theoretical and practical content.

Popular wisdom dictates that customs officers, although not accountants, must know how to calculate taxes; although not engineers, must know the production processes and inventory management; although not economists, must know about the components of trade balance and the importance of imports and exports; although not lawyers, must know how to apply administrative, criminal, and commercial laws to perfection; and although not diplomats, must know about the scope of international agreements.

As if that was not enough, now society demands that customs officials: "although not computer scientists, must know about data systems, encryption, and computer security."

As we can see, the areas of training are extensive and diverse. For this reason, the WCO elevated capacity building to the rank of Directorate since it understood that the key to effective customs management is to develop the human resources that drive customs administrations.

In addition to specific technical knowledge in some area of performance (classification, valuation, tax settlement, etc.), it is essential that customs officers acquire a holistic vision of their actions, projecting their work as an integral part of the system

H. H. Juárez Allende, *The World Customs Organization*, Law for Professionals,
https://doi.org/10.1007/978-3-030-85296-2_11

that constitutes global international trade. Understanding the whole will allow them to acquire skills in the parts.

In the customs context, capacity building is commonly understood as the means to develop or acquire the skills, competencies, tools, processes, and resources needed to improve the capacity of the administration to carry out its functions and achieve its objectives. It is a broad and comprehensive process involving all aspects of Customs administration and cannot be tackled successfully on a narrow technical or single-issue basis.

Capacity building requires a facilitating and motivating institutional environment with a responsive organizational model that promotes and rewards training in addition to adequate training infrastructure.

Implementing a learning culture involves the visualization of personnel training and development at each level within the Customs hierarchy, and in each step of their professional career.

The theme for the Fifth Session of the WCO Capacity Building Committee was "Strong People – Strong Organizations: Investing in People as the basis for Organizational Development." This theme reinforces the WCO's strong belief in a people-focus pathway to organizational development

The strategic document **"Customs in the 21st Century"**[1] identifies the need for a professional culture, based on knowledge and oriented towards the staff, where training within the organization is needed to support the competences of efficient and proactive personnel.

In this regard, it may be helpful to present some of the ideas that the Secretary General, Mr. Kunio Mikuriya, expressed in his speech on "Trade Facilitation: Benefits and Capacity Building for Customs," in the framework of the UNECE (Economic Commission for Europe) Forum on Trade Facilitation, held in May 2003 at the United Nations Office in Geneva, Switzerland.

On that occasion, Mr. Mikuriya explained that: "While technical assistance and training for each specific area is important, which many organizations including the WCO had been delivering, capacity building needs to go beyond a series of narrowly focused activities to embrace a more comprehensive and long-term approach designed to address all areas of Customs administrations."

In Mr. Mikuriya's words: "A well performing and ethical Customs administration can make a major contribution to effective revenue mobilization and can assist governments to facilitate trade and investment and increase confidence in the quality and integrity of government institutions, leading to good governance."

[1]The reader is advised to read the entirety of this important document at the following link: http://www.wcoomd.org/~/media/wco/public/global/pdf/topics/key-issues/customs-in-the-21st-century/annexes/annex_ii_en.pdf?la=en. Accessed May 10, 2021. Notwithstanding the above, the essential elements of this new Strategic Guidance for Customs launched in June 2008 are transcribed below: Globally networked Customs; Better coordinated border management; Intelligence-driven risk management; Customs-trade partnership; Implementation of modern working methods, procedures, and techniques; Enabling technology and tools; Enabling powers; A professional, knowledge-based service culture; Capacity building; Integrity.

The WCO Secretariat, following an extensive review of the global market for customs development and considering the development tools it should provide, has established a comprehensive strategy for the sustainable ongoing development of Customs and Border Management Services to meet the demands of member governments for the twenty-first century. This strategy was approved by the Council in 2003 and recognizes the key economic role of Customs, either as a primary or secondary function:

- Manage the international supply chain
- Provide social protection
- Generate economic statistical
- Maintain revenue streams

The WCO Capacity Building Strategy is an ambitious, dynamic, yet pragmatic approach to meet the role of Customs in the twenty-first century. Further, it reflects the need for individual members to take responsibility and ownership for their own development as well as to create and manage their own capacity development programs.

In this sense, it also has a transparent and well-oiled fundraising system from donor entities, and a range of Memoranda of Understanding with multilateral banks that offer their cooperation and financing.

It seeks to equip members with a blueprint to design comprehensive workforce development strategies and programs for Customs administrations as well as pooling methods on the related key concepts such as staffing, recruitment, development and learning, career paths and mobility and performance management.

Customs capacity building consists of developing and improving competencies and skills using instruments and tools specifically created for such purposes, and implementing them in the different areas of customs work. It is about taking decisions and delivering results. Implementation needs not be complicated, but to be successful there must be a strategic, holistic, and structured approach to prioritized, practical, operational activities based on proper needs assessment.

In that sense, the Capacity Building Directorate (CBD) is based on a standardized approach using the following flowchart (see Fig. 11.1):

These are the main and most important principles of the WCO capacity building strategy:

- Political will, leadership, and commitment are essential for successful capacity building.
- Holistic development, which looks at the impact of changes across the whole of the Customs service, must be coupled with a sustainable implementation approach.
- Customs services must be empowered to take full ownership of the capacity building program.
- There must be a steering vision of the results of capacity building, with concrete targets, recognized program management techniques, and measurement of implementation and results.

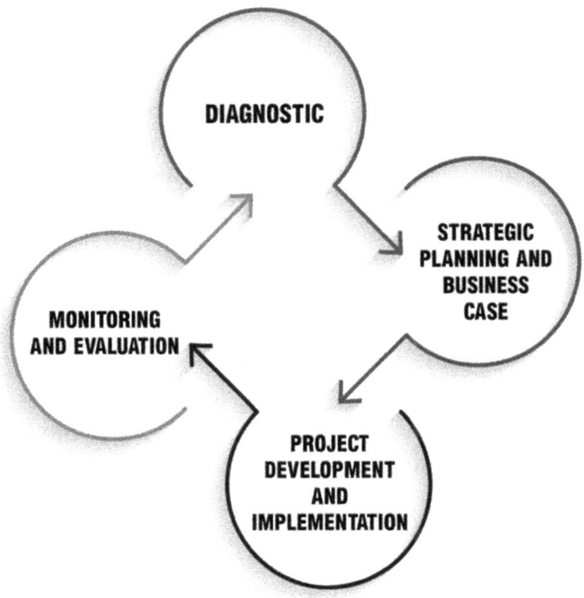

Fig. 11.1 Capacity building flowchart. **Source:** Author's elaboration based on information from the WCO

- Integrity must be an integral part of the capacity building program, implementation plans and projects.
- Partnerships at the global, regional, and institutional levels between Customs, trade, donors, development agents and academia are essential.

To support the implementation of the strategy several policies, tools, and services have been developed, among which we can mention the following:

- The Orientation Package for Decisionmakers— "Support for Customs Reform & Modernization"
- The Regionalization Policy
- The Integrity Development approach
- The Diagnostic Framework
- The Development Compendium
- The PICARD Development Programme
- The Training Development Strategy
- The Leadership & Management Development Programme
- Strategic Planning Support
- Programme Planning Support
- NII Procurement Support
- IT Procurement Support
- Expert Recruitment Support

11.1 Regionalization

The WCO Secretariat has devoted a great deal of attention to improving the quality, relevance and availability of its capacity building activities which led to the development of the WCO Capacity Building Strategy. Within this framework, and as an important link of its training system, this Capacity Building Strategy involves a "regional" approach which aims to encourage neighboring countries to share ideas and actions to achieve the same regional objectives, namely, economic growth and social development.

A regional approach to capacity building has various advantages: it ensures efficient and effective allocation of the WCO's limited capacity building resources and enables the capacity building initiative to focus on the areas where the maximum potential for regional cooperation and synergy lies.

Moreover, the WCO predicts that "regionalized" capacity building will facilitate regional cooperation and ensure greater coherence and synergy of capacity building activities pursued by different donors in each region, resulting in a significant increase in the quantum of funding and technical support currently available.

During its 2003 session, the WCO Policy Commission concluded that the regional approach should be considered a general framework of principles with possible regional variations and should be further developed considering the experience derived from pilot projects. Thus far, the two main examples of the regional approach are: the Regional Offices for Capacity Building (ROCB)[2] and the Regional Training Centers (RTCs).[3]

Regional Offices for Capacity Building

- The ROCB's mission is to assist Customs administrations with their training programs at the regional level. They generally formalize an agreement through a Memorandum of Understanding between the WCO and the government of the host country, helping them to:
- identify more accurate capacity building needs and possible solutions
- enhance the coordination of capacity building activities with regional members and the WCO Secretariat
- monitor projects
- improve networking with donor agencies and relevant organizations

[2]As of October 2020, the 6 Regional Capacity Building Offices are in Azerbaijan, Côte d'Ivoire, Kenya, Thailand, United Arab Emirates and Uruguay.

[3]Currently (October 2020) there are a total of 29 Regional Training Centers: seven in the Asia-Pacific region (China; Fiji; Hong Kong, China; India; Japan; Republic of Korea; and Malaysia), four in the East and Southern Africa region (Kenya; Mauritius; South Africa; and Zimbabwe), three in the Central and West Africa region (Burkina Faso, Republic of Congo, and Nigeria), seven in the European region (Azerbaijan; Hungary; Kazakhstan; Kyrgyzstan; North Macedonia; Russia; and Ukraine), two in the American region (Brazil and the Dominican Republic), and six in the North Africa and Near and Middle East region (Egypt; Jordan; Kuwait; Lebanon; Saudi Arabia; and Tunisia).

- use resources more cost-effectively
- coordinate the use and implementation of WCO tools and practices in the region

The Role and Responsibilities of the ROCB

- To coordinate Customs capacity building activities in the region
- To develop staff within the region to be able to support members with organizational development
- Support the implementation of international standards in customs and trade as reflected in WCO instruments
- To establish projects in individual members of economic regions
- To coordinate the activities of the Regional Training Centers
- To develop, promote, and maintain partnership with key regional stakeholders

Regional Training Centers

The RTCs are independent training units that work in a coordinated manner and at a regional level to cover the regional training needs in customs matters and to manage their group of specialized instructors. They are intended to train customs officers as well as for private sector foreign trade operators.

11.2 Columbus Programme

Since January 1st, 2006, the WCO has initiated a series of capacity-building programs and activities. The Columbus Programme is the largest and most comprehensive Customs Capacity Building initiative implemented to date. The objective of this program is the full implementation of the SAFE Framework of Standards, and other WCO Conventions and instruments, as well as best practices in the field of Customs administrations.

To achieve this development, the WCO needed an administrative reorganization (the creation of the Capacity Building Directorate) as well as to receive financial donations from members for this purpose. In addition, donor coordination and staff allocation were necessary.

The Columbus Programme consists of **three phases**:

Phase I: Needs Assessment

- A strategic assessment based on the WCO Diagnostic Framework tool that has been recognized by organizations such as the UN, OECD, World Bank, IMF, and others.
- A diagnosis carried out by capacity building experts through interviews with all stakeholders, including members of the business community.
- A diagnostic report covering the current situation, a gap analysis of full implementation and suggested ways forward through a series of recommendations.

Phase 2: Planning and Implementation

- Supporting the preparation of a global plan for the modernization of customs or action plans for specific projects.
- Supporting the development of project and business case proposals for submission to stakeholders and potential donors.
- Supporting the preparation and implementation of pilot projects towards sustainable implementation of modernization initiatives.
- Supporting the identification of potential sources of financial support.

Phase 3: Monitoring and Evaluation

The Capacity Building Directorate has developed a methodology for monitoring the progress of members who wish to review their reform and modernization efforts.

The tasks in Phase 3 seek to accomplish several specific objectives:

- Evaluate the implementation of Phase 1 recommendations.
- Evaluate the overall progress achieved in terms of modernization during a given period.
- Evaluate the results of the key actions taken to achieve this progress.
- Evaluate the way in which the reform has been carried out and managed.
- Issue recommendations to improve ongoing modernization efforts.
- Identify lessons learned for future application.

11.3 Picard Development Programme

PICARD is an acronym that stands for Partnership in Customs Academic Research and Development.

In 2005, the WCO held a series of meetings with universities and academic institutions. The representatives of the various educational organizations discussed the possibilities of cooperation between them and the customs administrations in capacity building. When the meetings ended, the creation of the International Network of Customs Universities (INCU)[4] was announced.

Since 2006, the WCO PICARD Programme aims to:

- Increase the professional knowledge and standing of Customs executives and practitioners.
- Encourage academic institutions and Customs administrations to increase their cooperation in the field of Customs education and research.
- Support initiatives related to this collaboration by promoting the development of Customs-specific educational products and research activities.
- Initiate new approaches to Customs whole-of-career development strategies.

---

[4] Available at: http://www.incu.org/.

The **PICARD 2020 Strategy** is a roadmap for promoting research and professionalism in Customs, which focuses on the following areas:

- Standardization building: PICARD professional standards are kept up to date according to the evolution of customs' competences.
- Customs Careers Development Paths: integrated strategic management of human resources and leadership and development of managerial capacities.
- Customs Qualification Recognition: building bridges between training courses for customs professionals and national education systems.
- Management of a proactive customs investigation agenda and a platform at the global and regional level.

PICARD Professional Standards

To meet the demands of an entirely globalized world, it is necessary to develop and apply new management techniques and technologies. Therefore, this new management style requires a different set of knowledge, skills, and behaviors that can only be provided through a more professional approach.

Along with the International Network of Customs Universities (INCU), the WCO developed international standards. Their objective is to provide the organization's "recognition" for the approved curricula and their graduates. At the June 2009 Council Sessions, the WCO approved the Guidelines for the Recognition of University Customs Curricula. Universities that wish to have their courses officially recognized as meeting PICARD professional standards may apply to the WCO.

The PICARD Professional Standards were finalized at the 2nd PICARD Conference and updated in 2019.[5]

In addition, in 2019, the WCO approved the Guidelines for the Recognition of University Customs Curricula[6] to ensure their conformity with PICARD professional standards.

PICARD Conferences

The annual PICARD conferences are academic and research forums where customs officials and academics meet to present their work and exchange ideas on customs and international trade issues, fostering the formation of networks that promote high levels of knowledge exchange.

Since its creation, 14 Picard Conferences have been successfully held. They have provided participants with the opportunity to interact with their government, business, and academic counterparts from around the world. These annual events have been held in Brussel (2006 and 2007), Shanghai (2008), Costa Rica (2009), Abu Dhabi (2010), Switzerland (2011), Marrakech (2012), St. Petersburg (2013), Puebla

[5] http://www.wcoomd.org/-/media/wco/public/global/pdf/topics/capacity-building/activities-and-programmes/picard/professional-standards/omd-normes-prof-uk-basse-def.pdf?la=fr. Accessed May 10, 2021.

[6] http://www.wcoomd.org/-/media/wco/public/global/pdf/topics/capacity-building/activities-and-programmes/picard/professional-standards/wco-recognition-of-university-customs-curricula-guidelines.pdf?la=fr. Accessed May 10, 2021.

(2014), Baku (2015), Manila (2016), Hammamet (2017), Malaysia (2018), and Skopje (2019).

11.4 Leadership and Managment Development Programme

Laying the foundation for the development of future leaders and managers of World Customs is a priority. For this reason, for over 30 years, the WCO has offered scholarships for a specialized training course called the Leadership and Management Development Programme aimed at outstanding senior officials of member Customs administrations to train them as potential leaders and managers of organizational change. The objective is, on the one hand, to create leaders who can improve their ability to lead and, on the other hand, to reform and modernize their organizations.

It is for these reasons that the WCO proposes the following:

- A project that brings together experts from member administrations, academia, and business to contribute to the development of future and potential customs leaders through a focus on the challenges and specificities of the customs operating environment.
- A program based on the components and principles of PICARD professional standards and international best practices in leadership development.

Objectives
Some of the program's main objectives include:

- Development of leadership qualities, managerial skills, and knowledge of Customs managers, improve of their capacity to contribute to the reform and modernization of their administration
- Provision of a well-balanced mix of theory and practice
- Increased ability to contribute to Customs reform through effective leadership
- Greater understanding of the role of Customs managers in sustainable organizational development
- Enhanced awareness of how to become a better leader and manager

Benefits

- Exposes middle managers to modern Customs instruments and practices
- Creates context for participants to build a network for Customs development
- Provides opportunity for participants to develop an adapted solution to meet their administration's challenges in a key area of Customs modernization

Program

- Introduction to the WCO
- Leadership and Management Development Workshop
- Research paper done by participants on a specific reform and modernization challenge in their administration

- Coaching from a WCO secretariat official to find optimum solutions
- Study trip to a modern Customs administrations in a specific area of research

Frequency: Annual sessions in English, French, and Spanish.

Duration: Four weeks at the WCO Secretariat combined with a two-week study trip in a modern Customs administration.

Sponsors: Belgium, Canada, European Union, France, Japan, Korea, the Netherlands, Norway, Sweden, Switzerland, and the United Kingdom.

In addition, a "WCO Orientation Package" for decisionmakers has been developed to help administrations obtain national support for reform processes. It provides a clear picture of modern customs functions.

11.5 Expert Recruitment Support

One of the fundamental tasks of the WCO is to provide technical assistance to its member states. Regarding training, it has developed a global network of professionals organized based on technical knowledge and distributed in accordance with the WCO's regional structure; specifically, its Regional Offices for Capacity Building and Regional Training Centers.

These experts may be drawn from the permanent staff of the WCO Secretariat, from member states, and if necessary, external advisors.

Based on skills, qualifications, and experience, the WCO has identified six categories of experts considering that some may be in more than one category:

1. Diagnostic Facilitators (DF): Senior and experienced customs officials with a solid understanding of the WCO Capacity Building Strategy and the WCO Customs Capacity Building Diagnostic Framework. DFs conduct comprehensive organizational assessments or review organizational reforms and modernization programs.
2. Customs Modernization Advisors (CMA): experienced customs officers who can accompany, guide and mentor organizations towards implementing global reforms and modernization activities and processes (corporate support, facilitation, and oversight functions).
3. Mercator Programme Advisors (MPA): experts with proven capabilities to support administrations in organizational (or governmental) gap analysis, planning and implementation of the WTO Trade Facilitation Agreement.
4. Technical and Operational Advisors (TOA): experts who have strong technical and specific skills in addition to knowledge of a particular field. They interact with senior and middle managers to advise on the organizational development of specific projects or programs. They are under the supervision of the head of the WCO in one of the following areas of expertise:

    - Authorized Economic Operators (AEO)
    - Data Model (DM)

- Intellectual Property Rights (IPR)
- Post Clearance Audit (PCA)
- Revised Kyoto Convention (RKC)
- Risk Managment (RM)
- Single Window (SW)
- Tariff & Trade Affairs (TTA) – Revenue Package
- Time Release Study (TRS)
- Transit

5. Expert Trainers (ETs): Expert Trainers specialize in specific Customs technical subjects such as Valuation, Origin, and the Harmonized System. Specialists with a high level of technical knowledge in a key and specific customs area, generally responsible for providing workshops or seminars. Expert Trainers also specialize in specific initiatives such as WCO Project Global Shield, WCO/UNODC Container Control Programme (CCP), the WCO Strategic Trade Controls Enforcement (STCE) Programme, the WCO COPES (Compendium of Customs Operational Practices for Enforcement and Seizures) Project and the INAMA Project (controlled delivery, investigation and operation planning, and command training), just to name a few.
6. Leadership and Management Development Advisors (LMDAs): specialists in the environment in which Customs operates and experience in management development and training. LMDAs are Customs managers with very strong facilitation and communication skills. They have both knowledge of the environment in which Customs operates and experience in management development and training. LMDAs are customs management specialists with strong communication skills.

By January 2019, there were a total of 698 "experts" (all specialties combined) at the WCO.[7]

11.6 Mercator Programme

The World Customs Organization has the necessary tools and knowledge to assist with the implementation of all legal, procedural, technological, and human resource measures related to trade facilitation.

Among these tools we find the MERCATOR Programme, developed as an instrument to facilitate the implementation of the World Trade Organization "Trade Facilitation Agreement" (TFA) through compliance with guidelines linked to the essential provisions of the TFA, the use of capacity building tools and

[7] http://www.wcoomd.org/-/media/wco/public/global/pdf/to-pics/capacity-building/resources/brochures/expert-guidance/experts_stats.pdf?la=en. Accessed May 10, 2021.

standards developed by the WCO to achieve simple, transparent, predictable, efficient, and coordinated border procedures.

The program was implemented in June 2014 and aims to achieve more effective cooperation among all stakeholders, especially in terms of raising the level of political will to take joint action to progress the trade facilitation agenda, bringing together all relevant government agencies and encouraging, for instance, efficient and coordinated border management, including meaningful partnerships with the private sector. Likewise, the WCO is strengthening its cooperation not only with the WTO through its participation in the National Trade Facilitation Committee, but also with other international organizations whose standards and norms are implemented by agencies present at the borders. This way, the WCO ensures that it supports the effective implementation of the WTO's TFA through a holistic and standardized approach agreed upon at the global level along with other parties involved in cross-border movements.

For those involved in the trade facilitation process, the MERCATOR Programme brings a unique opportunity to work side by side with the WCO to systematically implement measures under the TFA. The experience provides international knowledge and visibility, skill recognition and can provide new management career prospects.

The system is composed of "advisors" (Mercator Programme Advisors - MPA) who are responsible for capacity building missions, as well as for regional awareness among customs, trade ministries, private sector and international organizations emphasizing the TFA and the need to implement it with WCO tools. MERCATOR Programme Advisors are essentially experts in change management who guide, facilitate, or advise on strategic planning and implementation, team building, effective management, human resources management and implementation support.

To be accredited as an MPA, the following stages established by the WCO must be fulfilled:

i. National administrations respond to a WCO request for Customs officers who fill expected criteria, or chose among existing CMAs that show sufficient management skills.
ii. They participate in a five-day WCO accreditation workshop.
iii. Evaluation during an in-field mission with another qualified expert who will proceed according to the following parameters: (a) confirmation of accreditation, (b) recommendation to conduct at least one further infield mission, (c) recommendation to continue in another expert category, or (d) does not fulfill facilitation aptitude requirements.

As the main tool offered to implement the program, there is the "dual-track approach" which comprises a general request for assistance and a specific or "tailor-made" program. The former consists of thorough assistance related to the effective implementation of the TFA of the WTO by way of a customs administration status diagnosis, including recommendations to improve or enhance problems or shortcomings using more than 50 WCO instruments and tools compiled in the Implementation Guide for Section I of the TFA. The second provides a tailored response to a member interested in optimizing an aspect of TFA implementation, e.g., the Time Release Study (TRS), to improve border wait times.[8]

The MERCATOR Programme offers various benefits through its implementation. Originally designed for developing countries and least developed countries (LDCs), it allows countries to request and receive tailor-made technical assistance and capacity building according to their own identified needs to support the implementation of trade facilitation measures. In addition, it provides the necessary assistance to assess their needs with the WCO's expertise and benefits government institutions as they participate in diagnostic missions together with Customs administrations.

The WCO has extensive experience in managing technical assistance and capacity building projects along results-based management principles that meet the interests of these institutions. In this regard, to benefit these entities, priority is given to supporting the implementation of the TFA for countries that have joined in Category C.

In 2015,[9] the WCO recognized that it had to improve resource mobilization capacity; enhance donor coordination capacity; and prioritize efforts to ensure an effective level of absorptive capacity and optimize program and project management capacity. For this reason, the program is committed to donor coordination to make effective and timely delivery of capacity building support to members a crucial area for planning. While some sponsors implement long-term projects designed and planned in detail with project managers, other sponsors may fund "ad hoc" assistance requested by members and prioritized within the planning process. One of the key elements of the strategic planning process is to involve stakeholders and, when necessary, donors. In this regard, the WCO can offer capacity building assistance in issues such as how to engage stakeholders and organize national, sub-regional, or regional donor conferences. Interested development partners and institutions can contact the WCO Office of External Relations to express their desire for cooperation, including financial support for technical assistance and capacity building projects.

11.7 INCU

The International University Customs Network (INCU) is an international non-profit organization that was established to:

---

[8]To understand the importance of the program, keep in mind that in March 2017, the WCO had already organized more than 350 "general" missions and more than 144 "tailor-made" missions.

[9]WCO – OMD. Knowledge Academy – 2015—Trade Facilitation Track. Available at: https://www.eiseverywhere.com/file_uploads/c378e3d96e1a333598c1e0b859ada9dc_KnoweldgeAcademy2015-TradeFacilitationTrack-DonorSupportTF-RichardChopra.pptx Accessed May 10, 2021.

- Promote the academic standing of the Customs profession.
- Promote academic excellence in Customs matters
- Support research in Customs matters and promote the collective interests of its members
- Provide the World Customs Organization and other organizations with a single point of contact with universities and research institutes that are active in the field of customs research, education, and training
- Provide a global resource for governments and the private sector, and an educational source for students wishing to further their knowledge in the field of customs, international trade, and logistics

The INCU prints the World Customs Journal (WCJ). The publication is peer-reviewed,[10] and includes contributions from renowned customs specialists. It is offered to customs professionals, academics, researchers, and students, with the aim of sharing and developing customs knowledge.

The organization has a Management Committee composed of representatives of INCU members, and a Secretariat, based in Canberra (Australia), in charge of the administrative management and coordination of member and affiliate activities.

In support of its administration and with a view to enhancing its academic character, an INCU Advisory Board was formed. It is made up of specialists in customs matters from the public and private sectors.

Membership is free and open to universities, research institutes and customs-related bodies. To this end, Guidelines for the Recognition of University Customs Curricula[11] has been developed for those institutions who wish to join this global network. This document details the specific thematic content required.

11.8 CLiKC!

CLiKC![12] the WCO Training Portal gathers all training-related tools in a single portal. This website offers to the worldwide Customs Community a single-entry point for WCO training activities and a collaborative portal to share and foster Customs knowledge.

Over 250 h of courses on various customs topics are already available in English, French, Arabic, Spanish, and Portuguese. All officials from WCO member administrations can register and access the courses free of charge.

---

[10] Original research and theoretical papers that are submitted are subsequently reviewed using the so-called "double-blind" or "masked" procedure, whereby the identity of authors and reviewers remains unknown to each other.

[11] https://incu.org/resources/memberresources/download-info/wco-guidelines-for-recognition-of-university-customs-curricula-2019-english. Accessed May 10, 2021.

[12] https://clikc.wcoomd.org. Accessed May 10, 2021.

The CLiKC! portal is also used to capitalize and standardize WCO expertise, and manage knowledge created by both in-house experts and accredited experts.

This collaborative platform strengthens Customs training initiatives and networks by creating communities gathered around virtual tools to create, comment and design training contents and strategies.

Access to CLiKC! is free for all customs officers of WCO member administrations. Nominations are submitted through the national e-learning coordinator, a single point of contact designated by the administration to collect registration requests.

CLiKC! is based on the Moodle learning platform ran and coordinated by Moodle HQ—an Australian company that is financially supported by a network of over 60 Moodle partner services companies worldwide—and designed to provide educators, administrators, and students with a single robust, secure, and integrated system for creating customized learning environments.

The Moodle platform is trusted by institutions and organizations large and small, including Shell, the London School of Economics, the State University of New York, Microsoft, and the Open University. Moodle has more than 79 million users at both the academic and business levels, making it the most widely used multilingual learning platform in the world.

As a complement, and to provide training to interested parties who are not customs officers, on May 1st, 2018, a paid E-Learning Project called "WCO Academy" was launched,[13] This project has been positively received by the public and permanently increases the catalog of electronic courses and other training contents.

[13] https://academy.wcoomd.org. Accessed May 10, 2021.

Chapter 12
Integrity

12.1 Definition

According to the Oxford Advanced Dictionary,[1] "Integrity" means "the quality of being honest and having strong moral principles."

On a broader level, *Integrity* can be defined as the conduct of individuals and organizations vis-à-vis compliance with the rules and the rule of law. There are, on the one hand, ethical organizations in which we find individuals, isolated and exceptional cases, who deviate their behavior. On the other hand, there are organizations that structurally lack integrity and where honest individuals are the exception; these, reflect a particular cultural and social environment.

The Integrity Development Guide, prepared jointly by the WCO Secretariat and the Asia-Pacific region, defines integrity as: "A positive set of attitudes which foster honest and ethical behavior and work practices."

In other words, integrity is more than simply the absence of corruption. Rather, it involves developing and maintaining a positive set of attitudes and values that support the integrity strategy.

To effectively address Customs responsibilities for revenue collection, community protection, trade facilitation and national security, a high level of integrity is required. Only a perceived lack of integrity and/or the presence of corruption can destroy the legitimacy of Customs administration and greatly limit the ability to effectively fulfill its mission.

Corruption or lack of integrity in Customs implies:

- Revenue leakage
- Distortion of economic incentives

[1] Translator's Note (TN): The Spanish text refers to the Royal Spanish Academy's definition of "integrity" which is equivalent to the Oxford Advance Dictionary's definition.

H. H. Juárez Allende, *The World Customs Organization*, Law for Professionals,
https://doi.org/10.1007/978-3-030-85296-2_12

- Reduced trust of other nations, development agencies, and private companies that consider investing in a specific country
- Reduction in the level of trust and cooperation between Customs administrations and other government agencies
- Lower level of voluntary compliance with Customs laws and regulations
- Reduced national security and community protection
- Low personnel morale
- Increased costs which are ultimately borne by the community

All these elements lead to unnecessary barriers in international trade, thereby distorting trade and investment opportunities and undermining confidence in public administration.

To both minimize the negative consequences of corruption and to further develop and maintain public trust and confidence, Customs administrations need to address this issue in a logical and systematic way, as well as develop and implement solutions which are relevant to their needs.

This must be achieved without losing sight of the joint work with the private sector. We must not forget that acts of corruption are usually a two-way street: one party offers and the other accepts, or one party asks and the other pays. This issue must be tackled from a broad perspective that considers all system components.

Next, we will review the four WCO tools in connection with Ethics in Customs: The Arusha Declaration, The Integrity Development Guide, the Model Code of Ethics and Conduct and the Compendium of Integrity Best Practices. We will close with the contributions of the Integrity Sub-Committee and its operational structure.

12.2 The Arusha Declaration

In the late 1980s, when it was still taboo to openly discuss corruption in an international forum, the former Customs Cooperation Council recognized that corruption could be a significant threat for the efficiency and effectiveness of customs services. This led to the adoption of the **Arusha Declaration** at the 81/82 Council Sessions held in Arusha, Tanzania on July 7th, 1993. This declaration established that it is a top priority for governments to ensure that the Customs is free from corruption.

Since then, the WCO's integrity strategy and program have advanced in logical phases.

In October 1994, the **Columbus Declaration**, a document proposed by the World Customs Organization (WCO), was presented at the Symposium on Trade Efficiency in Columbus, USA.

In September 1997, during the 8th International Anti-Corruption Conference, the **Lima Declaration** was signed. This document was signed with the participation of representatives from 93 countries and called on international organizations such as the World Bank, IMF, UN, OAS, WCO and Interpol to act against corruption. In

January 2001, the Integrity Sub-Committee was established to function under the general direction of the WCO Council and the Policy Commission, with administrative support provided by the WCO Secretariat. In March 2002, African countries meeting in Maputo, Mozambique, issued a resolution recommitting themselves to the World Customs Organization's 1993 Arusha Declaration on Integrity in the Customs. In June 2003, during the 101/102 Council Sessions, the WCO reviewed the 1993 Arusha Declaration and made amendments to it with the aim of assisting Members in the implementation of the agreements. Five amendments were made to the original document.

Amendment No. 1

The Revised Declaration contains a clearer and more detailed description of the content. It provides a title for each factor and a brief descriptive text including several points clarifying the actual factor.

Amendment No. 2

The structure was reorganized to rationalize the number of key factors, merging the contents of various factors under more general headings.

The 10 key factors are presented below:

1. Leadership and commitment of senior and middle customs management.
2. Regulatory framework to simplify procedures and reduce costs.
3. Transparency that allows certainty of the application of standards for all, and includes the standard level of service that customers can expect from customs.
4. Automation to eliminate degrees of corruption and improve monitoring of records.
5. Reform and Modernization to avoid delays in procedures and avoid payments to have priority.
6. Audit and Investigation, carried out in a technical way and leading to take the necessary repressive actions when necessary.
7. A code of conduct that clearly indicates the expected attitudes of a customs official and the types of misconduct and sanctions that should be applied.
8. Human Resources management that covers salary, working conditions, recruitment, ethical values, promotion policies and staff placement, training and performance evaluation.
9. Morale and Organizational Culture, which promotes a sense of belonging in the employee and reinforces the empathy vital to their development and administrative career.
10. Transparent and productive relationship with the private sector. Users contribute ideas and solutions.

Amendment No. 3

The Declaration was reinforced by the consideration of the following aspects:

- The importance of long-term policy commitment.
- The strategic partnership with the private sector, which includes a consultative mechanism.

- The recognition that the personnel who manage customs have the primary responsibility of preventing corruption.
- The importance of ensuring that customs systems and procedures eliminate corruption risks.

Amendment No. 4
It emphasizes the custom's community's wish to combat corruption and provide a model for promoting integrity in Customs.

Amendment No. 5
The Council invites its Members to use the Integrity Development Guide, a new self-assessment tool in line with the Revised Arusha Declaration, which was developed by the Secretariat with assistance from the Asia/ Pacific Region.

Based on the above, it can then be said that the objective of the Revised Arusha Declaration is to provide basic principles for establishing integrity in customs administrations, especially with a view to combating corruption.

12.3 Intregrity Development Guide

The Integrity Development Guide is based on a self-assessment process with the aim of being a practical tool for Customs administrations. The Guide focuses on a set of issues central to the development of an efficient and effective ethics program. Additionally, it helps evaluate performance and identify opportunities to improve administrative and management strategies focused on Customs ethics.

The instrument defines three phases in the cycle to develop ethics:

Phase 1: Diagnostic and Self-Assessment

- Identify the key elements of an effective ethics strategy
- Serve as a practical guide, or checklist, to help Customs managers evaluate the usefulness of their current strategies and identify areas for future improvement

Phase 2: Analysis and Action Planning

- Include a variety of ethics development strategies
- Identify responsible officials
- Set implementation deadlines
- Define verifiable performance indicators

Phase 3: Assessment

- Conducted at least 12 months after the start of the implementation of the Ethics Action Plan
- Evaluate their ethics strategies to determine whether they have achieved the results anticipated in the Arusha Declaration

- Determine if there are areas that require further attention and/or new initiatives that could be presented
- Develop an enhanced Ethics Action Plan

12.4 Model Code of Ethics and Conduct

The Code of Ethics and Conduct describes, in clear and practical terms, the minimum standards of behavior required of all customs officials, who must practice these standards of behavior when making decisions and taking action.

To ensure public confidence in the integrity of Customs, all Customs officials must respect and adhere to their respective Codes of Conduct, which generally include the following key elements:

1. **Personal Responsibility**. All customs officers must accept personal responsibility for compliance with the Code of Ethics and Conduct.
2. **Compliance with the Law.** All customs officials must comply with the law.
3. **Relations with the Public**. The public expects their dealings with Customs employees to be conducted with integrity, courtesy, impartiality, honesty, and professionalism.
4. **Limitations** on acceptance of gifts, rewards, hospitality, and discounts from or granted by natural or legal persons who provide, or attempt to provide, to Customs, as well as those who carry out activities regulated by Customs.
5. **Avoiding Conflicts of Interest**. Conflicts of interest, or the appearance of a conflict of interest, may arise from official dealings with, or decisions made in respect to, individuals who share private interests.
6. **Limitations on Political Activity**. Customs employees should follow governmental guidance to ensure that official activities are not compromised, or give the appearance of being compromised, due to inappropriate political activities or public comments in the workplace
7. **Conduct in Money Matters**. Customs officers must meet all legitimate financial obligations, especially those imposed by law, such as paying their taxes, etc. Officials are urged not to carry out private financial transactions among themselves, and those between hierarchical superiors and their subordinates are strictly prohibited.
8. **Confidentiality and Use of Official Information**. All Customs employees have a duty not to disclose (without proper authority and lawful purpose) any non-public official information that has been obtained in the course of their official duties, such as proprietary business information and/or sensitive information related to enforcement of the law retrieved from automated Customs systems.

9. **Use of Official Property and Services**. Unless specifically and reasonably authorized, the use of Customs resources and property, as well as services paid for with official funds for personal purposes or gain is prohibited.
10. **Private Purchases of Government Property by Employees**. In common with other government employees, Customs employees are allowed, provided no restrictions apply, to purchase excess/retired articles of general government property that are on sale to the public, such as publications, surplus supplies and goods sold at government sales, unless:

    - Customs employees have, because of their official position, been able to obtain special knowledge about the condition of the goods being sold.
    - Customs employees have been officially associated with the disposal
    - Arrangements.
    - Customs employees receive the goods at a discount that would not be available to a member of the public.
    - Articles are being sold by or at the direction of Customs.

Work Environment. All employees have the right to a healthy and safe workplace, free of discrimination and harassment, in which individual and organizational objectives can be met. A good working environment is one that:

- is fair and equitable
- is safe and supportive
- is free of alcohol and drugs
- is free of harassment and discrimination

12.5 Compendium of Integrity Best Practices

Since the adoption of the revised Arusha Declaration, many efforts have been made to improve integrity in Customs at national, regional, and global levels.

In Korea, in June 2003, delegates attending the customs session of the 3rd Global Forum on Fighting Corruption and Safeguarding Integrity agreed that they were responsible for safeguarding the integrity of their countries' customs administrations.

Recognizing the importance of international cooperation to share best practices and address common problems, the World Customs Organization (WCO) agreed to develop a compendium of integrity best practices to facilitate the implementation of integrity development programs in customs administrations. The WCO Integrity Sub-Committee (ISC) assumed responsibility for the development of this Compendium.

The ISC recognized supply chain security and trade facilitation, the challenge of illicit drug trafficking and revenue collection as priorities. It focused on policy on practical steps to improve integrity and it I stressed that it was important to gather integrity best practices since integrity in Customs is considered a cornerstone for any Customs mission.

Between November 2003 and August 2004, the General Secretary surveyed the Customs administrations to request their contribution to the project of creating a Compendium of the best integrity practices. This survey was based on the key factors in the Revised Arusha Declaration. Over fifty surveys were received and reviewed by the ISC at its fifth meeting in March 2005 and the work of compiling the compendium was completed.

The Integrity Best Practices Compendium is a "Benchmarking" of best practices that identifies and measures the most successful operational standards or strategies available in the Customs community. This document may be one of the most effective tools to assist in the implementation and enhancement of organizational efficiency and productivity, especially for Members who are beginning integrity development efforts.

Chapter 13
Packages

For the purpose of facilitating technical assistance to its member administrations, the WCO has grouped its main instruments and tools into four extensive packages providing an integral modular action in the following areas: economic competitiveness, revenue, compliance and enforcement, as well as organizational development.

Hence, if a Customs administration aims to exhaustively strengthen any of these areas, when it requests the modular technical assistance the WCO will assist it in the implementation of all the units of the requested module.

This measure greatly facilitates access to internal or external funding by the requesting administration, since it does not require a budget for each strengthening unit, but creates it for the whole area to be strengthened. The entire evaluation, diagnostic and implementation process is conducted for all the functional units of the area, and not for each particular instrument.

As set forth below, there are some overlaps between the four packages as the same tool may contribute to achieving different objectives. For example, the Risk Management Compendium may contribute to revenue collection, economic competitiveness, and compliance and enforcement.

13.1 Economic Competitive Package

The **Economic Competitive Package** (ECP) is a matter of high priority at the World Customs Organization (WCO). Economic competitiveness starts with trade facilitation in which Customs administrations play an undeniable role. Indeed, preventing transactions from being blocked is one of the key objectives of the WCO, and the Organization has provided tools and instruments as well as technical assistance to this end.

The Revised Kyoto Convention is the major tool for this purpose. More recently, and in response to the growing need for an efficient supply chain in a rapidly

H. H. Juárez Allende, *The World Customs Organization*, Law for Professionals,
https://doi.org/10.1007/978-3-030-85296-2_13

changing world, the WCO further developed guides and best practices which were incorporated in the WCO ECP and adopted in 2012

The ECP also comprises all the other instruments, tools, and standards relating to supply chain facilitation and security, such as the SAFE Framework of Standards, the Risk Management and Single Window Compendiums as well as the Data Model, the Coordinated Border Management (CBM) to name a few. On trade, consideration has to be paid to small and medium sized enterprises (SMEs) as they may serve as an engine for economic growth. At the level of the Globally Networked Customs (GNC) cooperation among Customs administrations as well as cooperation with the private sector is enhanced.

13.2 Revenue Package

Revenue collection has been the cornerstone of Customs' responsibilities, especially in least developed countries or developing countries. In 2008, following the global financial crisis in that year, recession in international trade affected the revenue returns of administrations.

Within the framework of the global financial crisis, the World Customs Organization (WCO) developed the Revenue Package to increase the revenues of customs administrations or governments. Said package consists of all the available tools and instruments that are relevant for revenue collection and provides direct access, through hyperlinks, to these materials. It is available at the WCO members' website.

The package has been implemented in phases. In June 2012, the WCO Policy Commission and Council launched the first set of new tools and materials, known as Phase I, which consisted of materials related to valuation control, origin verification, tariff infrastructure and post-clearance audit. In June 2015, the Phase II Action Plan was completed and encompassed the development of a further series of tools and materials. The Phase III Action Plan began implementation at the 75th Session of the Policy Commission in June 2016. By the 79th session in June 2018, the mentioned phase was finalized with new and updated tools and materials designed to assist members in implementing the materials developed under Phases I and II to strengthen their capacity to identify and collect revenue.

Phase III initiatives,[1] related to the rules of origin include the *Practical Guide to the 2015 Nairobi Ministerial Decision on Rules of Origin for the LDCs*, the object of which is to simplify preferential market access for LCDs. In addition, Phase III incorporates the *Guide for Technical Update of Preferential Rules of Origin* that assists with the update the rules of origin in relation to changes in the Harmonized System; and new *Virtual e-learning modules on Origin* developed on topics such as certification, origin criteria, direct transportation, and verification.

[1]WCO Phase III Tools. http://www.wcoomd.org/en/topics/key-issues/revenue-package/revenue-package-overview.aspx. Accessed May 10, 2021.

As far as Customs valuation is concerned, Phase III contains the *Practical Implementation of the WTO Customs Valuation Agreement: A Guide for Least-Developed Countries* establishing a step-by-step approach for LDCs to effectively implement the WTO Agreement. It also includes the updated Practical Guidelines for Valuation Control with case studies, and the WCO Guide to customs Valuation and Transfer Pricing.

Regarding Customs Laboratories, the updated Customs Laboratory Guide incorporates best practices in sampling, test procedures and contact points, as well as the Procedures and requirements for establishing a Regional Customs Laboratory. Additional tools and materials were issued, e.g., Customs-Tax cooperation, guidelines to strengthen the collaboration and exchange of information between Customs and Tax authorities at the national level. Regarding Mineral Resources, a WCO tool was developed on control of mineral resources being exported and imported. Besides, in connection with Fragile Borders there are case studies on border management in post-conflict zones and the role of Customs in trade-hubs at border cities.

In connection with post-clearance audit, the WCO has worked hard on the audit of traders' systems and internal controls vis-a-vis customs requirements. During this Phase, the WCO prepared the Implementation Guidance on Post-Clearance Audit that provides the steps to be followed by Customs to assist in the development of PCAs in line with WCO recommendation practices. This Phase also includes the "How to audit" Typology, a document that provides field auditors with information on common irregularities, together with practical techniques for their detection. Finally, this Phase incorporates the updated PCA Guidelines Volume I and II to cooperate in the implementation of the WTO Trade Facilitation Agreement Article 7.5.

13.3 Compliance and Enforcement Package

The World Customs Organization has stated that "The Customs in the 21st Century Strategy calls on Customs administrations to implement modern working methods and techniques."[2] That is why the organization is currently focused on promoting and continuously developing capacity building instruments, tools, programs, and activities, grouped in the "Compliance & Enforcement Package" (CEP), to assist members in addressing the high-risk areas for Customs enforcement.

The CEP approach focuses on 4 key components: technology and infrastructure, partnerships, tools, and operational activities, all revolving around 5 key risk areas endorsed by the WCO Policy Commission in 2011:[3] revenue assurance (commercial

[2] Compliance & Enforcement Package Overview. http://www.wcoomd.org/en/topics/key-issues/cep/overview.aspx. Accessed May 10, 2021.

[3] CEP Guide. http://www.wcoomd.org/-/media/wco/public/global/pdf/topics/enforcement-and-compliance/overview/cep_flyer_final_en_hr_for-printing.pdf?db=web. Accessed May 10, 2021.

fraud activities: undervaluation, misuse of origin and preferential duties, misclassification, and drawback fraud), drug trafficking (cultivation, manufacturing, distribution and sale of substances which are subject to drug prohibition laws), health and safety/IPR (prohibition of fake or counterfeit pharmaceuticals, substandard items, tainted foodstuffs), security risks (terrorism, proliferation of weapons and materials of mass destruction, trafficking of small arms and explosives, and illicit diversion of dual-use goods), and environmental risks (illicit cross-border trafficking of endangered species, hazardous and toxic waste, ozone depleting substances). That is why assistance activities by the WCO focus on high-risk areas, while members are offered a collection of the tools.

The tools section of the CEP contains references to all relevant instruments that have been designed to assist members in the implementation of effective compliance and enforcement controls. They are grouped according to their nature in Agreements, Declarations, Resolutions, Recommendations, Technical Material/guidance documents and documents on technology and applications and regional support resources.

Regarding partnerships, the Package seeks to achieve an improved Customs-to-Government and Customs-to-Business cooperation. In terms of operational efficiency, the WCO provides technical assistance for the capacity building of its members to strengthen their national control programs and enhance their contribution against criminal groups, smugglers, and terrorist organizations at regional and international level. Thus, in terms of technology and infrastructure, an efficient management of these aspects enables risk assessment and timely and precise information and intelligence exchange, as key elements for the mitigation of illegal trade and fraud detection.

13.4 Organizational Development Package

The aim of the Organizational Development Package (ODP) is to support the development of Customs administrations so that they that can take ownership for their reform and progressively reduce their reliance on external assistance. This requires all efforts to be responsive and needs-driven to ensure that beneficiary Customs administrations obtain the support they need to pursue their reform and modernization.

Thus, for Customs administrations to develop capacities through reform and modernization, and, ultimately, be equipped to achieve their objectives, the WCO and its members have adopted the organizational approach method, in which reform and modernization are dealt with in a planned and structured manner and relying on three phases: 1. Diagnostic of the current situation: Thorough an examination of the current situation organizational capacity gaps and needs for development are identified; 2. Strategic planning and implementation of change: Based on findings of the diagnostic, the Customs administration, in cooperation with the WCO, develops a holistic reform and modernization plan that serves as the roadmap to enhance the capacities of the organization, where the WCO offers assistance in facilitating the development of strategic and modernization plans and in the implementation of key priorities to ensure the sustainability of the modernization process; 3. Monitoring and evaluation: This phase serves to identify new capacity gaps and, if needed, readjust the priorities for the development of the administration.

Additionally, the WCO recommends the application of three important factors as ODP enablers: the first one is political will, securing the commitment of policymakers is necessary to ensure that the Customs administration has the support it needs to implement its reform and modernization; the second one is people and staff , for which Customs administrations must create the right conditions, policies and programs to recruit, develop, and retain the best people available to perform the various duties within their organization; and third enabler corresponds to partnerships, as it is essential for Customs administrations to work closely with stakeholders from the private and public sectors to achieve sustainable reform and modernization.

Chapter 14
Other Instruments

14.1 Glossary of International Customs Terms

The Glossary of International Customs Terms[1] is a list in alphabetical order of definitions of customs terms that are considered relevant and necessary to facilitate the work of the WCO and their members (particularly when they have to draft Conventions of customs-related matters), of international organizations, and of trade operators who may need them. The Glossary provides a uniform approach to these concepts.

Although it is neither a binding nor an obligatory instrument, it is a of vital importance for the WCO's purpose of harmonizing and standardizing the customs' treatment of goods in international trade.

The Recommendation of the Customs Co-Operation Council concerning the use of International Customs Terms,[2] dated July 6th, 1993, asserts that "although the Glossary does not in in itself have the legal status of an international instrument, it has been approved by the Council and certain definitions within it have been accepted by the Contracting Parties to the principal international Customs Conventions."

It then recommends that members should "(1) make general use of the Council's Glossary of International Customs Terms, (2) refer to the definitions in the Glossary for terms used at international level, to ensure that a term is employed with the meaning attributed to it in the Glossary, except where it must be defined differently, for the purposes of an international instrument, (3) use the terms and their definitions in their legislation, in instruction, in training of Customs staff and in the performance

[1] http://www.wcoomd.org/-/media/wco/public/global/pdf/topics/facilitation/instruments-and-tools/tools/glossary-of-international-customs-terms/glossary-of-interntional-customs-terms.pdf?db=web. Accessed May 10, 2021.

[2] http://www.wcoomd.org/en/about-us/legal-instruments/recommendations/pf_recommendations/pfrecomm47glossaryintcustterms.aspx. Accessed May 10, 2021.

H. H. Juárez Allende, *The World Customs Organization*, Law for Professionals,
https://doi.org/10.1007/978-3-030-85296-2_14

of their duties, (4) where appropriate, bring the Glossary to the attention of public or private national and international bodies which for various reasons may be concerned with Customs questions."

The Glossary of International Customs Terms has been examined and reviewed by the Permanent Technical Committee (PTC) at several sessions, with the aim of updating and aligning it with developments having taken place in the Customs and international trade environment.

Due to several concerns, mainly of a procedural nature, raised by delegates and observers during the 195th/196th and 197th/198th sessions of the PTC, held in March and November 2012 respectively, the Committee was unable to reach consensus on the inclusion of the proposed new terms. Despite this, the discussions during these sessions underscored the fact that the PTC is the Committee responsible for keeping the Glossary up to date. Therefore, it is the responsibility of the PTC to decide which definitions should be included in the Glossary.

This issue was not discussed at the 199th/200th Sessions of the PTC held in March 2013 due to time constraints; however, the PTC agreed to set up a virtual group to facilitate discussions during the intersession. Out of the list of new terms proposed for inclusion in the Glossary, the PTC agreed that the virtual group should focus on definitions which had not yet been agreed by other Committees and on which the virtual group should make a proposal to the next PTC with a view to deciding on their inclusion in the Glossary.

As regards definitions endorsed by other Committees, the PTC agreed that its role was to include them in the Glossary or refer its comments back to the initiating Committee with a view to the latter proposing amendments.

A virtual group was formed during the intersession, comprising the Customs Administrations of Canada, Burkina Faso, Malawi, Spain, and Switzerland, as well as the International Federation of Freight Forwarders Associations (FIATA) which volunteered to join the group.

After analyzing the list of new definitions that should form part of the Glossary, the virtual group agreed that there were no technical or linguistic issues potentially preventing inclusion in the Glossary of terms that had been reviewed and approved by competent WCO bodies and, in some cases, incorporated in official instruments approved by the Council.

These terms include:

- Authorized Economic Operator (AEO)
- Customs Enforcement Network (CEN)
- Customs Enforcement Network Communication (CEN Comm)
- National Customs Enforcement Network (nCEN)
- Post Clearance Audit
- Risk Analysis
- Risk Management
- Screening and Scanning
- Unique Consignment Reference (UCR)
- Single Window

- WCO Data Model
- Time Release Study (TRS)
- Enquiry Point/Office
- Perishable Goods

The virtual group recommended that the PTC update the Glossary of International Customs Terms with the inclusion of the above definitions, which members endorsed in 2018.

Those who have participated in regional integration processes or in the elaboration of customs-related international trade facilitation agreements have experienced the utmost importance of this linguistic[3] tool that universally connotes and defines the specific terms found in the customs jargon. This Glossary facilitates international negotiations and paves the way for successful results.

Moreover, those who have been involved in drafting domestic customs rules are aware of the Glossary's valuable contribution as reference guide when defining their contents. Rules must necessarily be written in a natural language (although often ambiguous and vague) for comprehension of the community. We see that, contrary to formal languages (such as logic or mathematics), customs-related language cannot define its concepts with precision. Consequently, this group of universally agreed definitions represents a fundamental tool when legislating.

From another standpoint, the existence and development of an evolutionary glossary of technical terms contributes to perfect customs knowledge and its transmission for academic purposes

14.2 Performance Measurement Framework

With the aim of offering Customs a practical and dynamic instrument for measuring performance a basic set of performance indicators was developed. These indicators would enable a quick evaluation of an institution's progress in achieving Customs excellence. In fact, this is the name given to this instrument, "Achieving Excellence in Customs (AEC)."

The AEC depicts four main areas of work covered by the WCO: (i) Trade Facilitation and Security; (ii) Fair and Effective Revenue Collection; (iii) Protection of Society; and (iv) Institutional and Human Resource Development. These four core elements divide into 20 indicators that represent, in fact, the level of Customs excellence.

To illustrate, in Trade Facilitation and Security, the following eight indicators are identified in the AEC:

[3]The author has been involved in writing the MERCOSUR Customs Code on behalf of the Argentine Republic, among many other customs-related rules and international agreements.

- Revised Kyoto Convention
- SAFE Framework of Standards
- Time Release Study
- Electronic Declarations
- Data Model
- Coordinated Border Management (CBM)
- Authorized Economic Operator (AEO)
- Single Window

The reader is invited to go to Annex IV herein where we have incorporated the Performance Measurement Framework on one page. By completing the checklist of indicators one can assess the level of development of a Customs in particular.[4]

The purpose of this tool is to have a glimpse of the elements that have been "implemented," are "under development," and are "still to be done."

The AEC framework is used for self-assessment and not for Customs' categorization purposes.[5] It is strongly linked to first-level indicators to measure members' progress in the implementation of WCO instruments and tools.

It is very important to have objectively verifiable criteria to measure customs performance through an instrument that is developed by customs officers as experts in the field. Although some governments may prefer to base their assessment on instruments developed by international organizations such as World Bank's Doing Business or Logistic Performance Index that also contain data related to the business environment of a country, we shall bear in mind that the latter are created and implemented by persons who do not have direct experience with customs work, and who, consequently, lack the specificities of the operational reality.

Customs administrations needed their own performance measurement system, developed by the WCO, to produce a professional qualification that would not be used for political or advertising purposes but, rather, as an assessment tool to help Customs identify best practices to set and accomplish short, medium and long-term objectives.

The AEC performance measurement framework is expected to be backed up by a second layer that could be developed as a maturity model and whose work is still in progress.

[4]Those interested in further information regarding the Table may refer to the text available at: http://www.wcoomd.org/-/media/wco/public/global/pdf/topics/facilitation/ressources/permanent-technical-committee/211-212/pc0442e1.doc?la=en. Accessed May 10, 2021.

[5]The original intention was to gather members' information of the Performance Measurement Framework; however, after Council discussions delegates were of the view that the AEC data would not be published as its purpose was to help members excel, and not to compare or rank them.

14.3 Data Model

One of the World Customs Organization's objectives is to promote the exchange of information among Customs administrations, international organizations and other stakeholders.

To this end, we highlight the importance of the **WCO Data Model**, a standardized compilation of data elements, carefully combined and interrelated, that is regularly updated to meet the legal and operational requirements of Customs. This model is compatible with other international standards such as the United Nations Trade Data Elements, Directory (UNTDED). It is also a core element in the exchange of information among different global trade operators.

The Data Model version 1.0 was developed based on an initiative of the so- called Group of Seven (G7) designed to simplify and standardize data requirements to lodge Customs declarations of goods and cargo for it determined that confusing, redundant, and non-standard systems of data had become an on-tariff barrier to trade. The first version of the Data Model and the guideline for the implementation of messages were issued in 2002. Later versions broadened the scope of this instrument.

The WCO Data Model not only includes data sets for different customs procedures but also information needed by other Cross-Border Regulatory Agencies for the cross-border release and clearance. The WCO Data Model supports the implementation of a Single Window as it allows the reporting of information to all government agencies through the unique way it organizes regulatory information.

The Information Management Sub-Committee of the WCO (IMSC) is responsible for the maintenance of the WCO Data Model.

To ensure broad acceptance and use, the WCO Data Model includes: a comprehensive dictionary of the required cross-border data to exchange and process; standardized guidelines regarding electronic messages and other backup documents; and a maximum data set for export, import and transit transactions.

The WCO Data Model is managed by the Data Model Project Team (DMPT) in which participation is open to all interested parties. The DMPT, which reports to the IMSC, has established a transparent procedure and a method whereby requests for changes, deletions, and/or additions to the WCO Data Model of the above-mentioned items are made.

The Data Model is fundamental pillar or the WCO's initiative of the globally networked customs as it promotes cooperation providing all international trade government agencies and their private operators with a common vocabulary, language, and transactional syntax, thus, acting as a suitable platform for coordinated border management.[6]

[6]To see the implementation of the model in a specific case, visit the New Zealand Customs at website at: https://www.customs.govt.nz/business/trade-single-window/resource-material/technical-reference-documents. Accessed May 10, 2021.

14.4 Customs Laboratories

In the Customs environment processing chemical and scientific analyses is not essential only for the correct classification of products in the Harmonized System (HS), it is also critical to the fight against dangerous substances, for instance, chemical weapons, ozone depleting substances, pesticides, persistent organic products, and precursor drugs, etc. These analyses are performed by "Customs laboratories" which may be public or private but are specifically under the direction of a Customs administration, national laboratories that fall under the jurisdiction of another government agency, or private laboratories which undertake work on behalf of Customs. At the latter, ensuring good communication and coordination between Customs and the laboratories is crucial in terms of the relevance of test results. In addition, there are Customs (e.g., the US) that have implemented mobile laboratories that are deployed according to the operative needs.

The origin of these laboratories can be found at the beginning of the nineteenth century when in 1807 James Madison, the fourth president of the United States, recognized the importance of Customs duties, declaring that "the power of taxing people and their property is essential to the very existence of government,"[7] therefore, Authorities developed particular strategies to examine the merchandise and to collect Customs taxes. Preliminary inspections were carried out by appraisers, port officials and other Customs house officials, but their work was limited to visual examinations. When chemical analyses were required, local chemists or pharmacists were contracted as external experts or consultants. Some were appointed as drug inspectors to control the most relevant ports and national borders, focusing mainly on the study of drug and medicine purity, but dealing also with other types of goods for tax purposes when required. As this system proved to be inefficient, some countries decided to set up state-owned laboratories.

Their traditional work involves the chemical analysis to determine commodity codes and customs duties and taxes; however, over the last years their role has expanded due to changes in trade patterns and technical evolution. Customs laboratories differ from other laboratories in that they must analyze all types of products mainly for Customs classification purposes, with staff skilled in two disciplines: chemical analysis and Customs regulation. As well as solid training in analytical methods, industrial processes of manufacturing, and chemistry in general, the staff must have an in-depth knowledge of Customs procedures and regulations to evaluate the relevant elements pursuant to rules and regulations and the impact of their reports.

Considering these factors, the WCO has drawn up practical recommendations, as well as a comprehensive technical assistance and training program, to assist its members in improving the efficiency of their Customs laboratories and in

[7] Digital Magazine (2015) WCO News N0. 77. Focus on customs laboratories. http://www.wcoomd.org/-/media/wco/public/global/pdf/topics/key-issues/customs-laboratories/wco-magazine/focus-on-customs-laboratories-wco-news-77-june-215-en.pdf. Accessed May 10, 2021.

implementing such a facility or assessing its implementation feasibility and practicality.

The Organization developed, in particular, a Customs Laboratory Guide as a practical handbook for the establishment or improvement of Customs laboratories in developing countries. It includes "best practices" covering a variety of issues and operations: from the organizational structure, staff categories, design, space utilization, equipment, and information systems, to safety and pollution measures, sample preparation methods, recommended analytical methods, and operation and results reporting procedures.

Based on the WCO Customs Laboratory Guide, the WCO Secretariat provides technical assistance for the implementation or modernization of Customs laboratories, as well as specific training for laboratory staff. Assistance generally takes the form of expert assessment (WCO experts and external experts), training courses, workshops or seminars delivered at national or regional levels. Before the implementation of any assistance activity, the WCO Secretariat invites the future beneficiaries to precisely express the nature of the assistance requested and the objective sought, including a description of the status quo and plans for the Customs laboratory, its possible use, the volume of trade of target commodities, and the training required.

In addition, customs laboratories support the WHO INN lists with HS classifications. INN, international non-proprietary names (or generic names), identify pharmaceutical substances or active pharmaceutical ingredients with a name that is globally recognized and that is of public domain. Since its inception in 1953, the World Health Organization has published INN Lists twice a year; and since 1988 the Harmonized System Committee assisted by the Scientific Sub-Committee has classified around 4000 INNs in the Harmonized System (HS). After the WHO publishes each INN List, the WCO requests all its Contracting Parties' opinions to include the new INNs into the HS.

Lastly, laboratories assist in the authenticity and quality controls, e.g., the European Union (EU) Inter Laboratory Inventory of Analytical Determination (ILIADe),[8] The ILIADe is a shared directory of analytical methods. It was initially developed by the Italian Customs Agency and is currently hosted by the European Commission. Its main purpose is to improve the effectiveness of Customs Laboratories by providing them with an easily accessible and up-to- date compilation of analytical methods. The ILIADe database contains over 500 methods that include official analytical methods, international standards, and internally developed methods. This list of methods and contacts is also available for non-EU countries.

[8] *European customs laboratories: experience you can rely on. European Commission — Taxation and Customs Union. 2016 Available at: https://www.adm.gov.it/portale/do-cuments/20182/521620/CLEN_Brochure+laboratori+europei+delle+Dogane.pdf/ c18fd413-fc44-4e1f-9e88-238f44983369.*

14.5 Agreements of Assistance and Exchange of Information

14.5.1 Nairobi Convention

INTERNATIONAL CONVENTION ON MUTUAL ADMINISTRATIVE ASSISTANCE FOR THE PREVENTION, INVESTIGATION AND REPRESSION OF CUSTOMS OFFENCES (NAIROBI CONVENTION)

Historical Background
From the outset, the WCO has always sought means of cooperation that would assist Customs administrations in combating Customs offenses. On December 5th, 1953, it adopted the **Recommendation of mutual administrative assistance**. This Recommendation enabled the administrations that accepted it to establish close cooperation, based mainly on direct personal direct contact between the services concerned.

The 1953 Recommendation provided for mutual direct assistance between Customs in the field of enforcement (application and enforcement of customs rules) without having to go through a central or diplomatic agency. The Recommendation of June 28th, 1954 for the pooling of information concerning persons convicted of Customs offenses established a system whereby information was circulated by the Secretariat General of the Council. The Recommendation of June 8th, 1967 extended this system by providing for the pooling of information concerning not only persons convicted of customs fraud, but also information concerning places of concealment in means of transport, other methods of smuggling, goods particularly liable to be smuggled and known to be the subject of definite smuggling trends and fraud by forgery, falsification, or counterfeiting (documents, Customs seals, etc.).

On May 22nd, 1975, the Council adopted a new Recommendation on the pooling of information concerning Customs fraud, further broadening the scope of the 1967 Recommendation. In addition to persons finally convicted of Customs fraud, the new Recommendation also covered persons suspected of smuggling or other fraud or apprehended in the act of smuggling provided, however, that the national legislation did not prohibit the communication of such information to other countries. The role of the Council General Secretariat was extended, in that the latter was now required not only to administer the central index and circulate the information contained therein, but also to decide which information should be circulated and to use information from the index to prepare summaries and studies of trends in Customs fraud. A separate annex concerning vessels involved in smuggling was included in the new Recommendation.

In addition, in 1967, sharing the concern of many countries regarding the alarming increase in the abuse of narcotic drugs and psychotropic substances, the Council adopted a resolution inviting members to develop mutual assistance between their Customs administrations, to the greatest possible extent, with a view to preventing and detecting illicit traffic in narcotic drugs and psychotropic substances. This Resolution was followed by the Recommendation of June 8th, 1971 on the spontaneous exchange of information concerning illicit traffic in narcotic drugs and psychotropic substances. This Recommendation supplemented the legal means available to Customs services by enabling them to exchange operational intelligence, particularly where the success of an operation depended on speed of action; however, as pointed out in the text of this Recommendation, the sole purpose of this exchange of information was to reinforce the activities of the authorities with competence to take action against the abuse of narcotic drugs and psychotropic substances.

From 1973 onwards the Council's attention has been drawn to the problem of preventing and repressing the fraudulent exportation of works of art, antiquities and other cultural property, a matter of concern to the representatives of many countries. The importance of the UNESCO Convention on the means of prohibiting and preventing the illicit import, export, and transfer of ownership of cultural property (1970) and invited them to develop mutual administrative assistance to combat the smuggling of works of art and antiquities, by actively exploiting the possibilities offered by the Recommendations of 1953 and 1967 (as amended in 1975).

Creating these various legal instruments showed that the Council attached importance to international cooperation to combat Customs fraud, which was assuming an increasingly international character; and that it had adopted instruments dealing more specifically with the types of smuggling about which most concerned its members. Nevertheless, certain countries had trouble in granting administrative assistance merely based on Recommendations and considered that bilateral Conventions on mutual administrative assistance would provide a more effective means of action against Customs offenses. To facilitate and encourage such agreements, the Council proposed a model bilateral Convention on mutual administrative assistance, for consideration by the countries concerned.

In June 1967, the Council in fact adopted the **"Model bilateral Convention on mutual administrative assistance for the prevention, investigation and repression of Customs offences."** This model was given the form and wording of a potentially ready-made Convention. However, members remained free to delete or modify the provisions of the model as they saw fit, or insert additional provisions adapted to their needs. Alternatives were even included for certain articles of the model Convention. This enabled members wishing to conclude a bilateral agreement to choose the provision which best met their requirements.

Notwithstanding, it became evident that the conclusion of regional bilateral or multilateral agreements, although extremely fruitful and desirable for the countries concerned, could not provide an entirely satisfactory means of international action against Customs fraud, which was becoming increasingly growing. For this reason, in 1974, the Council instructed the Permanent Technical Committee to prepare a draft multilateral Convention on mutual administrative assistance, on the understanding that the resulting instrument should be sufficiently effective and binding, while being acceptable to as many countries as possible. This work culminated in the adoption, on June 9th, 1977, at the Council's meeting in Nairobi (Kenya), of an international Convention on mutual administrative assistance for the prevention, investigation, and repression of Customs offenses.

General Scope and Structure of the Convention

The Convention consists of a Body and 11 Annexes that may be accepted independently of one another. This system was adopted because it is flexible and allows countries that would not be able to implement all the provisions of a mutual administrative assistance Convention to become Contracting Parties to the Convention, accepting only certain annexes (at least one).

At the beginning, the original text of the Convention stated that no reservations were permitted (Article 18); however, during the efforts to promote the Convention, it was found that the provisions of Article 18 were one of the major obstacles to the full growth in the number of Contracting Parties.

Consequently, the Enforcement Committee decided to amend the provisions of Article 18 of the Convention. The Council, at its 81st/82nd Sessions, approved the recommendation that the simplified amendment procedure be applied. The original text of was replaced by the following "Each Contracting Party shall be deemed to have acceded to, or accepted all the provisions in, the Convention or the annexes thereto unless, at the time of acceding to the Convention or separately accepting an annex or at any time thereafter, it has notified the Secretary General of the Council of any reservations in respect or provisions to which it cannot subscribe. It shall undertake to examine periodically the provisions in respect of which it has entered reservations and notify the Secretary General of the Council in the event of the withdrawal of the reservations." This amendment entered into force on October 7th, 1995.

In addition to this amendment, there is an escape clause in Article 3 which provides that the requested State needs to grant assistance only to the extent that this would not infringe upon its sovereignty, security or other substantial national interest or prejudice the legitimate commercial interest of any enterprise, public or private.

It should also be noted that, as is generally the case in the field of mutual administrative assistance, the Convention is based on the concept of reciprocity, i.e., a Contracting Party has an obligation to render assistance to another Contracting Party only insofar as both have accepted the same annex.

14.5.2 Johannesburg Convention

INTERNATIONAL CONVENTION ON MUTUAL ADMINISTRATIVE ASSISTANCE IN CUSTOMS MATTERS (JOHANNESBURG CONVENTION)

The International Convention on Mutual Administrative Assistance in Customs Matters was adopted in the city of Johannesburg on June 27th, 2003 but has not entered into force yet.

The scope of this Convention is regulated by the provisions of Chapter II that state that Contracting Parties shall, through their Customs administrations, provide each other with administrative assistance for the proper application of Customs law and to ensure the security of the international supply chain.

Any activity carried out under this Convention by a Contracting Party shall be in accordance with its legal and administrative provisions and within the limits of its Customs administration's competence and available resources.

Contracting Parties may provide each other with different categories of information:

- Information for the application and enforcement of Customs Law that may involve new enforcement techniques having proved their effectiveness; new trends, means or methods of committing Customs offenses; goods known to be the subject of Customs offenses, as well as transport and storage methods used in respect of those goods; persons known to have committed a Customs offence or suspected of being about to commit a Customs offence; any other data that can assist Customs administrations with risk assessment for control and facilitation processes.
- Information relating to Customs offenses that have been committed or will be committed.
- Information for the assessment of import or export duties and taxes.
- Other particular types of information.

Additionally, the Convention establishes the different types of assistance that the Contracting Parties may provide each other:

- Surveillance over goods and/or persons
- Controlled deliveries
- Notifications
- Experts and witnesses
- Presence of officials in the territory of another contracting party
- Arrangements for visiting officials

Chapter 15
Research

The development of customs activities, together with the complexity they entail, has generated the need to resort to the active pursuit of knowledge through systematic inquiry, objective analysis, empirical evidence, and methodology of science. This will enable solid customs policies that may gradually move the "trial and error" techniques or the so-called "best practices." It should be noted that although some of these initiatives are viable in some countries, they are not in others.

The progress in social sciences has strongly influenced this development of approximation to human phenomena and the use of empirical evidence properly structured and contrasted with reality.

Thus, since 2009, the Research Unit that directly depends on the Secretary General and the Deputy Secretary General produces evidence-based analytical research and policy analysis on Customs and international trade topics. It also organizes international research events where scholars and professionals present their works and exchange opinions publicly, thus, promoting the development of scientific customs knowledge.

Undoubtedly, this is one of the structural changes regarding customs work, which has already shown the first results, and it is clearly the path to follow. Customs activity is a social phenomenon, and as such, modern scientific research methodologies must be used in its study.

Customs tasks are certainly dynamic and are influenced by several factors; therefore, we need to examine and predict their behavior to achieve the best degree of efficiency and effectiveness.

To accomplish these objectives, Customs administrators should know how to decipher change, understand its variations, and grasp their effects. Solid background and empirical data are required to enable a suitable analysis of the situation.

Reform strategies should not be "copied and pasted" from one country to another. Instead, we should analyze the specific circumstances of a particular Customs service as well as the political, social, economic, and administrative conditions influencing it.

H. H. Juárez Allende, *The World Customs Organization*, Law for Professionals,
https://doi.org/10.1007/978-3-030-85296-2_15

Again, it is worth mentioning the philosopher and epistemologist Dr. Mario Bung who, when referring to Social Sciences, wrote: “Scientists are expected to explore the world in order to understand it. They ask, answer, and argue. They observe facts – natural, social, or mixed – and invent hypotheses to explain or forecast them. They classify and construct systems of hypotheses, that is, theories, of various degrees of depth and breadth. They check data and guesses to find out whether these hypotheses are at least roughly true. They invent techniques to collect, check, or process data. And they argue over projects and findings broad and narrow.

Scientific researchers are expected to abide by the scientific method, which boils down to the following steps: previous knowledge, problem, candidate for the solution (hypothesis, experimental or technical design), test, evaluation of candidate, final revision of one or other candidate for the solution examining the procedure, the previous knowledge and even the problem.”[1]

The WCO Research Unit, through a multidisciplinary approach, produces research on matters that relate directly or indirectly with Customs and international trade.

By exercising its functions, we observe the accomplishment of two key objectives:

i. To publish and communicate high-quality research papers in renowned external publications such as *“Global Trade and Customs Journal”*[2] and *“World Customs Journal,”*[3] and in WCO publications, e.g., *“WCO News magazine.”*[4]
ii. To gather the best scholars and customs officers in international research conferences such as the annual PICARD Conference.

Over the last years, the Research Unit has examined several issues such as anti-terrorism, informal commercial practices, customs performance measurement, corruption, money laundering, implications for Customs of global warming, contribution of tobacco control to public health, wildlife protection, electronic trade, and cross-border customs practices.

Reference

Bunge M (1999) Las ciencias sociales en discusión (Social Science under Debate). Editorial Sudamericana SA, Buenos Aires

[1] Bunge (1999).

[2] Publication of Kluwer Law International. http://www.kluwerlawonline.com/toc.php?pubcode=GTCJ. Accessed May 10, 2021.

[3] Publication of INCU. https://worldcustomsjournal.org. Accessed May 10, 2021.

[4] WCO Publication. http://www.wcoomd.org/en/media/wco-news-magazine.aspx. Accessed May 10, 2021.

Chapter 16
Appraisal of Performance

The World Customs Organization, as any other international organization, has a strategic plan developed for guidance and goals accomplishment and which catalogs the identified priorities. The organ adopting the organization's decision, the Council, supports this plan. The purpose of this plan is to provide orientation and to reflect the customs and trade environment so that it can respond accurately to their needs.

Currently, the 2019–2022 Strategic Plan is in force (see Fig. 16.1). Its objectives are grouped in three large categories: Facilitation, Revenue collection and Protection of society. These three goals are supported by eight interrelated processes that provide the necessary tools for the development of international standards for the harmonization of customs procedures, reinforced cooperation among Customs and between Customs and other stakeholders, and the significant delivery of capacity building. Thus, assisting WCO members to achieve their objectives. These processes correspond to: SP1 Economic Competitiveness Package, SP2 Revenue Package, SP3 Compliance and Enforcement Package, SP4 Organizational Development Package, SP5 Joint Operations and Exchange of information, SP6 Sharing of knowledge and best practices, SP7 Technical assistance, training and tools for implementation of international standards, and SP8 Technical assistance, training, and tools on people development. In addition, the WCO Strategic Plan incorporates three learning and development objectives: LD1 Research and Analysis, LD2 Use of Technology and Data, and LD3 Raise Profile of WCO and Promote Customs' Role. The plan further includes two organizational capacity goals: ORG1 Specialized and Focused Work Allocation, and ORG2 Use of Budget Resources and Accountability.

To design the Strategic Plan, the WCO resorts to the annual plans in which the necessary strategic actions and related documents are defined. The WCO will

H. H. Juárez Allende, *The World Customs Organization*, Law for Professionals,
https://doi.org/10.1007/978-3-030-85296-2_16

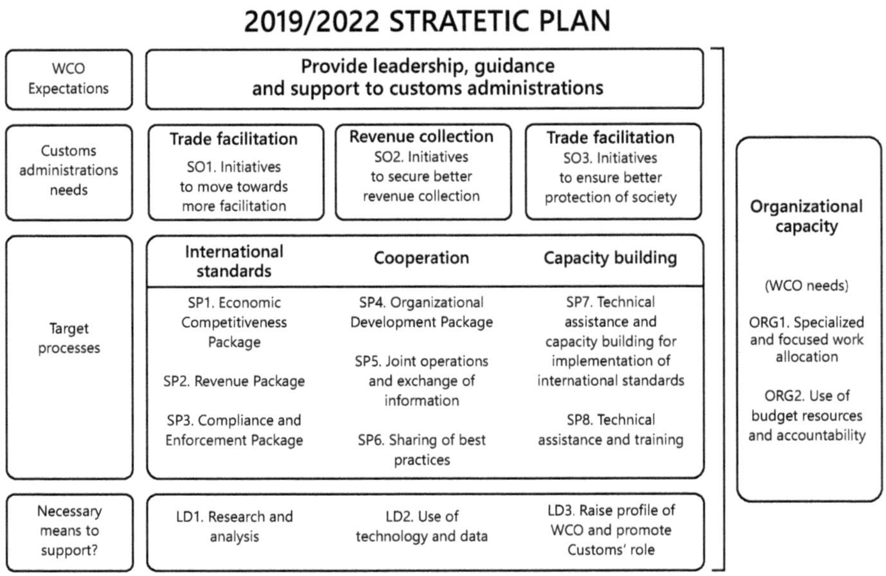

Fig. 16.1 Objectives of the 2019/2022 Strategic Plan. **Source:** Author's elaboration based on information from the WCO

regularly publish an updated report online,[1] to provide members with a permanent means of communication.

Currently, the WCO does not have mechanisms in place to measure the impact that its actions have on Customs administrations. As aforementioned, the strategic plan implementation report will be available in the future. In addition, it is worth noting that the Organization's annual reports encompass the goals that management has achieved in a global manner and do not specify how effective the different tools, instruments, or guidelines have been throughout the years.

In this sense, we can observe that in the international environment there are several organizations with expertise in tracking their management. For instance, since 2014 the World Bank (WB) has published, synthetically and directly, the measuring and reporting results of its twelve (12) development goals,[2] these results show the impact of the WB goals and enhance WB management transparency. The goals are specific and include defined terms to be accomplished; in addition, progress can be measured in real time as data are input as soon as they are made available. These data include information gathered by the bank through reports as well as comments made by citizens who have been affected by the financed projects. The goals cover transactions, financing, and the priorities regarding solutions of all

[1]WCO 2019–2022 Strategic Plan available at: http://www.wcoomd.org/-/media/wco/public/global/pdf/about-us/administrative-documents/wco-strategic-plan-2019-2022.pdf?-db=web. Accessed May 10, 2021.

[2]World Bank web results https://www.worldbank.org/en/results. Accessed May 10, 2021.

the institution, including the International Bank for Reconstruction and Development (IBRD), the International Development Association (IDA), the Multilateral Investment Guarantee Agency (MIGA), and the International Finance Corporation that deals with the private sector.

The latest edition of *Results and Performance of the World Bank Group*[3] concludes that the share of closed projects rated moderately satisfactory or above (MS+) on outcome rose from 69% in the FY2012-14 to 76% in the FY2015-17. Additionally, bank performance ratings rose in tandem, from 70% MS+ for projects closed in FY2012-14 to 76% for projects closed in FY2015-17.

In relation to the Universal Postal Union (UPU), this organization issues the annual Integrated Index for Postal Development (2IPD)[4] to measure postal development around the globe. The Index was created in 2013 and was applied for the first time two years later. Since 2016, it has regularly been updated and published. Thanks to this tool, governments can use the 2IPD indicators and results to design their own strategies to raise the postal network contribution to their socioeconomic infrastructure. Additionally, the Index enables regulators to identify the challenges they must face vis-à-vis development and enables them to benefit from international benchmark. Moreover, designated operators may profit from these data to compare the strengths and weaknesses of their business and exploitation model in relation to other operators with different level of development and in different geographic locations, with the aim of improving their results.

The objective of this tool is to measure the efficiency of postal services, the level of globalization of their services, the competitiveness of postal services in all key segments, and in particular, the potential to generate higher volumes. It also assesses the ability of postal services to withstand external shocks through adaptable business models. Overall, the 2IPD aims at providing a balanced view of postal development, without solely focusing on operational matters, e.g., delivery, but rather encompassing strategic affairs such as business portfolio management, or societal matters.

Other international organizations, such as the UNCTAD, use a component of this Index to calculate their own Business-to-Consumers E-Commerce Index.

The International Maritime Association is another organization that shows their results in a specific manner. This agency regularly identifies the main challenges through the systemic analysis of general trends and developments in the maritime transport industry. Therefore, in 2017[5] it designed a strategic plan that comprises: (1) the vision of the Organization; (2) the overarching principles; (3) the strategic directions that provide the Organization's; (4) the performance indicators related to

---

[3]Results and Performance of the World Bank Group 2018. https://ieg.worldbankgroup.org/evaluations/rap2018. Accessed May 10, 2021.

[4]Postal Development Report 2018. https://www.upu.int/UPU/media/upu/publications/postalDevelopmentReport2018En.pdf. Accessed May 10, 2021.

[5]Strategic Plan of the International Maritime Organization (IMO) 2018-2023. Available at: https://wwwcdn.imo.org/localresources/en/About/strategy/Documents/A%2030-RES.1110.pdf. Accessed May 10, 2021.

the strategic directions; and (5) the list of products for the two-year period. Every 2 years, through performance indicators, the IMO measures its performance against the strategic directions and analyzes the context for the Risk Management Framework of the Secretariat. To support the organization's biannual work, the Secretariat drafts a business plan to be endowed with sufficient financial resources to deliver the strategic results approved by the assembly.

The United Nations Conference on Trade and Development (UNCTAD) appraises its internal performance pursuant to the 2011 Evaluation Policy, which was established by the United Nations Evaluation Group to draw conclusions vis-à-vis the work done, make recommendations regarding the necessary improvements, and define lessons learned and best practices. These evaluations enable designing, planning, and executing future work; therefore, it is advisable for UNCTAD program managers to refer to previous reports and general aspects of the evaluations of UNCTAD activities before creating a new program. The UNCTAD Evaluation and Monitoring Unit coordinates the oversight activities within the organization that serve to ensure and enhance the quality and resonance of its programs and projects.

Considering the examples, it is evident that measuring results or the impact of policy implementation within international organizations is fundamental. Therefore, as the WCO is charged with enhancing Customs performance it is key to measure or quantify the effects of its recommendations or the use of its tools or instruments. By not openly communicating such measurements, the WCO may be considered as an organization that merely issues opinions or guidelines without knowing their effectiveness.

The renowned physicist and mathematician, William Thomson Kelvin (1824–1907) expressed "What cannot be defined, cannot be measured. What cannot be measured, cannot be improved. What cannot be improved, is always demoted."[6] This phrase remains relevant today; consequently, measuring through management indicators or strategic plan follow-ups are powerful and necessary tools for an organization's growth.

As far as the WCO is concerned, the Committees that produce its instruments can measure their results through management indicators that reveal if these actions have produced positive results or if, on the contrary, they should improve them. To this end, the Organization's current Strategic Plan[7] includes 29 performance indicators pursuant to the aforementioned 17 strategic goals, for example:

- Strategic Goal: SP1. Provide leadership, guidance, and support to Customs administrations. **Performance indicator**: Total initiatives or actions carried out

[6] What cannot be measured, cannot be improved. http://enciclopedia.us.es/index.php/Lord_Kelvin and https://www.aiteco.com/lo-que-no-se-mide. Accessed May 10, 2021.

[7] 2019–2020 Strategic Plan Implementation available at: http://www.wcoomd.org/-/me-dia/wco/public/global/pdf/about-us/administrative-documents/wco-implementation-plan-2019-2020.pdf?db=web. Accessed May 10, 2021.

to provide leadership, guide, and support Customs administrations/estimated initiatives or actions.

- Strategic Goal: SO1. Initiatives to move towards more facilitation. **Performance Indicator**: Number of initiatives developed or updated to move towards more facilitation (updated or new tools, cooperation, capacity building).
- Strategic Goal: SG. Provide leadership, guidance, and support to Customs administrations. **Performance indicator**: Total initiatives or actions carried out to provide leadership, guide, and support Customs administrations/estimated initiatives or actions.

On November 12th, 2019, the WCO launched the monitoring and reporting platform, available for members only, which will be updated regularly during the three-year implementation of the Strategic Plan 2019–2022. The report contains figures that cover all the initiatives conducted from July 2019 to the end of October 2019. Details include figures and data right down to specific actions performed under each of the strategic processes. The tool may be used as reference for WCO members and staff to keep up to date with the tasks completed, in progress, or planned for a later stage during the financial year.

Monitoring the implementation of the Strategic Plan opens the door to qualitative reporting and makes it possible to adapt quickly, without being held back by a strict three-year review process. Now, we shall see how effective the WCO is to amend and/or improve not so favorable scenarios, if one of its tools does not produce the desired effect.

Chapter 17
The Agenda of the Future

Since its establishment, the World Customs Organization has tried to be ahead of the eventual impacts that new industrial, trading, or technological developments could cause. Accordingly, in 2015[1] it created the Virtual Working Group on the Future of Customs that is made up of representatives from Customs administrations, universities and the private sector involved in international trade, and that has been working in the development of the document "The Future of Customs" that led to the more comprehensive report called "Study Report on Disruptive Technologies."[2]

The object of this study is to inform and help Customs administrations to better understanding what these technological advances are about, and how they could potentially be used in the years to come. This is so that the administrations are prepared to bring together all the appropriate measures to ensure proper and sustainable receipt and management, by fully exploiting the opportunities they provide, and neutralizing or decreasing the possible harmful side effects that could occur. To this end, understanding the depth and extent of those transformations is essential.

Let us take a closer look at the disruptive technologies under analysis and how they affect international trade management in general, and Customs management in particular.[3]

---

[1]The proposal was submitted at the 207th/208th Sessions of the Permanent Technical Committee (PTC) in March 2015.

[2]http://www.wcoomd.org/-/media/wco/public/global/pdf/topics/facilitation/instruments-and-tools/tools/disruptive-technologies/wco_disruptive_technologies_en.pdf?la=en. Accessed May 10, 2021.

[3]To view examples and case studies on each technical development, we suggest reading the author's article named "INFORME ESPECIAL: Las Aduanas ante la disrupción de las nuevas tecnologías" (SPECIAL REPORT: Customs in the face of the disruption of new technologies), available in Spanish at: https://tradenews.com.ar/aduana-block-chain-impresion-3d-internet-de-las-cosas-drones-inteligencia-artificial/as well as the TV report for "Estrategia Aduanera" on TV (México) available at: https://www.youtube.com/watch?v=IOrC99gRikw&t=4s. Accessed May 10, 2021.

H. H. Juárez Allende, *The World Customs Organization*, Law for Professionals,
https://doi.org/10.1007/978-3-030-85296-2_17

17.1 Blockchain

"Blockchain" is a concept that entails a giant revolution, which is not only applicable to economy or finances (where we can remember the Bitcoin or the Petro "cryptocurrencies") but can also be used in other environments to provide security and certainty in a chain of transactions.

The "Blockchain" is basically a recorded transaction that is added to a prior transaction to form a chain. Each of these blocks, once completed, is sealed and encrypted; therefore, to modify a transaction, all the participants in the blockchain must approve. This configuration grants the system enormous security on the transactions and the swift distribution of the information involved.

Blockchain technology may have a huge impact in customs processes: (i) in which there are several consecutive participants (freight carriers, shipping agents, customs brokers, custodians, importers, etc.); and (ii) which require security in their transactions (unalterable sworn statements). Consider, for instance, its use to issue certificates of origin, import licenses, or in single widow or integrated Customs management. Its development potential is huge to that effect.

The traceability and security of supply chains can be improved not only by reducing the number of intermediaries and paper or manual tasks, but also by providing certainty and predictability based on solid real-time information available to all supply chain stakeholders. This enables end-to-end traceability and visibility that increases supply chain security and facilitation. It is to be expected that blockchain-based solutions will significantly improve Customs' capacity for risk analysis and targeting, thus contributing to improved trade facilitation.

One aspect in which its huge potential will be appreciated is in the combat against the growing global tax base erosion. Lack of integration among the different operators in a supply chain has led to avoidance practices in which there are cross-trading transactions through the intervention of alleged intermediaries who distort prices with the aim of eroding the tax base or evading exchange rate controls. By having access to end-to-end transaction data, Customs services will be able to see the declared value of origin, as well as the places where goods are coming from, thus enabling the trigger of specific alerts and control mechanisms.

Yet, while benefits are visualized, challenges also arise: (i) their misuse as means of payment of illicit transactions, (ii) evasion of Customs duties and taxes, (iii) infringement of intellectual property rights, (iv) money laundering and (v) other financial crimes.

17.2 Artificial Intelligence (AI)

AI is the branch of computer science that develops processes that mimic the intelligence of living beings. Artificial intelligence involves several disciplines and fields (robotics, specialized systems), all of which share the creation of machines that can think. The idea is to build a machine able to execute tasks that require human intelligence. To this end tasks related to games, translation of languages, language understanding, diagnostics of faults, and robotics, among others, have been studied.

Some AI applications are already found in system controls, automated planning, the ability to respond to expert advice in different issues, carry out customer diagnosis and inquiries, and in handwriting, speech, and pattern recognition.[4]

Normal control procedures and customs audits are expensive and laborious tasks for officials who are responsible for verifying thousands or even millions of transactions. Use of artificial intelligence (AI) for fraud detection enables the discovery of "atypical points" helping officials to identify potential suspicious transactions.[5]

Some Customs have been working in the so-called "data mining" that is the intelligent use of information for the early (preventive) detection of suspicious transactions triggering "alerts" to the officials in charge of control.[6]

AI can also be used in: (i) tariff classification of goods, (ii) risk analysis, (iii) the analysis of images by X-ray scanners, (iv) logistical monitoring and control of Customs warehouses and cargo consolidation areas, (v) identification of high-risk passengers and vehicles, (vi) the enhancement of tax revenue services through the development of mobile applications, etc.

AI with specialized glasses (virtual reality or other) may be used by Customs for training purposes, as well as for shipment inspections and the detection of counterfeit and smuggled goods.

17.3 Internet of Things

The Internet of Things (IoT) is the inter-networking of physical devices, vehicles (also known as "connected devices" or "smart devices"), buildings and other items embedded with electronics software, sensors, and network connectivity that enable these objects to collect and exchange data.

It is estimated that over 20 billion devices will be connected to the network by 2020, 60% in consumer goods.[7]

---

[4]At the First WCO Global Communication Strategies Conference with the theme of "Communicating seamlessly in the digital age" held in Brussels, Belgium, on October 9, 2019, Indonesia Customs provided a specific example on how they implemented AI, through chatbots to provide up-to-date and 24/7 customer service. Available at: http://www.wcoomd.org/en/media/newsroom/2019/october/successful-conclusion-of-the-1st-wco-global-communication-strate-gies-conference-in-brussels. Accessed May 10, 2021.

[5]See full article in Spanish at: https://conexionintal.iadb.org/2018/03/27/la-facilitacion-del-comercio-america-latina-caribe-frente-la-revolucion-tecnologica. Accessed May 10, 2021.

[6]The Argentine Customs, which is integrated to the Internal Revenue and Social Security Resources Offices, uses this effective control methodology by exploiting the huge database it shares with these areas.

[7]Source: https://www.gartner.com/newsroom/id/2621015. Accessed May 10, 2021.

Among the main challenges the producers of IoT devices face, apart from connectivity and the possibility of exchanging information, the main concern is information security. Within the Customs context, the WCO considers the potentiality of the IoT in the implementation of the "Integrated Supply Chain Management" and in the "Single shipment reference."

Specifically, we can mention the advances in the Port of Hamburg, one of the leading institutions in the incorporation of the IoT into trading transactions.[8] The Port of Hamburg advances towards an intelligent structure, incorporating sensors and communicative abilities in their main assets. This includes motion sensor lighting, sensors monitoring the use of trucks, cranes, and infrastructure (e.g., roads, parking lots, warehouse storage rooms), storage systems with temperature, humidity, ventilation, and barometric pressure sensing ability that minimize the use of energy adjusting factors such as temperature and pressure. This results in a more efficient and secure[9] port operations.

In addition, China is implementing the IoT interconnection by allowing cargo shipment with the digital validation of container seals that activate exiting barriers, while vehicles are monitored through surveillance cameras and GPS systems. Likewise, the X-ray inspection system and the container weight verification system are interconnected to the weighing system, enabling the supervision of processes when assessing deviations.

At this point, we cannot fail to mention the initiative by the main container transportation industries that, in late 2018, created a non-profit entity with the object of boosting standardization, digitalization and interoperability in container transportation. In this sense, the harmonization of standards to widespread the implementation of satellite tracking systems of these loading units is being worked on.

The development and evolution of IoT will be deeply impacted and boosted by the fifth generation of wireless technology (5G) that will allow much faster connection speeds (between 100 and 250 faster than the fastest 4G networks), with connections of up to 20 gigabytes per second, and a latency rate of 1 millisecond (the delay between sending and receiving information), opening up a new ecosystem of emerging technologies that will allow to operate in (almost) real time, without any delays or perceptible latencies.

[8]For illustrative purposes only, we can mention the launching of the CONTAINER 42 project, a state-of-the-art container equipped with sensors that allow collecting information on the surrounding vibrations, tone, position, noise, air pollution, humidity, and temperature. This "smart" container left the Port of Rotterdam in May 2019, to set for a two-year research voyage in which it will gather valuable information on its journey to the major ports worldwide, sending the data to the cloud so it can be gathered and analyzed for a better port operation. The Container was built at the Port of Rotterdam in cooperation with IBM, Cisco, Esri, Axians, Intel, HvET Solar and DR Group. Further information available at: https://weare42.io. Accessed May 10, 2021.

[9]For further information: https://www.hamburg-port-authority.de/en. Accessed May 10, 2021.

17.4 Biometrics

Biometrics are statistical measurements and analyses of physiological and behavioral characteristics. The basic premise of this field is that each individual person is demonstratively unique and therefore, identifiable through their physiological or behavioral characteristics. This technology has produced major developments in facial, DNA, fingerprint, iris, palm vein, palm print and even odor recognition, allowing new information sources to verify an individual's identity.

Customs professionals may ask themselves why biometry, which focuses on people' identification (basically a migratory task), is relevant for the traditional and essential mission of Customs that focuses primarily on the movement of physical goods. To answer this, we should bear in mind that, except for unusual events (jetsam, forced arrival, movement of animals by their own means, etc.), in most cases the entry or removal of goods involves the participation of one human person (acting on their own behalf or on behalf of a third party). Therefore, thorough knowledge about his/her background (risk profile) will certainly be in the interest of Customs services.

Therefore, we can assert that the answer to the above question can be found in the potential of biometrics and its possible application as it can: (i) help to verify the identity of people sending shipments, (ii) control access to restricted areas (primary zones), (iii) secure levels of approval for process proceedings, (iv) identify subjects who have used franchises in special customs procedures (luggage, neighboring and cross-border transit, etc.), (v) replace vulnerability of security passwords and token equipment with the fingerprint or the iris reader (as mobile phones currently allow), among others.

17.5 Drones

The Oxford Advanced Dictionary defines a drone as an aircraft without a pilot. Initially, drones were used for recreational purposes, then for military purposes and currently for multiple purposes within which we can highlight commercial purposes.[10]

The Customs analyzes this issue from two standpoints: (i) as a new means of transport (remote-controlled aircraft) that may deliver legal goods as well as narcotic drugs, prohibited goods or other smuggled items, and (ii) as a new border control instrument.

From the first point of view, a series of questions with no uniform answers have arisen: What type of control measures should Customs develop to monitor cross-border movement of drones? Who will be responsible for the landing of drones

[10]From the commercial point of view, Couriers have been working on the transportation of packages in areas that are geographically remote or hard-to-reach.

carrying cargo? Will landing take place in traditional Customs stations or air cargo terminals? And, how can this be secured? How will data, including advance cargo information, be submitted to Customs, and by whom? Who will be responsible for the excess or shortage of cargo? How should the new class of actors in the supply chain-drone operators /owners be regulated? There is still a long way to go.

From the point of view of border control with drones, the United States Custom,[11] the Spanish Customs,[12] and the Ecuadorian Customs, among others, have been using this control instrument with excellent results as it facilitates surveillance in hardly accessible places as well as the detection of nocturnal movements by capturing infrared images in high resolution.

17.6 3D Printing

3D printing is a process of making three-dimensional solid objects from a digital file using a 3D printing machine and raw materials such as plastic, metal, nylon, or others.

These are products (houses, cars, weapons, etc.) with designs that are sent through the Internet and printed in other countries, without crossing any "physical" Customs. An industrial piece made in Germany could be "printed" in Argentina immediately after receiving its blueprint. This poses challenges regarding import taxes and even copyright as the piece may be printed endlessly.

This places us amid the so-called fourth wave of technological advancement: the digital industrial technology known as Industry 4.0, that features a transition from a centralized model to a decentralized, highly flexible, personalized, and digital smart mode of production of goods and services.

17.7 Intangibles[13]

One of the identified issues to be discussed is the WTO Ministerial Decision of December 19th, 2015 regarding the Electronic Commerce Programme (always promoted by the USA). This Decisions establishes that WTO members will keep

[11] The U.S. Customs and Border Protection has implemented the Unmanned aircraft system Predator-B (UAS) to patrol borders and combat illegal migration, control drug or weapon trafficking. Customs Border and Protection (CBP) currently maintains and operates a fleet of Predator-B units. Source: https://www.cbp.gov/border-security/air-sea/aircraft-and-marine-vessels. Accessed May 10, 2021.

[12] Further information available at: https://www.elindependiente.com/politica/2019/06/29/mas-drones-luchar-contrabando-narcotrafico. Accessed May 10, 2021.

[13] Although this matter is not currently being analyzed by the Virtual Working Group on the Future of Customs, it is included in this section as it could be one of the issues to be covered soon.

the current practice of NOT imposing custom duties (nor any other type of tax) to electronic transmissions.[14] Therefore, once again we should discuss whether Customs should only be involved with "tangibles" or if it can also venture in the "intangibles," to which purpose the concept of merchandise should be redefined with all its implications.[15]

Broadly speaking, trade of intangible assets refers to the digital or electronic transfer of products (e.g., software, music, movies, videos, books, etc.) by using information and communications technologies (ICT).

These electronic transmissions are no longer limited to the transfer of digital products for their final use or consumption, but also include digital designs to be used by manufactures that will then print the products in a tangible manner.

This trading modality, which few years ago was only emerging and barely generated transactions, has become a powerful player in global trade, taking the place of the large multinational factories of physical goods.[16,17]

Some Customs worldwide refuse to include intangibles as goods subject to Customs control,[18,19] others have begun to charge import and export duties to said

[14]The WTO, in its Decision of December 11, 2019 (WT/GC/W/794) on the World Programme on Electronic Commerce (WT/L/274), once again postponed this criterion until June 2020, stating that "…Members agree to maintain the current state of not imposing customs duties on electronic transmissions until the 12th session of the Ministerial Conference."

[15]This conceptual dispute appears not only in the field of customs law but also in physical sciences, as there are certain objects that look solid and firm to the human eye but that, using a microscope or laser or infrared lights, are not so. For example, an X-ray film shows that we are not as solid as we look because rays pass through us and project our more condensed elements (bones) on a receiving film. Moreover, the same holds true for radio or telephone waves. In the field of physical sciences, the "matter" concept is largely debated as there are theories that deem it as particles. waves or strings. Air provides a clear example, for it gives us the idea of being a vacuum or nothing, when it is actually made of elements and has consistency; e.g., it is a means through which sound travels; if we move our hands nothing seems to be there, but if we travel in a spaceship at high speed, friction with the air generates heat enough to burn it as a consequence of the resistance caused.

[16]Just by reading the Standard & Poor's rating, the S&P Global 1200, it can be seen that technological companies lead the list of most valuable companies by market capitalization, ahead of those linked to consumer goods and financial companies. Most of these companies are in a single country: United States. https://www.spglobal.com/spdji/en/indices/equity/sp-global-1200/#overview. Accessed May 10, 2021.

[17]From the 2019 WTO Word Trade Statistical Review, it arises that International Trade Services in 2018 amounted to USD 5.63 trillion, with a growth that was remarkably superior to the exchange of goods. https://www.wto.org/english/res_e/statis_e/wts2019_e/wts19_to-c_e.htm. Accessed May 10, 2021.

[18]The Singapore-Australia Free Trade Agreement (SAFTA) signed in 2003, in its Chapter 14, Article 3, Customs duties, expressly sets forth that: "Both Parties will maintain their current practice of not imposing customs duties on electronic transmissions between Australia and Singapore."

[19]Likewise, Article 14.3 of the Comprehensive and Progressive Agreement for Trans-Pacific Partnership (CPTPP) provides that: "1. Neither Party shall impose customs duties on electronic transmissions, including content electronically transmitted, between a person of a State party and a person of another State party."

transfers,[20] and a third group expects its treatment to be researched and analyzed globally, especially with respect to their most critical aspects:

(i) Classification, (ii) Valuation, (iii) Origin, (iv) Taxable event, (v) Control, (vi) Application of IPR (Intellectual Property Rights) and (viii) Illicit trading.

[20] Argentine Republic Customs Code: "Section 10: 1. For the purposes of this Code, merchandise is every object subject to being imported or exported. 2. The following are also considered – for the purposes of this Code – as if they were merchandise: c) The provision of services within the country, whose effective use or exploitation takes place abroad." (Subsection included by Section 78 of Law No. 27.467 Official Gazette 4/Dec/2018).

Chapter 18
Closing Words

When we look back to remote times (Neolithic period, approximately 8000 years BC), we observe that, after passing through a long nomad stage, human groups settled in territorial spaces that they considered their own, and over which they exerted the right to exclude other members of the species, external to their clan. These groups, who over time protected "their territories" with the different weapons that were available in each historical period, intended to defend themselves from the arrival of intruders.

This was the case until more advanced peoples, who developed agriculture, pottery, and craftwork, established cities and understood the advantages of trade, of the exchange of goods, and of relations with other peoples. They lifted military barriers and ceased the use of force. From that point on, peoples have entered a never-ending period which allows the entry of aliens bringing new and appealing goods from far-away geographical spaces controlled by "others."

Thus, cross-border goods entry and exit permits (borders that were generally the result of geographical characteristics, rivers, seas, mountain ranges) were granted through the payment of a right-of-way. A group of people who were strategically located at the land borders or seaports through which goods would necessarily arrive or depart were entrusted with the collection of this payment. These posts, charged with monitoring foreign traffic—entry and exit of goods—and collecting the right-of-way whenever applicable, were the Customs, one of the oldest institutions in the world.

Over time, Customs, along with their tax collecting activity, were also charged with preventing the entry or exit of goods that could affect local manufacturing industries, or jeopardize the interests of the treasury, health, or security of their populations. Therefore, Customs became responsible for protecting these interests and domestic production.

H. H. Juárez Allende, *The World Customs Organization*, Law for Professionals,
https://doi.org/10.1007/978-3-030-85296-2_18

Not to expand the historical account (which exceeds the purpose of this work),[1] we will jump to the Contemporary Age, where we observe that during the nineteenth century and up to World War I, the economic policies fostering free trade, free movement of goods, and non-intervention of the state in economic affairs were imposed in the West *("Laissez faire et laissez passer, le monde va de lui même" – "Let do and let pass, the world goes on by itself")*, limiting its role to safeguarding order and security.

In connection with Customs matters, protectionist practices were gradually removed, internal controls were abolished, and taxes were reduced to the point of not affecting free movement.

Once in the twentieth century, the effects of the economic crisis of the 1930s entailed the loss of vigor of global trade activities and the redesign of state economic policy through market intervention and regulation. This led to the fall of the liberal model that was replaced by a protectionist model in which the state had a strong presence in international trade.

The reimplementation of protectionist taxation measures and the establishment of direct restrictions on international trade implied the exclusion of Customs tariffs as a financial instrument of tax support. Then tariffs were replaced by internal taxes and states chose to subscribe bilateral agreements between countries as a new form of negotiation through which special and preferential tariff rates were set under the principle of reciprocity (bilateralism). This practice lasted until the end of World War II.

Once the world conflicts were over, pro-free trade ideas applied in the nineteenth and early twentieth century (now known as "neoliberalism") returned fostering the progressive liberalization of global trade, "multilateralism" (in replacement of bilateralism), and the creation of international organizations that command and regulate global trade worldwide.

Consequently, the World Bank, the International Monetary Fund, the International Trade Organization that led to the General Agreement on Tariffs and Trade (GATT) and is now referred to as World Trade Organization (WTO), and the Customs Cooperation Council today known as World Customs Organization gained prominence.

As we have seen throughout this book, this international matrix gave rise to the Agreements on Customs Valuation, on Rules of Origin, on the Harmonized System for the description and classification of goods and to the most ambitious Agreement Customs-wise (because of its "standardizing" nature), the Kyoto Convention.

International organizations surfaced as necessary platforms to reconcile the interests of sovereign states and the global community through various instruments that establish legal obligations and mechanisms that promote general welfare.

By observing the performance of the World Customs Organization, we can confirm that, in this sense, the mission has been fully accomplished, since through mutual cooperation, the WCO has been able to synchronize the efforts that have

[1] To this end, reading the following book is suggested: Asakura (2005).

supported the dramatic growth of global trade which we mentioned at the beginning of this book.

Cooperation, effectiveness, and efficiency are the three terms that best define the actions of the WCO. An agile and dynamic organization which, with limited budget and staff (when compared to other international organizations), has managed to bring together wills and to undertake unimagined projects (securing the supply chain, creating trusted operators with a permanent green channel, creating an information exchange network, among others).

Around the year 470 BC, Heraclitus, the Greek philosopher, would tell us: "The only constant in life is change". Today, in the international trade and Customs environment, we can affirm that we are undergoing a constant, dynamic, almost exponential change, in which modern technologies called disruptive, may very rapidly alter the way we trade and live.

By reducing downtime in the supply chain, the delivery time of products and commodities is reduced, boosting trust and the possibility of positioning perishable products that were previously excluded from international trade.

Distances shrink and trading markets grow.

New emerging technologies pose a true challenge to World Customs; fortunately, a specialized organization and the group of experts that comprise it and manage it, are already hard at work.

Reference

Asakura H (2005) World history of the customs and tariffs. World Customs Organization, Brussels, Belgium

Convention Establishing a Customs Co-operation Council

signed in Brussels on December 15, 1950 came into force on November 4, 1952

The Governments signatory to the present Convention,

Considering it advisable to secure the highest degree of harmony and uniformity in their Customs systems and especially to study the problems inherent in the development and improvement of Customs technique and Customs legislation in connection therewith,

Convinced that it will be in the interest of international trade to promote co-operation between Governments in these matters, bearing in mind the economic and technical factors involved therein,

Have agreed as follows:

ARTICLE I
A Customs Co-operation Council (hereinafter referred to as "the Council") is hereby set up.

ARTICLE II
a. The Members of the Council shall be:

   i. the Contracting Parties to the present Convention;
   ii. the Government of any separate Customs territory which is proposed by a Contracting Party having responsibility for the formal conduct of its diplomatic relations, which is autonomous in the conduct of its external commercial relations and whose admission as a separate Member is approved by the Council.

(continued)

H. H. Juárez Allende, *The World Customs Organization*, Law for Professionals,
https://doi.org/10.1007/978-3-030-85296-2

b. Any Government of any separate Customs territory, which is a Member of the Council under paragraph (a) (ii) above, shall cease to be a Member on notification to the Council of the withdrawal of its membership by the Contracting Party having responsibility for the formal conduct of its diplomatic relations.
c. Each Member shall nominate one delegate and one or more alternates to be its representatives on the Council. These representatives may be assisted by advisers.
d. The Council may admit representatives of non-Member Governments or of international organizations in the capacity of observers.

ARTICLE III

The functions of the Council shall be:

a. to study all questions relating to co-operation in Customs matters which the Contracting Parties agree to promote in conformity with the general purposes of the present Convention;
b. (b) to examine the technical aspects, as well as the economic factors related thereto, of Customs systems with a view to proposing to its Members practical means of attaining the highest possible degree of harmony and uniformity;
c. (c) to prepare draft Conventions and amendments to Conventions and to recommend their adoption by interested Governments;
d. (d) to make recommendations to ensure the uniform interpretation and application of the Conventions concluded as a result of its work as well as those concerning the Nomenclature for the Classification of Goods in Customs Tariffs and the Valuation of Goods for Customs Purposes prepared by the European Customs Union Study Group and, to this end, to perform such functions as may be expressly assigned to it in those Conventions in accordance with the provisions thereof;
e. (e) to make recommendations, in a conciliatory capacity, for the settlement of disputes concerning the interpretation or application of the Conventions referred to in paragraph (d) above in accordance with the provisions of those Conventions; the parties in dispute may agree in advance to accept the recommendations of the Council as binding;
f. to ensure the circulation of information regarding Customs regulations and procedures;
g. on its own initiative or on request, to furnish to interested Governments information or advice on Customs matters within the general purposes of the present Convention and to make recommendations thereon;
h. to co-operate with other inter-governmental organizations as regards matters within its competence.

(continued)

ARTICLE IV

The Members of the Council shall supply to the Council any information and documentation requested by it which is necessary for the execution of its functions provided that no Member shall be required to divulge confidential information, the disclosure of which would impede the enforcement of its laws, or which would otherwise be contrary to the public interest or prejudice the legitimate commercial interests of any enterprise, public or private.

ARTICLE V

The Council shall be assisted by a Permanent Technical Committee and a General Secretariat.

ARTICLE VI

a. The Council shall elect annually, from among the delegates of Members, a Chairman and not less than two Vice-Chairmen.
b. It shall establish its own Rules of Procedure by a majority of not less than two-thirds of its Members.
c. It shall establish a Nomenclature Committee as provided in the Convention on Nomenclature for the Classification of Goods in Customs Tariffs and a Valuation Committee as provided in the Convention on the Valuation of Goods for Customs Purposes. It shall also establish such other committees as may be desirable for the purposes of the Conventions referred to in Article III (d) or for any other purposes within its competence.
d. It shall determine the tasks to be assigned to the Permanent Technical Committee and the powers to be delegated to it.
e. It shall approve its annual budget, control its expenditure and give such directions as it may consider desirable regarding its finances to the General Secretariat.

ARTICLE VII

a. The Headquarters of the Council shall be in Brussels.
b. The Council, the Permanent Technical Committee and any committees established by the Council may meet elsewhere than at the Headquarters of the Council, if the Council so decides.
c. The Council shall meet at least twice a year. Its first meeting shall take place not later than three months after the entry into force of the present Convention.

ARTICLE VIII

a. Each Member of the Council shall have one vote except that a Member shall not have a vote on any question relating to the interpretation, application or amendment of any of the Conventions referred to in Article III (d) which is in force and which does not apply to that Member.

(continued)

b. Except as provided in Article VI (b) the decisions of the Council shall be taken by a majority of two-thirds of the Members present and entitled to vote. The Council shall not take a decision on any matter unless more than half of the Members entitled to vote on that matter are present.

ARTICLE IX

a. The Council shall establish such relations with the United Nations, its principal organs, subsidiary bodies and specialized agencies, and any other inter-governmental organizations, as may best assure collaboration in the achievement of their respective tasks.
b. The Council may make arrangements necessary to facilitate consultation and cooperation with non-governmental organizations interested in matters within its competence.

ARTICLE X

a. The Permanent Technical Committee shall be composed of representatives of the Members of the Council. Each Member of the Council may nominate one delegate and one or more alternates to be its representatives on the Committee. Representatives shall be officials specialized in technical Customs matters. They may be assisted by experts.
b. The Permanent Technical Committee shall meet not less than four times a year.

ARTICLE XI

a. The Council shall appoint a Secretary General and a Deputy Secretary General whose functions, duties, conditions of service and terms of office shall be determined by the Council.
b. The Secretary General shall appoint the staff of the General Secretariat. The establishment and staff regulations shall be approved by the Council.

ARTICLE XII

a. Each Member shall bear the expenses of its own delegation to the Council, to the Permanent Technical Committee and to any committees of the Council.
b. The expenses of the Council shall be borne by its Members in accordance with a scale to be determined by the Council.
c. The Council may deprive of its voting rights any Member which does not pay its contribution within three months of being notified of the amount thereof.
d. Each Member shall pay its full annual contribution for the financial year during which it becomes a Member of the Council and for the financial year during which its notice of withdrawal becomes effective.

(continued)

ARTICLE XIII

a. The Council shall enjoy, in the territory of each of its Members, such legal capacity, as defined in the Annex to the present Convention, as may be necessary for the exercise of its functions.
b. The Council, the representatives of Members, the advisers and experts appointed to assist them, and the officials of the Council shall enjoy the privileges and immunities specified in the Annex to the present Convention.
c. The Annex to the present Convention shall form an integral part thereof, and any reference to the Convention shall be deemed to include a reference to the Annex.

ARTICLE XIV

The Contracting Parties accept the provisions of the Protocol concerning the European Customs Union Study Group opened for signature at Brussels on the same date as the present Convention. In determining the scale of contributions provided for in Article XII (b), the Council shall take into consideration membership of the Study Group.

ARTICLE XV

The present Convention shall be open for signature until 31 March, 1951.

ARTICLE XVI

a. The present Convention shall be subject to ratification.
b. Instruments of ratification shall be deposited with the Belgian Ministry of Foreign Affairs, which shall notify all signatory and acceding Governments and the Secretary General of each such deposit.

ARTICLE XVII

a. When instruments of ratification have been deposited by seven of the signatory Governments, the present Convention shall come into force between them.
b. For each signatory Government ratifying thereafter the present Convention shall come into force upon deposit of its instrument of ratification.

ARTICLE XVIII

a. The Government of any State which is not a signatory to the present Convention may accede thereto as from 1 April, 1951.
b. Instruments of accession shall be deposited with the Belgian Ministry of Foreign Affairs, which shall notify all signatory and acceding Governments and the Secretary General of each such deposit.
c. The present Convention shall come into force for any acceding Government on the deposit of its instrument of accession, but not before it comes into force in accordance with paragraph (a) of Article XVII.

(continued)

ARTICLE XIX

The present Convention is of unlimited duration, but at any time after the expiry of five years from its entry into force under paragraph (a) of Article XVII, any Contracting Party may withdraw therefrom. Withdrawal shall take effect one year after the date of receipt by the Belgian Ministry of Foreign Affairs of the notification of withdrawal. The Belgian Ministry of Foreign Affairs shall notify each withdrawal to all signatory and acceding Governments and to the Secretary General.

ARTICLE XX

a. The Council may recommend amendments to the present Convention to the Contracting Parties.
b. Any Contracting Party accepting an amendment shall notify the Belgian Ministry of Foreign Affairs in writing of its acceptance and the Belgian Ministry of Foreign Affairs shall notify all signatory and acceding Governments and the Secretary General of the receipt of the notice of acceptance.
c. An amendment shall come into force three months after receipt by the Belgian Ministry of Foreign Affairs of notice of acceptance by all the Contracting Parties. When any amendment has been accepted by all the Contracting Parties the Belgian Ministry of Foreign Affairs shall notify all signatory and acceding Governments and the Secretary General of such acceptance and of the date on which the amendment will come into force.
d. After an amendment has come into force, no Government may ratify or accede to the present Convention unless it also accepts the amendment.

In witness whereof the undersigned, having been duly authorized thereto by their respective Governments, have signed the present Convention.

Done at Brussels on the fifteenth day of December, nineteen hundred and fifty (December 15, 1950) in the English and French languages, both texts being equally authentic, in a single original, which shall be deposited in the archives of the Government of Belgium which shall transmit certified copies thereof to each signatory and acceding Government.

ANNEX TO THE CONVENTION ESTABLISHING A CUSTOMS CO-OPERATION COUNCIL

LEGAL CAPACITY, PRIVILEGES AND IMMUNITIES OF THE COUNCIL

ARTICLE I DEFINITIONS

Section 1

In this Annex:

a. For the purposes of Article III, the words "property and assets" shall also include property and funds administered by the Council in furtherance of its constitutional functions;
b. For the purposes of Article V, the expression "representatives of Members" shall be deemed to include all representatives, alternates, advisers, technical experts and secretaries of delegations.

ARTICLE II JURIDICAL PERSONALITY

Section 2

The Council shall possess juridical personality. It shall have the capacity:

a. to contract,
b. to acquire and dispose of immovable and movable property,
c. to institute legal proceedings. In these matters the Secretary General shall act on behalf of the Council.

ARTICLE III PROPERTY, FUNDS AND ASSETS

Section 3

The Council, its property and assets, wherever located and by whomsoever held, shall enjoy immunity from every form of legal process except in so far as in any particular case it has expressly waived its immunity. It is, however, understood that no waiver of immunity shall extend to any measure of execution.

Section 4

The premises of the Council shall be inviolable. The property and assets of the Council, wherever located and by whomsoever held, shall be immune from search, requisition, confiscation, expropriation and any other form of interference whether by executive, administrative, judicial or legislative action.

Section 5

The archives of the Council and in general all documents belonging to it or held by it, shall be inviolable, wherever located.

Section 6

Without being restricted by financial controls, regulations or moratoria of any kind:

(continued)

a. the Council may hold currency of any kind and operate accounts in any currency;
b. the Council may freely transfer its funds from one country to another or within any country and convert any currency held by it into any other currency.

Section 7

The Council shall, in exercising its rights under Section 6 above, pay due regard to any representations made by any of its Members and shall give effect to such representations in so far as it considers that this can be done without detriment to the interests of the Council.

Section 8

The Council, its assets, income and other property shall be:

a. exempt from all direct taxes; it is understood, however, that the Council will not claim exemption from taxes which are, in fact, no more than charges for public utility services;
b. exempt from Customs duties and prohibitions and restrictions on imports and exports in respect of articles imported or exported by the Council for its official use; it is understood, however, that articles imported under such exemption will not be sold in the country into which they are imported, except under conditions agreed by the Government of that country;
c. exempt from all Customs duties and prohibitions and restrictions on imports and exports in respect of its publications.

Section 9

While the Council will not, as a general rule, claim exemption from excise duties and from taxes on the sale of movable and immovable property which form part of the price to be paid, nevertheless when the Council is making important purchases for official use of property on which such duties and taxes have been charged or are chargeable, Members of the Council will, whenever possible make appropriate administrative arrangements for the remission or return of the amount of duty or tax.

ARTICLE IV FACILITIES IN RESPECT OF COMMUNICATIONS

Section 10

The Council shall enjoy, in the territory of each of its Members, for its official communications, treatment not less favourable than that accorded by that Member to any other Government including the latter's diplomatic mission, in the matter of priorities, rates and taxes on mails, cables, telegrams, radiograms, telephotos, telephone and other communications, and press rates for information to the press and radio.

(continued)

Section 11

No censorship shall be applied to the official correspondence and other official communications of the Council.

Nothing in this section shall be construed to preclude the adoption of appropriate security precautions to be determined by agreement between the Council and any of its Members.

ARTICLE V REPRESENTATIVES OF MEMBERS

Section 12

Representatives of Members at meetings of the Council, the Permanent Technical Committee and committees of the Council shall, while exercising their functions and during their journeys to and from the place of meeting, enjoy the following privileges and immunities:

a. immunity from personal arrest or detention and from seizure of their personal baggage, and in respect of words spoken or written and all acts done by them in their official capacity, immunity from legal process of every kind;
b. inviolability for all papers and documents;
c. the right to use codes and to receive papers or correspondence by courier or in sealed bags;
d. exemption in respect of themselves and their spouses from immigration restrictions or aliens' registration in the State which they are visiting or through which they are passing in the exercise of their functions;
e. the same facilities in respect of currency or exchange restrictions as are accorded to representatives of foreign Governments or temporary official missions;
f. the same immunities and facilities in respect of their personal baggage as are accorded to members of comparable rank of diplomatic missions.

Section 13

In order to secure for the representatives of Members at meetings of the Council, the Permanent Technical Committee and committees of the Council complete freedom of speech and complete independence in the discharge of their duties, the immunity from legal process in respect of words spoken or written and all acts done by them in discharging their duties shall continue to be accorded, notwithstanding that the persons concerned are no longer engaged in the discharge of such duties.

Section 14

Privileges and immunities are accorded to the representatives of Members, not for the personal benefit of the individuals themselves, but in order to safeguard the independent exercise of their functions in connection with the

(continued)

Council. Consequently, a Member not only has the right but is under a duty to waive the immunity of its representatives in any case where, in the opinion of the Members, the immunity would impede the course of justice, and where it can be waived without prejudice to the purpose for which the immunity is accorded.

Section 15

The provisions of Sections 12 and 13 are not applicable in relation to the authorities of a State of which the person is a national or of which he is or has been a representative.

ARTICLE VI OFFICIALS OF THE COUNCIL

Section 16

The Council will specify the categories of officials to which this Article shall apply. The Secretary General shall communicate to the Members of the Council the names of the officials included in these categories.

Section 17

Officials of the Council shall:

a. be immune from legal process in respect of words spoken or written and all acts performed by them in their official capacity and within the limits of their authority;
b. be exempt from taxation in respect of the salaries and emoluments paid to them by the Council;
c. be immune, together with their spouses and relatives dependent on them, from immigration restrictions and aliens' registration;
d. be accorded the same privileges in respect of exchange facilities as are accorded to officials of comparable rank of diplomatic missions;
e. be given, together with their spouses and relatives dependent on them, the same repatriation facilities in time of international crises as officials of comparable rank of diplomatic missions;
f. have the right to import free of duty their furniture and effects at the time of first taking up their post in the country in question, and to return such furniture and effects free of duty to their country of domicile on the termination of their functions.

Section 18

In addition to the privileges and immunities specified in Section 17, the Secretary General of the Council shall be accorded in respect of himself, his spouse and children under the age of 21, the privileges, immunities, exemptions and facilities accorded to heads of diplomatic missions in conformity with international law.

(continued)

The Deputy Secretary General shall enjoy the privileges, immunities, exemptions and facilities accorded to diplomatic representatives of comparable rank.

Section 19

Privileges and immunities are granted to officials in the interest of the Council only and not for the personal benefit of the individuals themselves. The Secretary General shall have the right and the duty to waive the immunity of any official in any case where, in his opinion, the immunity would impede the course of justice and can be waived without prejudice to the interest of the Council. In the case of the Secretary General, the Council shall have the right to waive the immunity.

ARTICLE VII EXPERTS ON MISSIONS FOR THE COUNCIL

Section 20

Experts (other than officials coming within the scope of Article VI) performing missions for the Council, shall be accorded such privileges, immunities and facilities as are necessary for the independent exercise of their functions during the period of their missions, including the time spent on journeys in connection with their missions. In particular they shall be accorded:

a. immunity from personal arrest or detention and from seizure of their baggage;
b. in respect of words spoken or written or things done by them in the performance of their mission and within the limits of their authority, immunity from legal process of every kind;
c. inviolability for all papers and documents.

Section 21

Privileges, immunities and facilities are granted to experts in the interests of the Council and not for the personal benefit of the individual concerned. The Secretary General shall have the right and the duty to waive the immunity of any expert in any case where, in his opinion, the immunity would impede the course of justice and it can be waived without prejudice to the interests of the Council.

ARTICLE VIII ABUSES OF PRIVILEGES

Section 22

Representatives of Members at meetings of the Council, the Permanent Technical Committee and committees of the Council, while exercising their functions and during their journeys to and from the place of meeting, and officials within the meaning of Section 16 and Section 20, shall not be required

(continued)

by the territorial authorities to leave the country in which they are performing their functions on account of any activities by them in their official capacity. In the case, however, of abuse of privileges of residence committed by any such person in activities in that country outside his official functions, he may be required to leave by the Government of that country provided that:

i. Representatives of Members of the Council, or persons who are entitled to diplomatic immunity under Section 18, shall not be required to leave the country otherwise than in accordance with the diplomatic procedure applicable to diplomatic envoys accredited to that country.
ii. In the case of an official to whom Section 18 is not applicable, no order to leave the country shall be issued other than with the approval of the Foreign Minister of the country in question, and such approval shall be given only after consultation with the Secretary General of the Council, and if expulsion proceedings are taken against an official, the Secretary General of the Council shall have the right to appear in such proceedings on behalf of the person against whom they are instituted.

Section 23

The Secretary General shall co-operate at all times with the appropriate authorities of Members of the Council to facilitate the proper administration of justice, secure the observance of police regulations and prevent the occurrence of any abuses in connection with the privileges, immunities and facilities enumerated in the present Annex.

ARTICLE IX SETTLEMENT OF DISPUTES

Section 24

The Council shall make provision for appropriate modes of settlement of:

a. disputes arising out of contracts or other disputes of a private character to which the Council is a party;
b. disputes involving any official of the Council who by reason of his official position enjoys immunity, if immunity has not been waived in accordance with the provisions of Sections 19 and 21.

ARTICLE X SUPPLEMENTARY AGREEMENTS

Section 25

The Council may conclude with any Contracting Party or Contracting Parties supplementary agreements adjusting the provisions of the present Annex so far as that Contracting Party or those Contracting Parties are concerned.

Protocol to the Agreement between the Kingdom of Belgium and the Customs Cooperation Council

H. H. Juárez Allende, *The World Customs Organization*, Law for Professionals,
https://doi.org/10.1007/978-3-030-85296-2

PROTOCOL VAN OVEREENKOMST

tussen het Koninkrijk België en de Internationale Douaneraad, betreffende het behoud van de zetel van de Wereld Douane Organisatie in Brussel

DE REGERING VAN HET KONINKRIJK BELGIË, enerzijds,

en

DE INTERNATIONALE DOUANERAAD, anderzijds,

verlangende de praktische en financiële modaliteiten te regelen betreffende het behoud van de zetel van de Wereld Douane Organisatie in Brussel, ten gevolge van het besluit van de Raad van de Organisatie van 6 december 1996,

zijn overeengekomen hetgeen volgt:

Artikel 1

Overeenkomstig het besluit van de Internationale Douaneraad van 6 december 1996 om de zetel van de Wereld Douane Organisatie in Brussel te behouden, op grond van het door België voorgesteld definitief aanbod, verbindt het Koninkrijk België er zich toe aan de Internationale Douaneraad een jaarlijkse bijdrage te verlenen voor de periode tijdens welke deze laatste een jaarlijkse vergoeding betaalt in toepassing van de erfpachtovereenkomst met optie tot aankoop van het terrein en het gebouwencomplex te Brussel, die werd gesloten tussen Tijdelijke Vereniging «BURCO-CDP» en de Internationale Douaneraad op 7 februari 1997 en dit gedurende de zevenentwintig jaar tijdens welke de Organisatie in de gebouwen aanwezig is.

Artikel 2

De financiële tussenkomst van het Koninkrijk België beloopt vijftig miljoen Belgische frank voor het eerste jaar, vanaf 1 juli 1998, of, indien de erfpachtovereenkomst niet begint te lopen vanaf deze datum, vanaf de aanvangsdatum van deze erfpachtovereenkomst, en dit tot de afloop van deze overeenkomst.

Deze tussenkomst van het Koninkrijk België volgt de ontwikkeling van het geheel van de jaarlijkse vergoeding die door de Internationale Douaneraad verschuldigd is, in functie van en overeenkomstig de bepalingen van de erfpachtovereenkomst met de Tijdelijke Vereniging «BURCO-CDP» van 7 februari 1997.

Artikel 3

Indien, bij het einde van de erfpachtovereenkomst, de Internationale Douaneraad beslist de optie tot aankoop te lichten, verbindt hij er zich toe aan het Koninkrijk België de mogelijkheid te bieden 50% van de eigendom in onverdeeldheid te verwerven door middel van een aanbod van de helft van de optie tot aankoop waarover de Internationale Douaneraad inzake het goed beschikt en dit voor de som van 1 Belgische frank of zijn equivalent op dat ogenblik. Een dergelijke afstand kan slechts geschieden mits akkoord van de Belgische Regering die haar beslissing dient kenbaar te maken binnen een maand, te rekenen vanaf de tijdige notificatie door de Internationale Douaneraad.

Artikel 4

Indien, bij het einde van de erfpachtovereenkomst, de Internationale Douaneraad beslist om zijn optie tot aankoop niet te lich-

PROTOCOLE D'ACCORD

entre le Royaume de Belgique et le Conseil de Cooperation Douanière relatif au maintien du siège de l'Organisation Mondiale des Douanes a Bruxelles

LE GOUVERNEMENT DU ROYAUME DE BELGIQUE, d'une part,

et

LE CONSEIL DE COOPÉRATION DOUANIÈRE, d'autre part,

désireux de régler les modalités pratiques et financières relatives au maintien du siège de l'Organisation Mondiale des Douanes à Bruxelles, comme suite à la décision du Conseil de l'Organisation du 6 décembre 1996, y relative

sont convenus de ce qui suit:

Article 1

Conformément à la décision du Conseil de Coopération douanière du 6 décembre 1996, de maintenir le siège de l'Organisation Mondiale des Douanes à Bruxelles, sur base de l'offre définitive présentée par la Belgique, le Gouvernement du Royaume de Belgique s'engage à donner une subvention annuelle au Conseil de Coopération douanière durant la période où celui-ci doit s'acquitter d'une redevance annuelle en application du contrat de bail emphytéotique avec option d'achat du terrain et du complexe immobilier sis à Bruxelles, contrat passé entre l'Association Momentanée «BURCO-CDP», et le Conseil de Coopération douanière, le 7 février 1997, et ce pendant les vingt-sept années de présence de l'Organisation dans ces bâtiments.

Article 2

L'intervention financière du Royaume de Belgique s'élève à cinquante millions de FB pour la première année, à partir du 1 juillet 1998 ou à défaut de la prise de cours du bail d'emphytéotique à cette date, à partir de la date de prise de cours de ce bail et jusqu'à l'expiration de ce bail.

Cette intervention du Royaume de Belgique suivra l'évolution de la totalité de la redevance annuelle due par le Conseil de Coopération douanière, en fonction de et d'après les stipulations de son bail emphytéotique avec l'Association momentanée «BURCO-CDP» du 7 février 1997.

Article 3

Au terme du bail emphytéotique, si le Conseil de Coopération douanière décide de lever son option d'achat, le Conseil de Coopération douanière s'engage à offrir au Royaume de Belgique la possibilité d'acquérir 50% indivis de la propriété par une offre de la moitié de l'option d'achat dont le Conseil de Coopération douanière dispose sur ledit bien, et ce pour la somme de 1 FB ou son plus proche équivalent existant à cette époque. Une telle cession ne pourra intervenir qu'avec l'accord du Gouvernement belge qui disposera d'un délai d'un mois pour notifier sa décision à dater de la notification du Conseil de Coopération douanière qui lui aura été faite à temps.

Article 4

Au terme du bail emphytéotique, si le Conseil de Coopération douanière décide de ne pas lever son option d'achat, celui-ci

ten, verbindt hij er zich toe zijn optie tot aankoop aan te bieden aan het Koninkrijk België voor 100%.

Een dergelijke afstand kan slechts geschieden mits akkoord van de Belgische Regering, die haar beslissing dient kenbaar te maken binnen de drie maand, te rekenen vanaf de tijdige notificatie door de Internationale Douaneraad.

Artikel 5

Ingeval het Koninkrijk België, de eigendom van het terrein en het gebouwencomplex, in onverdeeldheid, geheel of gedeeltelijk zou verwerven, gaat het de verplichting aan om geen huurgeld te vragen aan de Internationale Douaneraad zolang de Wereld Douane Organisatie het gebouwencomplex benut, alsook om geen eis te stellen om uit de onverdeeldheid te treden zonder het akkoord van de Internationale Douaneraad. Deze laatste verbindt zich om de huurlasten, zoals vastgesteld in de Belgische wetgeving, te zullen dragen.

Artikel 6

Als het gebouwencomplex waarover sprake in het contract tussen de Internationale Douaneraad en de Tijdelijke Vereniging «BURCO-CDP» niet beschikbaar zou zijn overeenkomstig de bepalingen en voorwaarden van dit contract, dan verbindt het Koninkrijk België er zich toe een gepaste huisvesting ter beschikking te stellen van de Organisatie tot op het ogenblik dat het gebouwencomplex naar behoren ter beschikking kan gesteld worden zonder dat de bijdrage van de Internationale Douaneraad groter zou zijn dan het bedrag dat hij had moeten betalen indien hij over het complex had kunnen beschikken op 1 juli 1998.

Als tegenprestatie verbindt de Internationale Douaneraad zich ertoe de vergoeding wegens vertraging, die hem betaald zal worden door de verpachter, overeenkomstig het contract tussen de Internationale Douaneraad en de Tijdelijke Vereniging «BURCO-CDP», te bestemmen voor de bijkomende onkosten ten laste van het Koninkrijk België voor deze huisvesting, eventueel onder voorbehoud van de opeenvolgende minderingen op de werkelijk door de Internationale Douaneraad opgelopen schade als gevolg van de vertraagde ingebruikneming van het gebouwencomplex, dit alles te beoordelen in overleg met de Belgische Regering.

Artikel 7

Elk geschil betreffende de interpretatie of de toepassing van dit Protocol dient voorgelegd te worden aan een Commissie, die samengesteld is uit vertegenwoordigers van beide Partijen. Deze Commissie vergadert op verzoek van de meest gerede partij en zonder ongerechtvaardigde vertraging.

Artikel 8

Elke partij deelt aan de andere partij de vervulling mee van de volgens haar wetgeving vereiste procedures voor de inwerkingtreding van dit Protocol.

Ten blijke waarvan de ondergetekende vertegenwoordigers, die daartoe gemachtigd wreden, dit Protocol ondertekend hebben.

Gedaan te Brussel, op 7 februari 1997, in twee originelen, in de Nederlandse en de Franse taal, zijnde de twee teksten gelijkelijk rechtsgeldig.

s'engage à offrir au Royaume de Belgique son option d'achat à concurrence de 100%.

Une telle cession ne pourra intervenir qu'avec l'accord du Gouvernement belge, qui disposera d'un délai de trois mois pour sa décision et pour la notifier, à dater de la notification de la décision du Conseil de Coopération douanière faite en temps voulu.

Article 5

Pour le cas où le Royaume de Belgique acquerrait, en partie ou en totalité, la propriété du terrain et du complexe immobilier indivis, le Royaume de Belgique s'engage à s'abstenir de toute demande de loyer à l'égard du Conseil de Coopération douanière aussi longtemps que l'Organisation occupera le complexe immobilier et à s'abstenir de toute demande de sortie d'indivision sans l'accord du Conseil de Coopération douanière. Celui-ci s'engage à assumer les charges locatives définies par la législation belge.

Article 6

Si le complexe immobilier visé par le contrat passé entre le Conseil de Coopération douanière et l'Association momentanée «BURCO-CDP» n'était pas disponible selon les dispositions et les conditions dudit contrat, le Royaume de Belgique s'engage à garantir un logement adéquat à l'Organisation jusqu'à ce que le complexe immobilier puisse valablement être mis à sa disposition, sans que la contribution du Conseil de Coopération douanière soit supérieure au montant qu'il aurait dû payer s'il avait pu disposer de ce complexe au 1er juillet 1998.

En contrepartie le Conseil de Coopération douanière s'engage à affecter les indemnités de retard que lui versera la bailleresse emphytéotique, conformément au contrat conclu entre le Conseil de Coopération douanière et l'Association momentanée «BURCO-CDP», au paiement des frais complémentaires encourus par le Royaume de Belgique pour ce logement, sous réserve éventuellement de déductions consécutives au dommage réellement subi par le Conseil de Coopération douanière du fait de ce retard d'occupation, à évaluer conjointement avec le Gouvernement belge.

Article 7

Tout différend relatif à l'interprétation ou à l'application du présent Protocole doit être soumis à une commission, composée de représentants des deux Parties. Celle-ci se réunit à la demande de la Partie la plus diligente et sans délai injustifié.

Article 8

Chacune des Parties notifie à l'autre Partie l'accomplissement des procédures requises par sa législation pour la mise en vigueur du présent Protocole.

EN FOI DE QUOI, les Représentants soussignés, dûment autorisés, ont signé le présent Protocole.

FAIT à Bruxelles, le 7 février 1997, en deux originaux, en langues française et néerlandaise, les deux textes faisant également foi.

1-1017/1 - 1997/1998 (10)

VOOR HET KONINKRIJK BELGIË:	POUR LE ROYAUME DE BELGIQUE:
Carlos VAN WALLEGHEM	Carlos VAN WALLEGHEM
Directeur-Generaal, Administratie der Douane en Accijnzen	*Directeur Général, Administration des Douanes et Accises*
Ministerie van Financiën	*Ministère des Finances*
VOOR DE INTERNATIONALE DOUANERAAD:	POUR LE CONSEIL DE COOPÉRATION DOUANIÈRE:
Leonid LOZBENKO	Leonid LOZBENKO
Adjunct-Secretaris-Generaal	*Secrétaire Général adjoint*

Source: Senate of the Kingdom of Belgium. Session 1997–1998

PROTOCOL OF AGREEMENT
between the Kingdom of Belgium and the Customs Cooperation Council regarding maintenance of the World Customs Organization's headquarters in Brussels.[1]

THE KINGDOM OF BELGIUM of the one part, and

THE CUSTOMS COOPERATION COUNCIL, on the other part,

Desiring to regulate the practical and financing terms and conditions in connection with the maintenance of the World Customs Organization's headquarters in Brussels pursuant to the Council's decision of December 6th, 1996 have agreed as follows:

Article 1

In accordance with the Customs Cooperation Council's decision of December 6th, 1996 related to maintaining the World Customs Organization's headquarters in Brussels based on the definitive offer submitted by Belgium; the Government of the Kingdom of Belgium commits itself to providing an annual subsidy to the Customs Cooperation Council during the period in which the latter shall pay an annual fee pursuant to the emphyteutic lease with the option to purchase the land and building complex in Brussels according to the agreement entered into between "Association Momentanée BURCO-CDP"[2] and the Customs Cooperation Council on February 7th, 1997 and during the twenty-seven years of presence of the Organization in these buildings.

(continued)

[1] Non-official translation.

[2] Translator's note: Translation into English from a non-official Spanish translation. In Belgian Law an "Association Momentanée is a partnership set up without legal personality with determined and limited commercial goals, and not allowed to develop any other type of activity as partnership (Article 53 of the Belgian Company Law).

Article 2
The financial intervention of the Kingdom of Belgium shall be fifty million of Belgian francs during the first year, as of July 1st, 1998, or in the absence of a lease agreement on this date, as of the date of the lease and until the date of its termination.

This intervention of the Kingdom of Belgium shall follow the evolution of the total annual fee owed by the Customs Cooperation Council pursuant to the provisions of its emphyteutic lease with "Association Momentanée BURCO-CDP" of February 7th, 1997.

Article 3
Upon termination of the emphyteutic lease, if the Customs Cooperation Council decides to use its option to purchase, the Customs Cooperation Council commits itself to offer the Kingdom of Belgium the possibility to acquire 50% of the undivided property through an offer of half of the available purchase option for the Customs Cooperation Council upon said property, for 1 (ONE) Belgian Franc or its closest existing equivalent at that moment. Said transfer could only be possible with the agreement of the Belgian Government which shall have one month to notify its decision as of the date of the notification of the Customs Cooperation Council that would have made on time.

Article 4
Upon termination of the emphyteutic lease, if the Customs Cooperation Council decides not to exercise its option of purchase, it commits itself to offer the Kingdom of Belgium its purchase option at 100% of market value.

Said transfer could only be made with the agreement of the Belgian Government which shall have three months to make its decision and notify it as of the date of the notification of the Customs Cooperation Council made on due time.

Article 5
In case the Kingdom of Belgium acquires partially or totally the undivided property of and building complex, the Kingdom of Belgium commits itself to restrain from any leasing request to the Customs Cooperation during all the time that the Organization occupies the building complex, and from any request to leave the joint tenancy without the agreement of the Customs Cooperation Council. The Council commits itself to bear the lease expenses defined by the Belgian legislation.

(continued)

Article 6

If the building complex object of the agreement between the Customs Cooperation Council and the "Association Momentanée BURCO-CDP" were not available pursuant to the terms and provisions of said agreement, the Kingdom of Belgium commits itself to provide suitable premises for the Organization until the building complex is made available, without a higher Customs Cooperation Council's contribution than the amount that would have been payable, if it had had access to the building complex on July 1st, 1998.

In return, the Customs Cooperation Council commits itself to apply the late payment penalties, which the emphyteutic lessor shall pay to it pursuant to the agreement entered into between the Customs Cooperation Council and the "Association Momentanée BURCO-CDP", to the payments of additional expenses incurred by the Kingdom of Belgium for this property, subject to the eventual deductions derived from the actual damage suffered by the Customs Cooperation Council as a result of the delay in occupancy, to be jointly evaluated with the Belgian government.

Article 7

Any dispute related to the interpretation or application of this Protocol shall be submitted to a commission made up of representatives of both Parties. Said commission shall meet upon the request of the most diligent Party and without unjustified delays

Article 8

Each Party shall notify the other of the conclusion of the proceedings required by their legislation for the entry into force of this Protocol.

IN WITNESS WHEREOF, the undersigned Representatives, being duly authorized thereto, have executed this Protocol.

DONE at Brussels, on February 7th, 1997 in two originals in the French and Dutch languages, each text being equally authentic.

FOR THE KINGDOM OF BELGIUM Carlos VAN WALLEGHEM
Director General, Customs and Excise Administration
Ministry of Finance FOR THE CUSTOMS COOPERATION COUNCIL
Leonid LOZBENKO Deputy Secretary General

Conventions of the Customs Cooperation Council

H. H. Juárez Allende, *The World Customs Organization*, Law for Professionals,
https://doi.org/10.1007/978-3-030-85296-2

	CONVENTION ESTABLISHING A CUSTOMS COOPERATION COUNCIL	NOMENCLATURE	BRUSSELS VALUATION (BDV)	HARMONIZED SYSTEM	COMMERCIAL SAMPLES	PROFESSIONAL EQUIPMENT	FAIRS
MEMBER COUNTRIES							
AFGHANISTAN	10-Aug-04						
ALBANIA	31-Aug-92			16-May-12			
ALGERIA	19-Dec-66		18-Aug-77	24-Oct-91	3-Nov-88	5-Sep-72	31-Oct-88
ANDORRA	3-Sep-98			11-Jul-06			
ANGOLA	26-Sep-90			4-Apr-11			
ANTIGUA AND BARBUDA	10-Apr-17						
ARGENTINA	1-Jul-68			11-Jan-94			
ARMENIA	30-Jun-92			5-Jan-09			
AUSTRALIA	5-Jan-61	22-Sep-87		22-Sep-87		4-Dec-67	20-Dec-62
AUSTRIA	21-Jan-53	22-Sep-87		22-Sep-87	9-Mar-62	5-Oct-62	20-Sep-62
AZERBAIJAN	17-Jun-92			7-Jul-00			
BAHAMAS	16-Aug-74			13-Sep-11			
BAHRAIN	1-Jul-78			14-Dec-01			24-Jan-97
BANGLADESH	7-Jan-99	22-Sep-86		22-Sep-87			
BARBADOS	16-Aug-74						
BELARUS	16-Dec-93			21-Oct-98			
BELGIUM	11-Dec-52	22-Sep-87		22-Sep-87	27-Jun-63	7-Sep-65	6-Jul-67
BELIZE	22-Apr-08						
BENIN	9-Nov-98			24-Jul-06			
BERMUDA	1-Jul-90						
BHUTAN	12-Feb-02			27-Oct-06			
BOLIVIA	14-Aug-97			27-Apr-04			
BOSNIA AND HERZEGOVINA	4-Jul-08			14-Aug-12			
BOTSWANA	25-Aug-78	13-Feb-87		13-Feb-87			
BRAZIL	19-Jan-81			8-Nov-88			
BRUNEI DARUSSALAM	1-Jul-96			28-Jun-14			
BULGARIA	1-Aug-73			30-Oct-90	5-Aug-69	31-Jul-64	31-Jul-64
BURKINA FASO	16-Sep-66			25-Sep-90			
BURUNDI	20-Oct-64			18-Jan-17			
CAMBODIA	3-Apr-01			27-Jun-02	20-Feb-63		20-Feb-63
CAMEROON	9-Apr-65			16-May-88			
CANADA	12-Oct-71	14-Dec-87		14-Dec-87			
CAPE VERDE	1-Jul-92			19-May-08			
CENTRAL AFRICAN REP.	28-Jul-86			11-Jun-98	23-Feb-62	1-Apr-62	1-Apr-62
CHAD	16-Feb-05			5-Sep-90			
CHILE	1-Jul-66			17-Feb-05			
CHINA	18-Jul-83			23-Jun-92			27-Aug-93
COLOMBIA	1-Jul-93			21-Oct-02			
COMOROS	1-Jul-93			7-Jan-13			
CONGO (Dem. Rep. of the)	26-Jul-72			27-Mar-07			
CONGO (Republic of the)	2-Sep-75			10-Nov-87			
COSTA RICA	29-Aug-01			3-Jul-12			
COTE D'IVOIRE	2-Sep-63			25-Jan-90			2-Jun-78
CROATIA	1-Jul-93			29-Sep-94	29-Sep-94	29-Sep-94	29-Sep-94
CUBA	11-Jul-88			3-Nov-95	31-Oct-63	3-Dec-62	2-May-62
CURAÇAO	1-Jul-01						
CYPRUS	31-Aug-67			21-Mar-94		15-Dec-72	2-Jun-78
CZECH REPUBLIC	1-Jan-93	9-Dec-87		16-Nov-93	1-Jan-93	1-Jan-93	29-Sep-94
DENMARK	19-Oct-51	22-Sep-87		22-Sep-87	15-Dec-61	14-Apr-65	2-May-62
DJIBOUTI	19-Mar-08			12-Jun-15			
DOMINICAN REPUBLIC	28-Jul-04			7-Sep-06			12-Dec-62
ECUADOR	16-Dec-97			22-Oct-08			
EGYPT	26-Oct-56			27-May-99	25-Mar-63	25-Mar-63	25-Mar-63
EL SALVADOR	7-Jul-05						
ERITREA	8-Aug-95			17-Jan-03			
ESTONIA	18-Jun-92			26-May-93			
ETHIOPIA	6-Aug-73			1-Mar-95			
FIJI	1-Jul-97			23-Dec-97			
FINLAND	27-Jan-61	22-Sep-87		22-Sep-87	23-Apr-65	1-Aug-64	1-Aug-64
FRANCE	6-Oct-52	22-Sep-87		22-Sep-87	26-Jan-61	31-Mar-62	22-Jun-64
GABON	18-Feb-65			7-Jul-00			

ATA CARNET	WELFARE MATERIAL FOR SEAFARERS	SCIENTIFIC EQUIPMENT	PEDAGOGIC MATERIAL	KYOTO CONVENTION	REVISED KYOTO CONVENTION (as amended)	NAIROBI	ISTANBUL	JOHANNESBURG
					6-Apr-13	6-May-01	28-May-09	7-Mar-05
2-Jul-73	5-Mar-69	5-Aug-69	16-Jun-71		26-Jun-99	27-Oct-88	8-May-98	
2-Sep-98							2-Sep-98	
					23-Feb-17			
			3-Jan-73		19-Jun-15			
					19-Jul-13		3-Jul-18	
14-Jun-67	9-Jan-67	30-Jun-69	25-Jun-71		10-Oct-00	11-Mar-86	9-Jan-92	
20-May-63		29-Mar-72	10-Oct-72		30-Apr-04	16-Jun-78	29-Sep-94	
					2-Mar-06	25-4-2002		
					31-May-12		31-May-12	
					27-Sep-12			
			7-Mar-75					
7-May-98					1-Oct-11	9-Jul-00	7-May-98	26-Jun-04
22-Feb-66	20-Jun-66	12-Nov-70			30-Apr-04		18-Jul-97	
		16-Jan-69	5-Feb-71		1-May-17			
					15-Sep-14			
							7-Apr-10	
					26-Jun-06			
							4-May-11	
31-Jul-64					17-Mar-04		11-Mar-03	
					7-Aug-17			17-May-04
				25-Jun-74				
					28-Jun-14			26-Jun-04
		5-Dec-69	29-Jun-71		18-Nov-14			
10-Jul-72		24-Jul-74			11-Sep-00	19-Sep-90		
					27-Jun-13			
		30-Jun-69						
		3-Apr-70					3-Mar-04	
27-Aug-93					15-Jun-00		27-Aug-93	
				24-Oct-77	14-Dec-17			
14-Jun-62	26-Sep-78				27-Jun-13	10-Oct-83		
29-Sep-94	29-Sep-94	29-Sep-94			11-Feb-05	17-Oct-00	1-Mar-99	
24-Sep-63					24-Jun-09	11-May-95		
25-Oct-76		12-Feb-71	30-Nov-73		25-Oct-04	30-May-01	25-Oct-04	
1-Jan-93		1-Jan-93			17-Sep-01	29-Jun-99	24-Nov-99	
14-Apr-65	16-May-66	5-Jun-69			30-Apr-04		18-Jun-97	
					28-Jun-12			
		23-Sep-69						
11-Jan-68	20-Oct-67	26-May-70	21-Jan-71		1-Aug-08			
					28-Jul-06		17-Jan-96	
		17-Mar-71			26-Jan-10			
1-Aug-64	17-May-68				30-Apr-04	6-Jul-85	18-Jun-97	
20-Dec-62	6-Jul-66	22-May-69	15-Mar-73		22-Jul-04	4-Dec-01	18-Jun-97	
		25-Aug-69			15-Nov-12			

	CONVENTION ESTABLISHING A CUSTOMS COOPERATION COUNCIL	NOMENCLATURE	BRUSSELS VALUATION (BDV)	HARMONIZED SYSTEM	COMMERCIAL SAMPLES	PROFESSIONAL EQUIPMENT	FAIRS
GAMBIA	14-Oct-87						
GEORGIA	26-Oct-93			27-Mar-09			
GERMANY	4-Nov-52	22-Sep-87		22-Sep-87	11-Jul-69	11-Jul-69	9-Jun-67
GHANA	1-Aug-68			29-Jun-07			
GREECE	10-Dec-51			15-Jul-88		19-Jul-62	19-Jul-62
GUATEMALA	22-Feb-85			18-Sep-14			
GUINEA	30-Oct-91			23-Sep-97			
GUINEA-BISSAU	19-Aug-10			23-May-13			
GUYANA	29-Jul-76						
HAITI	31-Jan-58		31-Jan-58	17-Jan-00			
HONDURAS	8-Dec-05						
HONG KONG, CHINA	1-Jul-87						
HUNGARY	16-Sep-68			27-Aug-90		4-Feb-63	4-Feb-63
ICELAND	15-Feb-71	28-Oct-87		28-Oct-87		8-Dec-70	8-Dec-70
INDIA	15-Feb-71	23-Jun-86		23-Jun-86			20-Jun-88
INDONESIA	30-Apr-57			5-Jul-93			
IRAN (Islamic Republic of)	16-Oct-59			28-Feb-95	16-Apr-68	16-Apr-68	16-Apr-68
IRAQ	6-Jun-90						
IRELAND	23-Sep-52			22-Dec-87	15-Sep-65	15-Apr-65	15-Apr-65
ISRAEL	23-May-58		26-Feb-81	5-Aug-87	2-Jun-61	1-Feb-66	16-Dec-64
ITALY	20-Nov-52			31-May-89	30-May-63	20-Sep-63	9-Nov-63
JAMAICA	29-Mar-63						
JAPAN	15-Jun-64	22-Jun-87		22-Jun-87		1-Aug-73	1-Aug-73
JORDAN	1-Jan-64	10-Oct-85		10-Jun-85			
KAZAKHSTAN	30-Jun-92			26-Mar-04			
KENYA	24-May-65		13-Mar-67	29-Jul-88	31-Aug-83	31-Aug-83	
KOREA (Republic of)	2-Jul-68	27-Nov-87		27-Nov-87	21-Oct-75	4-Apr-78	21-Oct-75
KOSOVO	25-Jan-17						
KUWAIT	4-Oct-93			27-Nov-03			
KYRGYZSTAN	10-Feb-00			4-Jan-07			
LATVIA	16-Jan-07						
LAO PEOPLE'S DEM. REP.	16-Jan-07			0-Jan-00			
LEBANON	20-May-60			3-May-96		11-Dec-79	11-Dec-79
LESOTHO	2-Aug-78	12-Dec-85		12-Dec-85	27-Jan-82	27-Jan-82	27-Jan-82
LIBERIA	7-Jan-75			25-Jun-10			
LIBYA	11-Jan-83			17-May-93			
LITHUANIA	18-Jun-92			20-Jun-94			
LUXEMBOURG	23-Jan-53			11-Jul-88	12-May-64	28-Jan-66	16-Feb-71
MACAU, CHINA	7-Jul-93						
MADAGASCAR	18-Feb-64			22-Dec-87		12-Apr-62	12-Apr-62
MALAWI	6-Jun-66			25-Oct-88			
MALAYSIA	30-Jun-64	12-Dec-87		15-Dec-87			
MALDIVES	8-Sep-95			7-Jul-00			
MALI	7-Aug-87			15-Jun-94			3-Mar-89
MALTA	6-Jul-68			20-Dec-89		11-May-88	11-May-88
MAURITANIA	2-Oct-79			3-Apr-01			
MAURITIUS	29-Mar-73	10-Jun-85		10-Jun-85			
MEXICO	8-Feb-88			6-Sep-91		7-Nov-00	13-Nov-00
MOLDOVA	28-Oct-94			10-Jun-04			
MONGOLIA	17-Sep-91			30-Sep-91			
MONTENEGRO	24-Oct-06			23-Mar-07			
MOROCCO	1-Jul-68			27-Feb-92			16-Nov-62
MOZAMBIQUE	1-Jul-87			11-Oct-12			
NAMIBIA	1-Jul-92			5-May-04			
NEPAL	22-Jul-85			25-Aug-06			
NETHERLANDS	23-Jan-53	22-Sep-87		22-Sep-87	21-Nov-62	17-Jan-64	16-Nov-62
NEW ZEALAND	16-May-63	22-Sep-87		22-Sep-87		17-May-77	16-Nov-62
NICARAGUA	24-Sep-98						
NIGER	1-Jul-81			16-Mar-90		14-Mar-62	14-Mar-62
NIGERIA	21-Aug-63			15-Mar-88			
NORWAY	6-Aug-51	22-Aug-87		27-Aug-87	21-Nov-61	30-Mar-62	23-Sep-63
OMAN	11-Sep-00			12-May-16			
PAKISTAN	16-Nov-55	22-Sep-86		22-Sep-87			
PALESTINE	24-Mar-15		14-Oct-57	10-Mar-17			
PANAMA	8-Mar-96			24-Aug-98			
PAPUA NEW GUINEA	18-Mar-02			18-Dec-13			
PARAGUAY	3-Oct-69			12-Jan-07			
PERU	27-Jan-70			9-Jul-98			
PHILIPPINES	1-Oct-80			28-Jun-01			
POLAND	17-Jul-74			12-Sep-95	29-Jun-65	19-Jul-69	19-Jul-69
PORTUGAL	26-Jan-53	4-Nov-87		4-Nov-87	23-May-90	15-Mar-62	31-Mar-62
QATAR	4-May-92			28-Sep-04			
ROMANIA	15-Jan-69			5-Dec-96	23-Dec-66	26-Mar-68	15-Jan-64
RUSSIAN FEDERATION	8-Jul-91			18-Jun-96			
RWANDA	3-Mar-64			29-Jul-92			

ATA CARNET	WELFARE MATERIAL FOR SEAFEARERS	SCIENTIFIC EQUIPMENT	PEDAGOGIC MATERIAL	KYOTO CONVENTION	REVISED KYOTO CONVENTION (as amended)	NAIROBI	ISTANBUL	JOHANNESBURG
				16-Jan-74				
						12-Mar-09	1-Apr-10	
15-Oct-65	11-Jul-69	10-Jun-69	10-Jun-71		30-Apr-04		18-Jun-97	
		15-Jan-69						26-Jun-04
23-Oct-75	18-Jan-71	23-Jan-74	23-Jan-74		30-Apr-04		18-Jun-97	
							15-Feb-95	
22-Nov-65		25-Feb-76	25-Feb-76		29-Apr-04		31-Jan-05	
16-Jun-70					10-Aug-15	29-Jun-78		
5-Jul-89		9-Mar-71	4-Dec-73		11-Mar-05	20-Jun-88		24-Jun-05
					22-Aug-14	19-Aug-93	17-Nov-14	
16-Apr-68	21-Jan-70	21-Jan-70	24-Apr-72		23-Feb-16	1-Jun-98		
			2-Dec-71					
15-Apr-65	27-Feb-67				30-Apr-04	29-Sep-93	18-Jun-97	
25-Aug-66	13-Sep-71	5-Nov-70	5-Apr-73	30-Mar-77				
19-Jun-64	26-Mar-68	6-May-75			30-Apr-04	18-May-93	18-Jun-97	
1-Aug-73	15-Jun-68				26-Jun-01			
			25-Jun-71		12-Aug-06	6-Sep-78	24-Jun-92	26-Jun-04
					19-Jun-09		21-Aug-13	
	6-Mar-67	31-Aug-83			25-Jun-10	31-Aug-83		
4-Apr-78	21-Oct-75	18-Jun-82	18-Jun-82		19-Feb-03			
					14-Apr-17		3-Dec-17	
					20-Sep-01	3-Apr-97	16-Jul-99	
					7-Jun-16			
11-Dec-79	31-Aug-65	7-May-71	16-Feb-71					25-Jun-04
10-May-83		27-Jan-82	27-Jan-82		15-Jun-00			
		18-Jun-69						
					27-Apr-04	24-Nov-00	26-Feb-98	
10-Jun-66	27-Feb-75	9-Mar-72			26-Jan-06		18-Jun-97	
	30-Sep-66				27-Jun-07		2-Jun-08	26-Jun-04
						23-Jun-78		
13-Jun-88					30-Jun-08	26-Mar-79		
		31-Jul-87	10-Dec-70		5-Apr-10		8-Oct-04	
22-Nov-83	1-Jul-66				5-Nov-10		8-Jan-01	
22-Apr-82					24-Sep-08	2-Jan-85	7-Jun-95	
13-Nov-00		19-Jul-72						
						20-Jul-01	2-Feb-09	
					7-Jan-06		5-Jun-03	
					23-Jun-08		23-Jun-08	
19-Nov-96		22-Jun-78	3-Aug-73		16-Jun-00	21-Feb-80		
					7-Nov-12			
					2-Mar-06			
					2-Mar-17			
17-Jan-64	9-Nov-66	20-Oct-70	6-Jun-86		30-Apr-04		18-Jun-97	
28-Nov-77	3-Jun-65	28-Nov-77	28-Nov-77		7-Jul-00	30-Oct-84		
8-Dec-78	28-Jul-65	21-Feb-69	21-Mar-72		13-Feb-15	9-Aug-89		
1-Oct-73		0-Jan-00			28-Jun-12	25-Jun-84	10-Jun-93	
29-Oct-64	10-Sep-65				1-Sep-07	25-Mar-85		
					1-Jun-15		11-Jan-12	
	27-Sep-66				10-Jan-04	29-Jul-79	18-May-04	
					31-Jan-14			
		10-Apr-73	20-Apr-71		25-Jun-10			
19-Jul-69	28-Sep-65	14-Jun-71	29-Aug-72		7-Sep-04		12-Sep-95	
20-Apr-66	10-Nov-67	19-Oct-71	3-Jun-75		15-Apr-05		18-Jun-97	
					13-Jul-09	9-May-03	10-Sep-14	
7-Mar-67	7-Mar-67	7-Dec-70			22-Feb-11		26-Nov-02	
18-Apr-96					4-Apr-11	13-Dec-94	18-Apr-96	
			5-Nov-70		21-Nov-11			

	CONVENTION ESTABLISHING A CUSTOMS COOPERATION COUNCIL	NOMENCLATURE	BRUSSELS VALUATION (BDV)	HARMONIZED SYSTEM	COMMERCIAL SAMPLES	PROFESSIONAL EQUIPMENT	FAIRS
SAINT LUCIA	12-May-05		1-Jun-64				
SAMOA	1-Oct-01						
SAO TOME AND PRINCIPE	23-Sep-09			2-Jul-13			
SAUDI ARABIA	8-May-73			10-Mar-88			
SENEGAL	10-Mar-76			21-Sep-89			
SERBIA	27-Mar-01		16-Oct-78	9-Jan-02	27-Dec-01	4-Feb-02	27-Dec-01
SEYCHELLES	25-Jul-00						
SIERRA LEONE	6-Nov-75			12-Jun-15			
SINGAPORE	9-Jul-75			30-Nov-05			
SLOVAKIA	1-Jan-93			7-Jun-93	5-Feb-93	5-Feb-93	5-Feb-93
SLOVENIA	7-Sep-92			23-Nov-92	23-Feb-93	23-Feb-93	23-Feb-93
SOMALIA	4-Oct-12						
SOUTH AFRICA	24-Mar-64	25-Nov-87		25-Nov-87	11-Oct-73	28-Sep-71	28-Sep-71
SOUTH SUDAN	18-Jul-12						
SPAIN	13-Jul-52	28-Sep-87		28-Sep-87	8-Jan-65	11-Feb-63	11-Feb-63
SRI LANKA	29-May-67			3-May-88		23-May-91	14-Jul-81
SUDAN	8-Jun-60			10-Dec-93			28-May-74
SURINAME	26-nov.-18						
SWAZILAND	15-May-81	22-Nov-87		26-Nov-85			
SWEDEN	17-Oct-52	22-Sep-87		22-Sep-87	21-Mar-61	19-Mar-64	19-Mar-64
SWITZERLAND	19-Dec-52	22-Sep-87		22-Sep-87	30-Apr-63	30-Apr-63	30-Apr-63
SYRIAN ARAB REPUBLIC	3-Nov-59			12-Nov-07			
TAJIKISTAN	1-Jul-97			6-Jul-05			
TANZANIA	17-Nov-64		9-Dec-77	24-Jan-08			
THAILAND	4-Feb-72			16-Dec-91		30-Sep-94	30-Sep-94
THE FORMER YUGOSLAV	1-Jul-94			31-Mar-95		4-Mar-96	3-Apr-96
TIMOR-LESTE	19-Sep-03						
TOGO	12-Feb-90			12-Feb-90			
TONGA	1-Jul-05						
TRINIDAD AND TOBAGO	15-Oct-73					5-Jan-81	5-Jan-81
TUNISIA	20-Jul-66	1-Jan-89		28-Oct-87		21-Apr-72	21-Apr-72
TURKEY	6-Jun-51			15-Dec-88	27-Dec-65	23-Aug-74	23-Aug-74
TURKMENISTAN	17-May-93						
UGANDA	3-Nov-64			11-Jul-89	9-Jan-70	11-Jul-89	11-Jul-89
UKRAINE	26-Jun-92			26-Aug-02			
UNION OF MYANMAR (Rep. of	25-Mar-91			5-Dec-94			
UNITED ARAB EMIRATES	7-Feb-79			27-Jun-02			
UNITED KINGDOM	12-Sep-52	22-Sep-87		22-Sep-87	1-Apr-77	25-Mar-63	25-Mar-63
UNITED STATES	5-Nov-70			31-Oct-88		3-Dec-68	
URUGUAY	16-Sep-77			17-Oct-11			
UZBEKISTAN	28-Jul-92			17-Nov-98			
VANUATU	17-Nov-09			28-Mar-18			
VENEZUELA	1-Jul-96			23-Oct-98			
VIETNAM	1-Jul-93			26-Mar-98			
YEMEN	1-Jul-93			30-Sep-02			
ZAMBIA	27-Sep-78	22-Dec-87		22-Dec-86			
ZIMBABWE	19-Mar-81	11-May-86		5-Nov-86	18-Feb-87	18-Feb-87	
WCO MEMBERS - CONTRACTING PARTIES	183	33	8	156	38	55	61
2018 - Percentage of adhesio	100%	18%	4%	85%	21%	30%	33%

ATA CARNET	WELFARE MATERIAL FOR SEAFEARERS	SCIENTIFIC EQUIPMENT	PEDAGOGIC MATERIAL	KYOTO CONVENTION	REVISED KYOTO CONVENTION (as amended)	NAIROBI	ISTANBUL	JOHANNESBURG
					27-Oct-16			
					5-Aug-17			
					5-Apr-11	18-Mar-85	4-May-11	
14-Oct-77		19-May-71	2-Sep-75		21-Mar-06	18-Mar-92		
27-Dec-01	27-Dec-01				18-Sep-07		7-Jul-10	
						29-Mar-12		
	7-Sep-66				6-Dec-15			
14-Nov-83		8-Sep-69						
5-Feb-93		5-Feb-93			19-Sep-02	2-Oct-00	22-Sep-00	
23-Feb-93	23-Feb-93				27-Apr-04		23-Oct-00	
			29-Jun-71					
18-Dec-75	27-Sep-65	28-Sep-71	18-Dec-75		18-May-04	8-Oct-93	18-May-04	12-Jul-07
6-Apr-64	7-Oct-66	26-Feb-71	17-Nov-72		30-Apr-04		18-Jun-97	
14-Jul-81		23-May-91	23-May-91		26-Jun-09	19-Dec-84		
					16-Aug-09			
					31-Oct-12	1-Dec-00		
19-Mar-64	15-Feb-66				30-Apr-04	5-Mar-83	18-Jun-97	
30-Apr-63	22-Aug-68	14-Nov-73	14-Nov-73		26-Jun-04		11-May-95	
	30-Apr-75	24-Oct-74						
						20-Aug-97	27-Aug-97	
	8-Dec-75							
30-Sep-94		16-Oct-70			6-Dec-15		5-Jan-07	
3-Apr-96					28-Jul-09		21-Apr-06	
			21-Dec-70		28-Jun-14	15-May-91		
5-Jan-81							29-Aug-11	
10-Mar-71	14-Jul-65		20-Oct-71		24-Jul-17	28-Sep-83		
23-Aug-74	17-May-91	17-May-91	17-May-91		5-Mar-06	25-Aug-82	15-Dec-04	
	19-Jun-67	11-Jul-89	11-Jul-89		27-Jun-02	7-Nov-89		
					15-Jun-11	7-Nov-00	22-Jun-04	
					31-May-10		14-Sep-10	
19-Jul-63	25-May-66	30-Jun-69			30-Apr-04	18-Mar-83	18-Jun-97	
3-Dec-68					12-Jun-05			
					30-06-2018			
					1-Aug-08			
					27-Jun-13			
					7-Jan-06	21-May-84		
		5-Nov-86	18-Feb-87		2-Oct-03	14-Jun-82	17-Nov-92	
63	42 1 Signatories (subject to ratification)	55	38	4	115	52 2 Signatories (subject to ratification)	69	3 7 Signatories (subject to ratification)
34%	23%	30%	21%	2%	63%	28%	38%	2%

Source: Author's elaboration based on information from the WCO

Institutional Self-assessment Template

H. H. Juárez Allende, *The World Customs Organization*, Law for Professionals,
https://doi.org/10.1007/978-3-030-85296-2

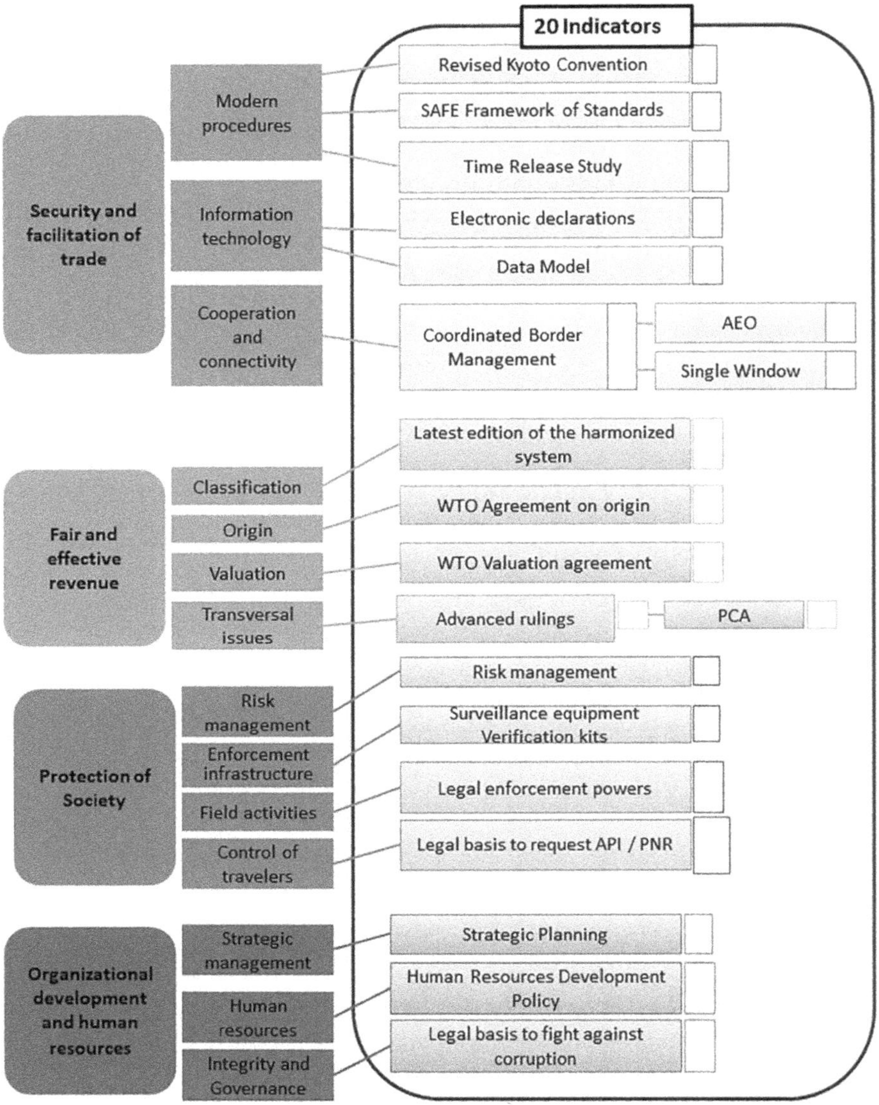

Source: Author's elaboration based on information from the WCO

Bibliography

Alais HF (2008) Los Principios del Derecho Aduanero. Marcial Pons. Buenos Aires, Argentina

Álvarez Gómez-Pallete JM (2002) La Organización Mundial de Aduanas y sus Convenios. Centro de Investigación Aduanera y de Comercio Internacional (CIACI). Mexico

Asakura H (2005) World history of the customs and tariffs. World Customs Organization. Brussels, Belgium

Barboza J (2008) Derecho Internacional Público. Zavalía Editor. Buenos Aires, Argentina

Barreira et al (2011) Código Aduanero Comentado. Abeledo Perrot. Buenos Aires, Argentina

Basaldua RX (2007) La Organización Mundial del Comercio y la regulación del comercio internacional. Lexis Nexis. Buenos Aires

Basaldua RX, Lidia A (2019) El Régimen de Origen de las Mercaderías. Guía Práctica y Ediciones IARA S.A. Buenos Aires, Argentina

Berr CJ, Tremeau H (2006) Le droit douanier, Communautaire et national. Economica. Paris, France

Bouheben J (2004) Itineraire d'un douanier gascon: Du service de la France aux Organisations Internationales. Abacus

Bueno ME (2005) El valor en Aduana de las mercaderías. IARA S.A. Buenos Aires, Argentina

Bunge M (1979) Treatise on basic philosophy. Vol. 4: Ontology II: a world of systems. D. Reidel Publishing Company

Cabello Pérez M, Cabello González JM (2012) Las aduanas y el comercio internacional. Ed. ESIC. Spain

Carvajal Contreras M (1986) Derecho Aduanero. Editorial Porrúa. Mexico

Cotter JP (2018) Derecho Aduanero y Comercio internacional. Guía Práctica y Ediciones IARA S.A. Buenos Aires, Argentina

Couture EJ (1960) "Vocabulario Jurídico con especial referencia al derecho procesal uruguayo". Library of Official Publications of the School of Law and Social Sciences of the "Universidad de la República". Montevideo

Dewulf L, Sokol JB et al (2005) Manual para la Modernización de Aduanas. World Bank

Heli (2012) Investigación sobre la Organización Mundial de Aduanas y su Sistema Legal. Law Press. China

Hoguet JH (2004) Au service de l'Etat à travers la Douane 1954-1996. L'Harmattan

Juárez Allende et al (2018) Manual de Aduanas. Guía Práctica y Ediciones IARA S.A. Buenos Aires, Argentina

Lyons T (2008) EC customs law, 2nd edn. Oxford University Press, New York, USA

H. H. Juárez Allende, *The World Customs Organization*, Law for Professionals,
https://doi.org/10.1007/978-3-030-85296-2

Pardo Carrero et al (2015) Relevancia Tributaria del Valor en Aduana de la mercancía importada. Instituto Colombiano de Derecho Tributario (ICDT). Bogota, Colombia

Pardo Carrero et al (2019) Derecho Aduanero (2 volumes). Tirant lo Blanch. Valencia, España

Tiuna Benito F (1998) Fuentes y Practicas del Derecho Aduanero Internacional. Alin Editora S.A. Honduras

Trevisan R (2017) Imposto De Importacao E O Direito Aduaneiro Internacional. Aduaneiras. São Paulo, Brazil

Ingram Content Group UK Ltd.
Milton Keynes UK
UKHW020136050723
424579UK00003B/191

9 783030 852955